Grasses in the Garden

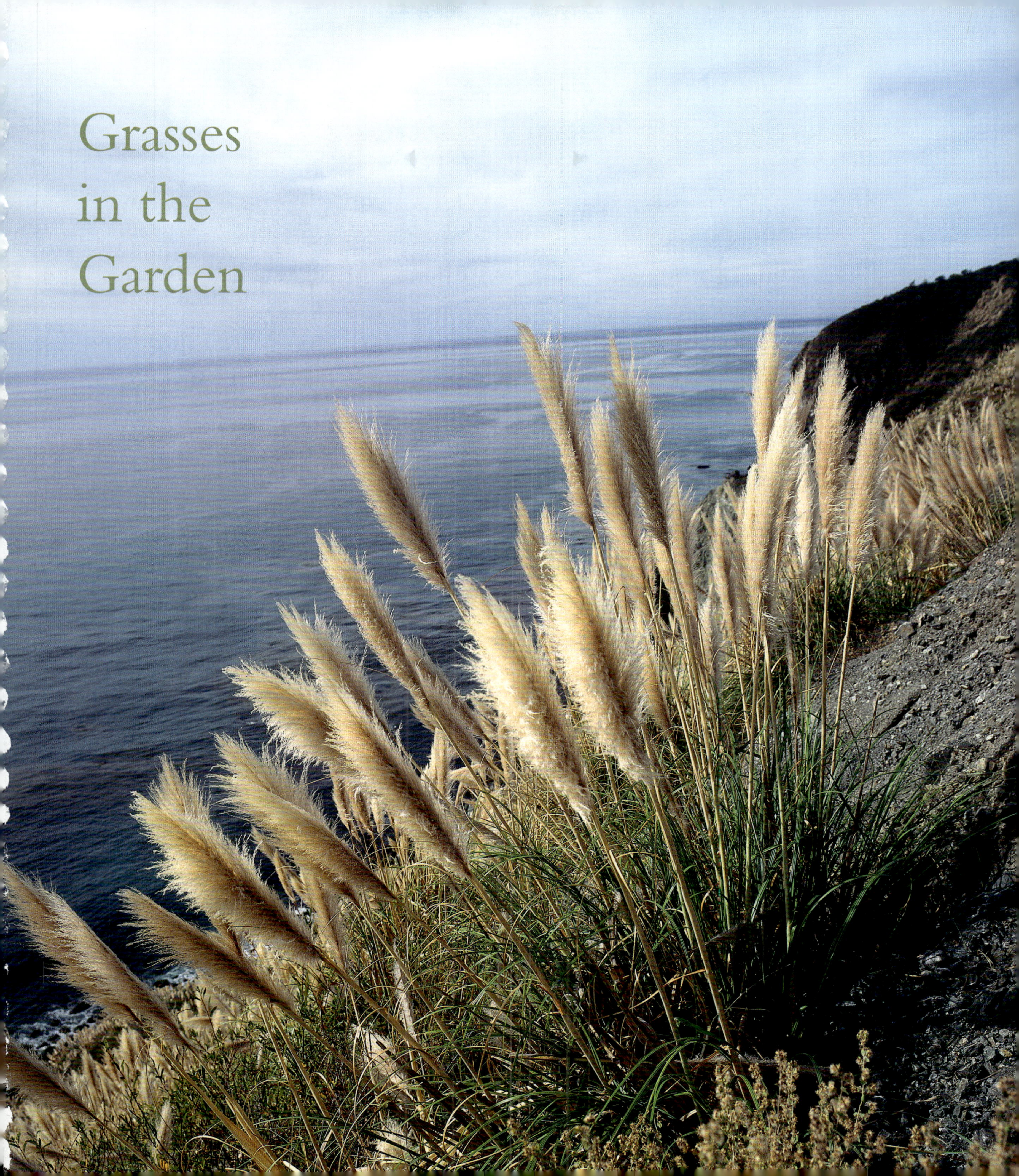

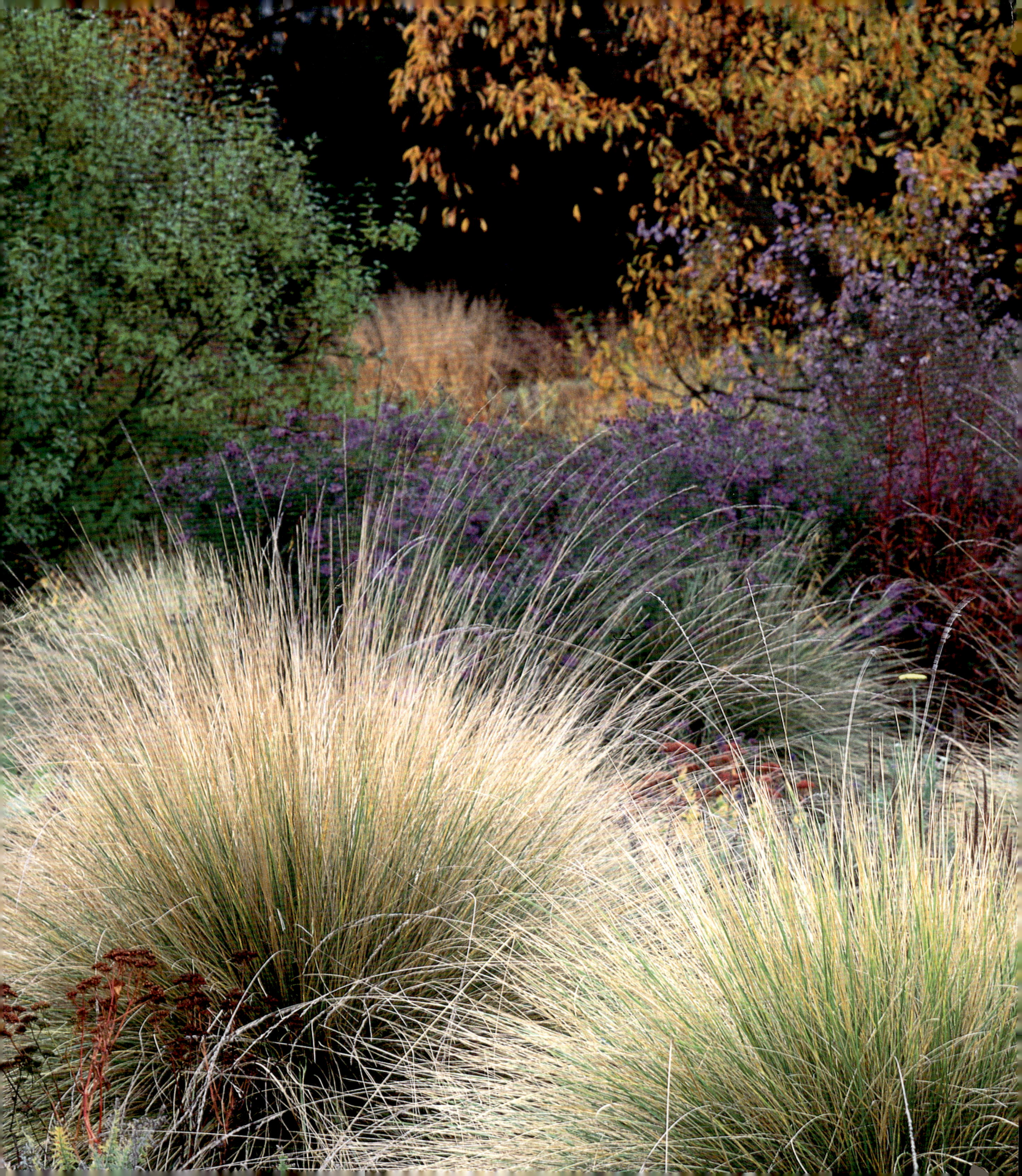

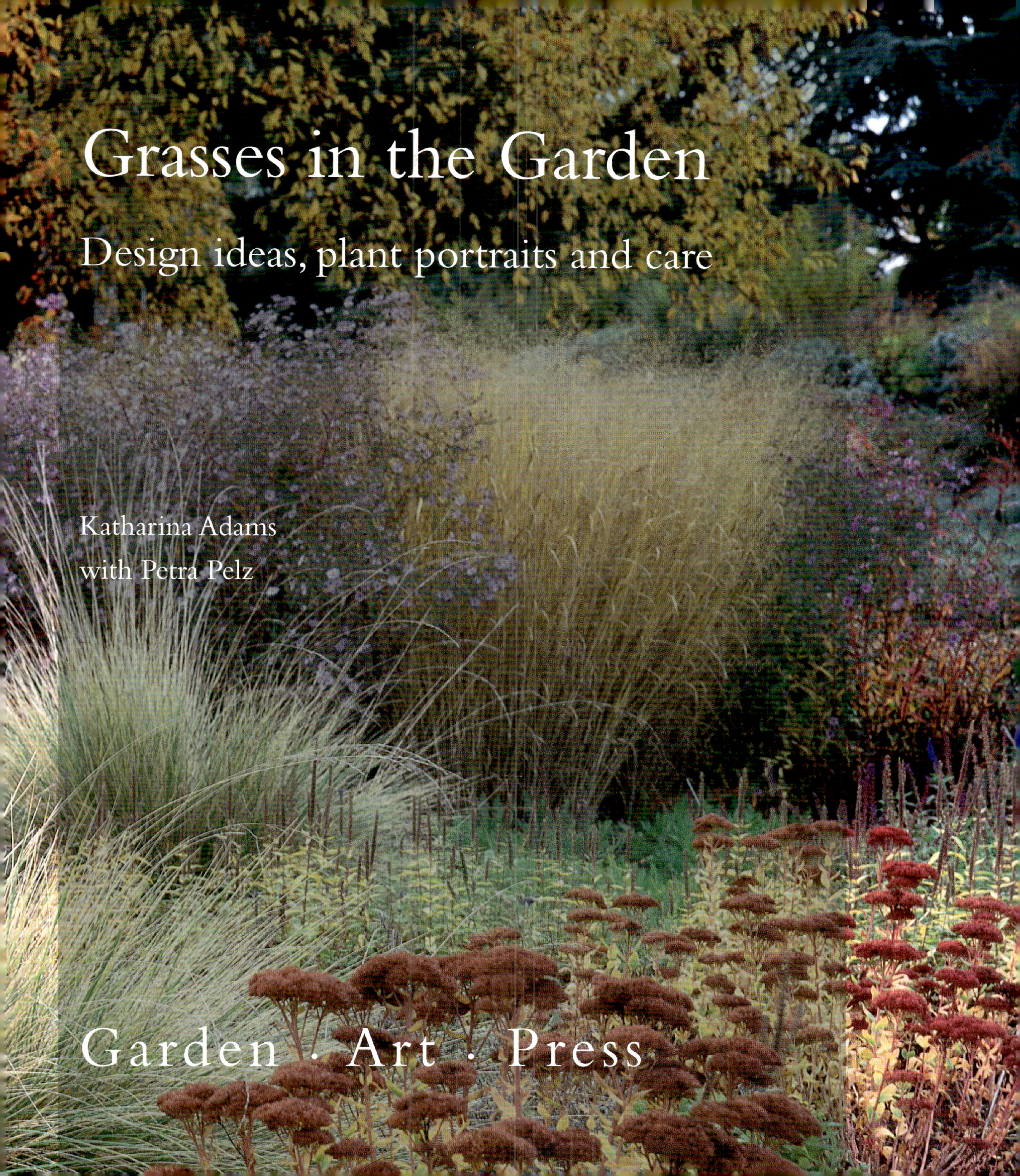

Grasses in the Garden

Design ideas, plant portraits and care

Katharina Adams
with Petra Pelz

Garden · Art · Press

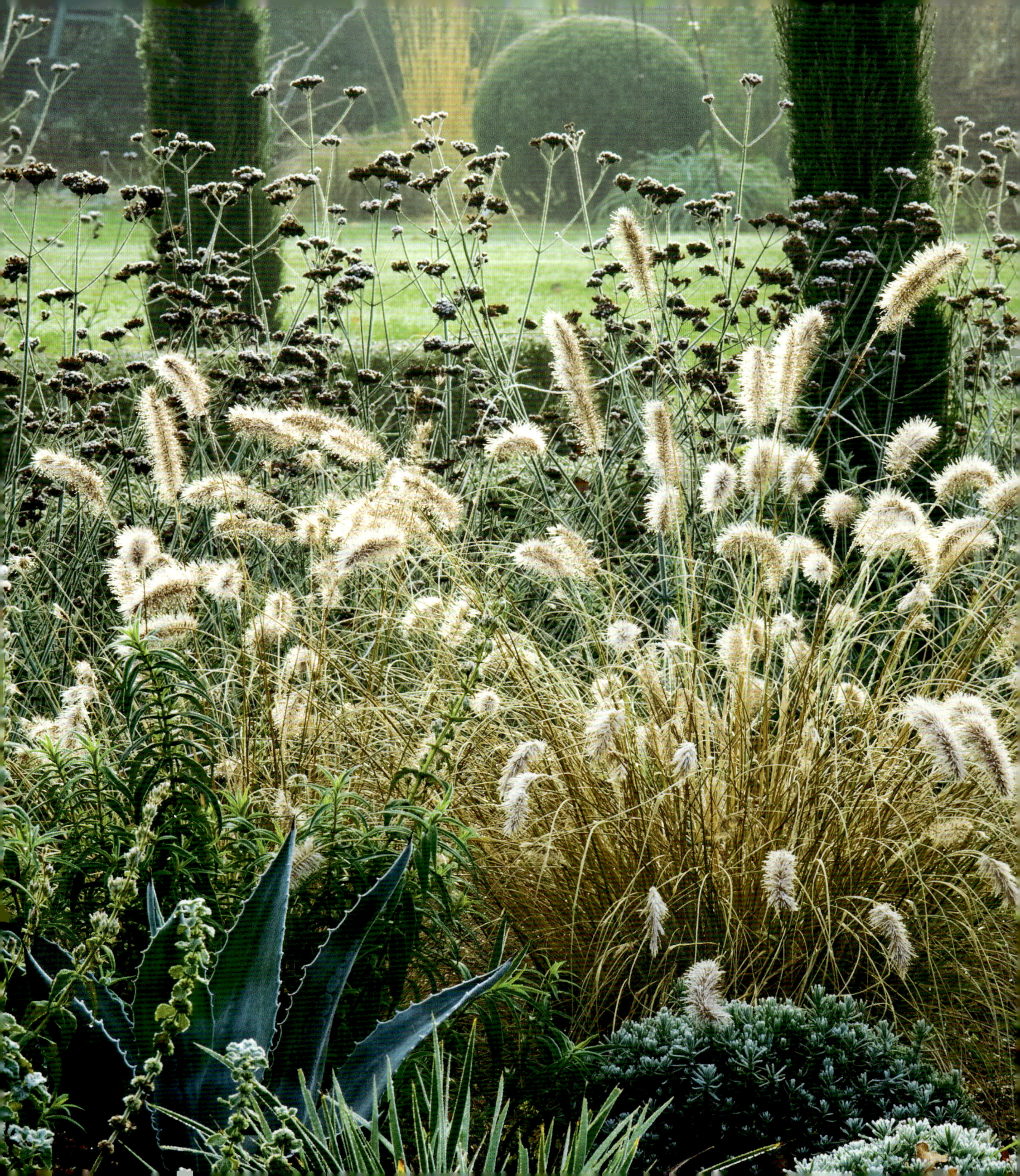

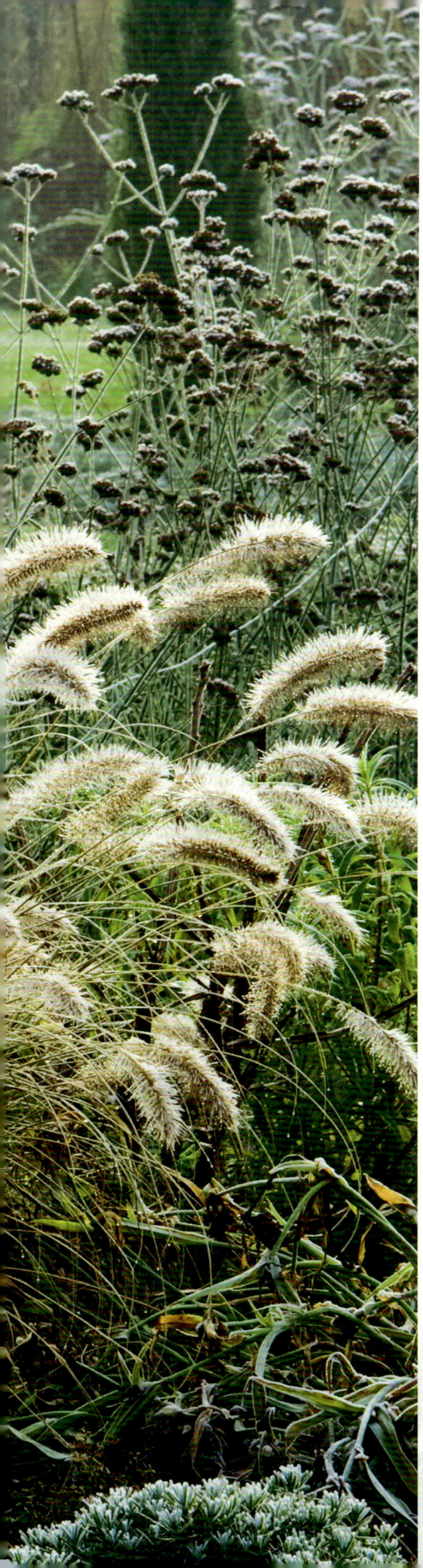

Contents

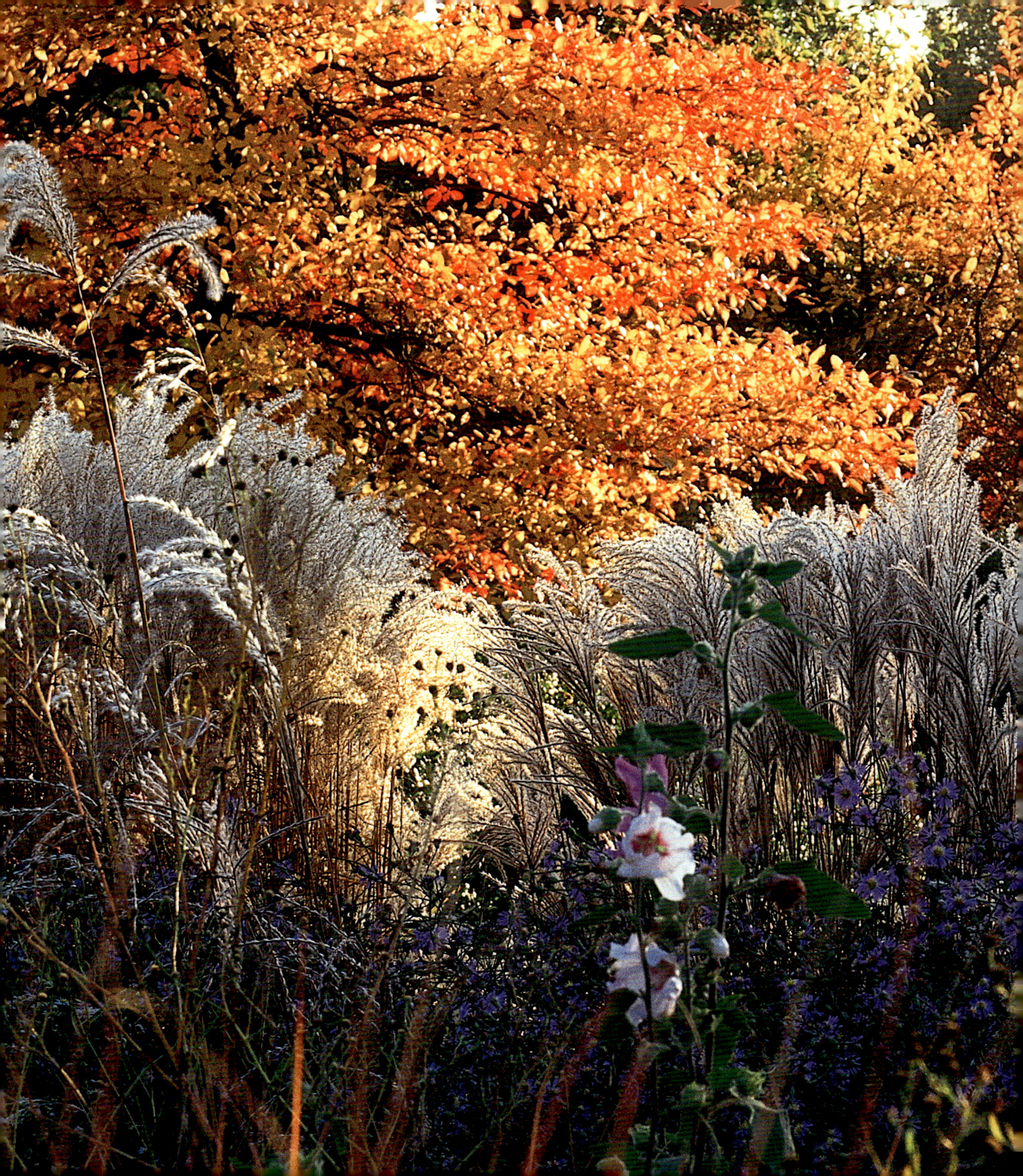

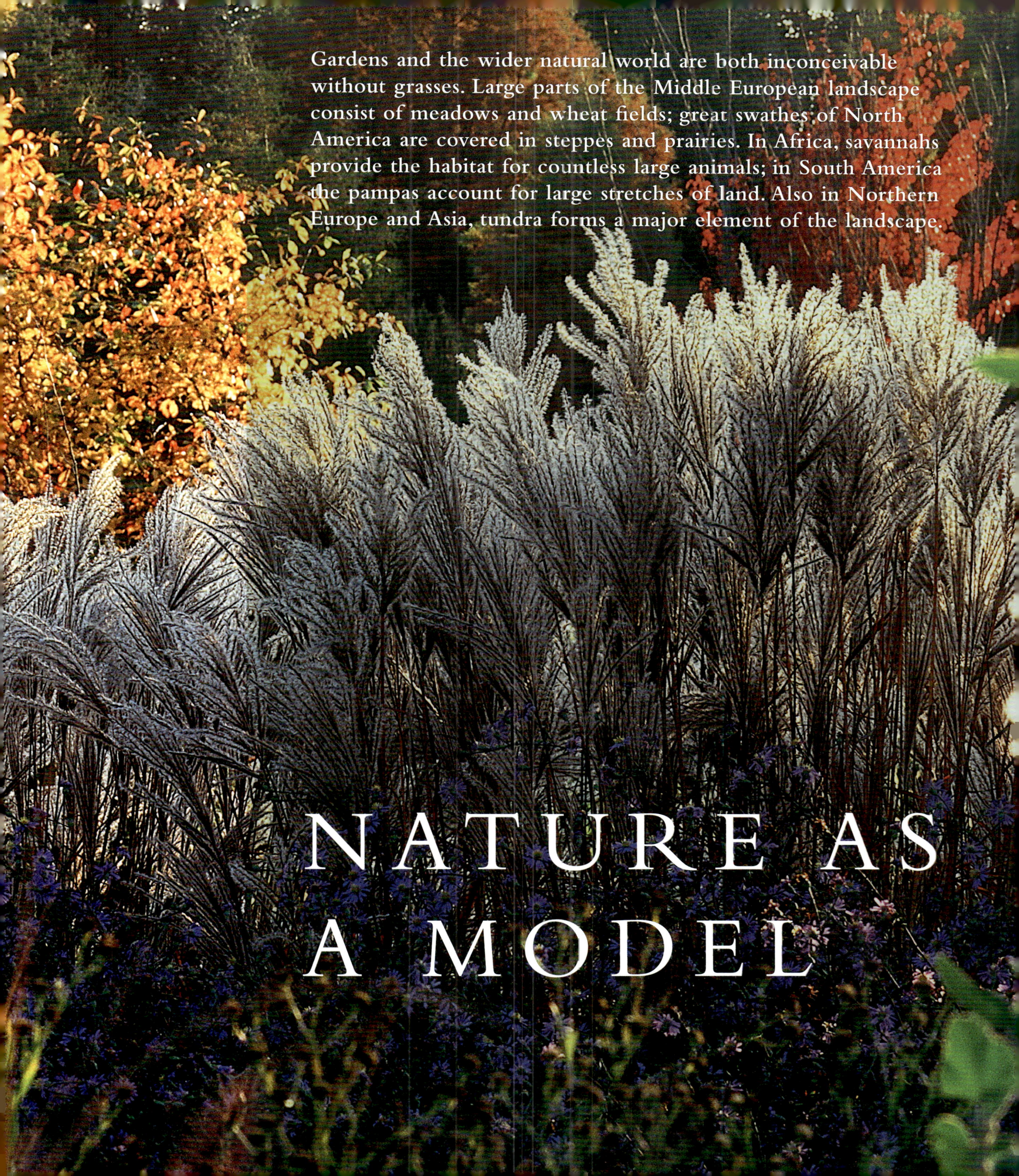

Gardens and the wider natural world are both inconceivable without grasses. Large parts of the Middle European landscape consist of meadows and wheat fields; great swathes of North America are covered in steppes and prairies. In Africa, savannahs provide the habitat for countless large animals; in South America the pampas account for large stretches of land. Also in Northern Europe and Asia, tundra forms a major element of the landscape.

NATURE AS A MODEL

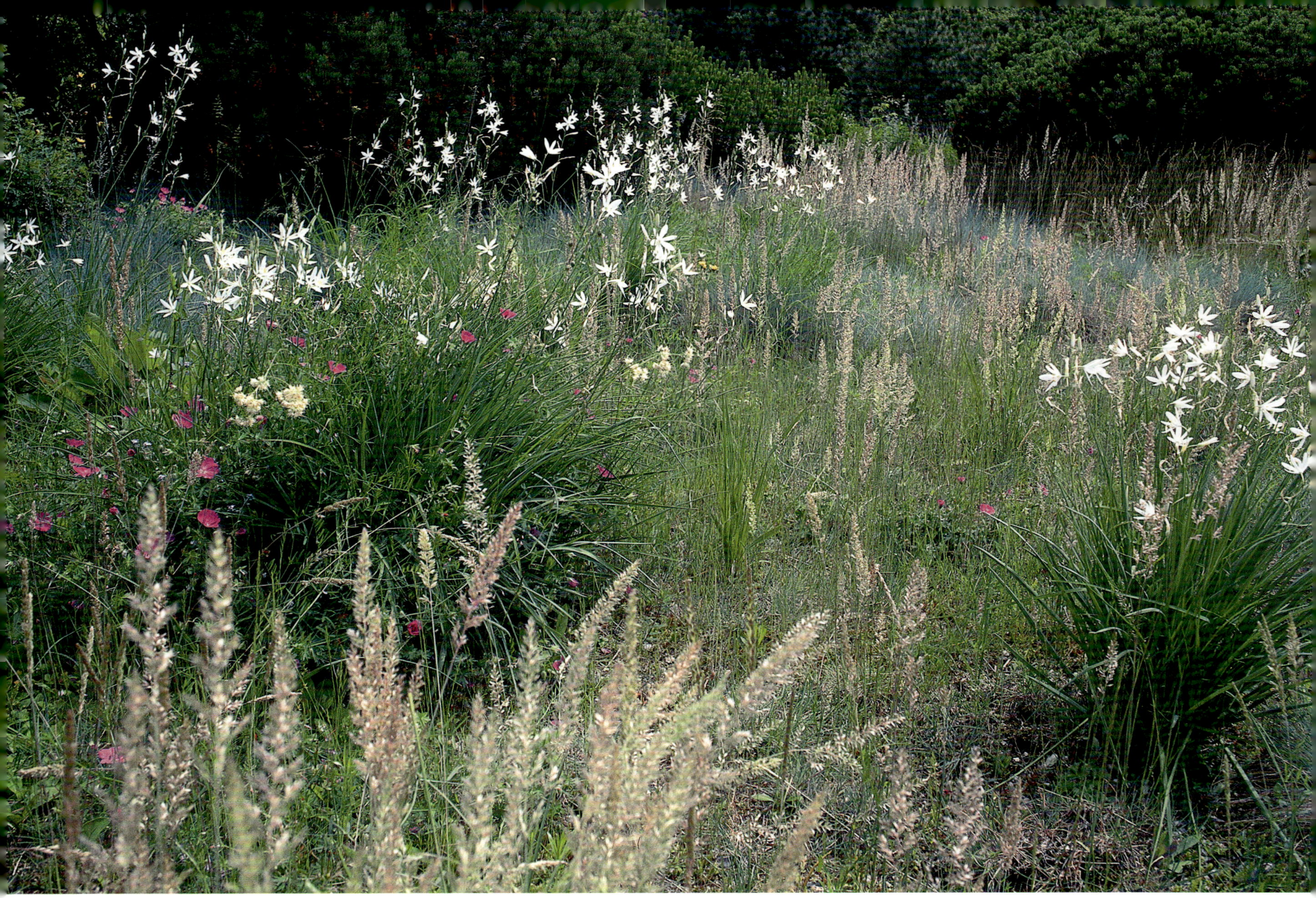

Colourful meadow in early summer
In drier habitats shrubs are found with grassy foliage such as *Asphodeline*, an attractive accompaniment to various grasses.

Seas of Grass

Waving grass as far as the eye can see – in the natural world grasses make up whole landscapes and ecosystems

Without grasses in their many different shapes and sizes both nature and gardens would be anything but green. Large parts of the Middle European landscape consist of meadows and wheat fields, which provide an important source of nutrition for humans and animals alike. In other parts of the world, grasses also play a major role: in the steppes and prairies of North America, the pampas of South America and the savannahs of Africa or the tundra of Northern Europe and Asia. Depending on the season and the amount of rainfall, these can be unattractive wastelands or luxurious green seas of grass interspersed with a host of blooming plants. Grasses have adapted astonishingly well to diversity of natural habitats. On the coast,

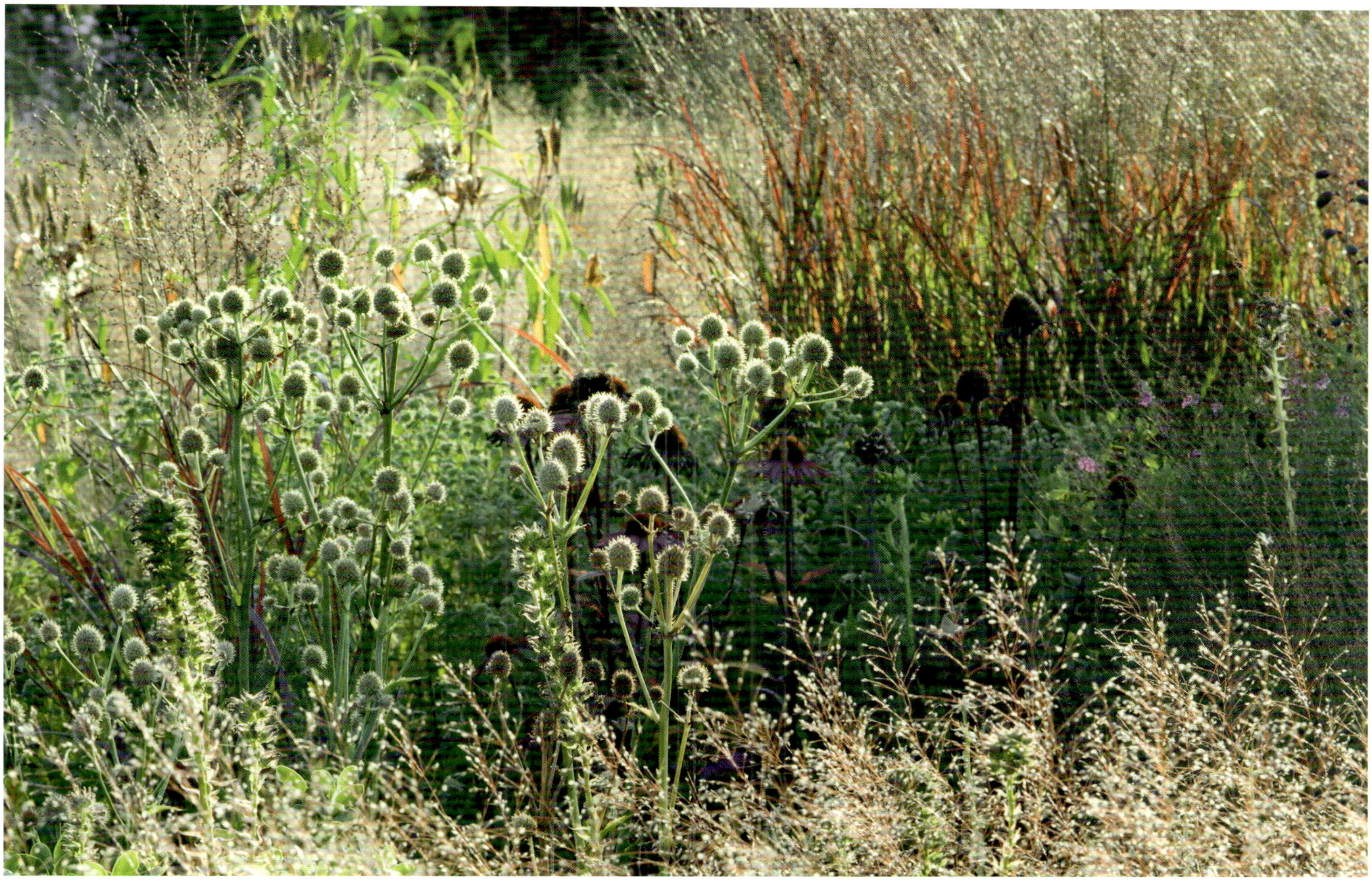

their root systems ensure that sand dunes are not washed away and thus they act as a form of coastal defence. Rice, the main staple of large sections of the human population, has perfectly adapted to the periodic flooding of its habitat.

GRASSES IN THE GARDEN

Grasses can be used in almost as many ways in the garden as can be observed in the natural world. There are suitable grasses for every part of the garden and every location; the range of types is overwhelming. In herbaceous borders, tall grasses can function as specimen shrubs, while smaller filigree grasses can define the space between the full-size shrubs and knit all different plants together. Many forms of sedge *(Carex)* can thrive in the deep shade under trees, and at the edge of ponds reeds create an ideal contrast with the broad leaves of the bog plants. Even the famous English lawn is made up of grasses, as are the various seed mixtures used in regular domestic gardens.

MEADOWS

Fenced areas for grazing cows or sheep, clearings in the soft morning light where deer browse, mountainsides scented with a blend of grasses and herbs – meadows are tremendously diverse. The meadows of our cultivated landscapes reach their apogee in early summer. That is when typical meadow perennials such as meadow cranesbill and meadow sage, corn poppies and yarrow come into full bloom. After the first mowing the colours are more muted, but the perennials continue

Billowing meadow in autumn
In the weak light of late summer the first grasses change colour and give a hint of the autumn display to come.

Prairie after a bush fire (left)
Grass fires are part of the rhythm of life on the North American prairie.

Perennials of the prairie (right)
The prairie is home to numerous wild perennials, such as this *Baptisia bracteata*.

New spring growth (below)
After the winter, the new green grass shoots colour the dry yellow prairie in fresh green.

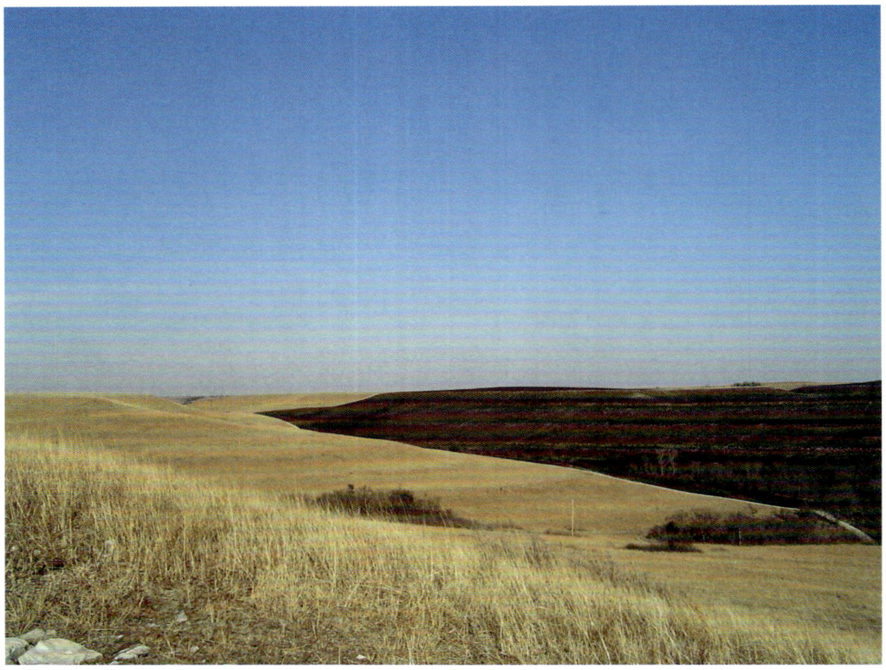

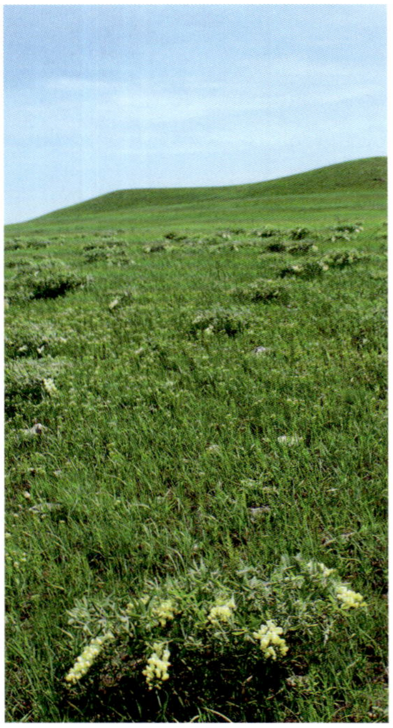

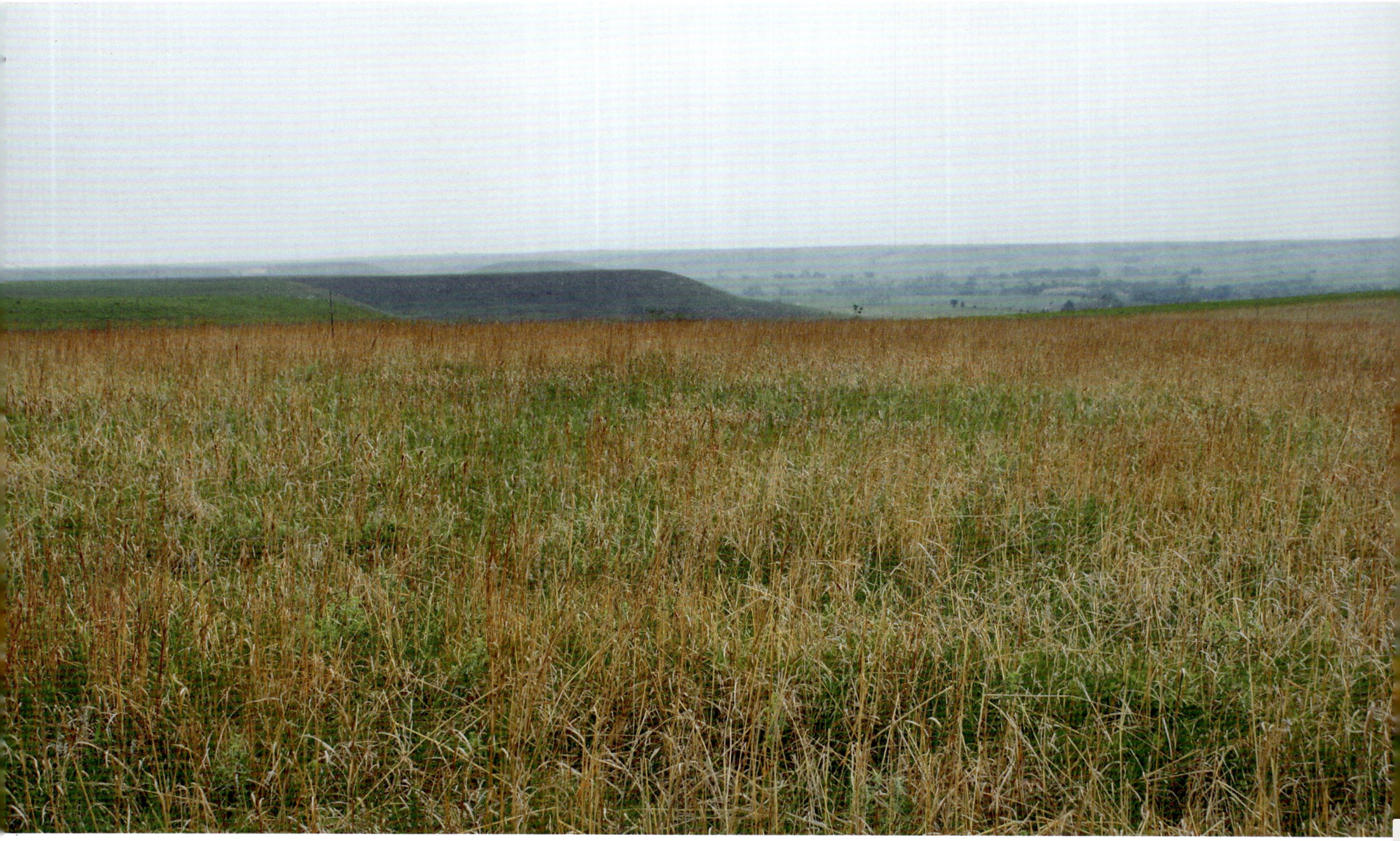

to flower among the grass blades right through until autumn. Depending on the soil type and the geographical location, a whole variety of perennials can grow side by side. In wet meadows, for example, we might find certain types of mint, comfrey and buttercups, while Campion, St John's wort or viper's bugloss are typical plants in dry grasslands on chalky soils.

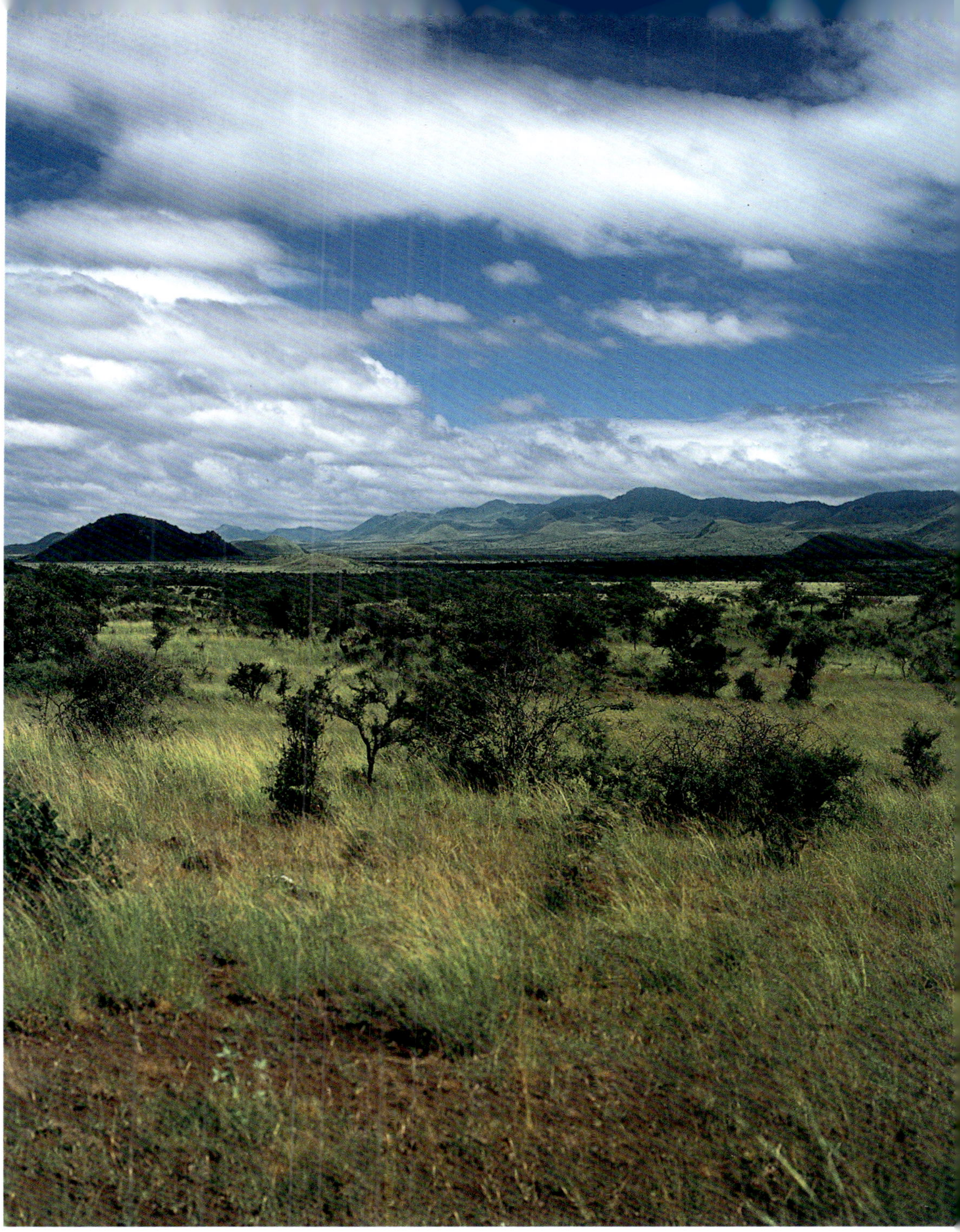

SAVANNAHS AND STEPPES

The savannah, a tropical ecozone, is characterised by open vegetation and sparse trees. Savannahs are particularly common in Africa, but this grass-dominated ecosystem can also be found in India, Australia and parts of northern South America. The savannah is the link between the desert and the tropical rainforest. As on the prairie, fire plays an important role, because the regular cull of young trees by bush fires favours grass growth. The burned remains of plants serve as a source of nutrients for new vegetation.

In contrast to the tropical savannah, grasslands in the temperate zones of the northern and southern hemisphere are referred to as steppe, prairie, puszta or pampas. They are also characterised by clear shifts between dry and rainy seasons and by fire. As well as grasses, the steppes contain mosses and lichens, low-growing heather and types of flowering shrubs. Many cereals were originally native steppe plants.

PRAIRIES

Many grasses require a sunny location with well-drained soil and are thus ideal partners for perennials in sunny locations such as open spaces or steppe-inspired planting schemes. Even sunny edges of woods provide a habitat for these grasses. Species and types that lend themselves to being combined are Korean feather reed grass, also known as diamond grass *(Calamagrostis brachytricha)*, with its delicate inflorescences, where the morning dew glistens like diamonds – *nomen est omen* – as well as feather reed grass *(Calamagrostis x acutiflora)*, with its stiff, upright ears. It has architectural accents and turns an impressive brownish yellow in late summer. With its large overhanging panicles, North American wild oats or spangle grass *(Chasmanthium latifolium)* is an inspiring grass that turns a reddish brown. The spikes of the Chinese fountain grass *(Pennisetum alopecuroides)* resemble small bottle brushes and are incomparably beautiful, especially in the morning, when small dew drops sparkle inside them. The dwarf variety *(Pennisetum alopecuroides 'Hameln')* is especially suited to the front of beds. Also not to be overlooked is needle grass *(Stipa)*, with long awns attached to its panicles, which tilt over elegantly and sway like finely shredded ostrich or heron feathers in the wind. The different types grow to between between 60 and 180cm – the design possibilities are, therefore, virtually limitless.

African savannah
On the savannah, grasses share space and water with small shrubs and trees. They are the main food source for the large herd animals of the African continent.

BARREN DESERT

In order to survive in the desert, grasses – similar to all plants that thrive in this habitat – need the ability to survive long periods of drought. During the short rainy periods, they must be able to lay up a reserve in as short a time as possible to tide them over throughout the next dry period. Special root tissue makes survival possible because, unlike succulents, grasses have no memory cells in their leaves or stem. Some grasses, for example, *Aristida pungens*, which grows up to 2 metres, thus manage to survive in the Sahara, and several species of the genus *Stipa* are to be found in the deserts and semi-deserts of Northern Asia.

Cold deserts (right)
Cortaderia pilosa grows in the Antarctic, forming dense clumps.

Hot deserts (below)
Even in hot deserts, grasses manage a meagre existence. They are in constant danger of being swallowed up by the drifting dunes.

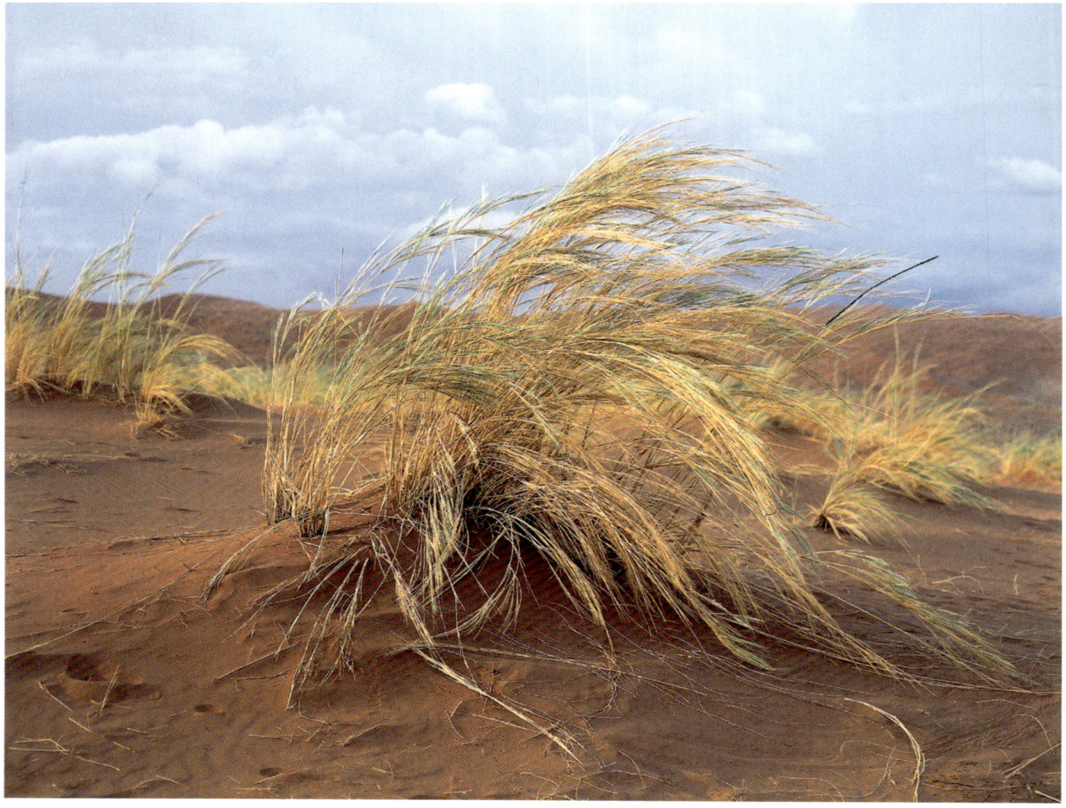

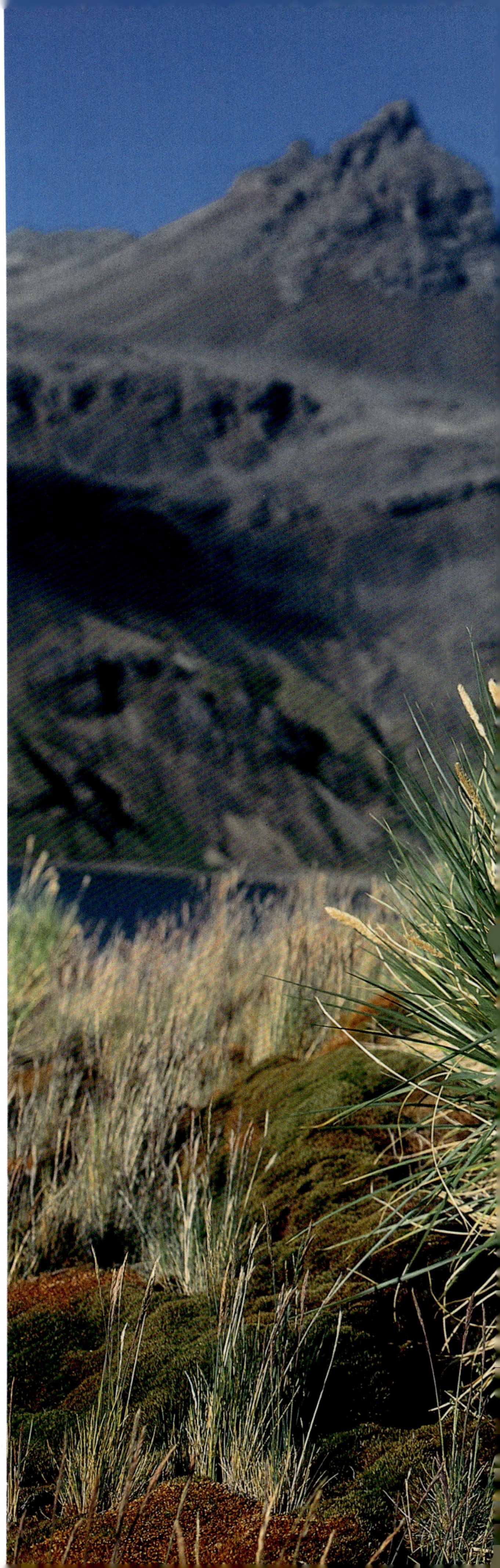

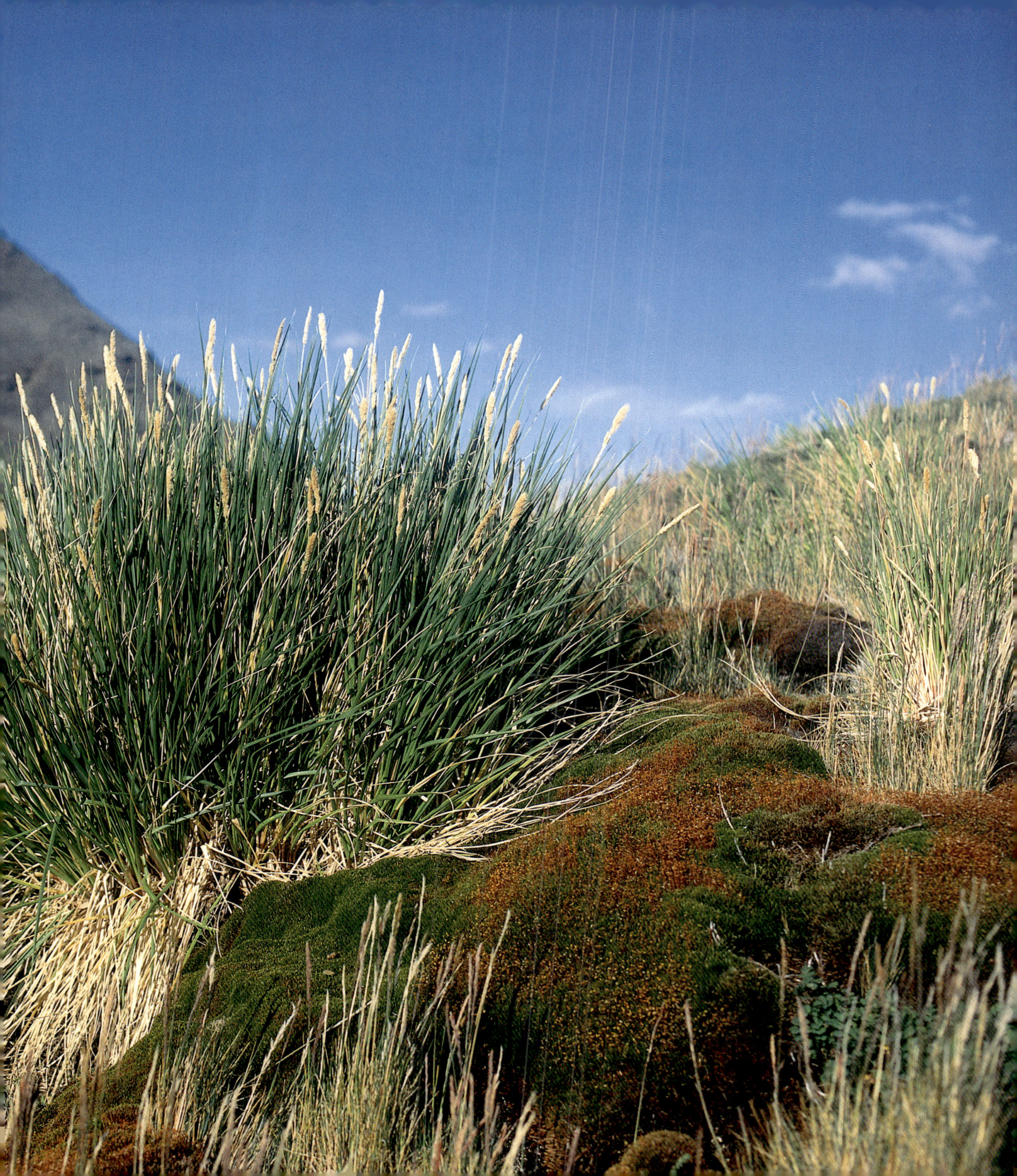

Bogs and Marshes

Mist, blades of grass glistening with dew and cotton grass heads swaying in the wind – bogs and marshes are home to a wide variety of grasses.

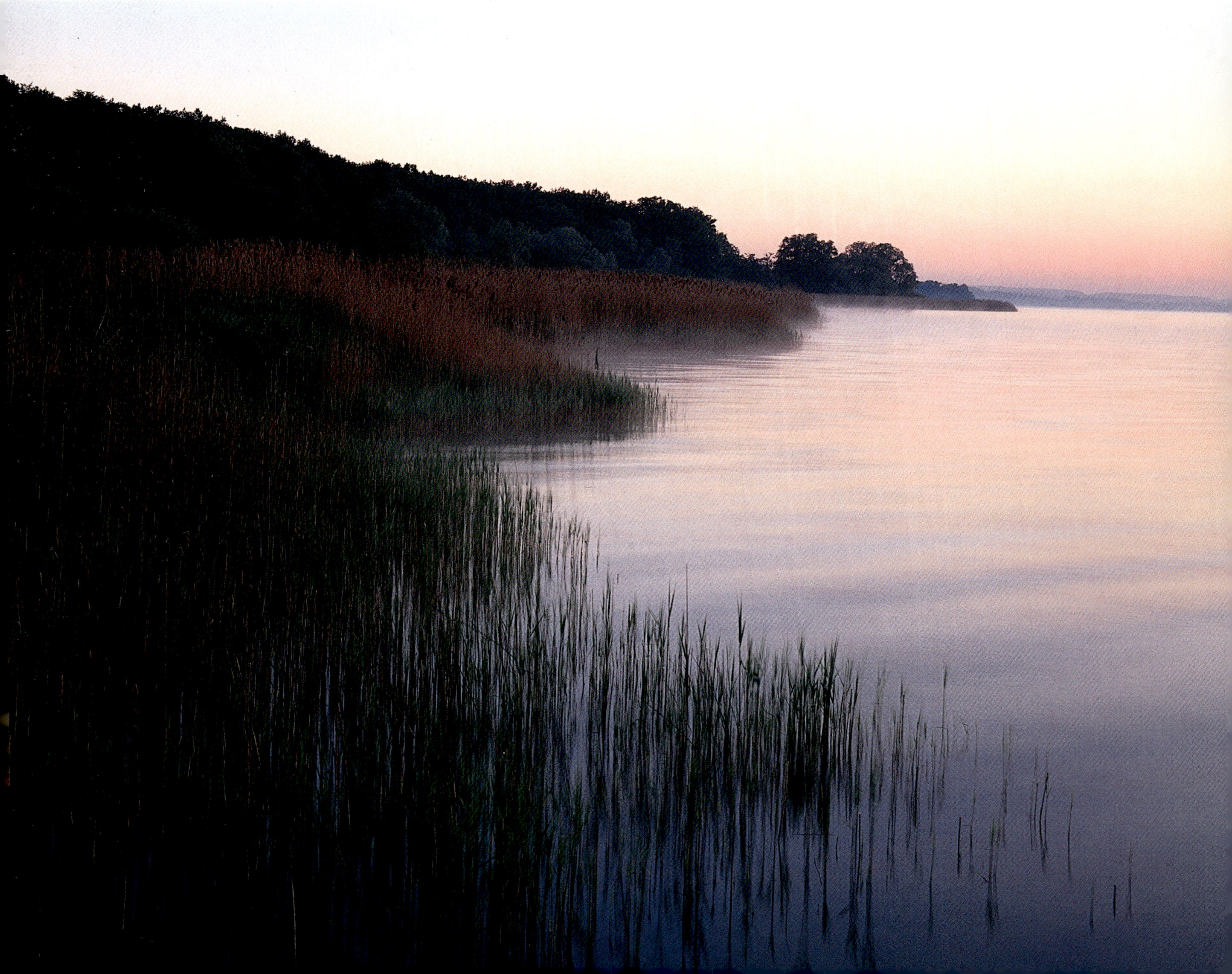

Cold fog wafting over low tufts of grass, a sallow moon in the background, a faint gurgling noise from underground and perhaps the odd rustle of an animal scurrying by: the stuff of horror stories and legends. Bogs and marshes are often seen as scary places, especially as they are usually far from the nearest civilisation. However, they provide a natural habitat for a number of plant and animal species that are threatened with extinction. Due to peat extraction and drainage for agricultural purposes, the creatures of the marshes are now restricted to quite limited areas. Cotton grasses *(Eriophorum)* are typical of marshes. The elongated perianth bristles of the fruits form a woolly-white tuft that gives cotton grass its name. Alongside them, in the marshes and bogs, are to be found various sedges *(Carex)* and rushes *(Juncus)*.

Cotton grasses (top)
The woolly white flower heads of the *Eriophorum* stand along the lake's edge as far as the eye can see.

Pond planting inspired by nature (bottom)
The grasses around the edge of this pond complement each other perfectly.

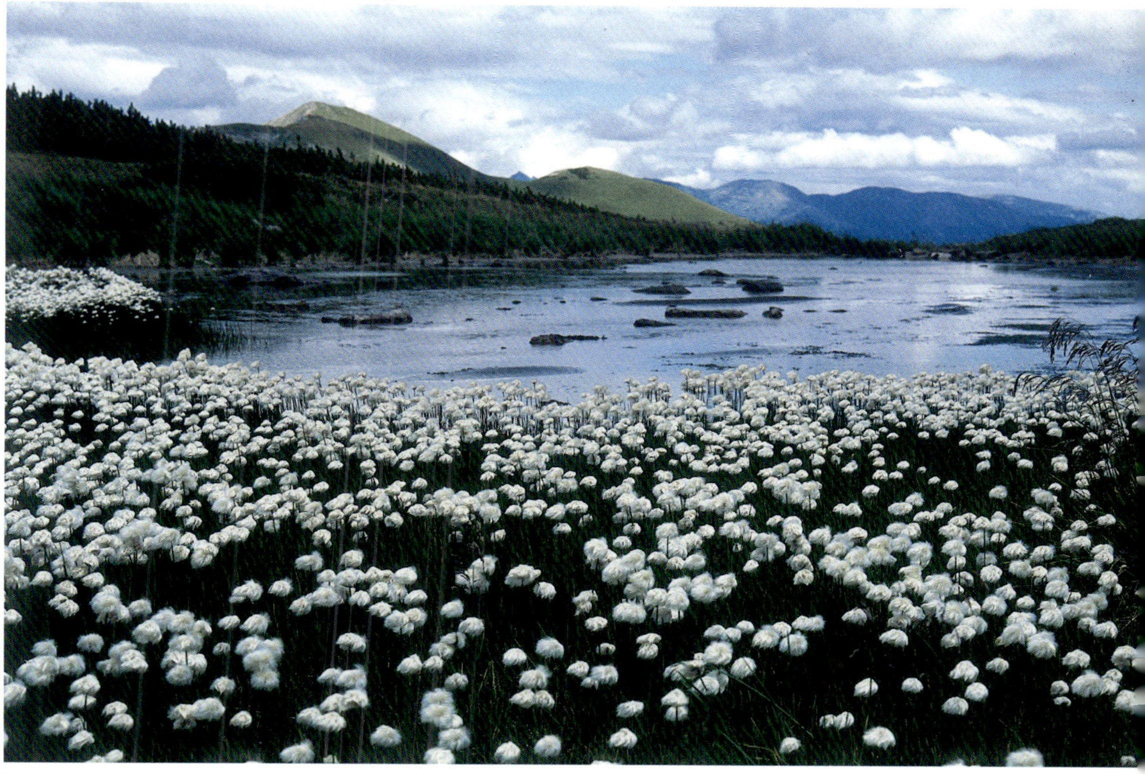

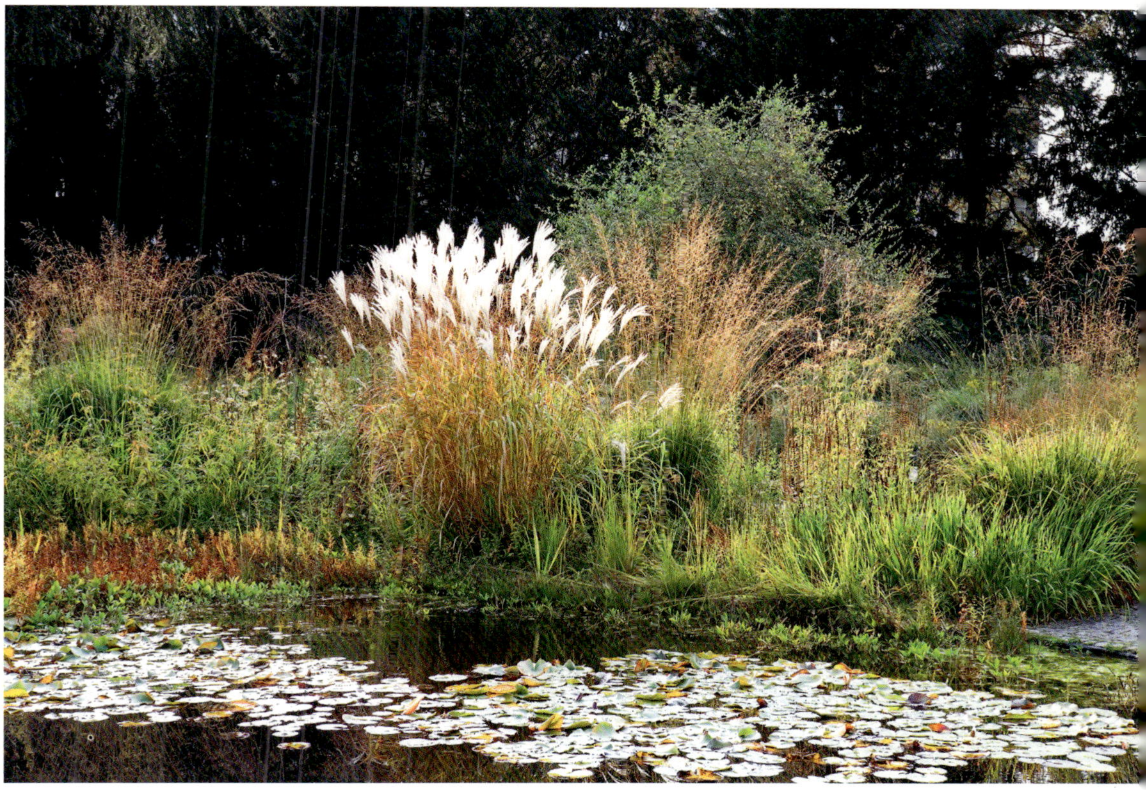

Wispy morning mist on the lake (left)
The reed beds are a habitat for many birds and other animals.

Woods and Woodland Edges

Whether on the dry and sunny fringes of the forest or in the deep, cool shade beneath the towering trees – grasses colonise every niche of this habitat.

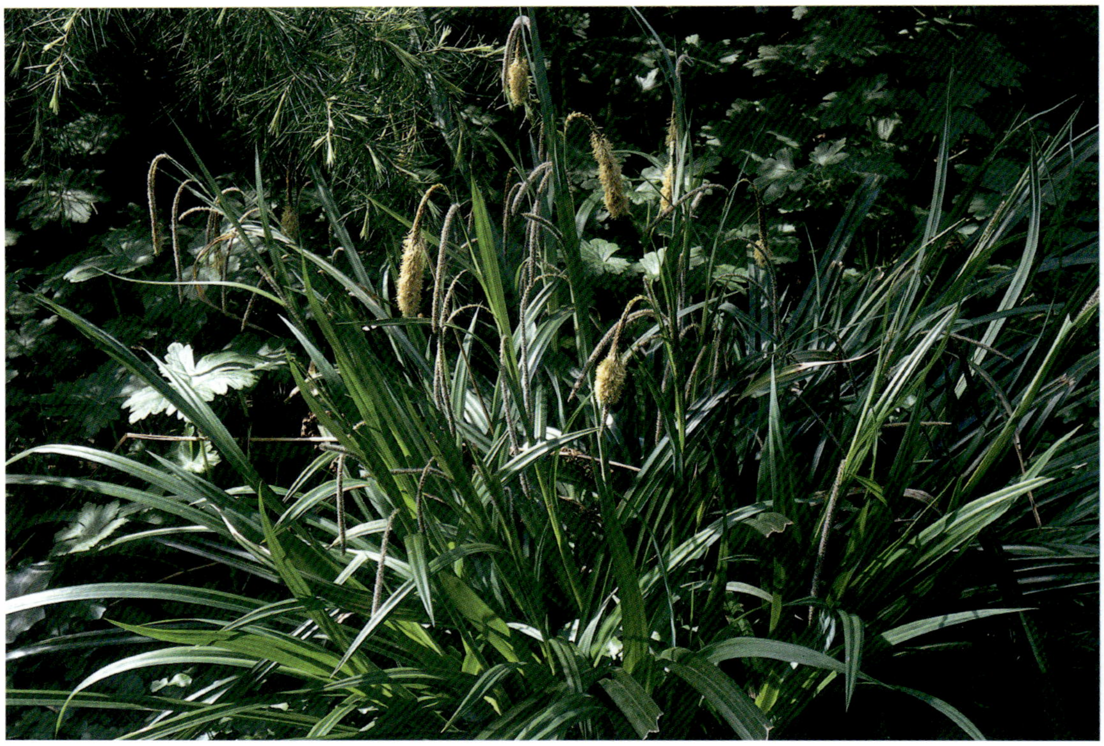

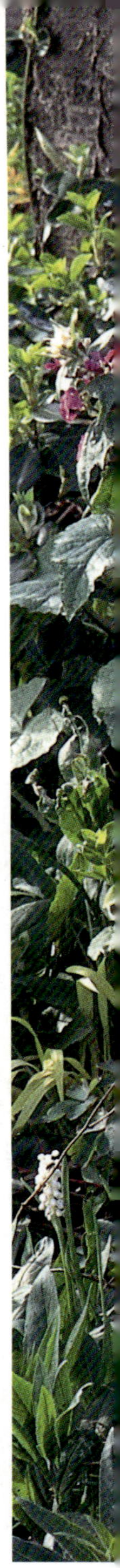

Weeping sedge
Carex pendula provides striking accents in the shade between different ground-covering plants.

If you are going for a walk in the woods and, instead of gazing at the tree canopy, you cast a glance at the forest floor, you will find a surprisingly varied range of vegetation made up of shrubs and small trees. Only in very dense coniferous forests, where the light and the nutrients in the soil are so meagre, the ground under the thick layer of acidic needle litter so hostile to life, is there almost nothing to see there. Typical inhabitants of the Middle European forest are wood millet *(Milium effesum)* and tor grass *(Brachypodium pinnatum)*, both of which are true grasses, as well as several types of sedge *(Carex)*, which belong to the Cyperaceae family, and rushes *(Juncaceae)*, such as wood-rush *(Luzula)*. In clearings and woodland edges, a variety of grasses grow alongside typical woodland-edge perennials such as bluebells, geraniums and foxgloves. Similarly, in the garden, grasses from woodland habitats mingle very well with perennials from the same habitats. Carpets of low grasses come into their own beneath spring-flowering shrubs such as rhododendrons and azaleas and, interwoven with ground-cover perennials and bulbs, can

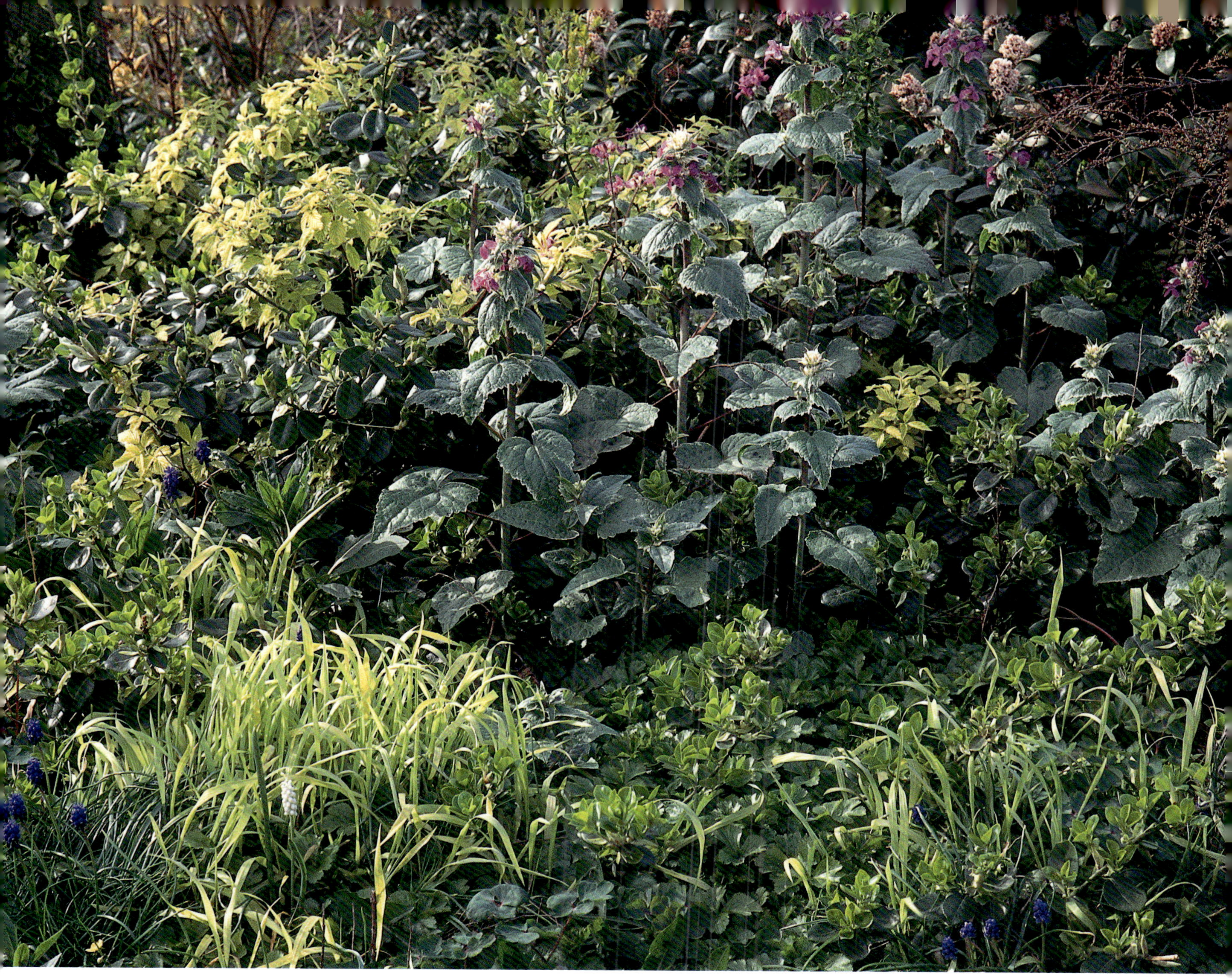

Grasses at the woodland edge
The golden yellow flush of *Milium effusum* 'Aureum' glows between spring-flowering perennials and bulbs.

produce a very natural effect. Here once again sedges are the plants of choice, as there are many evergreen varieties that provide attractive aspects throughout the year and display their qualities especially well in combination with the equally evergreen rhododendron. Colour in the undergrowth is provided by the many variegated, hence multicoloured, varieties. For example, *Carex morrowii* 'Silver Sceptre' and *Carex ornithopoda* 'Variegata' have white-striped leaves, while *Carex morrowii* 'Aureomarginata' and *Carex oshimensis* 'Evergold' have a yellow colouring.

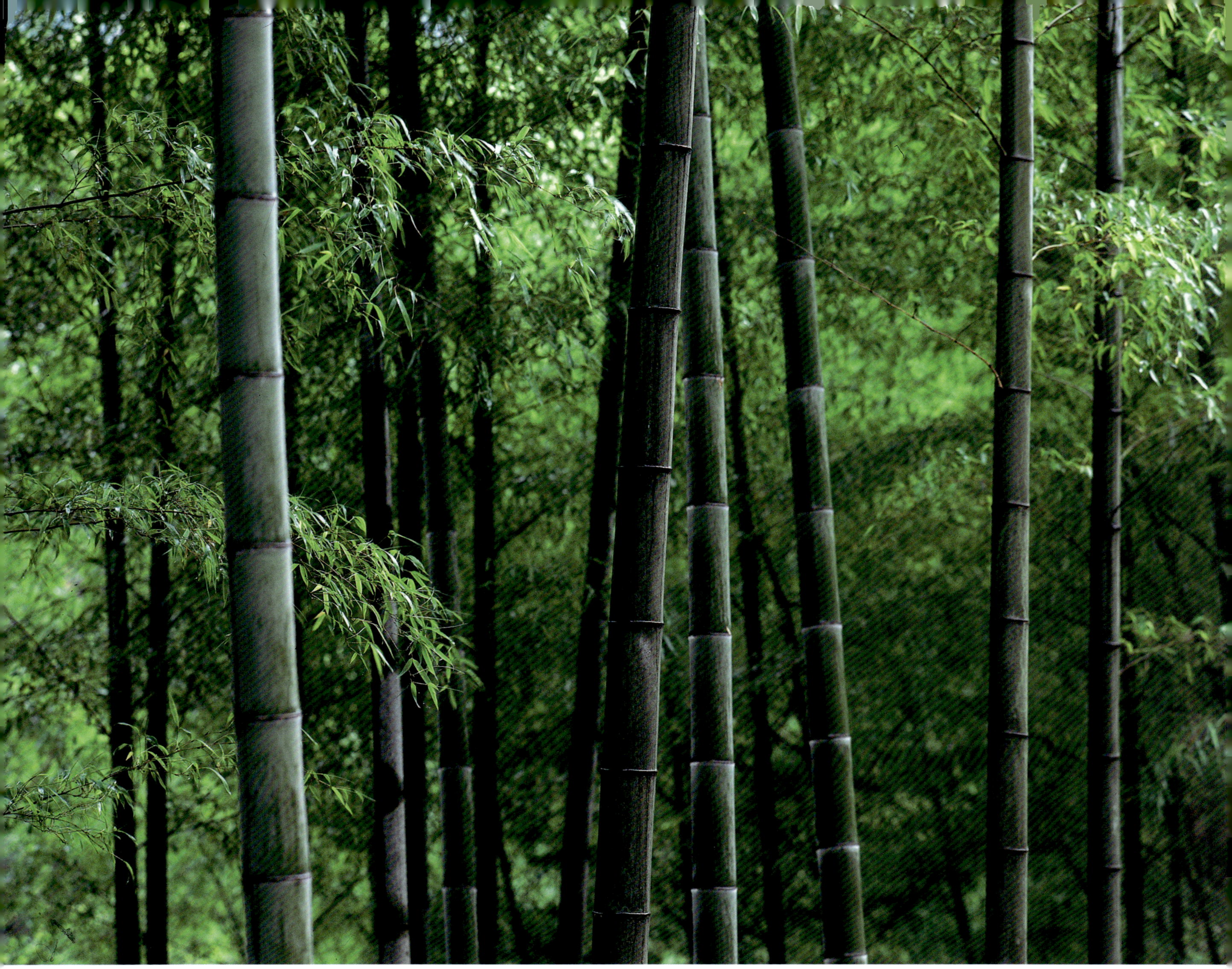

Grass-stalk Forests

Forests of grass? In many tropical regions some species of giant bamboo grow as high as 40 metres and form thick forests.

From a botanical point of view, bamboos belong to the grass family, although in garden centre and nursery catalogues they are usually classified as woody plants. This is no doubt due to the rapid lignification of their perennial stalks, unlike many grasses, and of course with the height to which many bamboos can grow. So we can indeed talk about bamboo forests. And these giant grasses have another distinctive feature: bamboos do not flower every year, like other grasses, but only once in a while, and then almost all plants of a particular species bloom together. This flowering is not seen by gardeners as a welcome byproduct or climax of growth, but rather as a minor catastrophe, because the plants usually die off soon afterwards. The flowering of the bamboo *Fargesia murielae* many years ago meant that almost all the plants in the gardens and parks of Europe were lost, because they were mostly propagated from a single parent plant. Within a very short space of time there were hardly any examples of this plant, and the few that did remain were virtually unsellable, as they were likely to flower at any moment. Meanwhile, new plants have been grown from the resultant seed and good species selected that will now be propagated. It should be a few decades before the plants bloom again, although the greater diversity of species should mean that they don't all bloom at the same time.

As well as these tall, woody bamboos there are some small and dwarf types, which according to their habitat and character are better defined as grasses. They lend themselves perfectly for use as ground cover and over larger areas, and some of them are well suited as low hedges.

THE BEAUTY OF GRASS STALKS

Tall bamboos are fascinating especially because of their stalks: some winter-hardy Middle European varieties reach heights of up to 15 metres with a diameter of more than 10cm. Typically, they are divided into segments, which are separated by ridges, or 'nodes'. This creates an impression of horizontal stripes. From these nodes sprout stems with leaves. But it is not only these nodes or knots in the stalks that create the decorative effect and are arranged differently in different species, the stalks themselves have great ornamental value. They are often multicoloured, sometimes striped, spotted or speckled as if painted by an artist's brush. Many species and varieties also have red, orange, yellow or black stalks. In their juvenile phase these can be white, grey or blue or can change their colour more than once over the course of their development – an additional accent and charm that brings excitement to any garden.

WORLD CHAMPION GROWER

With an established tall bamboo, you can almost see it growing. A plant that is only a shoot poking out of the ground in the morning can be as much as a metre tall by the end of the day. In the first years after planting, the growth is much lower, and also the stalks take years to thicken. Bamboos spread via underground rhizomes, which push new shoots up towards the light. Depending on the length of the rhizomes and the speed at which they are formed, a bamboo can become invasive or remain 'civilized' and clump-forming. The invasive types can quickly become a problem in the garden as they take over all remaining space and drive out other plants. A suitable rhizome block introduced at the planting stage can restrict their spread. Alternatively, they can be planted in containers, but that weakens their overall growth. Most species of the genus *Phyllostachys* are of invasive, strongly growing bamboos of this type, but they are among the most attractive in terms of stalk colouring. The species of the genus *Fargesia*, on the other hand, grow to form clumps and spread only very slowly. They are also more delicate, with thinner stalks and seldom grow taller than 3 metres.

Bamboo forests (opposite)
In Asia various bamboo species are the predominant plants in forests.

Tropical bamboos (below)
Gigantochloa reaches heights of 10–15 metres. Bamboo forests provide a habitat for many endangered species, such as the giant panda.

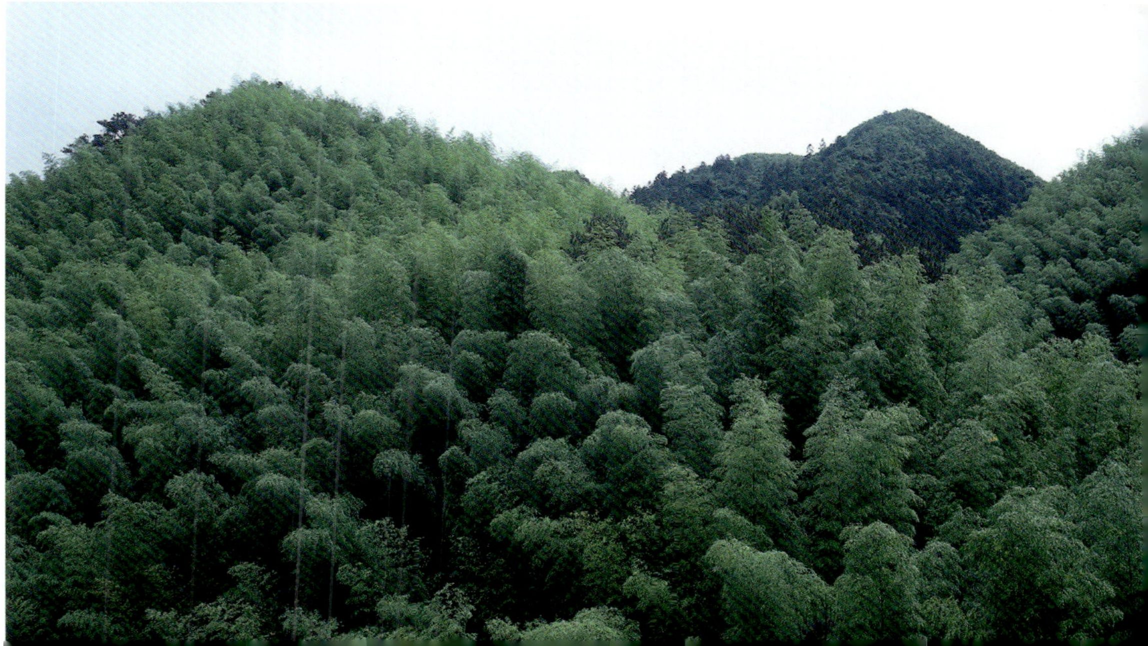

Grasses and People

Humans have had a strong connection with grasses for millennia. They have used them as a source of nutrition, as feed for their animals and as building materials.

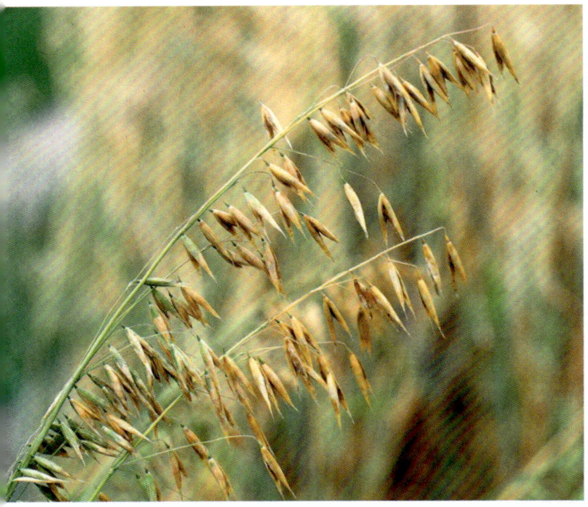

Oats (above)

The various cereals are the most important source of human nutrition.

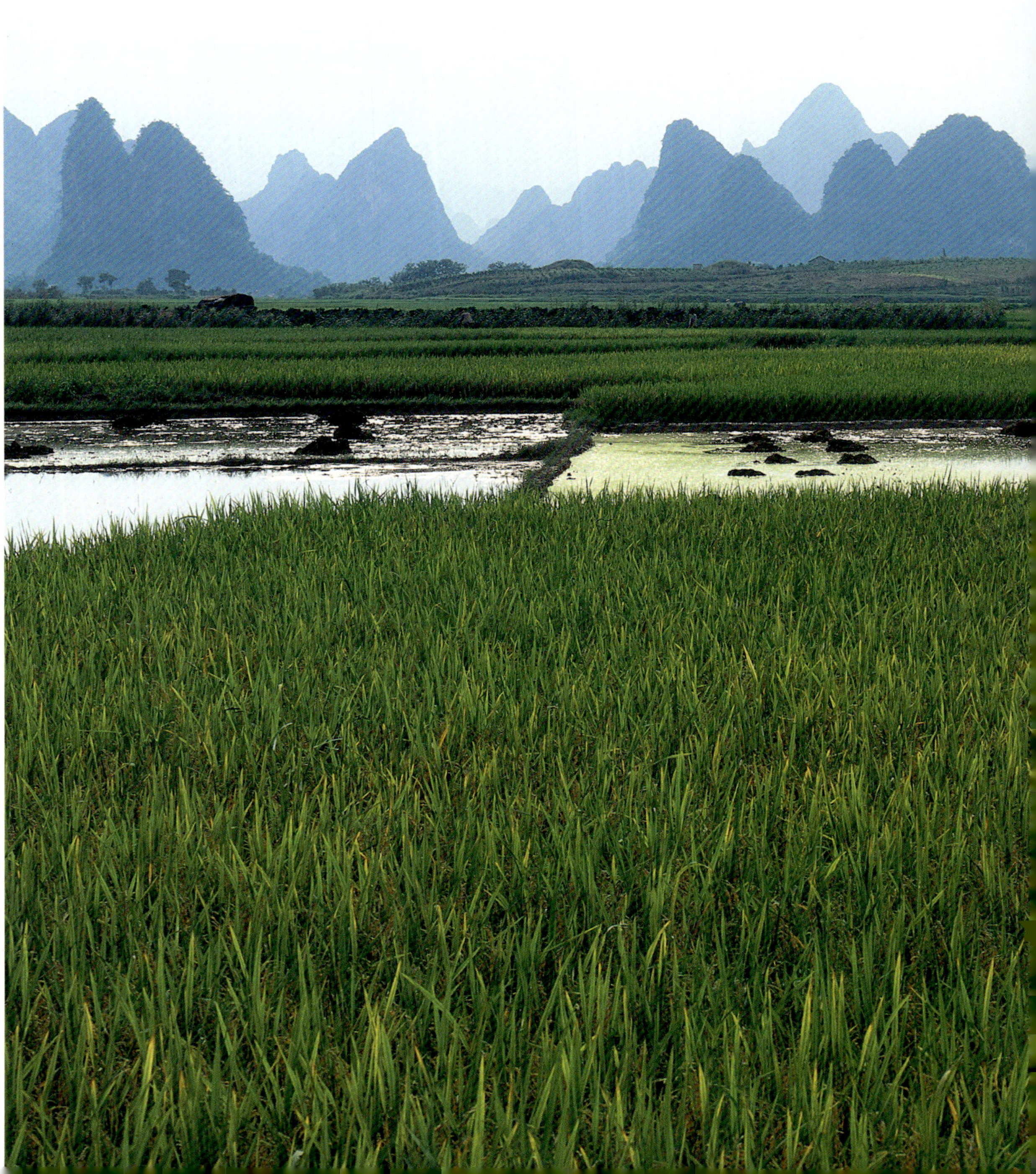

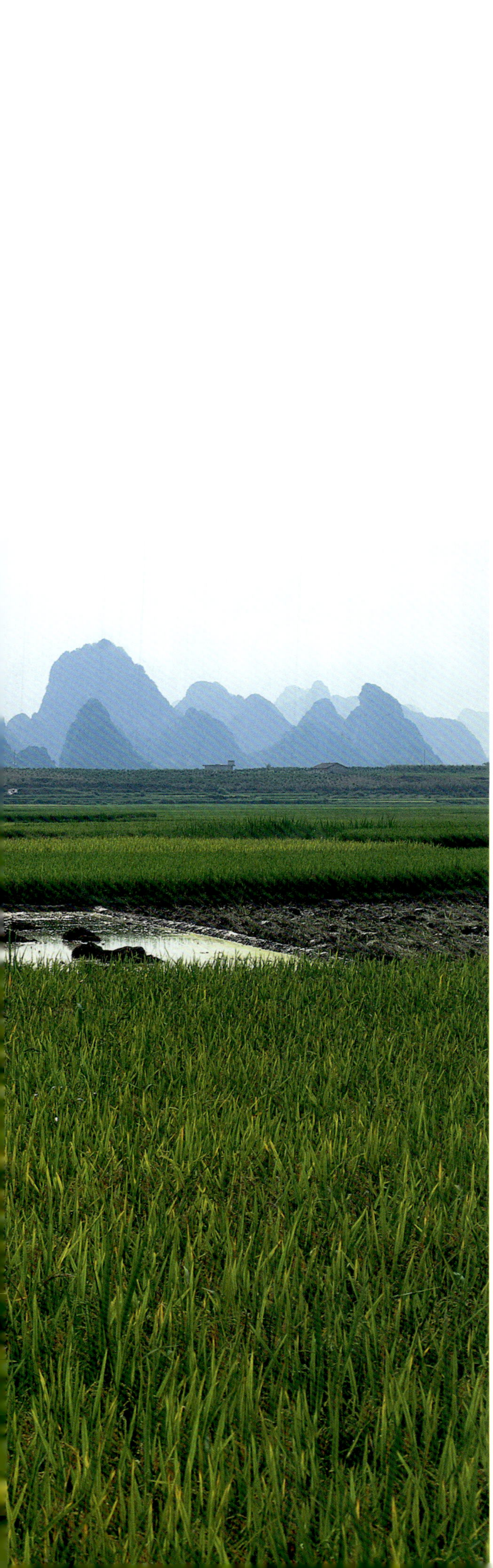

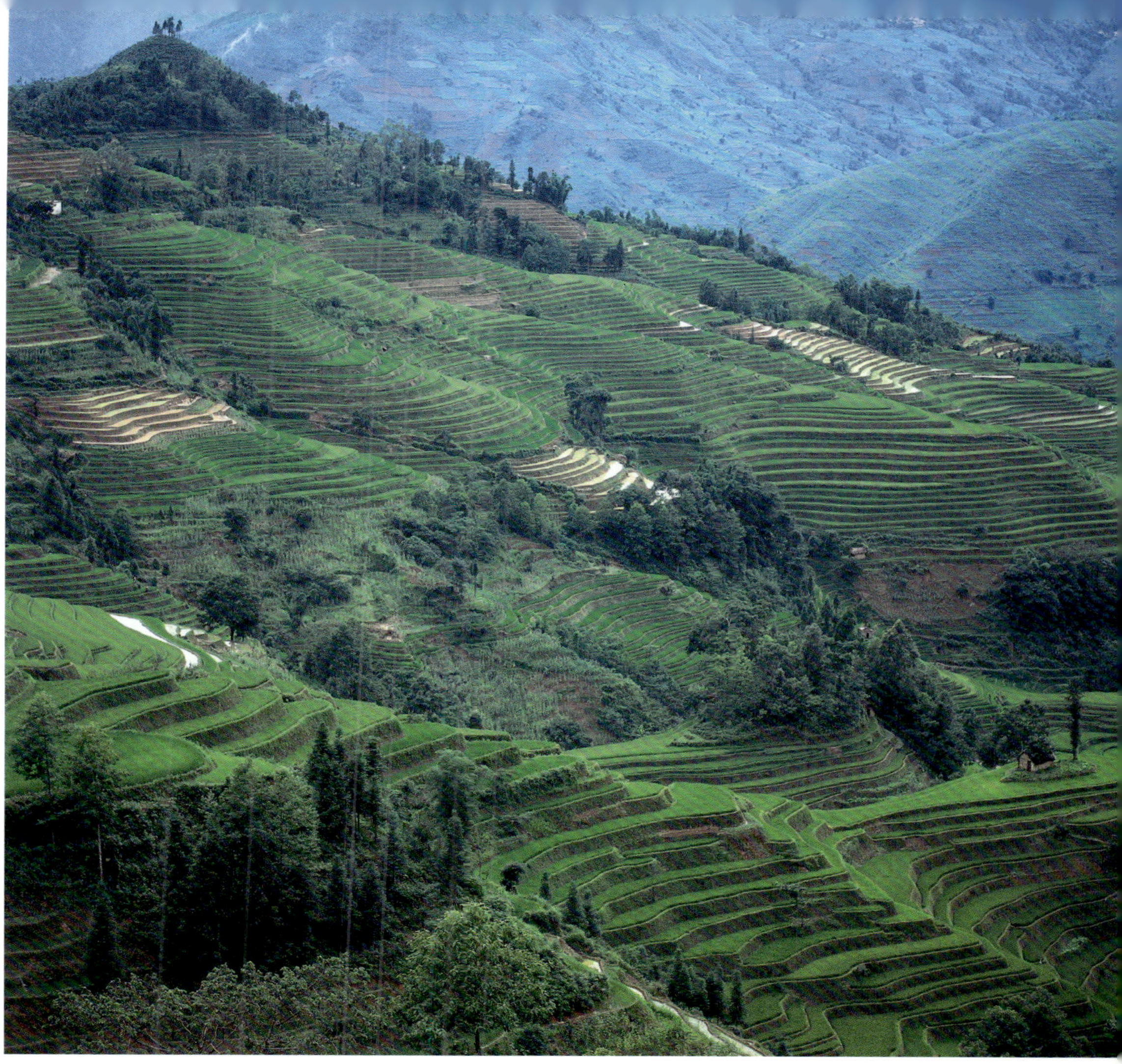

Rice terraces in China (above)

In mountainous regions such as the Ailao Mountains of China rice is grown on artificial terraces. Thus, the moisture is retained in the fields.

Rice fields (left)

Rice is a bog plant, so rice fields are flooded for most of the year.

Grasses have been part of human life for thousands of years. Ever since the earliest people were able to cultivate plants with edible seeds, and then store and mill these seeds, human life expectancy and wellbeing have increased significantly. Most of these edible seeds were derived – and still are today – from grasses.

CEREALS

The first cultivated cereals can be seen as the archetypes of the cereals we know today. Kamut, which was cultivated by the ancient Egyptians, is known as the 'mother of wheat'. Archaeological finds, such as those at Dashare, where earthenware pots containing ears of kamut were discovered in 1948, are evidence of this. Due to many years of selection and directed breeding, modern cereal crops are more productive, but also need more fertiliser and care in order to achieve their greater yields. However, organic farmers and those dealing with Third World food shortages have found it quite rewarding to return to the old species. For example, kamut has 40 per cent more

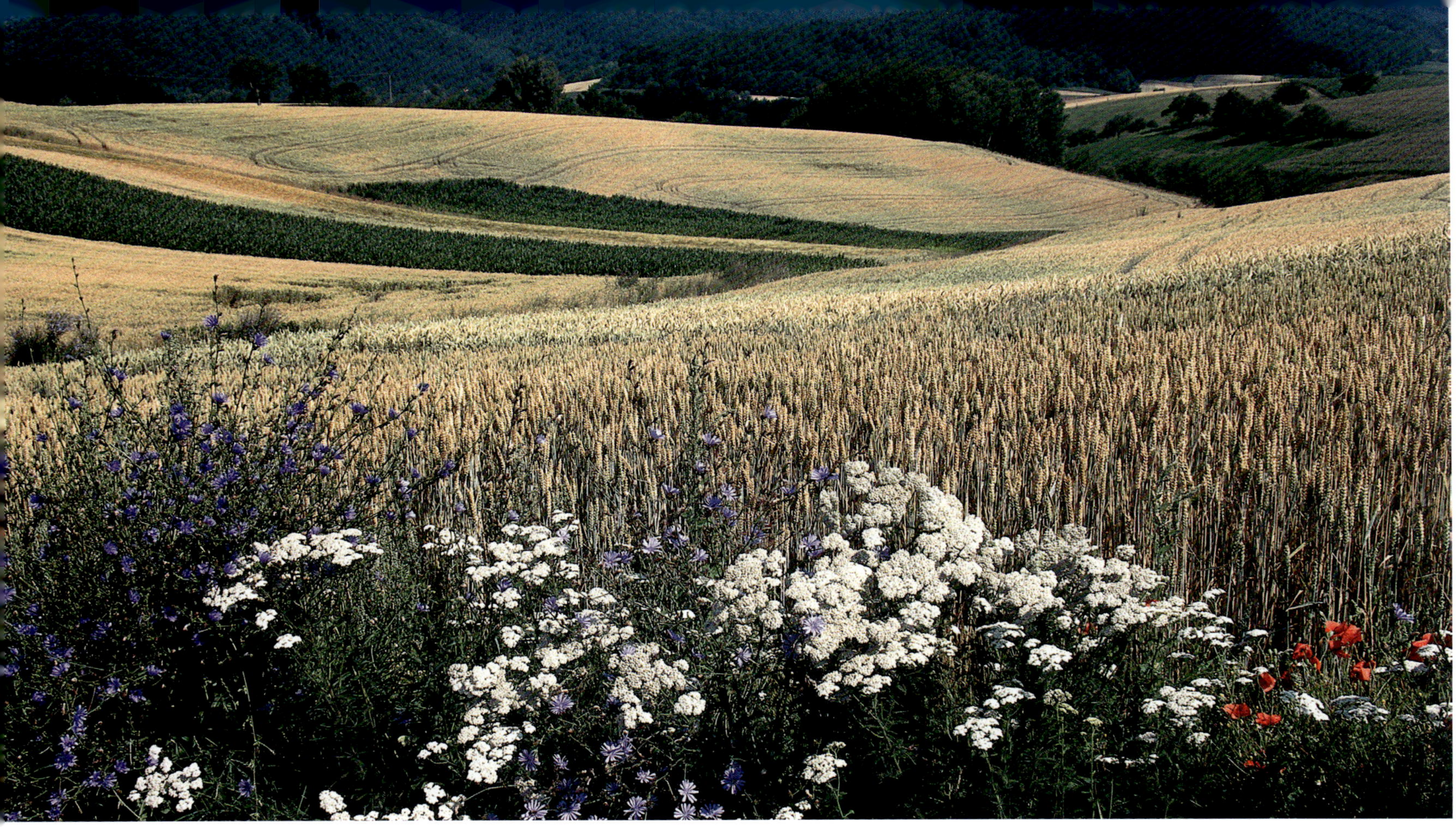

Cereal fields

Over the centuries high-yielding varieties have been bred from simple wild grain. Combined with meadows and natural field margins, they can create interesting and varied landscapes.

protein and minerals than modern cultivars and has particularly good adhesive properties, which are important when it comes to be processed.

RICE

Throughout the Asian continent and also in parts of Africa rice is the main food staple. Rice is predominantly grown wet, that is, in flooded fields. Through the use of dams and the construction of terraces with irrigation systems, rice fields are flooded most of the time. The impressive sight of these terraces across whole landscapes underlines the importance of this crop in Asia. The flowing water carries fertile mud to the fields through a complex system of dams and provides the necessary fertiliser for the crop. In the USA, too, rice has been cultivated since the seventeenth century and has become established as an important cereal.

GRASSES AS BUILDING MATERIAL

In those parts of the world where there are no large trees to provide wood as a building material, people have to fall back on grasses. In the broad alluvial plain of the Nile in Africa or in the reed beds around the high Andean lakes, rushes are used as building material for boats, huts and furniture. The Uru people, the original inhabitants of Lake Titicaca on the border between Peru and Bolivia, spend most of their lives on home-made islands constructed out of totora bulrushes.

Bamboo has been used as a building material in garden design. Fences, trellises and sightscreen walls made out of bamboo harmonise with both formal and heavily planted gardens. Bamboo poles are also excellent for treehouses and other children's playthings. Due to their toughness and their smooth surface they can be kept outdoors all year round without any further weatherproofing. Despite this, bamboos are easily worked with saws, drills and hammers. For temporary structures, bamboo poles can be lashed together with rope or string. This is how scaffolding is made in Asian countries: these apparently precarious scaffolding structures are used even in the construction of high-rise buildings. Bamboo has the advantage of being light but strong, and hence fairly elastic. Nevertheless, the workers who climb up aloft these structures must have a good head for heights …

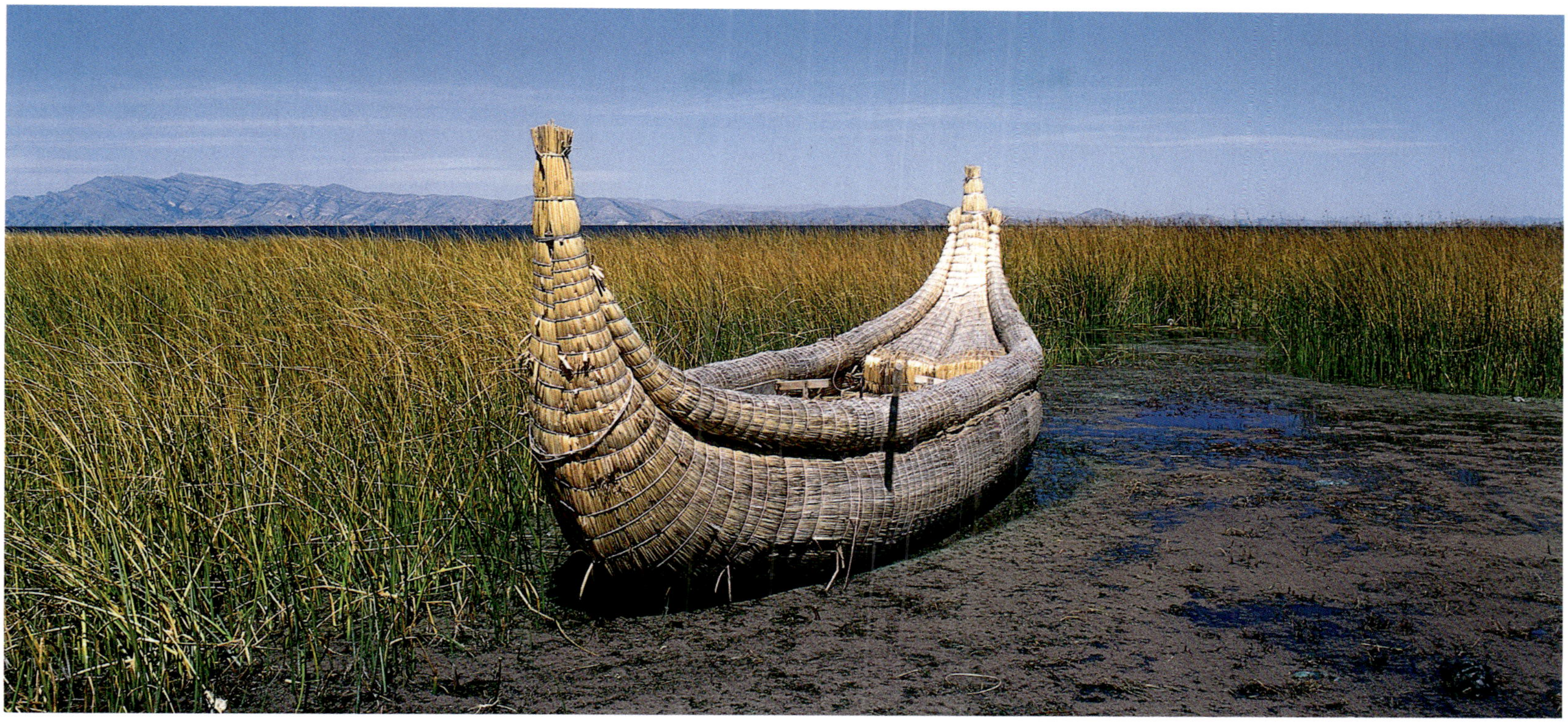

Boat on Lake Titicaca
Lacking other building materials, the inhabitants of Lake Titicaca in the Andes make their boats out of the stalks of Totora bulrushes.

Bamboo has become quite a fashionable material in recent years in interior design. It is useful for parquet flooring as it needs to be 'worked' much less than the traditional woods that are used. The regular stripe of the grain produces an elegant effect, and it is also possible to achieve different hues by the application of heat during fabrication. Bamboo has also been successfully employed in small items of furniture and kitchenware – chopping boards, trays and bowls look stylish and fit in with any décor.

GRASSES AS A RENEWABLE RESOURCE

Long known and utilised in China, giant silver grass *(Miscanthus giganteus)* is now being used more in Middle Europe. This plant possesses a whole range of qualities that makes it interesting for a wide variety of applications. It is suitable as biomass for the generation of energy, such as in the form of pellets for small block heating power stations or plants producing biogas.

Another interesting application is as a natural building material. The crushed plants are mixed with cement to make a sort of concrete. The result is a very stable building material impervious to environmental influences such as damp, salt, mould or the like. According to the proportions used, and whether or not the miscanthus is ground up coarse or fine, the properties of the concrete can be varied. It can be used in solid form as a construction material or screed, and in its lighter, more porous form for heat and sound insulation; as such it is a useful insulating material for walls and roofs. In Britain, miscanthus is already used in the plastics industry, in conjunction with polymers made from rapeseed oil. The result is a light, flexible plastic that could be used in the car industry, for example.

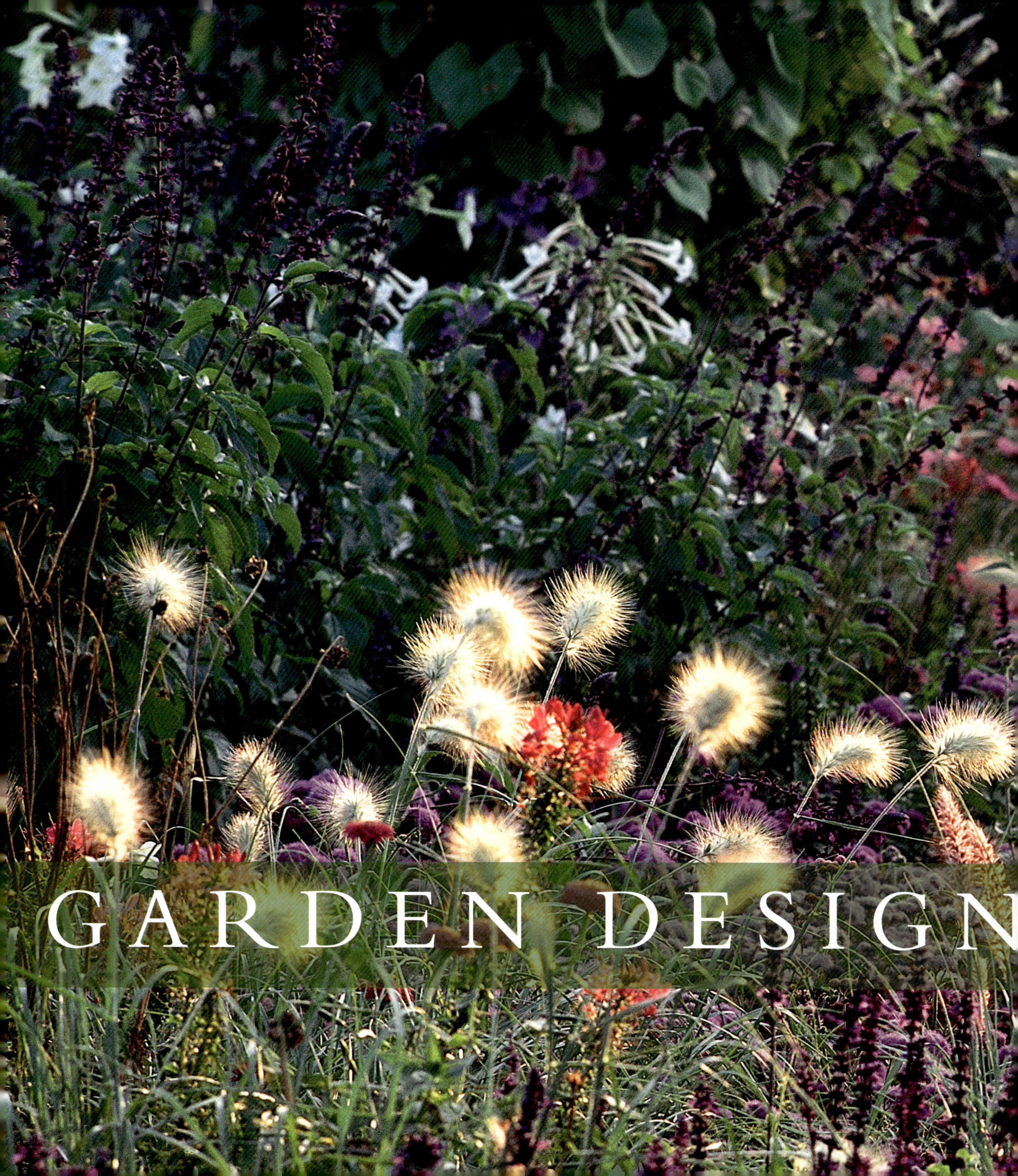

GARDEN DESIGN

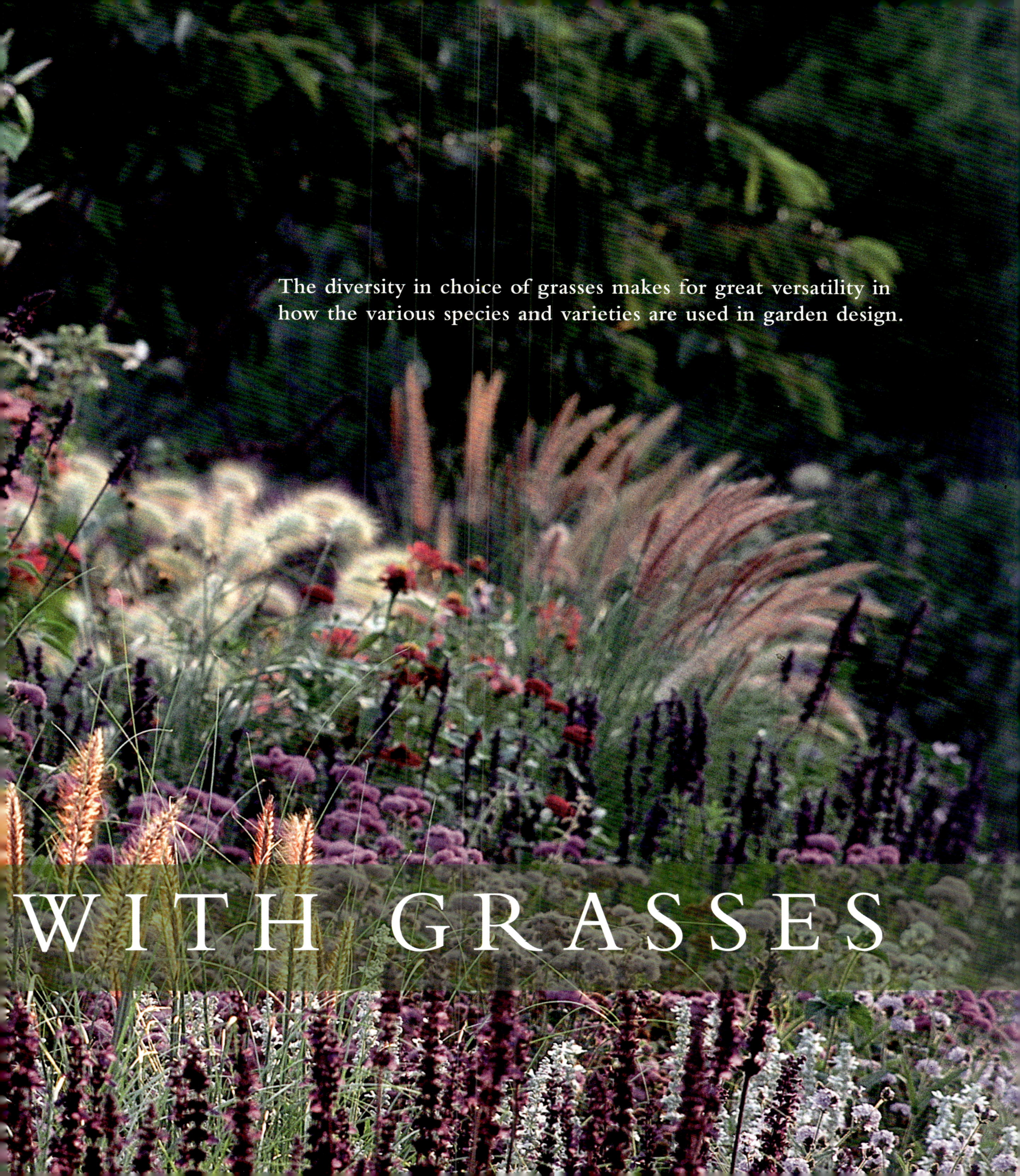

The diversity in choice of grasses makes for great versatility in how the various species and varieties are used in garden design.

WITH GRASSES

Lines and Accents

Giant grasses and dwarf cushion grasses – when it comes to grasses in the garden, the design possibilities are endless.

Grass types range from ornamental giant grasses, which grow to heights of 4 metres, to dwarf cushion plants, which can conceal themselves in the crevices between stones. Many grasses are conspicuous for their distinctive habits. Some grow straight upright, others tip over, many cascade like a waterfall to the ground. These distinctive forms can be exploited as design elements in the garden, both in combination with each other and alongside shrubs and trees. Even buildings and other constructions can be emphasised and enhanced by the introduction of grasses. Giant grasses cut a splendid figure when standing alone – showing their monumental habit to best advantage.

LINES

Grasses as far as the eye can see, swaying wheat fields stretching to the horizon – nature plays with horizontal lines. And this play can be echoed in the garden, albeit on a much smaller scale. It is important, however, to be liberal: better

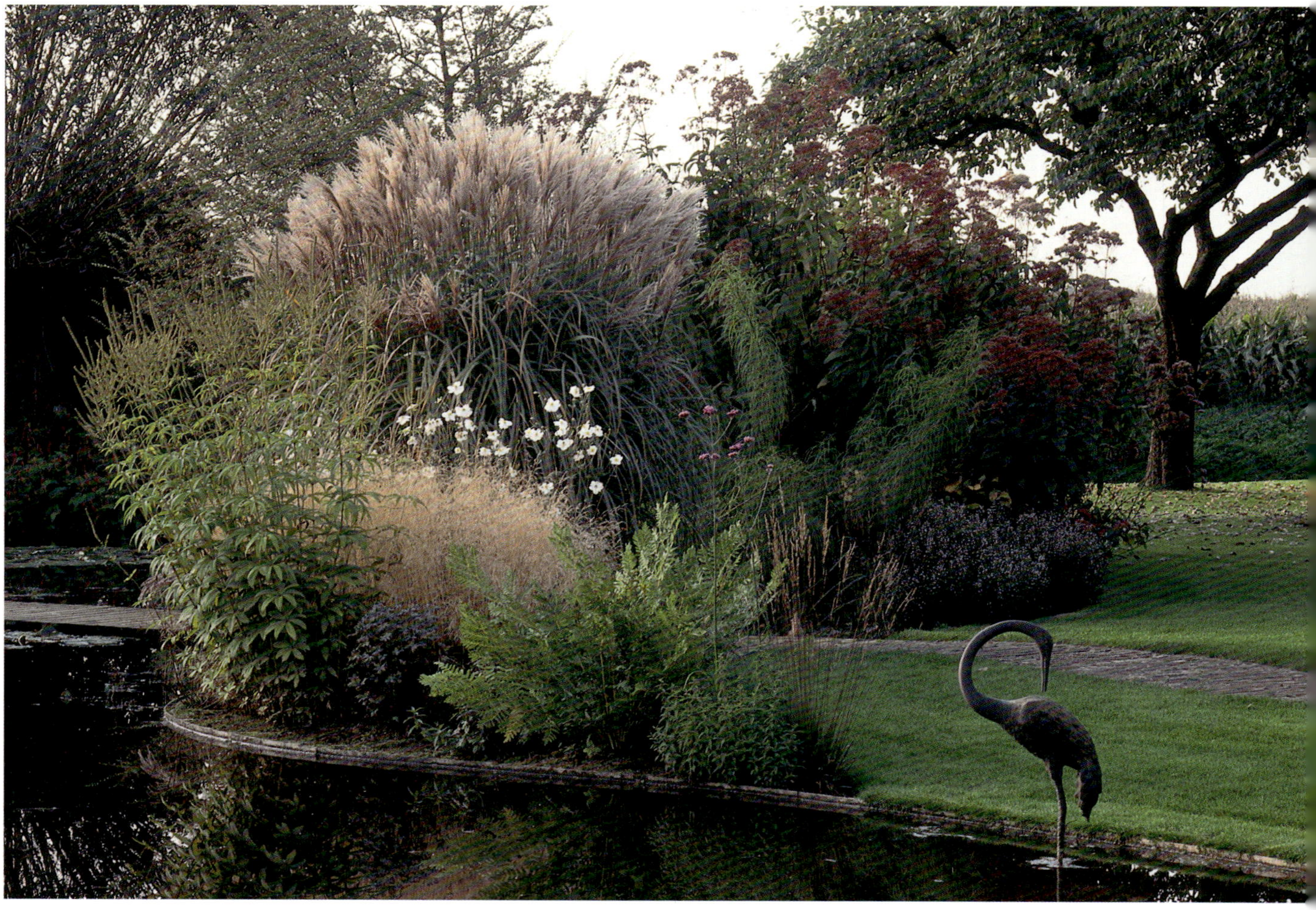

Lines at the edge of a pond
The high-arching Eulalia *(Miscanthus sinensis)* picks up the elegantly curved water's edge. Its planting partners are Culver's root *(Veronica virginica)*, hair grass or tussock grass *(Deschampsia)*, royal fern *(Osmunda regalis)*, boneset *(Eupatorium)*, willow-leaved sunflowers *(Helianthus salicifolius)*, catmint *(Nepeta)* and Japanese anemone *(Anemone japonica)*.

to work with only a few varieties of grasses but use them in large quantities. In this way you can create expressive strips, so-called drifts. This type of plant usage comes from the USA and is starting to establish itself in Europe. Drifts work best with thin-stemmed grasses, which sway in the breeze. Through a subtle gradation of height and the use of various leaf and stalk colours, even pure grass drifts can be exciting. One can also combine grasses with suitable flowering shrubs. Care should be taken, however, to use plants that have a capped growth and uniform height in order to achieve the desired 'horizontal' look.

In contrast, there are grasses that lend themselves to arrangements using vertical lines. These are characterised either by erect, relatively upward-growing foliage or by rigid flower stalks. With the right mix of vertical and horizontal elements, beds can be given the desired depth and structure.

CURVES

While linear arrangements can often seem a little rigid, curves are often associated with terms such as 'soft', 'supple' and 'pliable'. Many grasses grow in a curved shape, their thin foliage bending gracefully in all directions. Adjectives like 'vase-shaped', 'overhanging', 'dome-like' or 'cushiony' describe the soft lines particularly well. Elegant overhanging giant grasses need plenty of space to be shown to their best advantage. They should, therefore, be located at the rear and preferably to one side of a planting scheme, so that they aren't crowded by neighbouring plants. Especially attractive grasses with curved shapes, such as the many varieties of miscanthus, work best when they are planted between lower partners. In this way they can display their habit appropriately.

Smaller, cushion grasses, such as most of the fescue *(Festuca)* varieties, work best in small or larger groups. Especially in rock gardens or gravel beds, they form a nice contrast with the hard, non-

Paths and stepping stones
Grasses and shrubs were planted in segments of this circular paved area. This especially emphasises the variety of leaf shapes and colours.

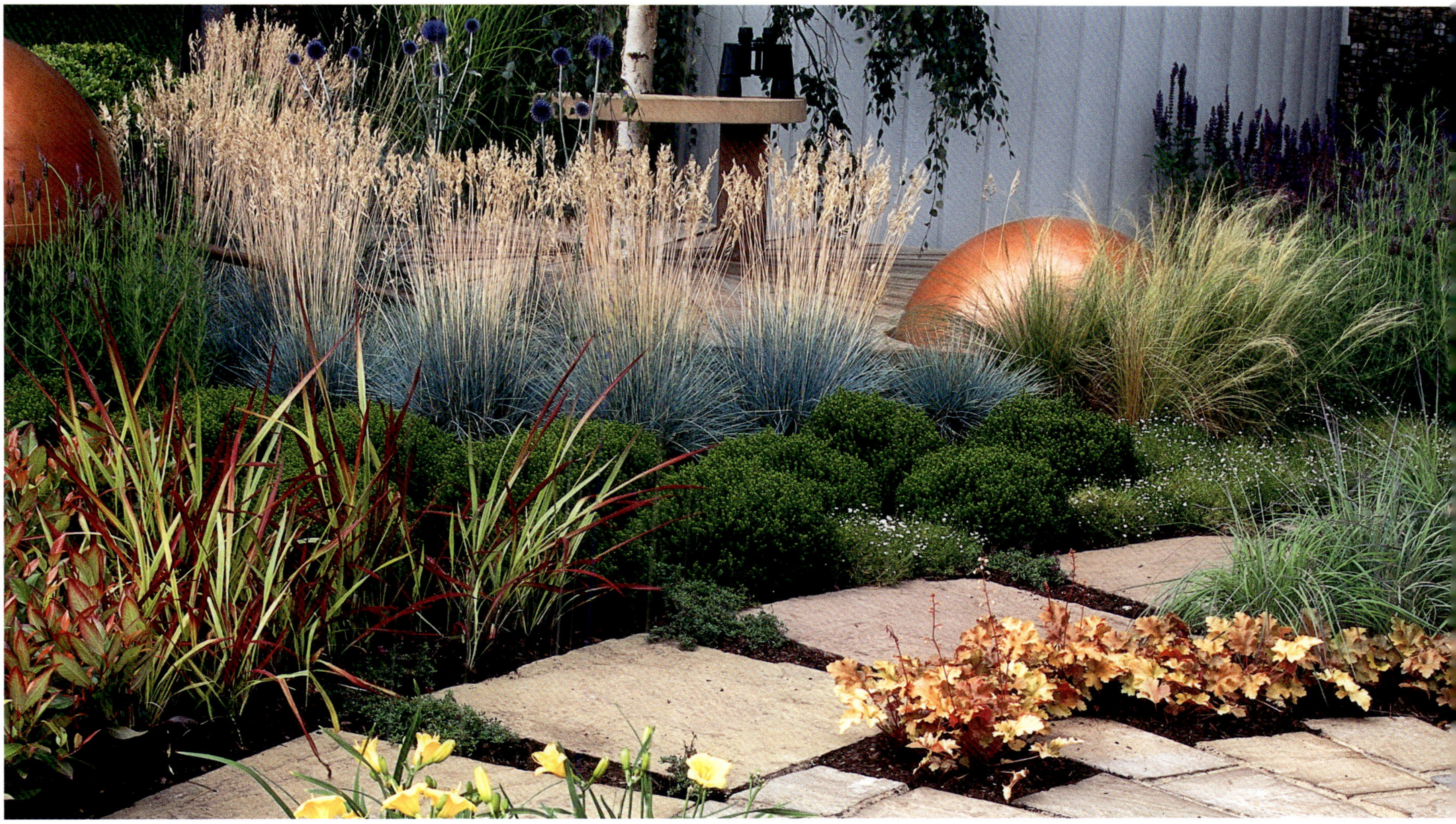

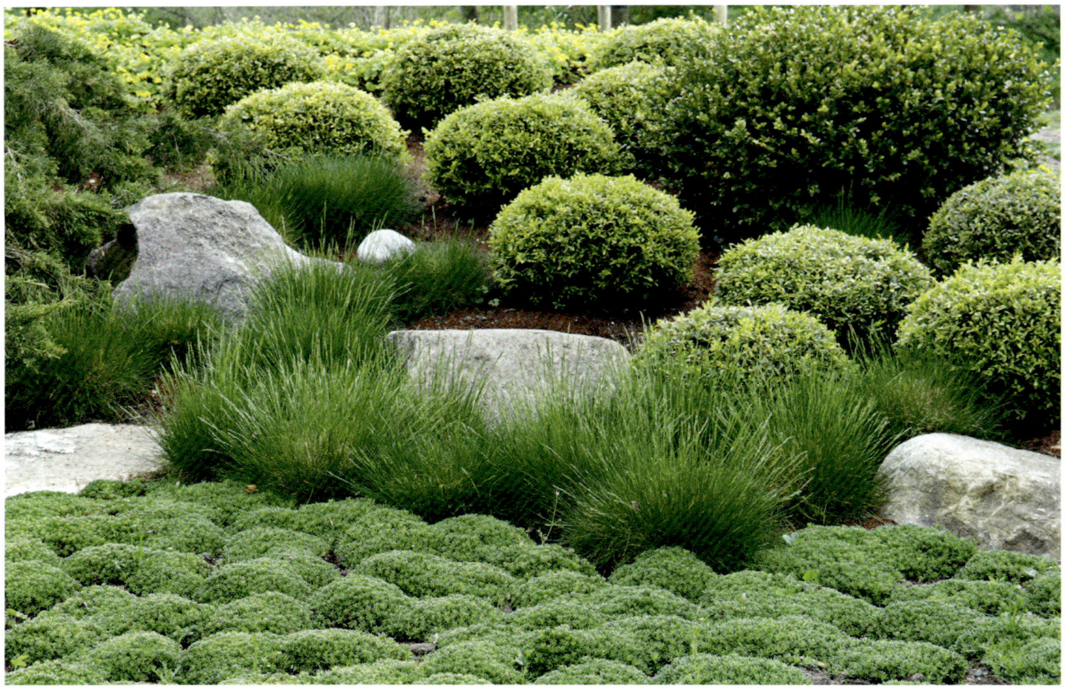

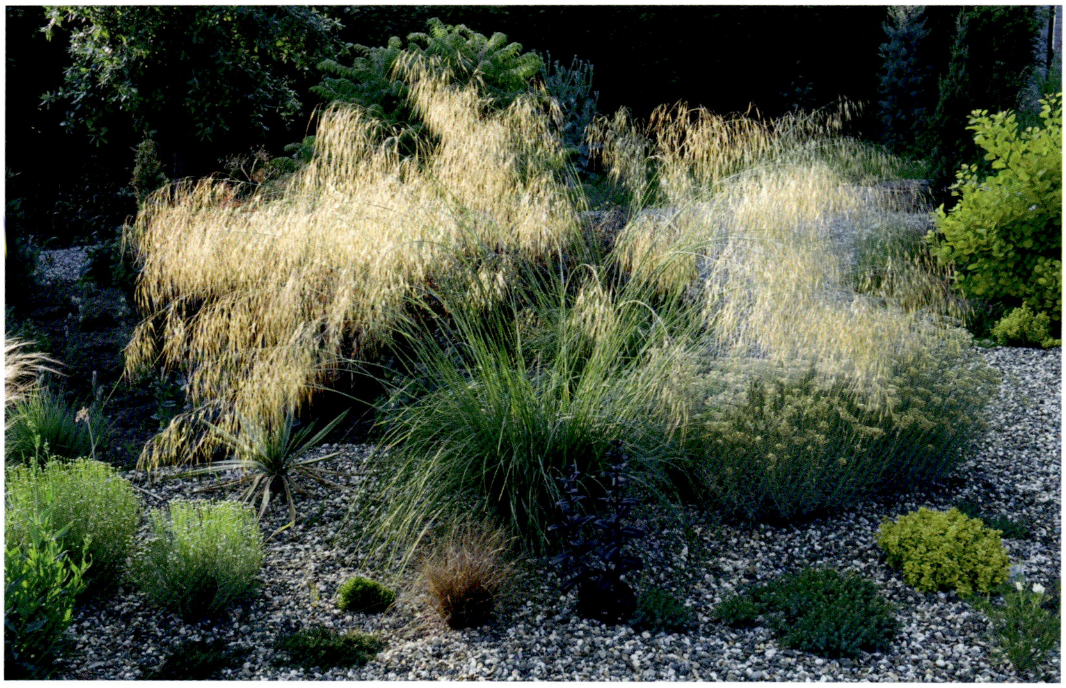

Globes of different sizes (above, top)
Topiary shrubs and grasses of all sizes are the basic theme of this very formal design. The bearskin fescue *(Festuca scoparia)* naturally forms the right shape.

Accents in a gravel bed (above, bottom)
Grasses and silver-leafed shrubs provide accents to a sunny gravel bed.

organic materials; they soften angular rocks and play around the straight lines of walls and paths.

Even the overhanging species, which are suitable for the foregrounds of beds, mediate between the planting and the hard structures. Corners and edges disappear gracefully under soft curves.

ACCENTS

With single grasses and small groups of grass you can create points of accent. They act as quasi exclamation marks that catch the eye and draw attention to themselves, or provide repeating elements between relatively uniform groups of plants. The most striking accents are created with tall, erect grasses. They act like lighthouses in seas of grasses or flowers. Even the long-distant effect of a planting scheme can be enhanced by the strategic placement of strong giant grasses. In this case the same rules apply as in the design of a classical border: a harmonious scheme is achieved through the combination of specimen shrubs and filler planting, a considered use of height gradations and an exciting structure made up of horizontal and vertical elements.

Specimen shrubs play a particularly important role in design by providing the vertical accents. They are the visual framework of the planting. Typical examples among grasses are pampas grass *(Cortaderia selloana)*, giant silver grass *(Miscanthus giganteus)* and the rather more upright sorts of Eulalia *(Miscanthus sinensis*, for example 'Malepartus', or 'Strictus'). The tall specimen shrubs should be offset and supplemented by so-called companion shrubs. The specimen shrubs emphasise the vertical aspect of the border, while the companion plants provide a horizontal counterpoint to create an exciting interplay.

In order to make the planting look dense and enclosed, filler planting needs to be introduced. They should be of an airy habit and be visually unobtrusive, so that they can fulfil their allotted function. Many transparent grasses such as melic *(Melica)* and fescue *(Festuca)* belong in this category, as do filigree plants such as gypsophila, lady's mantle *(Alchemilla)* and rose campion *(Lychnis coronaria)*.

Even medium-sized plants can stand out from their surroundings and create accents, especially when the surrounding plants are a lot lower. Areas with full ground cover work better and are enhanced when they are interspersed with accent plants. Even in shady spots under trees striking grasses such as Gray's sedge, or Mace Sedge, *(Carex grayi)* or Bowles' golden grass (*Milium effesum* 'Aureum') can give unattractive ivy- or pachysandra-covered areas some necessary structure. When choosing grasses you should always make sure that they are thoroughly sturdy and that they have enough root space between the ground-cover plants. The grasses themselves should not be ground-cover, otherwise the desired accentuation will be lost over the course of time.

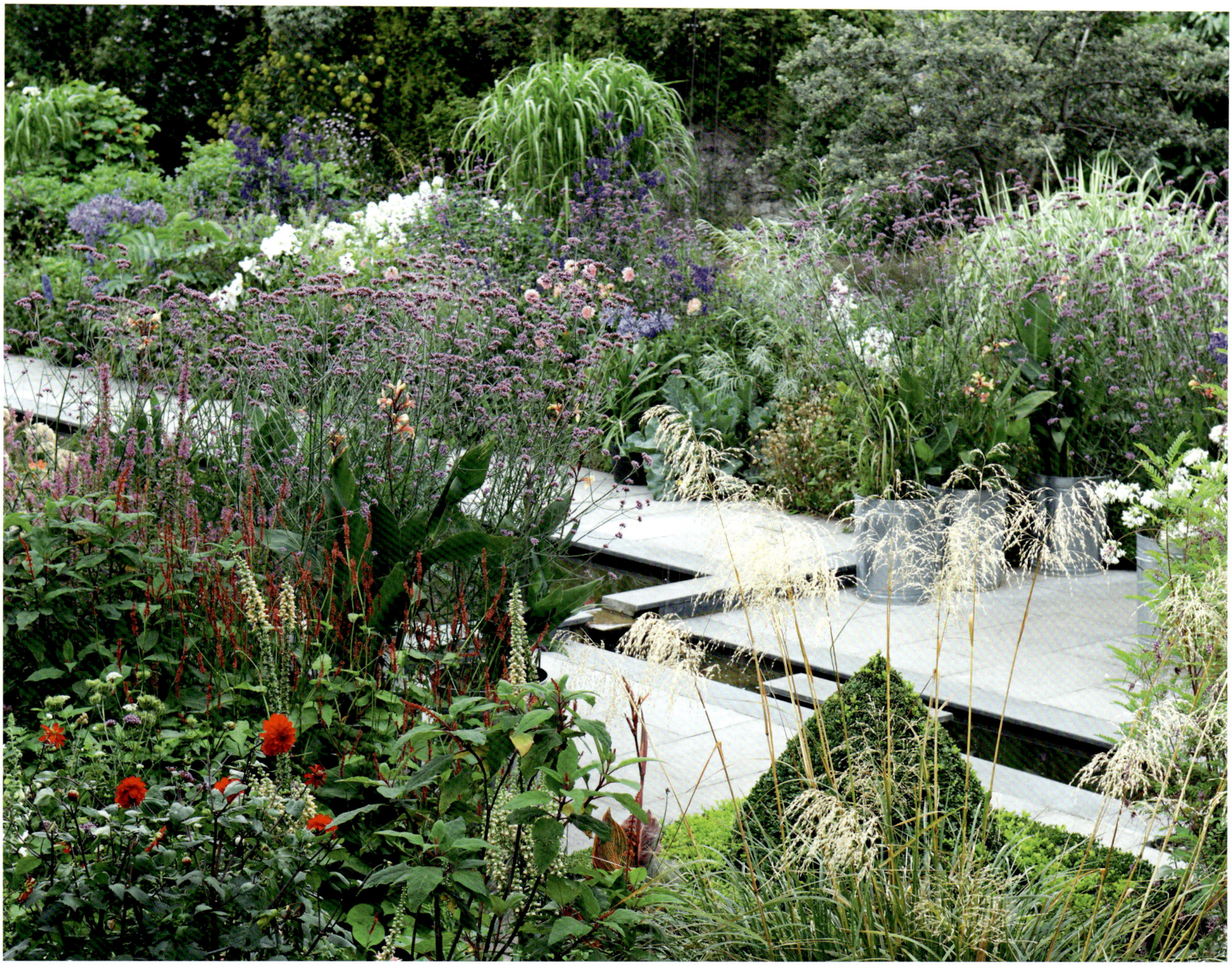

Tall grasses at the edge of a pool
Various tall grasses form the background for the planting alongside a formal water feature.

Habitats

Habitats in the wild provide a model for the use of grasses in the garden.

When you base the planning of your beds on the available habitats in the garden and combine the plants most suitable for them, you get lasting beautiful beds with healthy plants. And the costs of upkeep are also kept within reasonable limits. In practice, the different habitats have been classified, and the following are relevant for garden design using grasses.

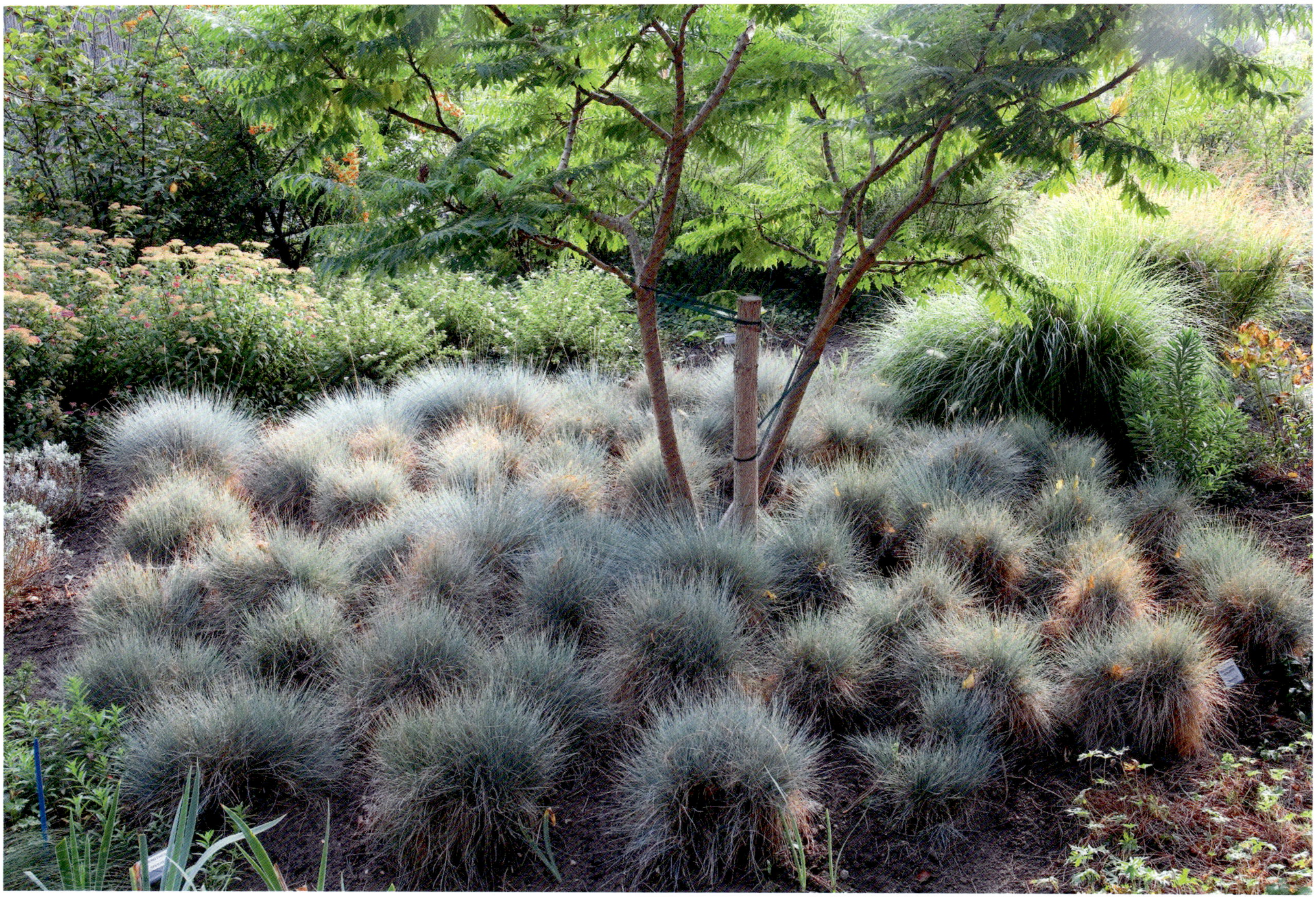

WOODLAND

In this habitat those grasses and shrubs do best that have a close relationship to trees. They need shade or at least half shade and prefer humus-rich, ideally fresh, hence damp and not dried-out soils. To this group belong native woodland grasses and shrubs that can bear root pressure and thus can survive well between the powerful roots of trees, but also foreign species that make greater demands on the soil and thrive without difficulty in the shade so long as they are given sufficient water and nutrients.

WOODLAND EDGES

Many parts of the garden spend some hours each day in shade but are also open to the sun, for example at the edge of woods, next to walls and alongside buildings. Depending on their aspect, the plants spend a few hours in full sun and the rest of the day in shade. Beneath sparsely leafed bushes, on the other hand, the foliage acts as a sort of filter, and this is often described as dappled or semi-shade. The soil conditions in half shade can vary greatly, depending on whether there are tree roots to contend with, whether or not the soil is porous or whether buildings provide shelter from rain.

FULL SUN

Depending on the humidity of the soil, this habitat has the character of a steppe or meadow. Wild shrubs and grasses or lightly bred species and varieties are at home in this habitat. Several types of grasses also do well on the steppe and combine well with shrubs from the sun-baked regions of America. Many plants from this habitat are sensitive to prolonged winter damp, so the soil must in any case have good drainage. Heavy soil should be improved with sand and grit. On nutrient-rich, fresh soil native meadow flowers congregate with splendid shrubs, so you should restrict yourself to natural-looking, and thus not over-bred, species with single blooms. They are hardier than their highly bred cousins, which frequently have to be tied up and can often appear too dominant to the eye.

ROCK GARDENS

Plants for this habitat are mostly low-growing. Many grow as creepers or mounds. As well as regular rock gardens, dry walls, stone steps, scree and gravel beds are all examples of this habitat. Most rock garden plants prefer full sun or at least a predominantly sunny location, though there are some specialist plants that prosper on north-facing walls and depend on the higher air humidity that predominates there.

BORDERS

Borders are where the numerous types of decorative, highly bred shrubs find their place. The designation 'border' is in fact somewhat misleading, since other habitats are effectively borders. A cultivated herbaceous border is what is meant here.

The plants suited to this habitat need deep, sufficiently moist, but well-drained soil, well supplied with nutrients, in order to thrive. They are all sunseekers and wilt and suffer severe curtailment of their flowering performance if they get too much shade. Preparing the soil well before setting out a border is therefore a top priority. In dry weather, regular watering is required, tall grasses and shrubs often need to be supported, and many shrubs have to be taken up and divided every few years so that they don't grow weak and to ensure that they bloom dependably year after year. The unsurpassed display of flowers more than makes up for all the effort involved.

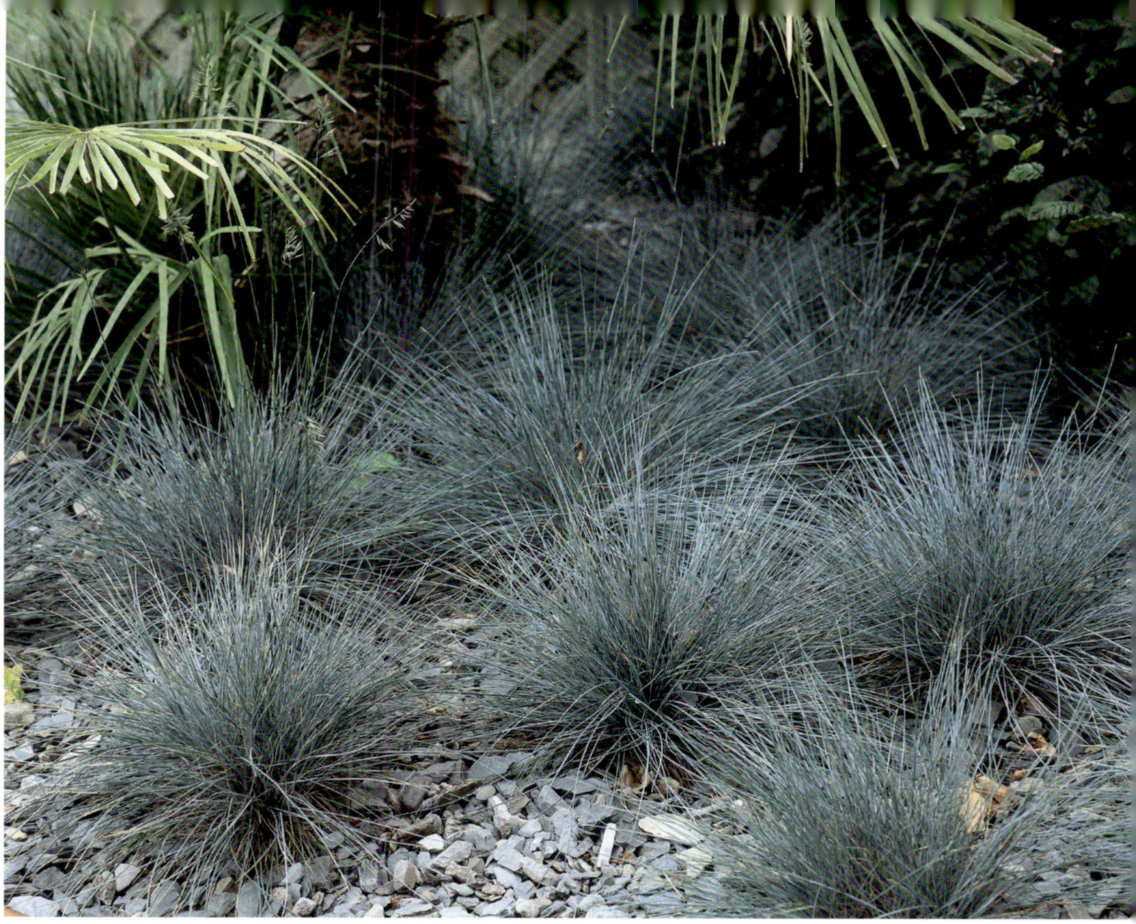

Full sun habitat
The steel-blue stalks of the common blue fescue *(Festuca cinerea)* serve as a contrast with the rough pebbles. In the background, a Chinese windmill or Chusan palm *(Trachycarpus fortunei)*.

Woodland edge habitat (opposite)
Common blue fescue *(Festuca cinerea)* in semi shade. The individual mounds do not overlap.

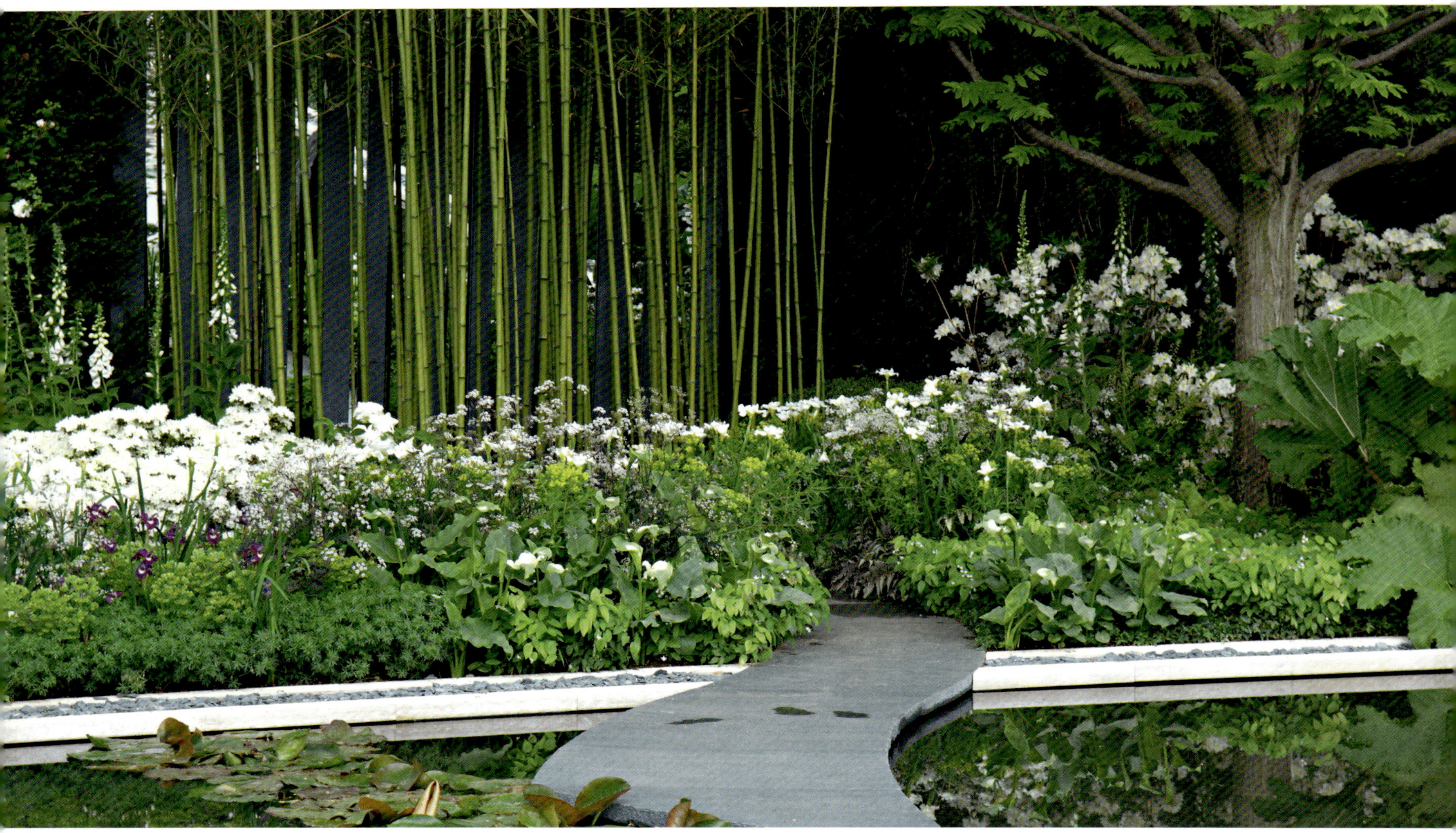

Waterside habitat
Tall bamboo stalks make an ideal backdrop for various shade-loving shrubs.

Rock garden habitat (right)
Switch grass *(Panicum virgatum)* offer a filigree adornment to a group of boulders.

Rock garden habitat (opposite)
A lot of contrast in a confined space. Mexican feather grass *(Nassella tenuissima)* with the succulent broad-leaved glaucous spurge *(Euphorbia myrsinites)*.

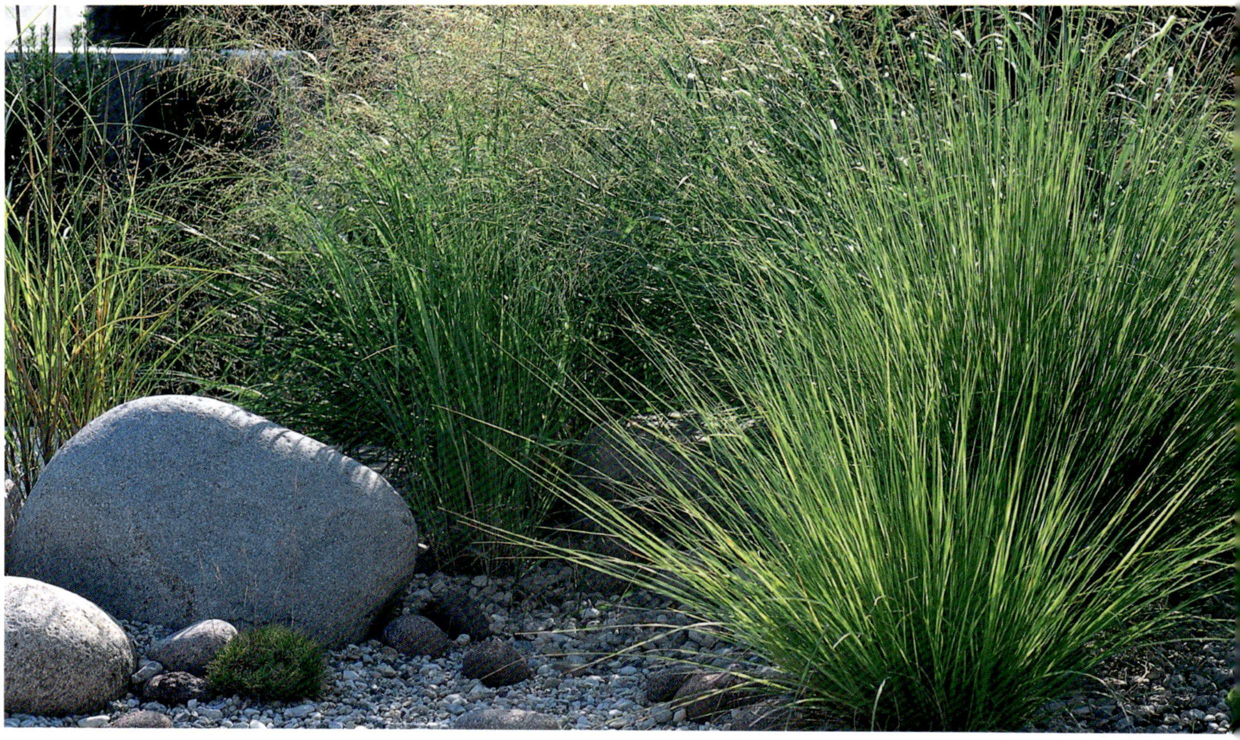

WATER'S EDGE

The edges of garden ponds are usually damp to boggy. The shallows, where there is a constant depth of water of about 10cm, also counts as part of this habitat. Even for this habitat there is a full range of shrubs. Native shrubs that grow in damp meadows in the wild are suitable for waterside planting, as are bog grasses and rushes. Notably, among the specialist plants for waterside locations, there are many shrubs with beautiful ornamental foliage.

AQUATIC

The deeper parts of ponds and lakes are the typical habitat of various aquatic plants, whose roots either float in the water or are anchored in the pond bed and have long stems up to the surface of the water. A few grasses manage to cope with water depths of 20-40 cm and can therefore be suited to the watery habitat. Among them, for example, are species such as the cyperus or hop sedge *(Carex pseudocyperus)* and the club-rush *(Schoenoplectus lacustris)*.

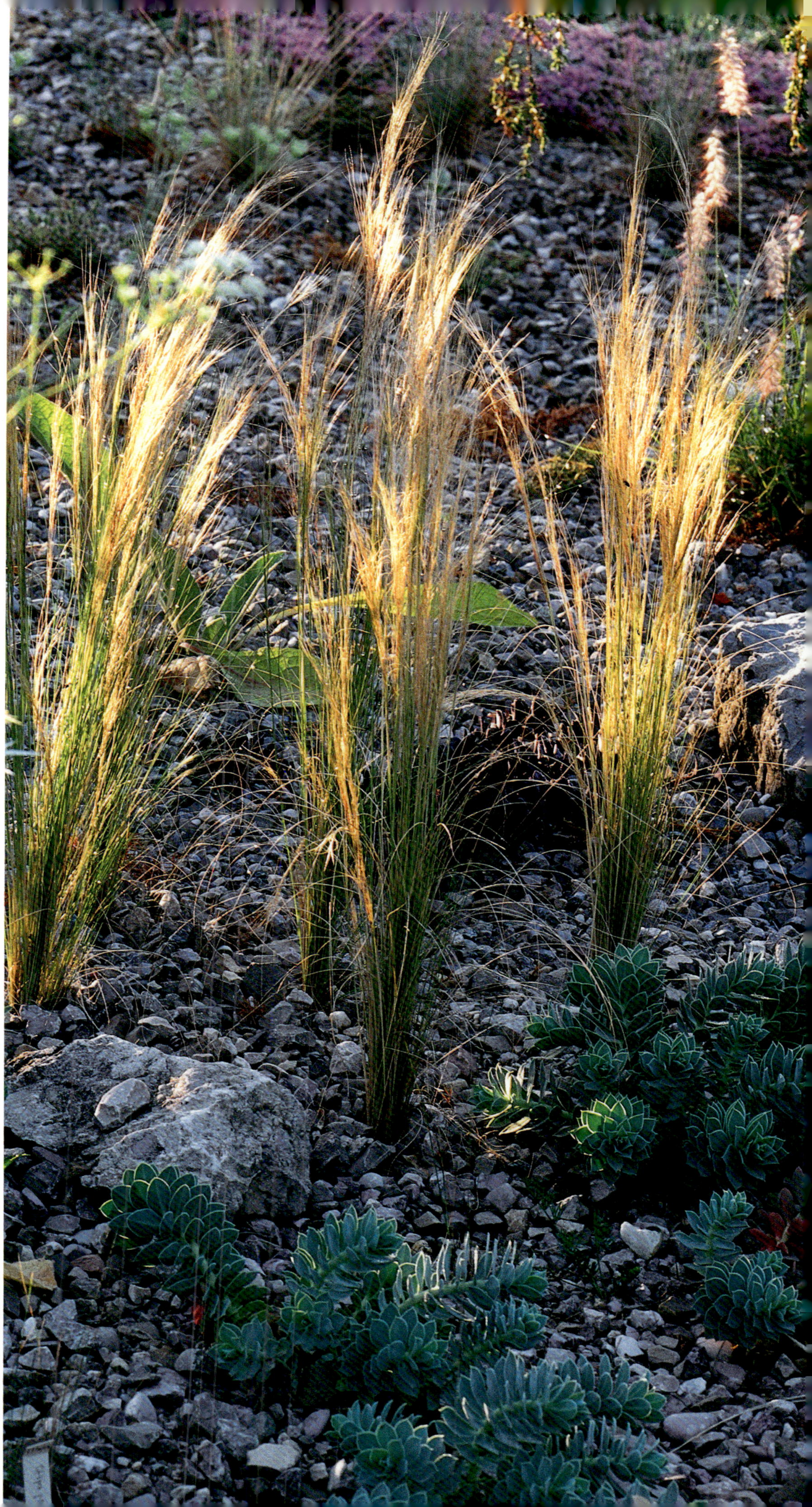

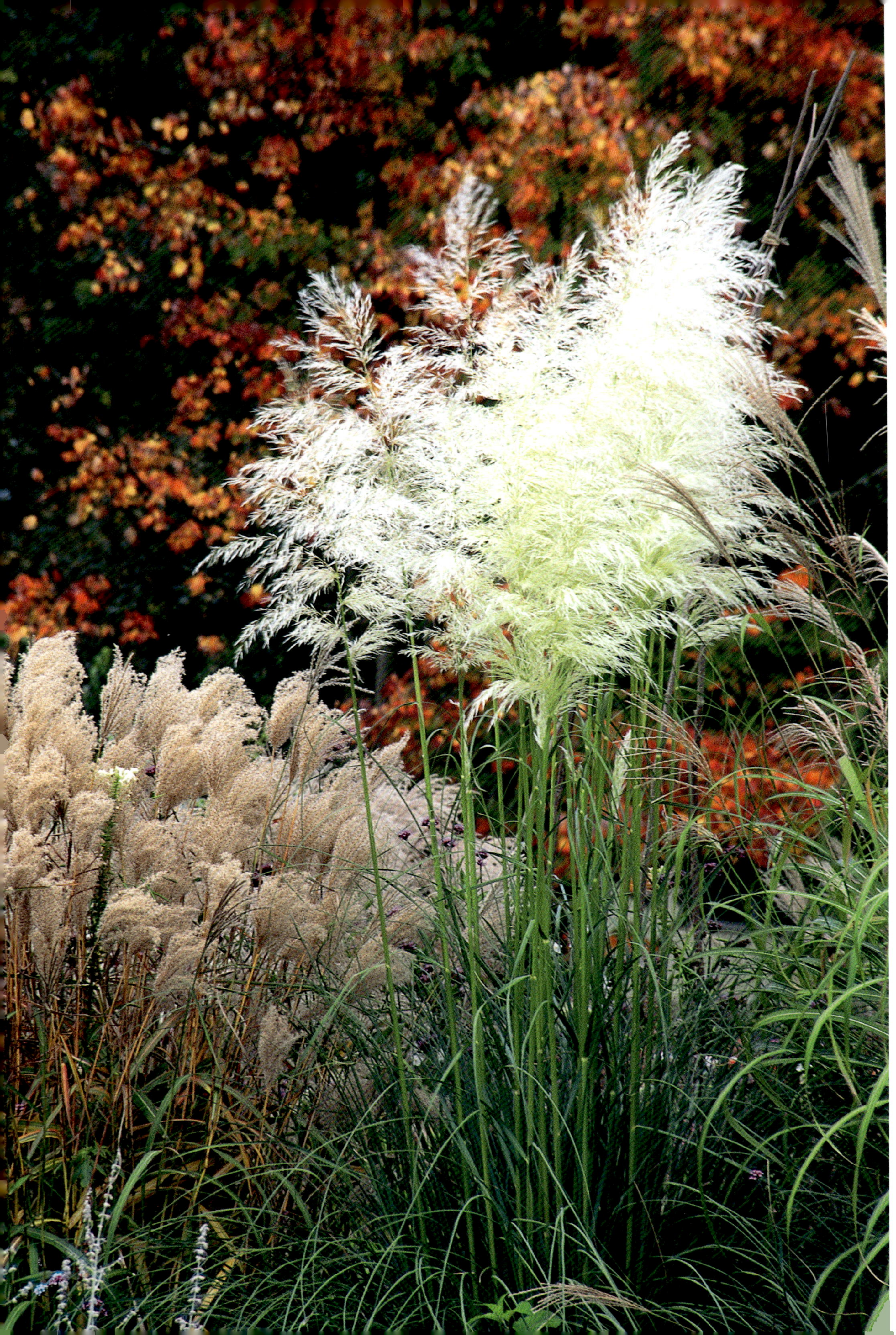
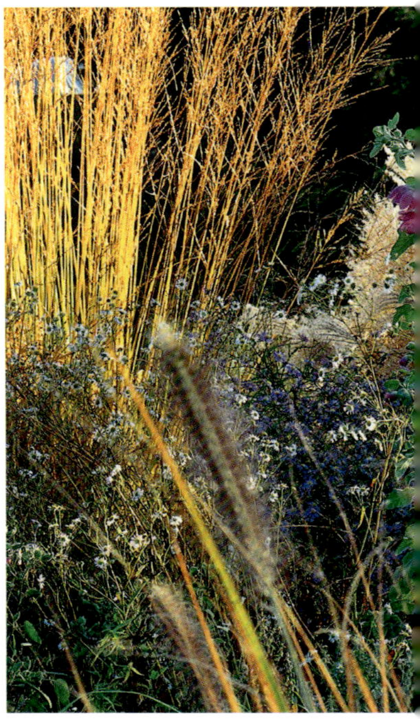
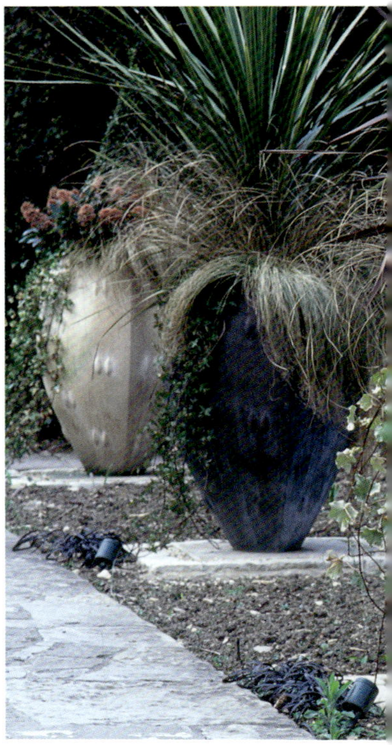

Design

Every garden is different, but grasses can be combined with shrubs, summer flowers and trees.

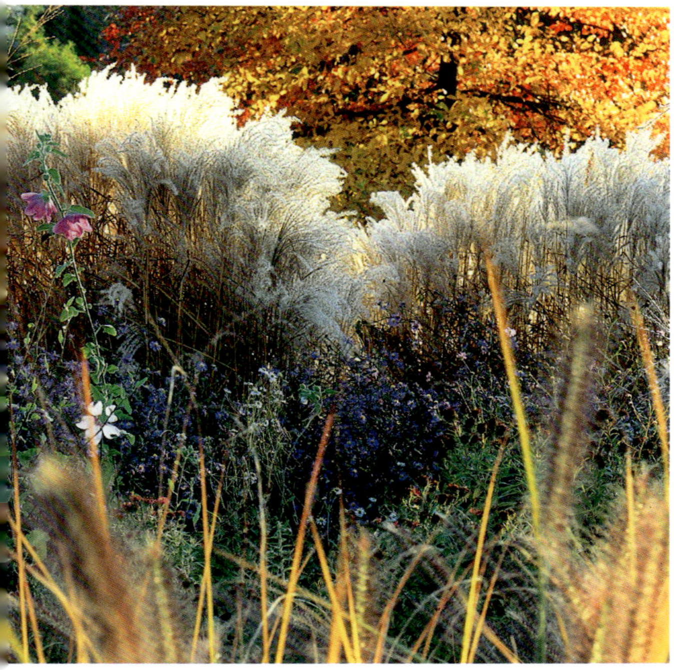

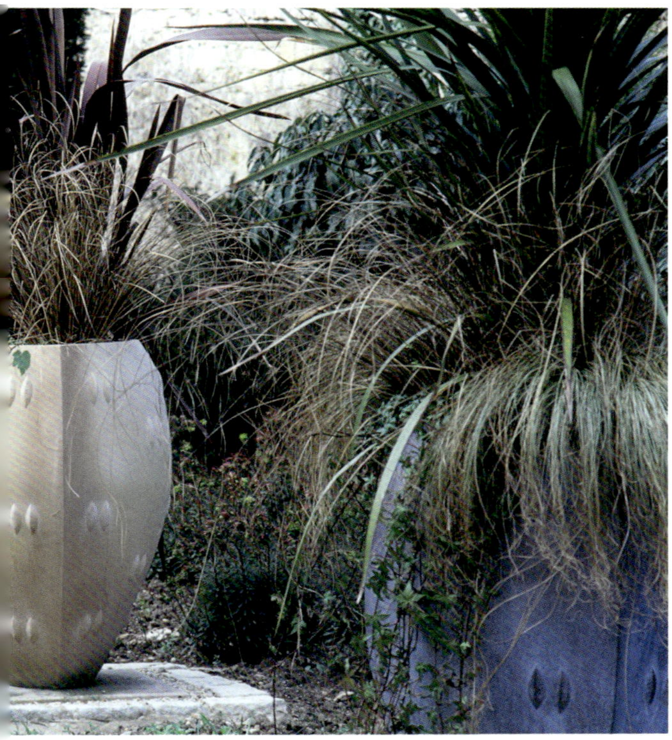

The combination of various grasses and shrubs with each other or in large groups of the same species and variety can create harmonious but also quite dramatic effects. So there are many different ways to design a planting scheme. Often the first consideration is a purely aesthetic one. Favourite colours and preferred shapes can play just as big a part in garden design as they do in interior design. So it is logical to proceed from these principles. Then questions of fashion can play a significant, even if sometimes unconscious, role in the selection of plant combinations. Trends and fashions, even those in furniture and architecture, are in our mind's eye all the time, so they can exert a subtle influence in our decisions. So there are fashionable undercurrents at work in the planting. This can be seen in the new varieties being developed.

In recent years grasses have received much more attention from shrub- and plant-breeders – happily, since for a long time grasses were mainly seen as solitary plants or as accompaniments to other planting. Fifty years ago Karl Foerster strongly promoted the 'introduction of grasses and ferns into the garden'. Nowadays, at least grasses have reached our gardens and truly enriched them.

BEAUTIFUL WILD CONFUSION

Plant schemes based on lush meadows are simply spectacular. As in the wild, tall grasses and filigree shrubs stand together side by side. The plants are thus interwoven with each other, either individually or in small groupings. The overall impression is, despite the size of the plants used, one of a number of smaller sections, undifferentiated from a distance. And there are plant combinations whose structures and textures are visible from the middle distance and close

Fireworks of colour in autumn (left, top)
Chinese silver grass *(Miscanthus sinensis)* with developing seed heads in front of splendidly coloured tress.

Accents in containers (left, bottom)
These tall thin pots are the perfect complement to sedge *(Carex comans)*, underplanted New Zealand flax *(Phormium)* and cordyline.

Fluffy plumes (opposite)
Filigree seed heads of pampas grass (*Cortaderia selloana* 'Sunningdale Silver') in the autumn light.

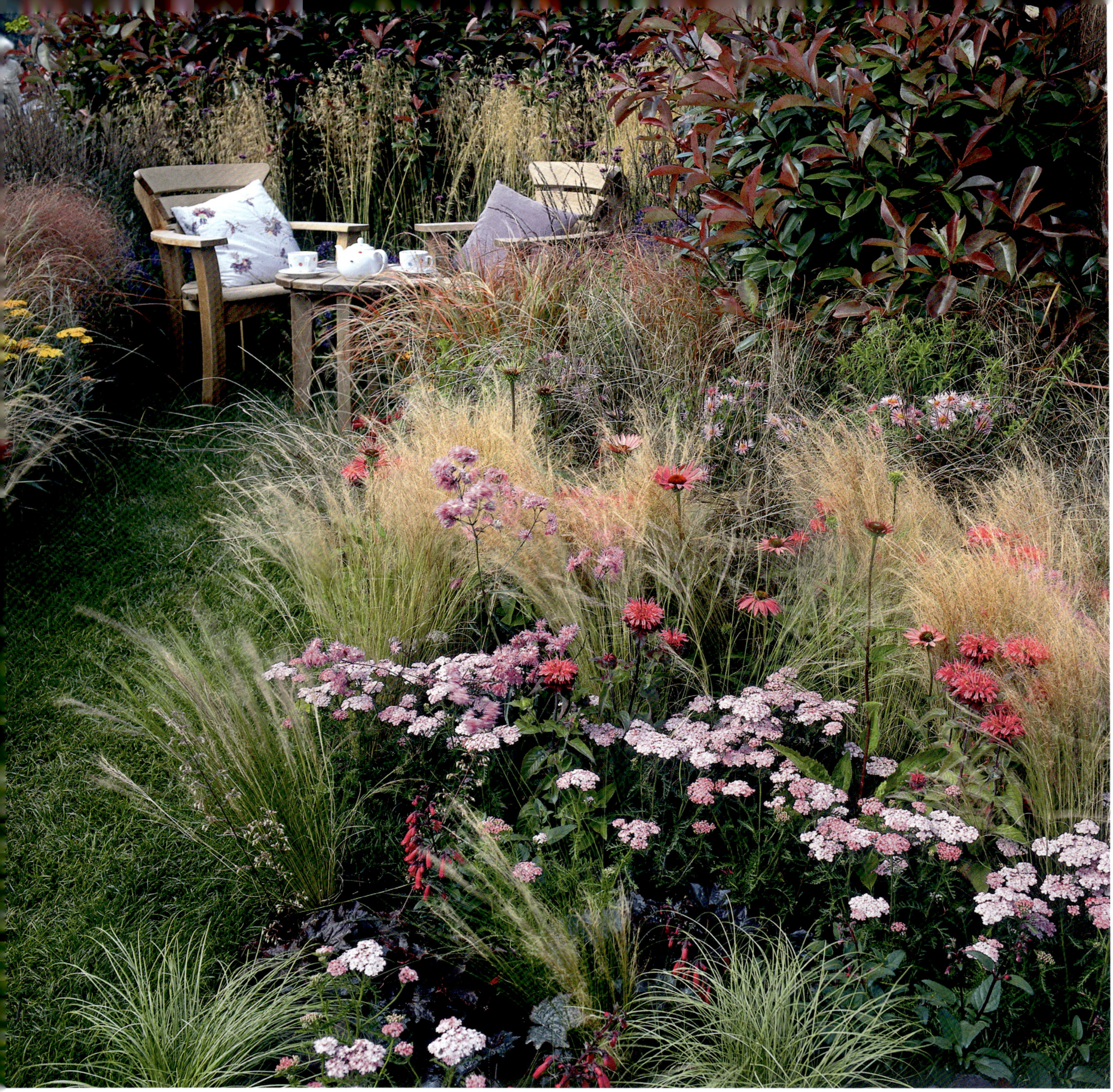

Seating area in the meadow

A brightly coloured mix of grasses and meadow shrubs surround this hidden seating area in the garden.

up. The high proportion of grasses also dampens down the colours of the flowering shrubs. You could say that a soft-focus lens covers everything harsh and garish with a thin haze. As most grasses reach their peak in late summer and autumn they need as accompaniment other shrubs that also bloom at this time. Many large shrubs are sufficiently filigree to fit well into this concept. Among them, for example, are found the group of umbelifers, which offers giants such as angelica, parsley *(Selinum)*, and fennel *(Foeniculum)*. Willow-leaved sunflowers *(Helianthus salicifolius)* only bloom after warm summers, but even their 3 metre-high stems and their exuberant foliage

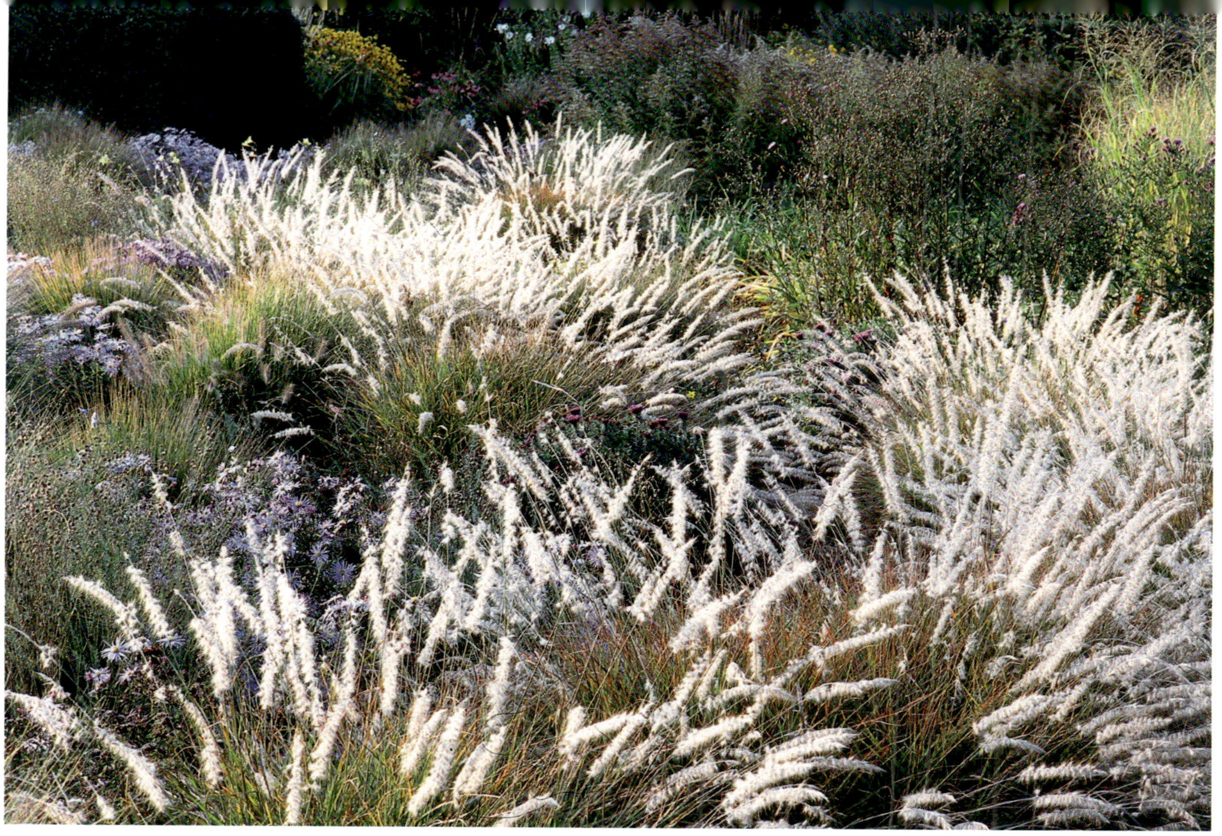

Steppe planting
Delicate oriental fountain grass (*Pennisetum orientale*) in perfect combination with Michaelmas daisies (*Aster pyrenaeus*).

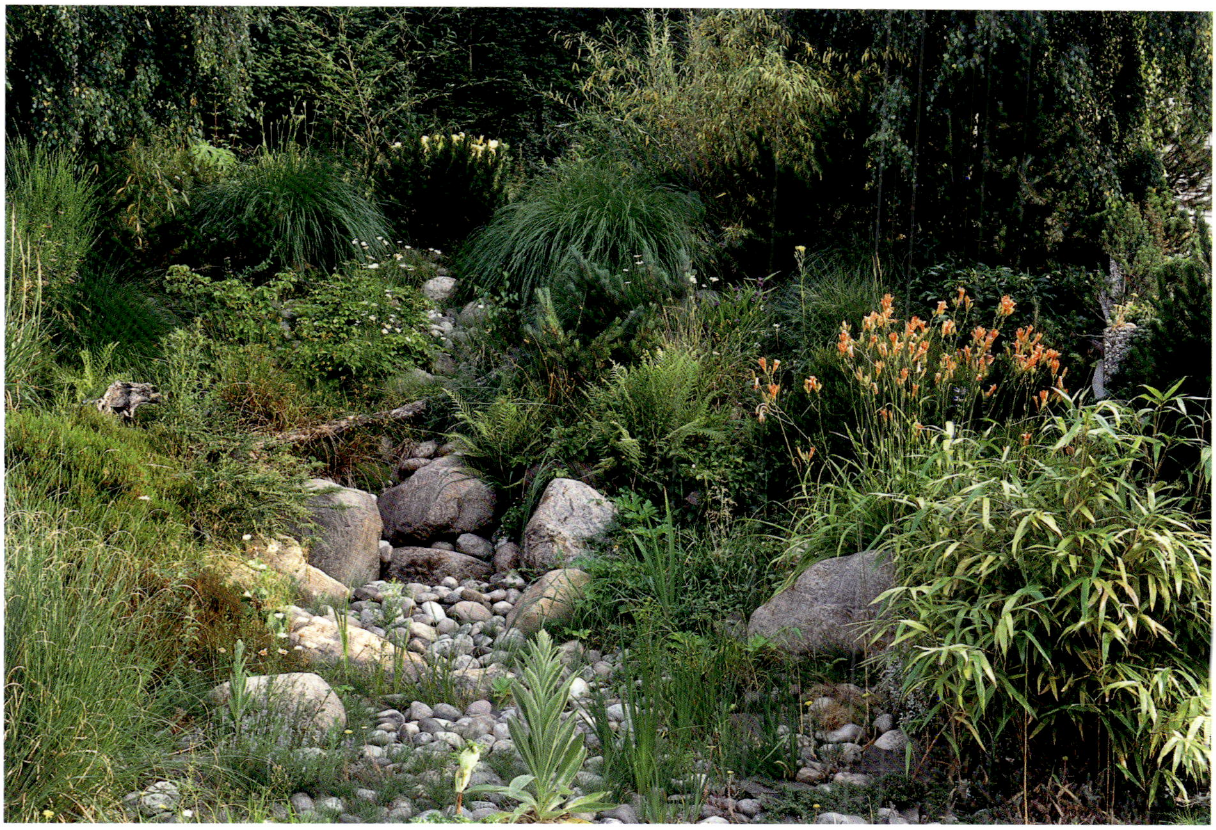

Rocky stream bed
Bamboos, shrubs and various grasses form the edge planting for this shingly stream bed.

are a feast for the eyes. Among the grasses that work well with this design are the many types of miscanthus, especially the loosely growing forms. These include 'Flamingo', with its somewhat overhanging, rose-tinted flowers, 'Graziella', also overhanging, or the relatively new variety 'Nishidake', which is very loose growing. But this group also includes switch grass *(Panicum virgatum)* and frost grass *(Spodiopogon sibiricus)*. There are many good new varieties of switch grass, after a long period when only 'Rehbraun' and 'Hänse Herms' were available. Not all varieties develop the desired red autumn colouring, though 'Strictum' and 'Squaw' are very reliable.

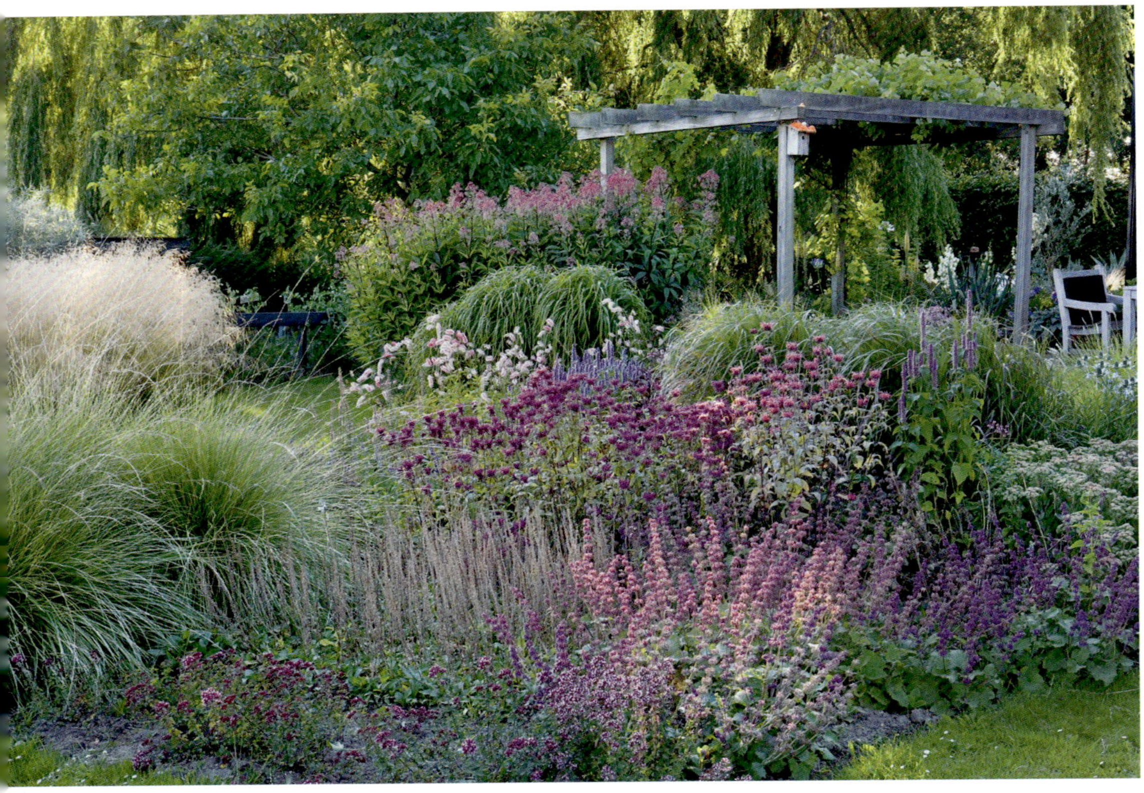

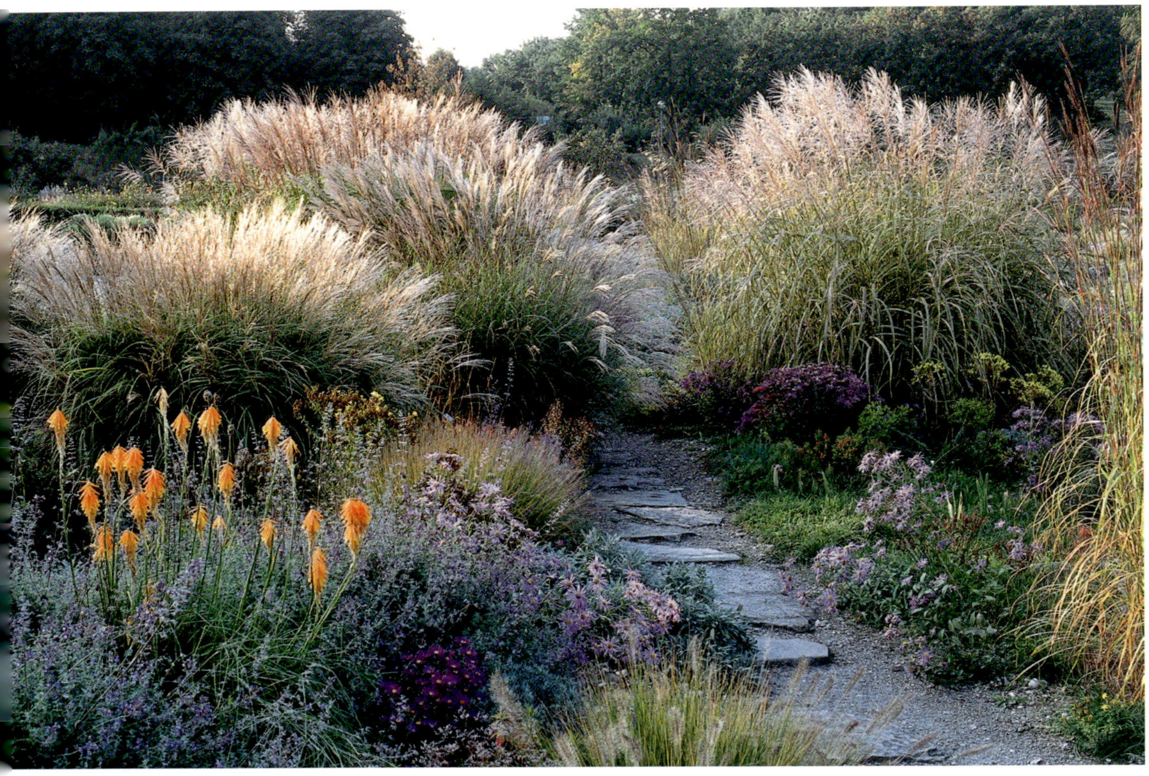

GRASSES ON THEIR OWN

Planting schemes consisting purely of grasses can be very attractive. Of course, their highpoint comes in summer through to autumn, but in winter their seed heads can be decorative and should in no circumstances be cut down. The morning after the first night of frost shows clearly why you should not be too quick to tidy the garden in autumn. As in a herbaceous border, a grass bed should be laid out according to the rules of plant arrangement.

In classical beds plants are arranged in height gradations – the lowest species and varieties in the foreground, the middle-sized ones behind, and the giants at the back. Such height gradation is especially effective when the bed is in front of a wall or a hedge, against which the colours of the grass flowers will really stand out.

For beds in the middle of a lawn, or open on two sides, the same rules apply in principle. Here you plant the tallest grasses in the centre and the smaller ones around the edges. Apart from the aesthetic aspect, height gradation has the advantage of allowing all the plants to get enough sunlight, as the smaller plants are not shaded by the larger ones. Exceptions to this are spring bulbs that have been integrated into the bed. They should be planted in the centre. During their blooming period the fresh grass shoots are still quite small, and later on their fading foliage will be better hidden by the grasses and shrubs.

Secluded seating area (above)

Tall grasses act as a screen.

Sunny location (below)i

Shrubs and grasses enclose a stone path.

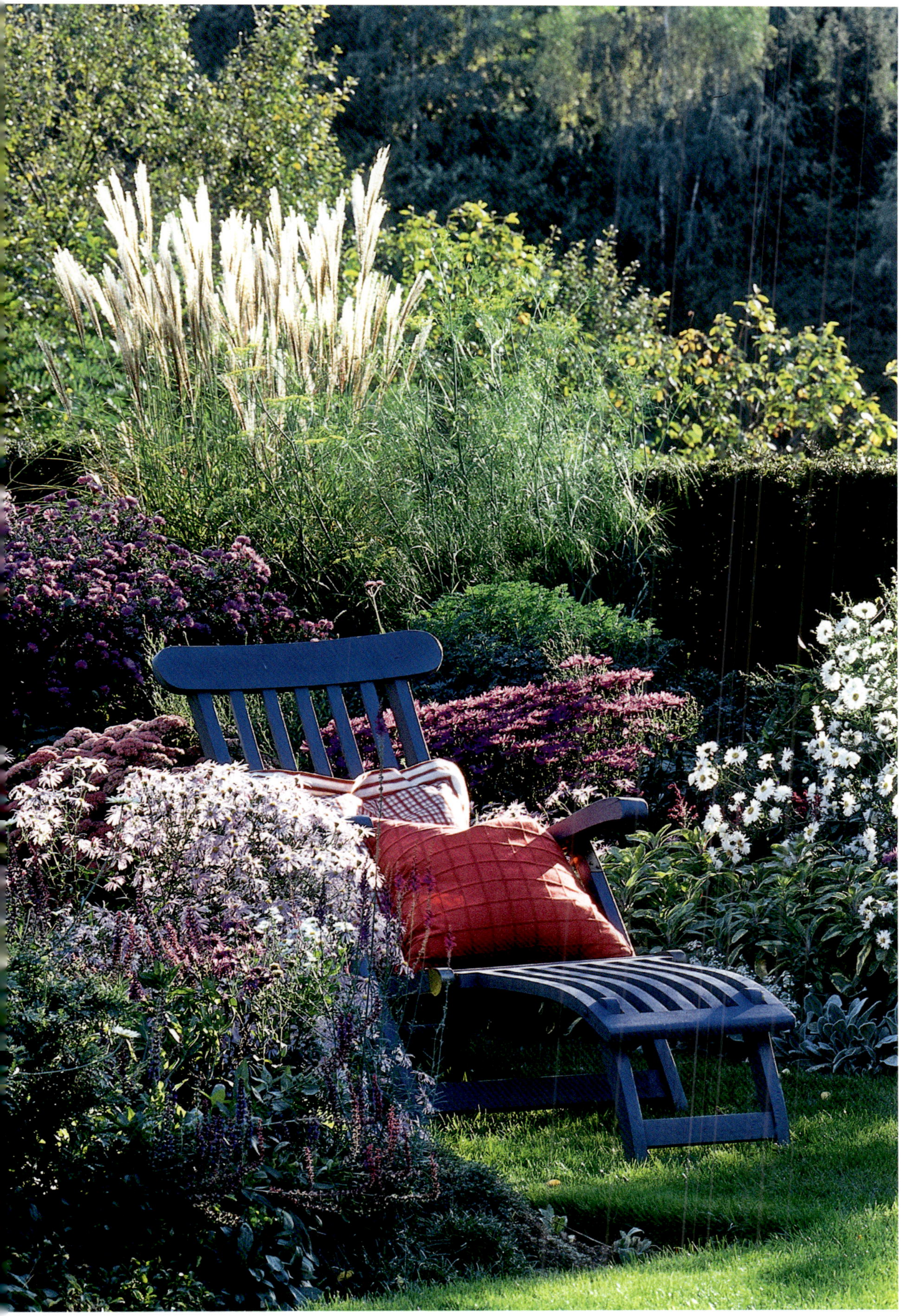

Invitation to relax

The silvery flower heads of the Eulalia or silver grass (*Miscanthus sinensis* 'Kleine Fontäne') create a gentle rustling effect in the garden.

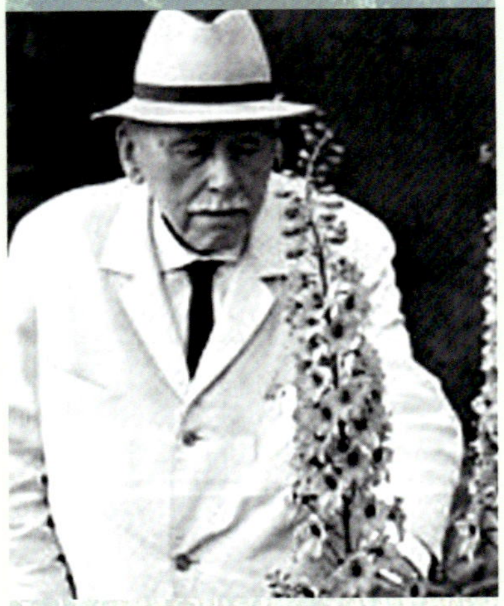

Karl Foerster

Karl Foerster was a pioneer in the use of grasses in garden design.

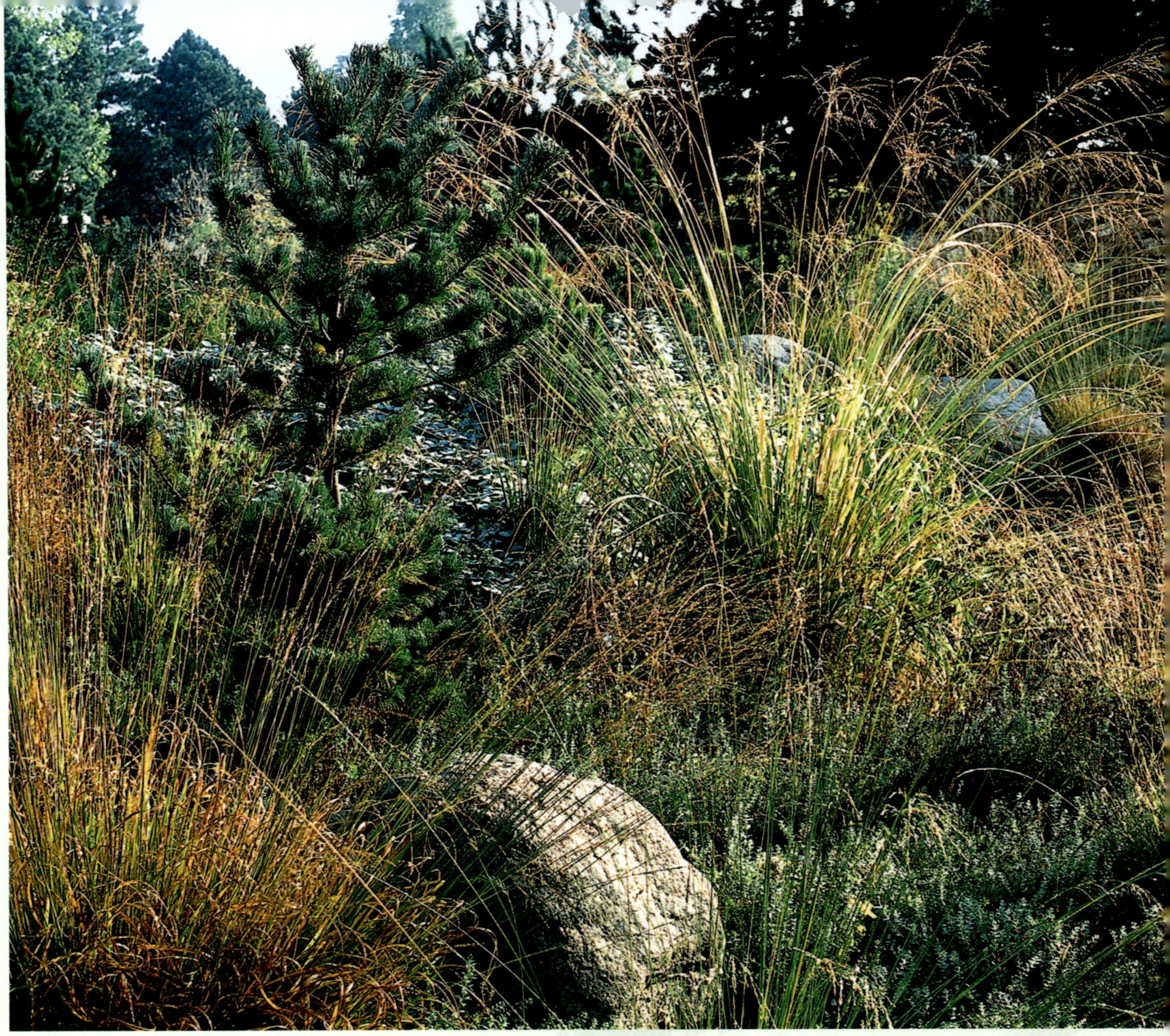

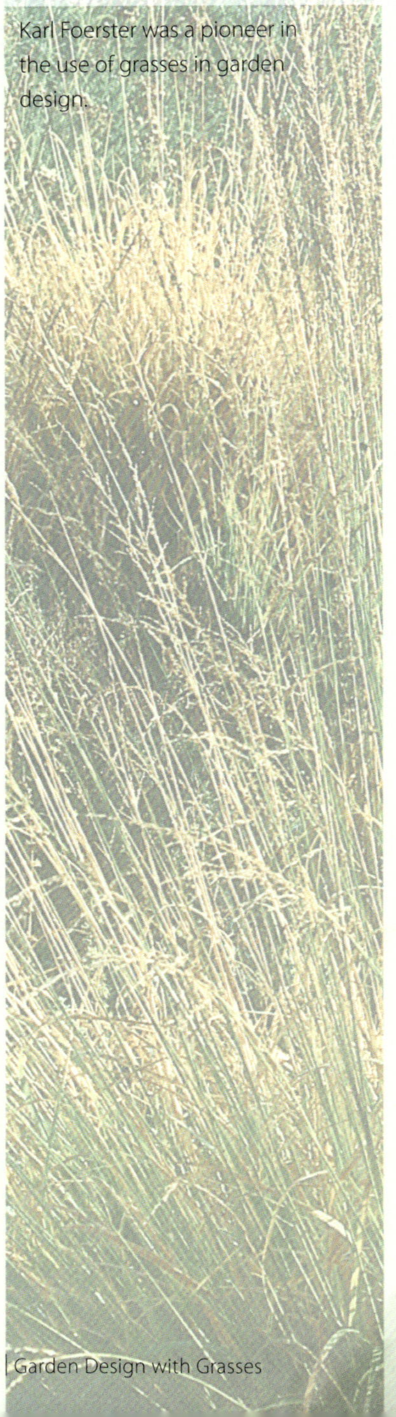

The Hair of Mother Earth

Karl Foerster – an advocate for the use of grasses as accompaniments to flowering shrubs.

Karl Foerster, born in 1874, was one the most influential gardeners and breeders of shrubs in the twentieth century; he set up his famous nursery in the Bornim district of Potsdam in 1911. He was an author, one might even say a poet, of gardening books, and published thirty-seven during his lifetime. In his work *Einzug der Gräser und Farne in die Gärten (Introduction of Grasses and Ferns into the Garden)* he took an in-depth look at the use of grasses in garden design. He called grasses 'the hair of Mother Earth' and argued for the use of grasses as accompaniments to flowering shrubs or as natural ground cover. In this book, which quickly became a standard reference work, he described the origins, properties and gardening uses of numerous grasses. His incomparable turn of phrase is best shown by the following quotations from *Einzug der Gräser und Farne in die Gärten:*

"How beautifully the tufts of the waist-high heron's feather grass sway in the gentle breeze! How enticing are the waving head-high blond flower stalks of blue oat grass above their thick light-blue-green foliage. What a novel sight, even in completely dry places, is provided by the upright, monumental grass bush of the giant miscanthus, which, wrapped in blue and white bindweed, towers up before the storm clouds."

"You can see, in dew and morning light, in moonlight and light snow, in the green of spring and the ripe maturity of autumn, wonderfully beautiful things in them [grasses] that you will never forget and which will become longstanding features of your garden. They often organise their surroundings so well and create such a mysterious harmony with their neighbouring plants that, when they are removed, it is as if an orchestra has lost its conductor."

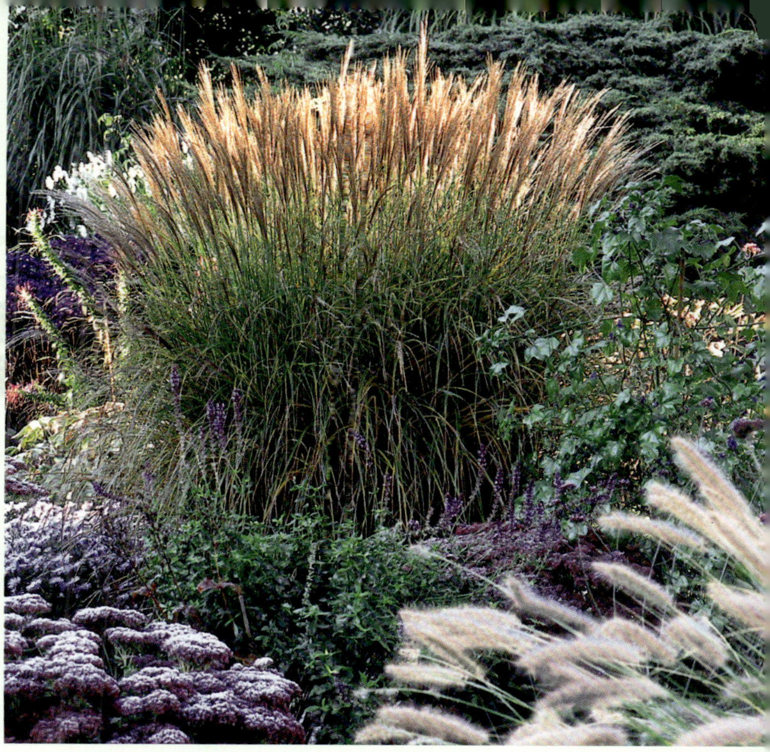

In the sunken garden in Bornim (above)
Miscanthus sinensis in the Foerster sunken garden in Potsdam-Bornim.

Heathland planting (opposite)
Tall moor grass (*Molinia arundinacea* 'Karl Foerster').

These quotations, so full of poetry and passion, display his respect for, and love of, grasses. Karl Foerster cultivated many new shrubs and took wild shrubs and grasses from nature and made use of them. Many varieties familiar today emerged from years of careful selection based on hardiness as well as aesthetic considerations. He created a type of plant for the gardens of today: one might say new plants for new gardens.

His catalogue, however, includes primarily flowering shrubs rather than grasses – plants such as *Aster amellus, A. dumosus, A. novae-angliae and A. novi-belgii, Campanula, Chrysanthemum, Delphinium, Helenium* und *Phlox*.

The sunken garden in Bornim, which he laid out along with Hermann Mattern, was both an experimental garden and a show garden, a magnet for experts and garden lovers alike – and it remains so to this day.

In 1928, together with the garden architects Herta Hammerbacher, Hermann Göritz, Walter Funcke and Hermann Mattern, founded the association 'Garden Design in Bornim', the so-called 'Bornim circle'. However, this association also attracted painters, poets and sculptors who shared Karl Foerster's philosophy. From this collaborative work, inspired by a suggestion from Karl Foerster, came a show and study garden built on the Freundschaftsinsel (Friendship Island) in Potsdam. For the 2001 Bundesgartenschau, the biennial German horticultural show, around 200 different varieties were newly planted in the garden on the Freundschaftsinsel, winter hardy flowering shrubs as well as grasses and ferns, that can still be viewed there today.

Near the sunken garden in Bornim and the garden on the island, you can also visit the 'Karl Foerster Garden' in the Berlin-Marzahn 'Gardens of the World', which was reworked by Christian Meyer and reopened in 2007.

Karl Foerster died in 1970. Today a foundation manages his estate and takes care of youth development with the aim of fostering a good practically oriented use of plants.

Accents in a grass garden (below)
The bright yellow autumn colouring of the feather reed grass (*Calamagrostis x acutiflora* 'Karl Foerster') remains well into the winter.

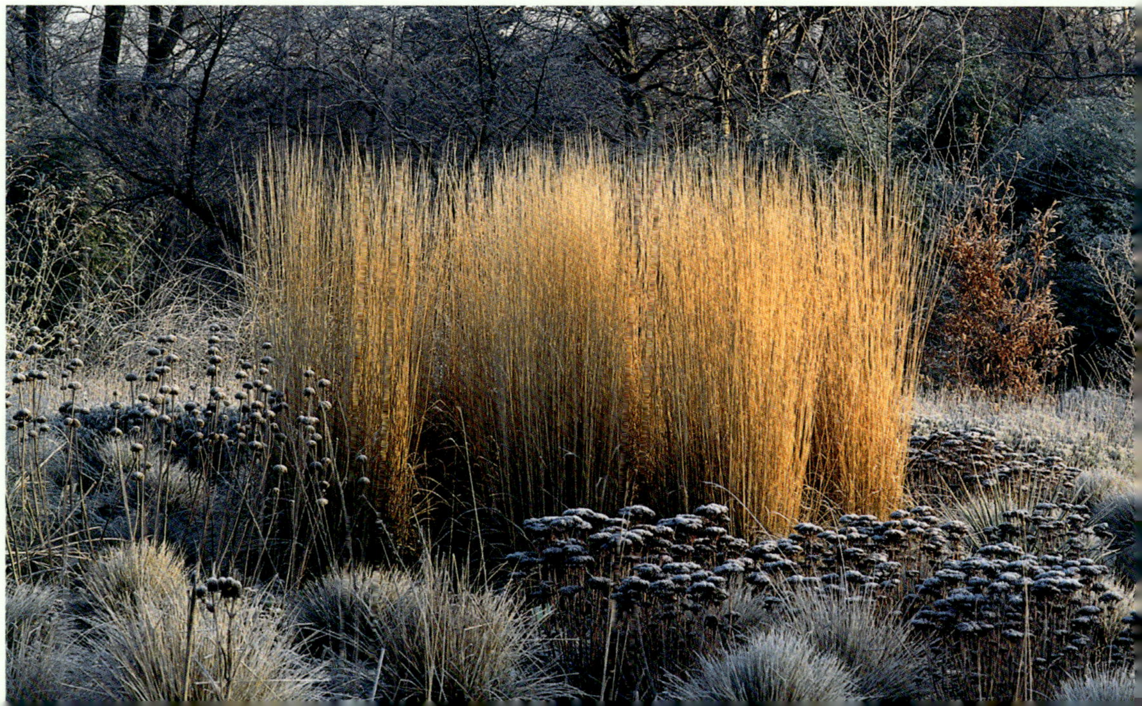

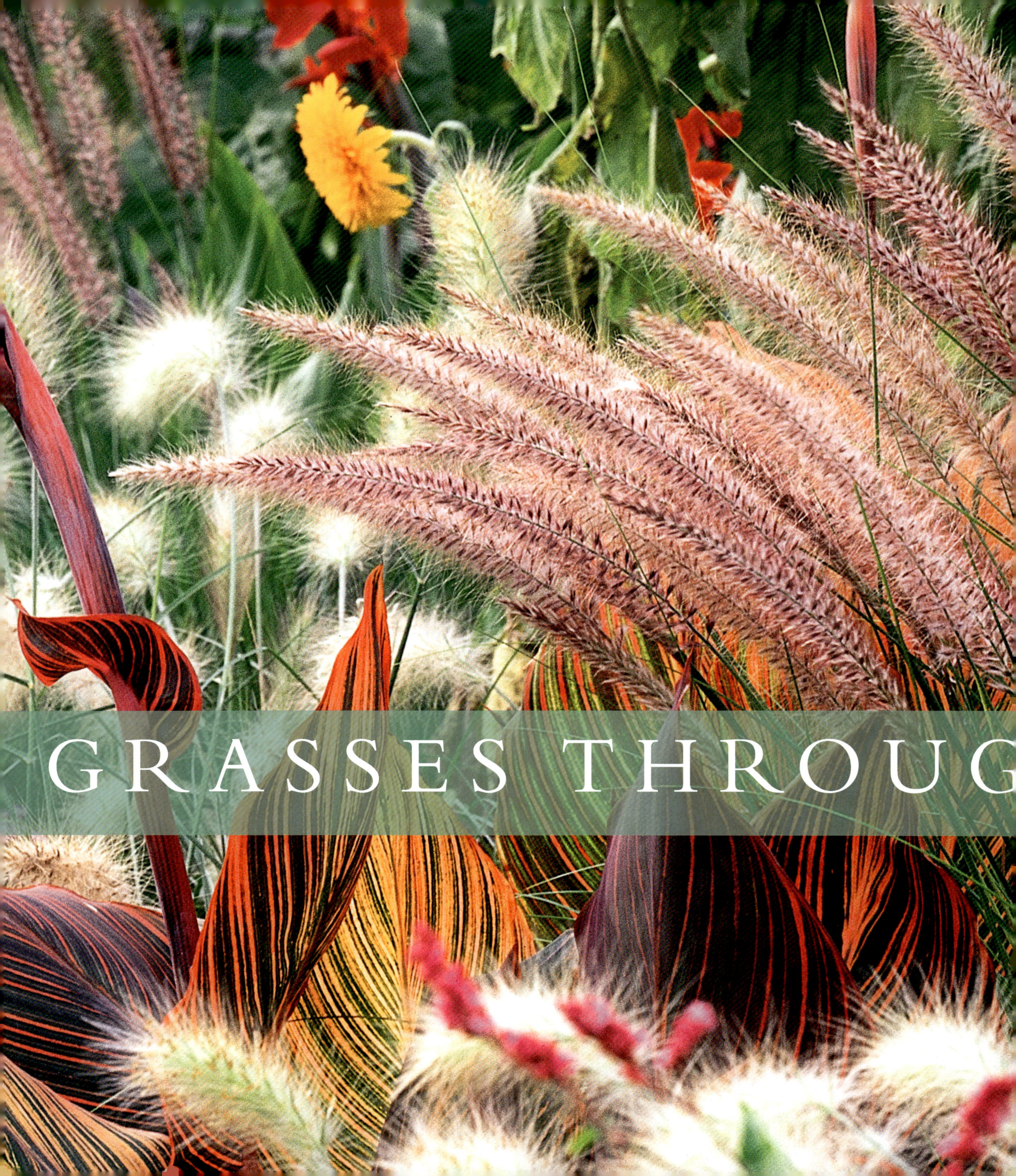

GRASSES THROUG

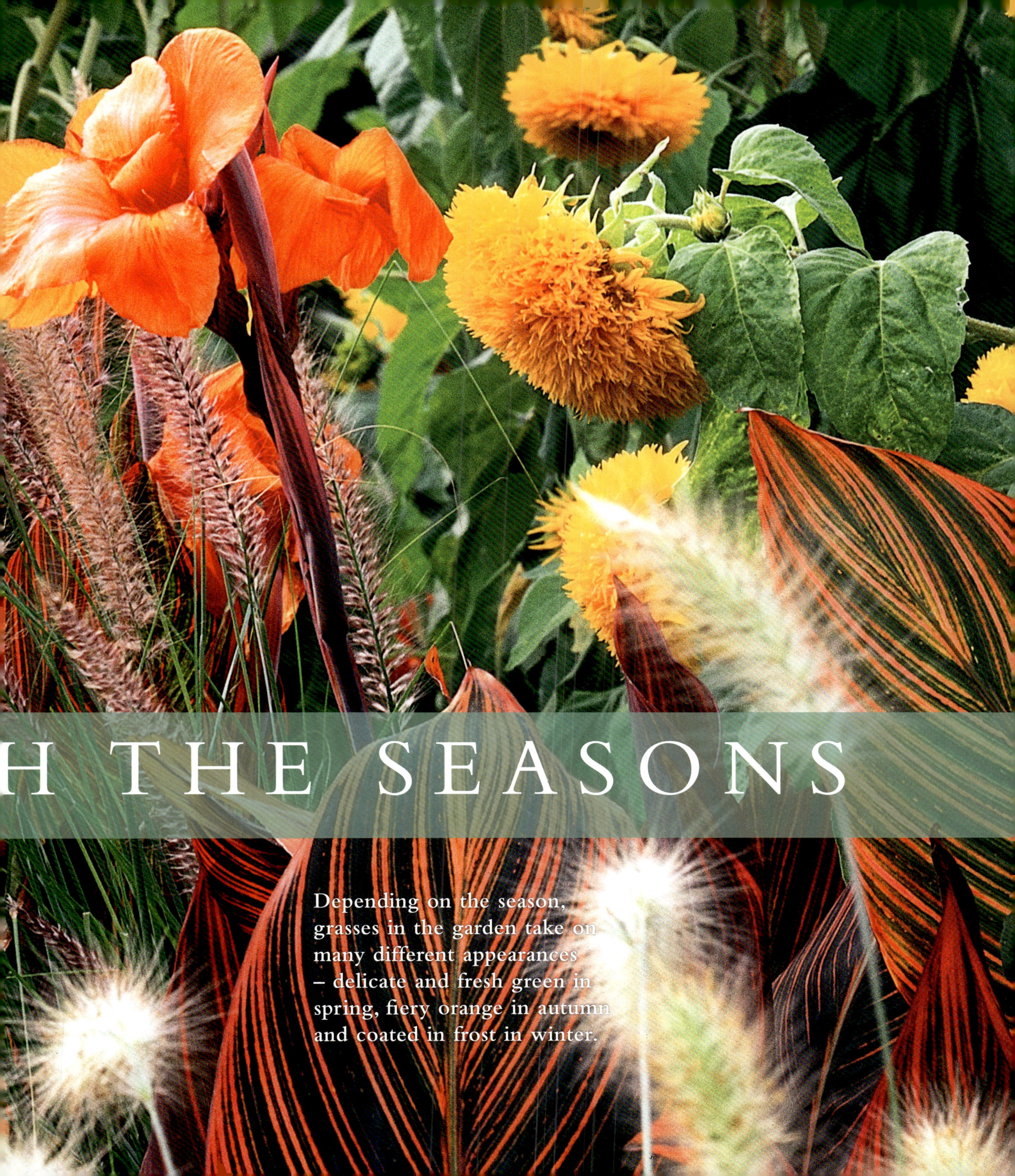

H THE SEASONS

Depending on the season, grasses in the garden take on many different appearances – delicate and fresh green in spring, fiery orange in autumn and coated in frost in winter.

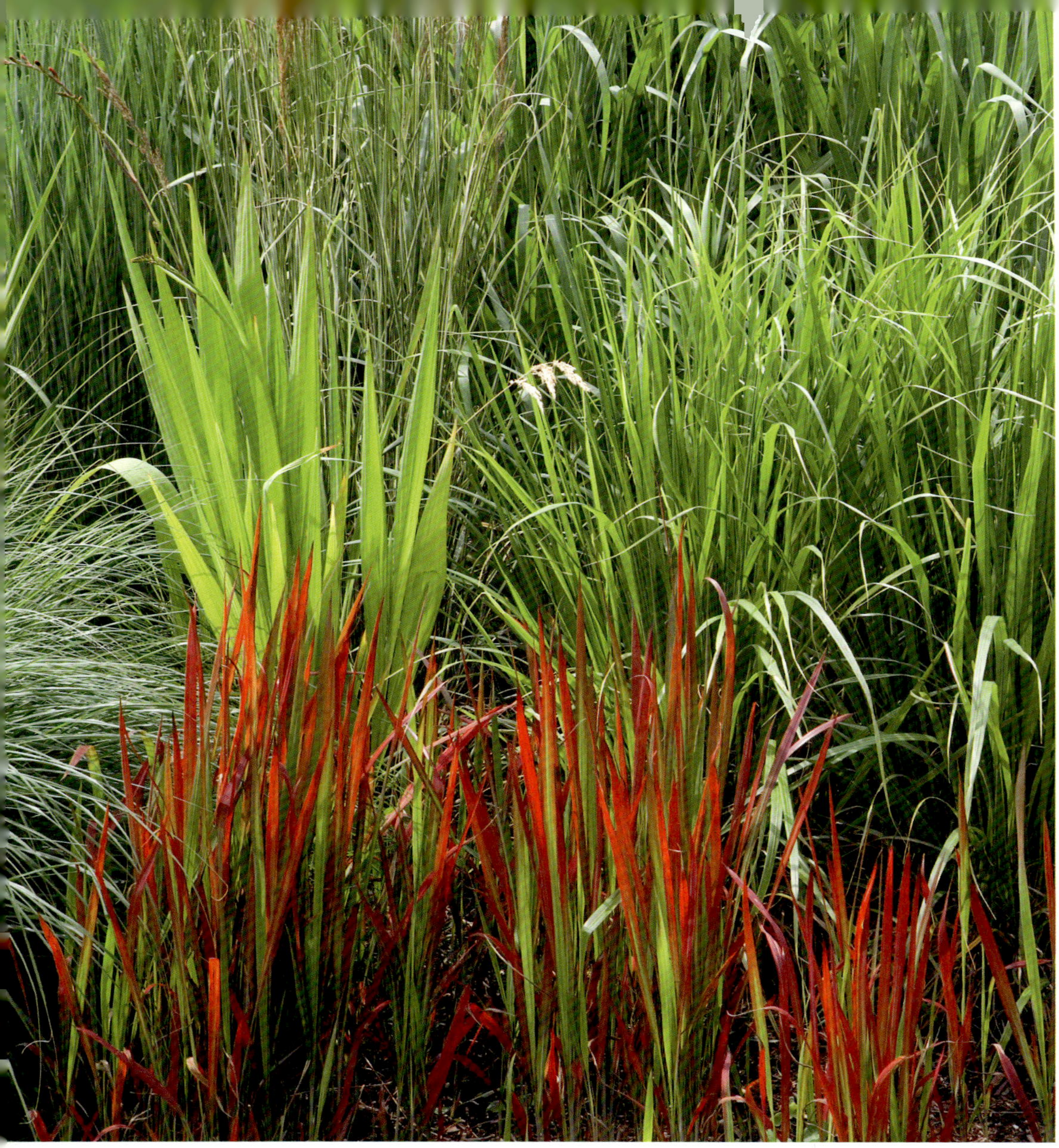

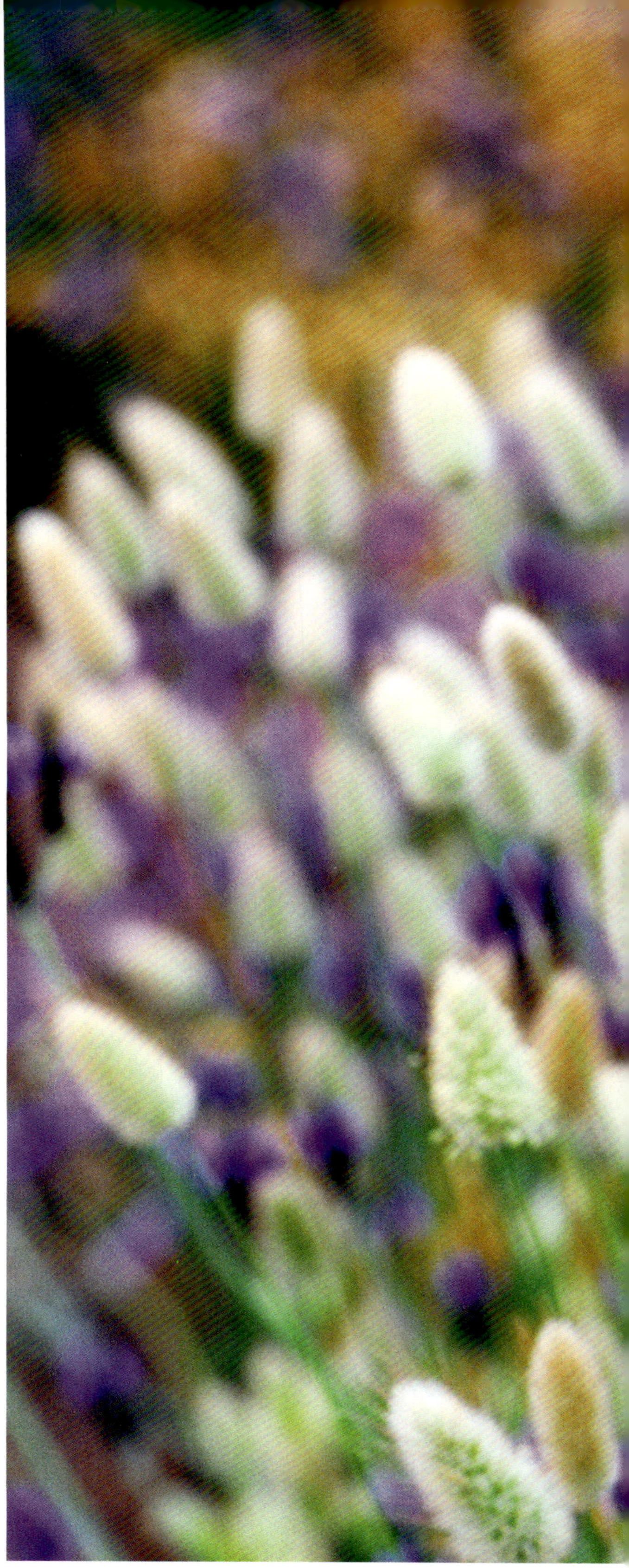

Spring

Most grasses are still dormant in early spring and only begin to sprout in March/April.

The seed heads and stalks from the previous year's growth are cut back in early spring, along with the dead foliage, which creates space for the new growth to come. Evergreen varieties put on new growth, so here too dead and unsightly foliage should be removed.

However, a few early varieties begin to bloom in March. This group includes such species of the genus *Sesleria*, moor grass. The Blue moor-grass *(Sesleria albicans)* blooms in March. Dark violet flowering spikes sprout above the rounded tussocks of leaves, which grow no higher than about 30cm. It thrives on well-drained, chalky soils. *Sesleria heufleriana* is somewhat bigger, the

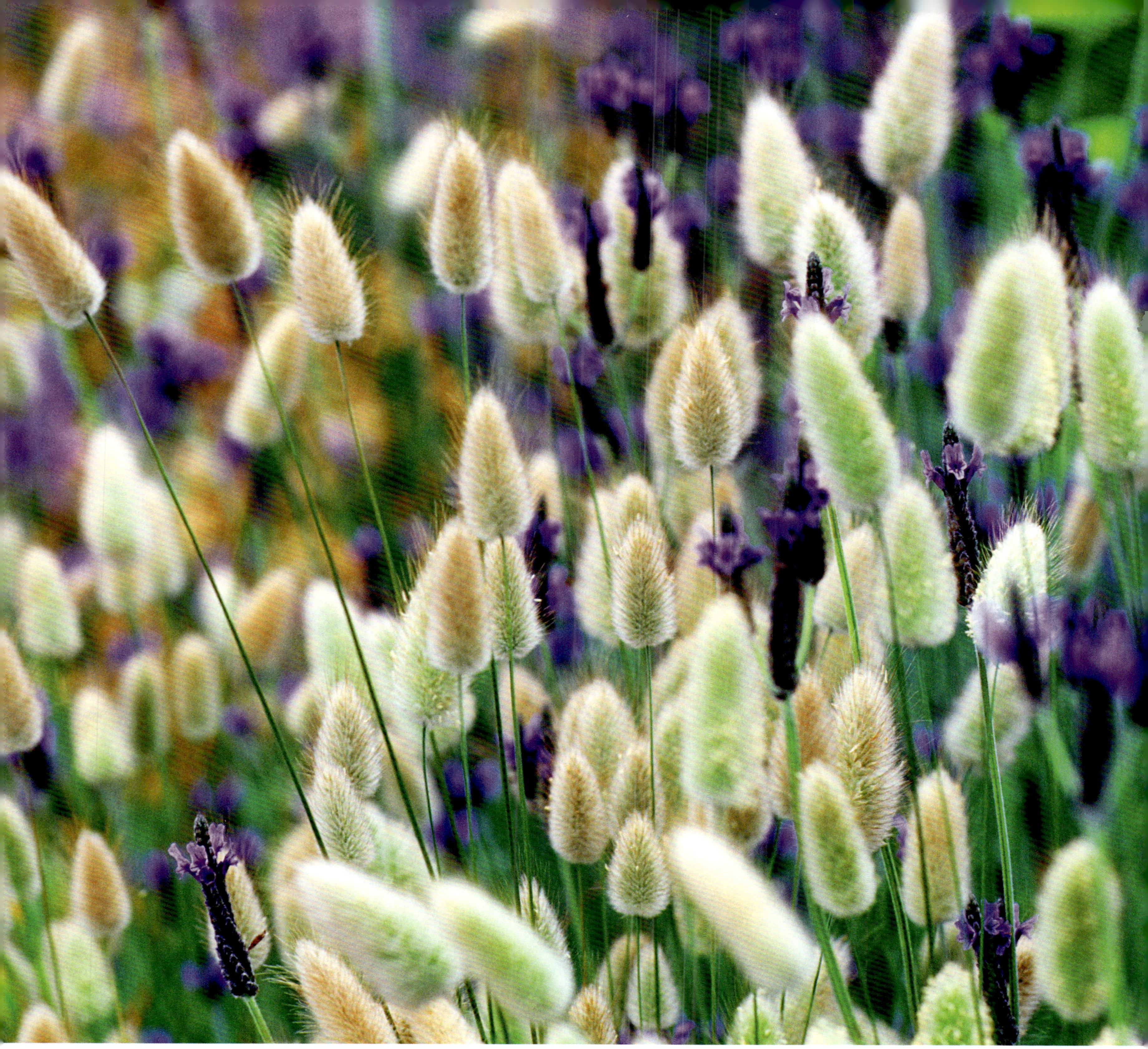

flower panicles are almost black, and it prefers semi shade, such as woodland edges, and shaded, not too dry locations in rock gardens. They offer a good accompaniment to early flowering bulbs.

Brilliant display in early summer
The flowers of the hare's tail grass *(Lagurus ovatus)* sway in every breath of wind and offset the deep blue lavender.

Fiery spring growth (opposite)
Japanese bloodgrass or Cogon grass *(Imperata cylindrica)*.

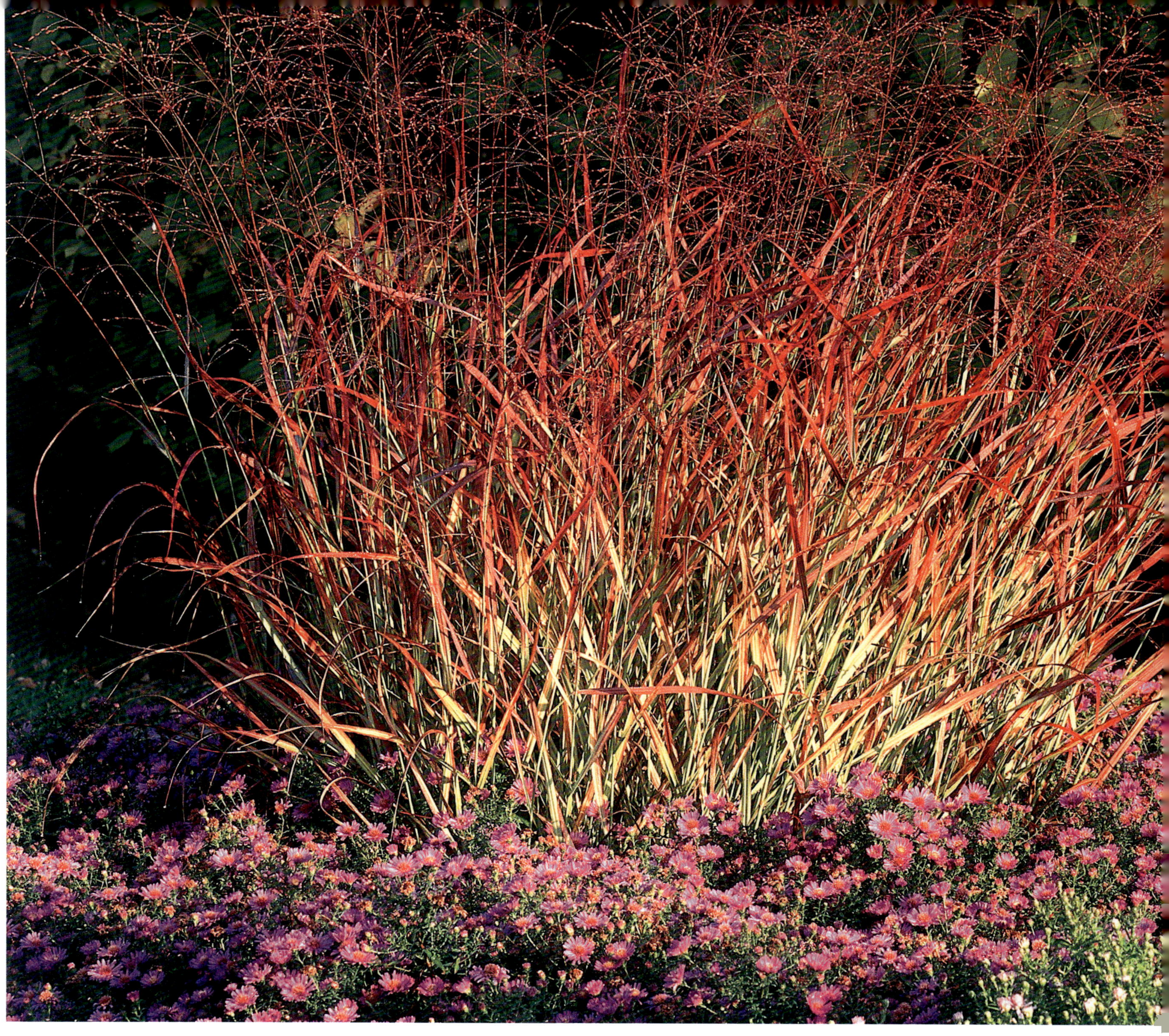

Garden scene in late summer
With their blazing red colouring, the many varieties of switch grass *(Panicum virgatum)*, such as 'Hänse Herms' und 'Rotstrahlbusch', here underplanted with Michaelmas daisies *(Aster dumosus)*, can be inspiring. Above the stems dangle delicate flower panicles.

Summer

In June the early-flowering shrubs reach their peak. Autumn-flowering tall grasses such as miscanthus also put on a fine display.

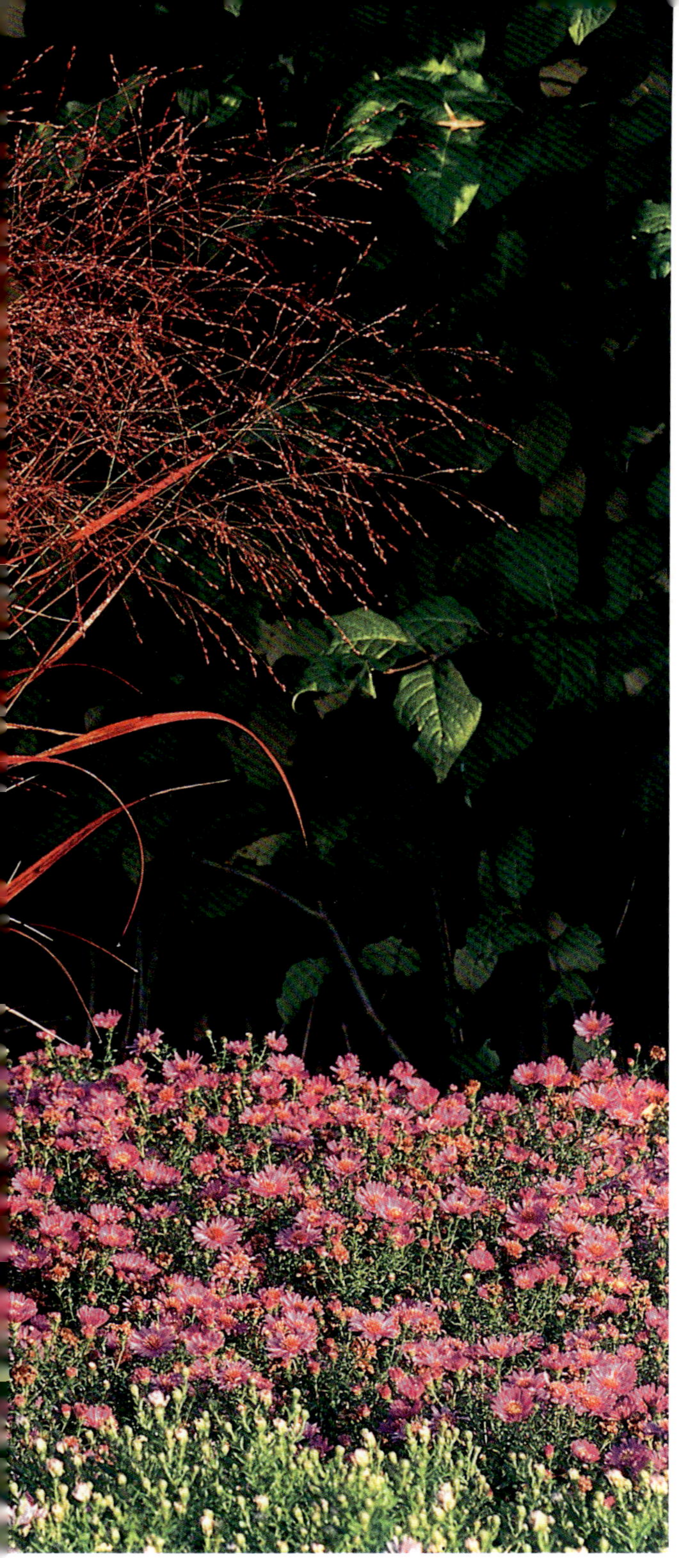

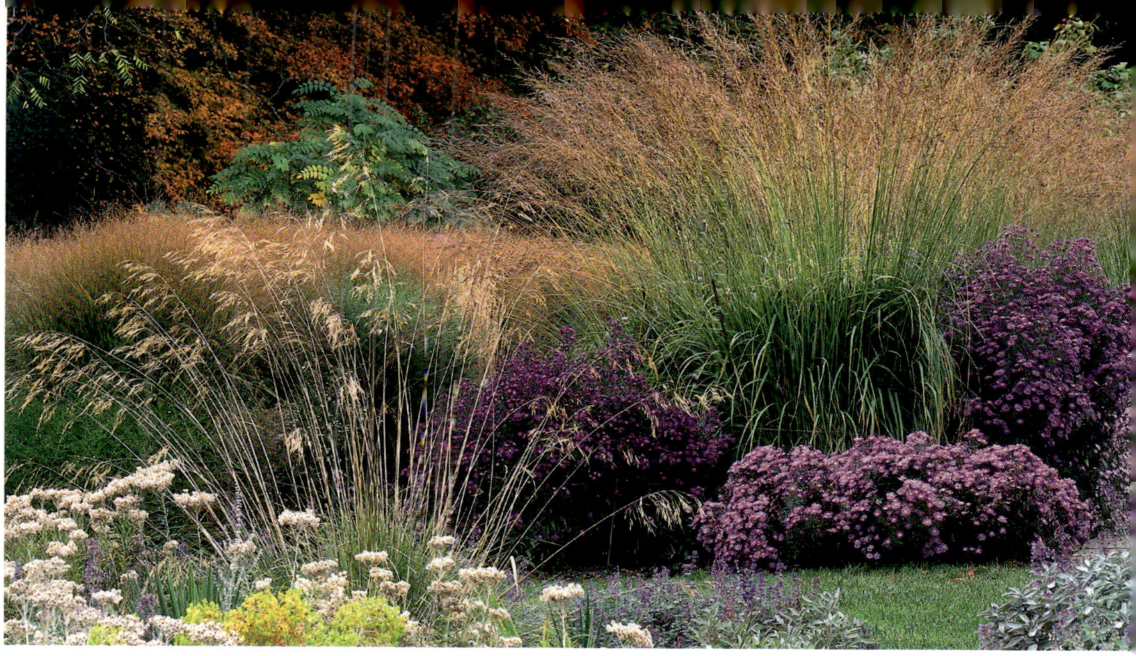

Grass accents

The flower panicles of the purple moor grass *(Molinia caerulea)* and the giant feather grass or golden oats *(Stipa gigantea)* create a sparkling fountain above the western pearly everlasting *(Anaphalis margaritaceum)* and asters.

A few species come into bloom in early summer and so provide an ideal accompaniment to shrubs, annuals and summer bulbs. Among these are, for example, feather reed grass *(Calamagrostis x acutiflora)*, giant feather grass or golden oats *(Stipa gigantea)* and tufted hair grass or tussock grass *(Deschampsia caespitosa)*. Either solitary or in groups, but in a recurring rhythm, they can add lightness to the classical border combinations of delphiniums, campions *(Lychnis)*, tall bellflowers *(Campanula)*, phlox and others. Many grasses also look great alongside roses, a combination seen far too rarely. Particularly suitable here are the essential *Miscanthus sinensis*: filigree types such as 'Samurai', 'Vorläufer' or 'Gracillimus' work best of all. Even the latter do not bloom in most summers, but instead have even prettier, perfectly overhanging slender foliage.

For half shade the hanging or weeping sedge *(Carex pendula)* is virtually essential. It is very versatile for combination with other plants and is outstanding as a backdrop to hostas or between aquilegia, wide-leaved bellflowers *(Campanula latifolia var. macrantha)* and meadow-rue *(Thalictrum)*. During flowering, the hanging spikes glow dark yellow and they lose nothing of their attractiveness in the months following blooming.

Annual grasses are an important element of summer garden design and border planting. In the wild, numerous summer flowers such as red flax *(Linum grandiflorum)*, cornflowers *(Centaurea cyanus)* and corn poppy *(Papaver rhoeas)* grow at the edges of fields, in other words in wheat fields and meadows. In domestic gardens, then, they should be accompanied by the corresponding grasses. Foxtail barley *(Hordeum jubatum)* and foxtail millet *(Setaria italica)* work very nicely here. This selection also pleases the corn-eating domestic bird population.

Autumn and Winter

Autumn and winter are definitely the highpoint for most grasses. Many of them don't flower until late in the year, while others have distinctive decorative seed heads at this time of year.

First impressions of autumn
The pale morning light hazy with frost-covered grasses.

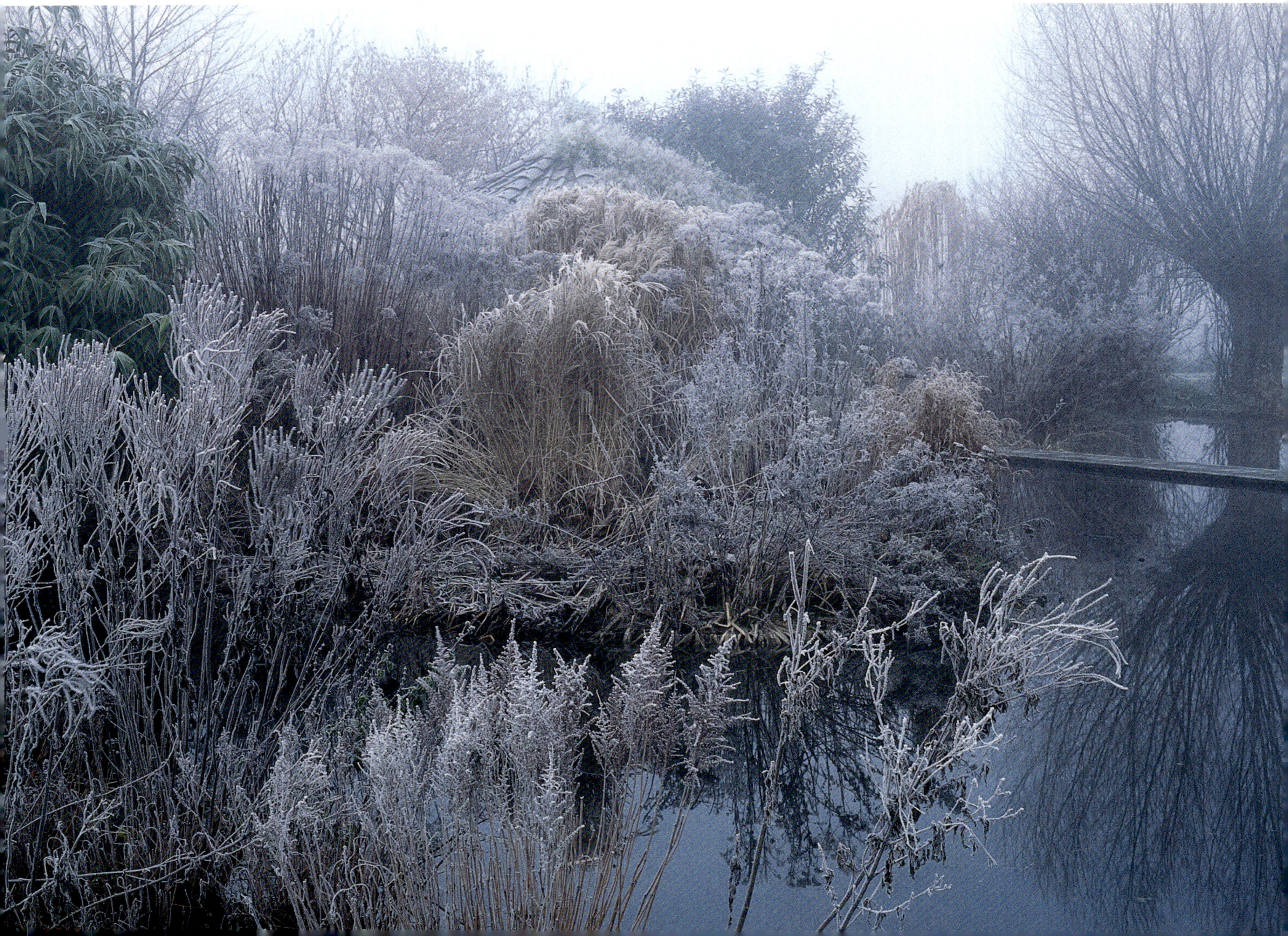

The spectacular autumn colouring of many species and varieties should never be overlooked. It is especially harmonious with autumn-blooming flowering shrubs.

Among the prettiest autumn-colouring grasses are the varieties of switchgrass *(Panicum virgatum)*. The 'Rehbraun', 'Hänse Herms' and 'Squaw' varieties turn from brown to red in late summer; the colours are at their best in warm summers. The 'Warrior' variety changes colour again in autumn to a glowing yellow. Yellow and red are the dominant tones of autumn. The leaves of the miscanthus too change to both colours as well as various other shades in between. 'Malepartus' is especially colourful and when backlit in the evening resembles a blazing fire. 'Rotsilber', 'Sioux' and 'Ferner Osten' also have especially impressive autumn colouring. Pheasant tail's grass, or New Zealand wind grass, (*Anemanthele lessoniana,* formerly called *Stipa arundinacea*) presents a fantastic leaf colouring of golden orange and greenish yellow. But it needs to be in a dry location to be reliably hardy over winter.

The upright forms of feather reed grass *(Calamagrostis x acutiflora)* glow straw-yellow and provide good vertical structure in borders. Due to their height of up to 1.5 metres they act as sentries between the loosely growing shrubs, which lean against them. Even the delicate feather grasses begin to stand out once they change colour from green to yellow in late summer. The long awns of *Stipa capillata*, the weak awns of *Stipa tirsa* and *Nasella tenuissima*, which bend in such a picturesque fashion in the slightest breath of wind, all bring a wonderful glow to autumn borders. Seeing them, you can understand what Karl Foerster meant when he described grasses as harps, without which an orchestra would be incomplete.

Pampas grass *(Cortaderia selloana)* has effective flower heads, and later seed heads. Thick, candy floss-like clumps sit on top of straight, strong stalks. Of course, the plants are generally rather upright, and it is not easy to blend them in to a mixed planting scheme. In contrast, *Cortaderia richardii* is overhanging, and though its loose flower panicles can be as high as 2.5 metres, they are much more delicate. The flowers of miscanthus are, depending on the variety, silvery red to pearl white, but always delicate and feathery in structure. They look especially attractive when backlit by the low autumn sun. This is when the details are set off to best advantage. The flowers cascade like small, rushing waterfalls of wavy strands of hair.

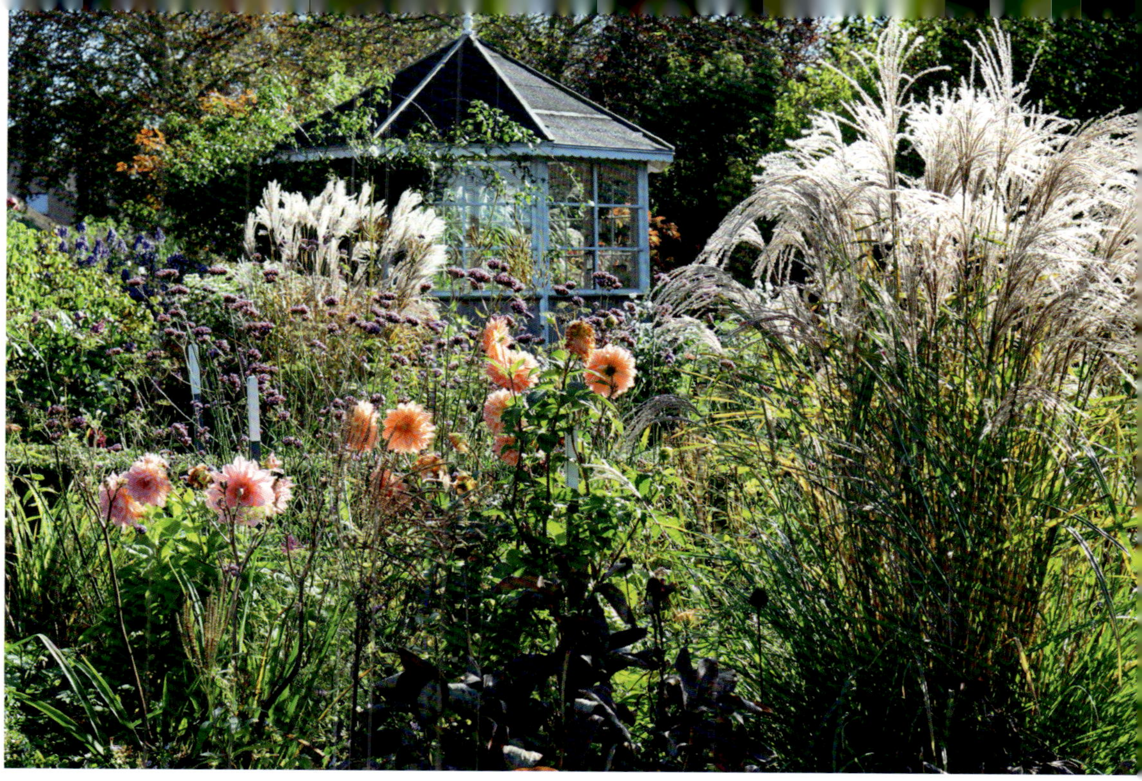

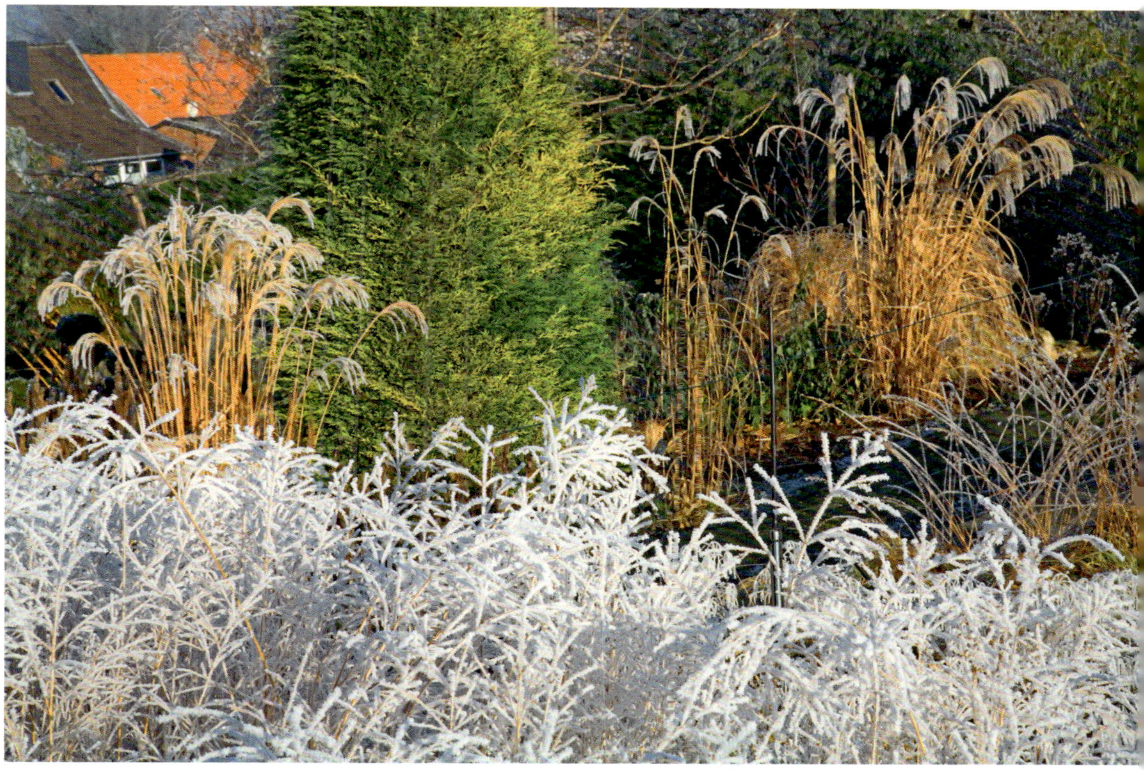

Garden magic through backlighting (above)
Miscanthus again. There are so many varieties that there is one for every garden.

Frost in late autumn (below)
After the first cold night in autumn, frost glistens on the grass panicles. The display unfortunately soon melts away in the sunlight.

Pampas grass

The seed heads of the normally upright *Cortaderia selloana* bend over elegantly under the weight of the frost.

SHRUBS AS ACCOMPANIMENT

With the right shrubs alongside them, autumn grasses reach the peak of their form. The choice of shrubs is so huge and diverse that countless impressive combinations can be created. There are asters in all their brightly coloured diversity, late-flowering perennial sunflowers and, of course, crysanthemums in abundance. The best known are the tall autumn asters (*Aster novae-angliae* and *A. novi-belgii*), whose flowers cover the spectrum from white to pink to dark violet. The violet tones in particular stand in wonderful contrast with the glowing orange and red colouring of the grasses. The *Aster* genus, however, has a lot more to offer: tall wild asters such as *Aster laevis* and *A. lateriflorus* have light-blue flowers, *Aster turbinellus* have dark-blue; they work best in combination with tall grasses, against which they can lean. *Aster ericoides* and *A. x frikartii* grow no higher than 50–70 cm. The delicate flowers of these wild species suit slender grasses exceptionally well and form a counterpart to the latter's autumn colouring. Perennial sunflowers such as *Helianthus decapetalus* and late-flowering black-eyed Susans (*Rudbeckia* 'Herbstsonne') as well as verbesina *(Verbesina alternifolia)* are strong forms and work best with tall miscanthus varieties. Their golden yellow flowers create a glowing counterpart to the silvery flower heads of the grasses. Other yellow winter bloomers are the tall calliopsis or tickseed *(Coreopsis)* and goldenrods *(Solidago)*. Goldenrod flowers have almost the same shape as those of the miscanthus – an attractive example of the multiple possibilities that exist for combining grasses and shrubs. They interveave with each other extremely well. The purple-pink cones of the boneset *(Eupatorium)* are at the same height as the dark lilac cones of the Arkansas ironweed *(Vernonia arkansana)* and can also tower over tall grasses.

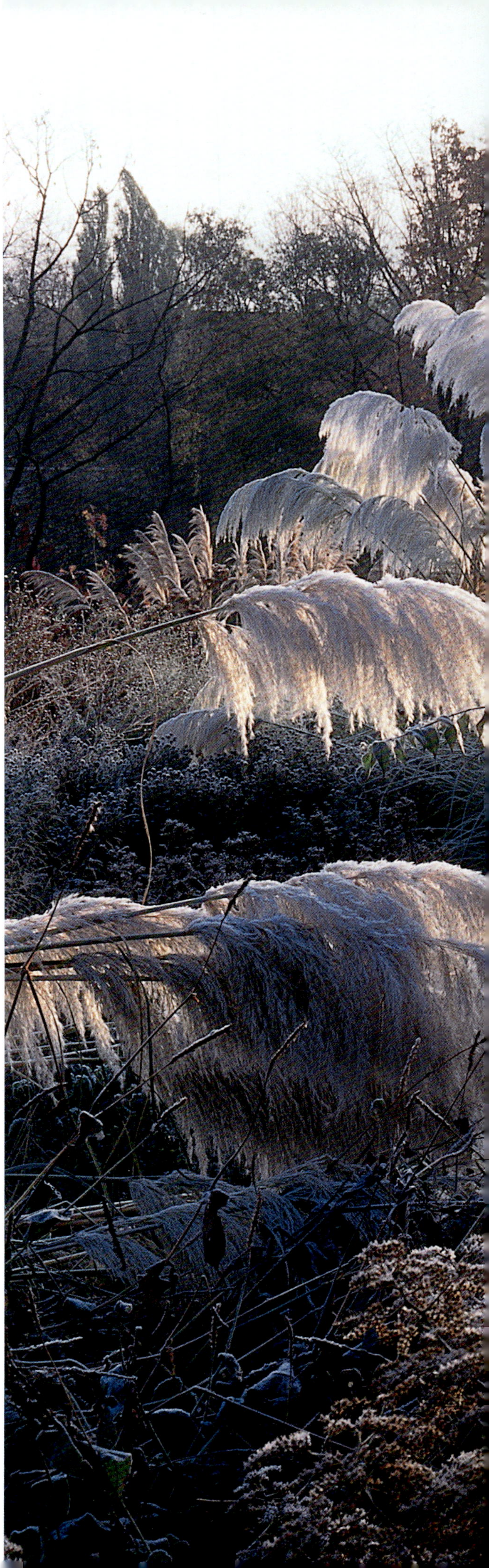

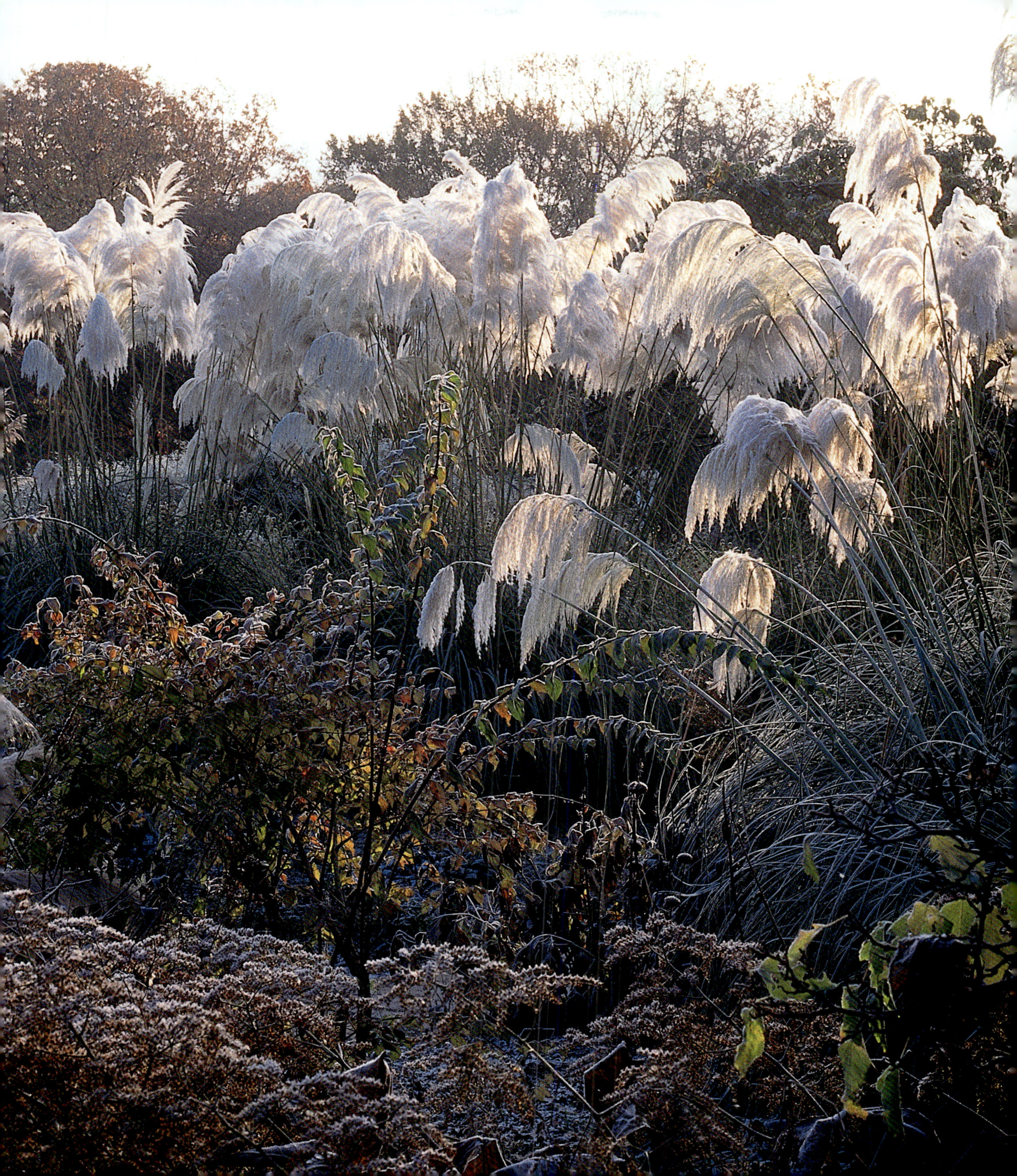

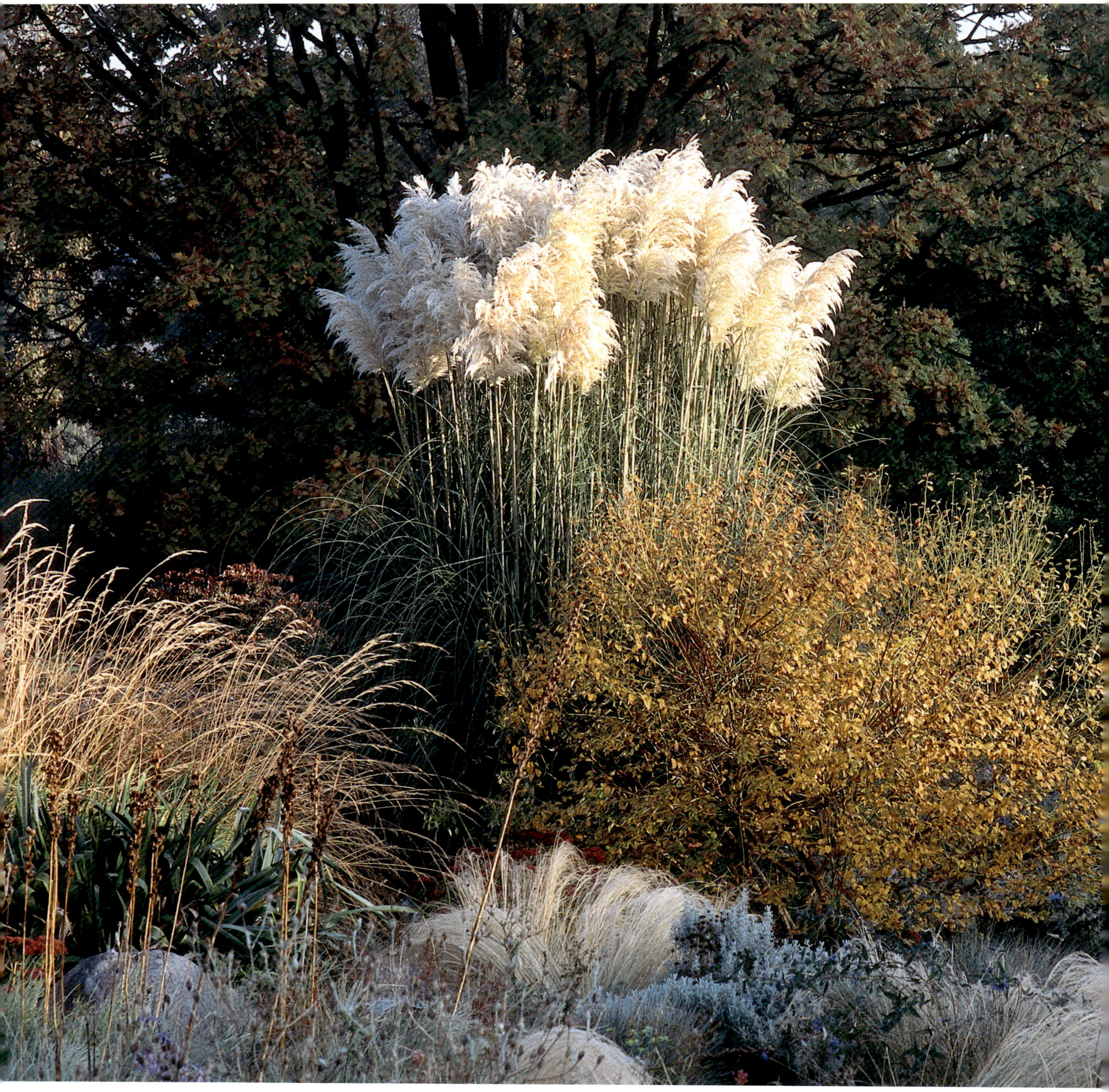

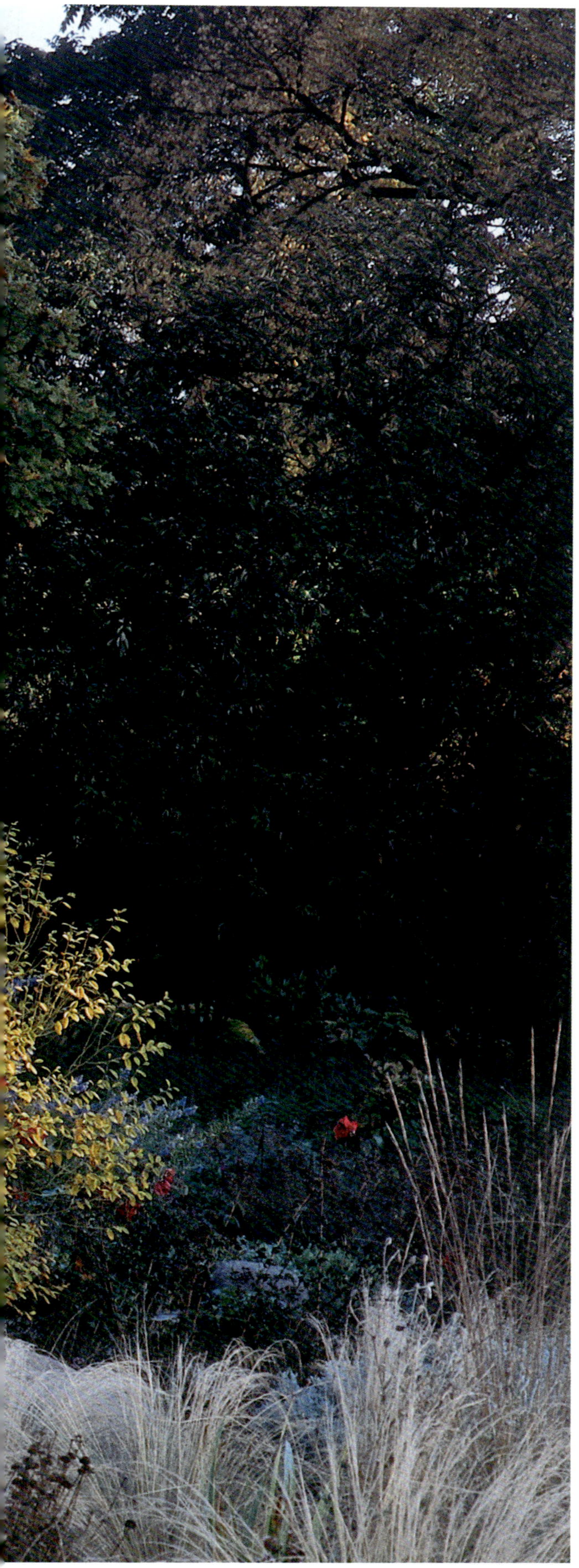

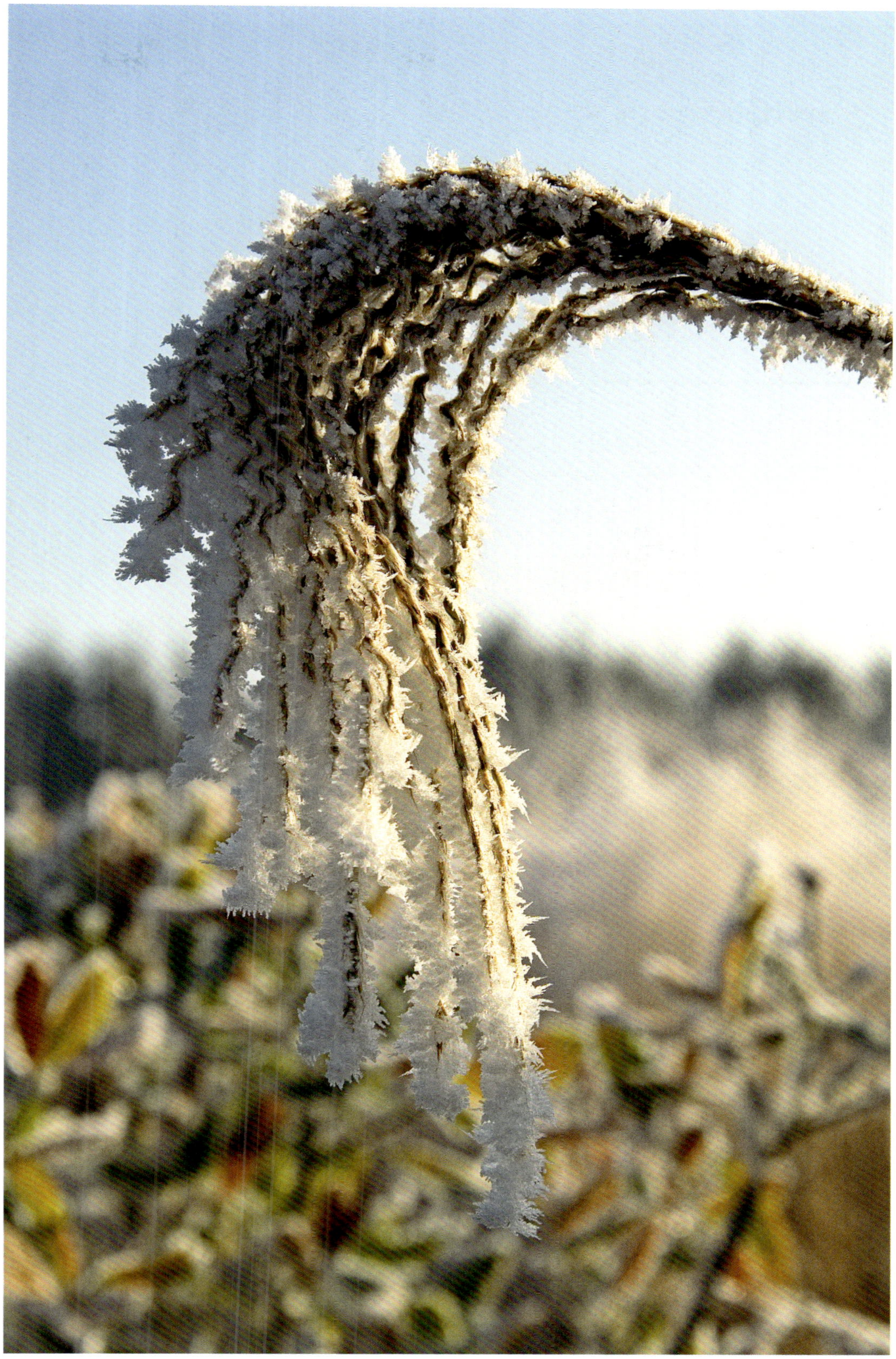

Impressive free-standing grasses (left)
Because of its imposing height, pampas grass *(Cortaderia selloana)* is the ideal grass for backdrops.

Icy fur (above)
After clear, frosty nights the flowers of the miscanthus are overgrown with ice crystals.

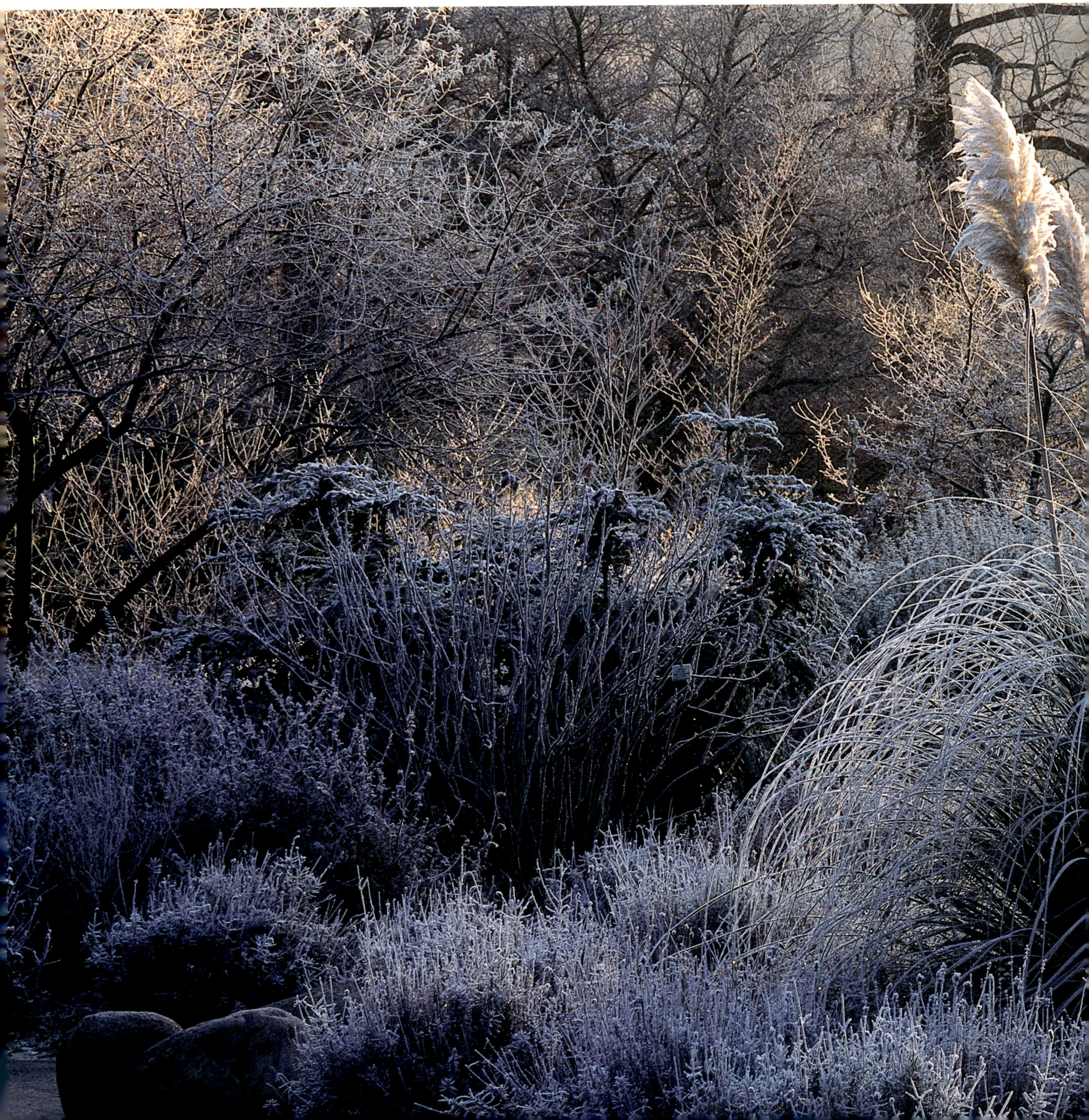

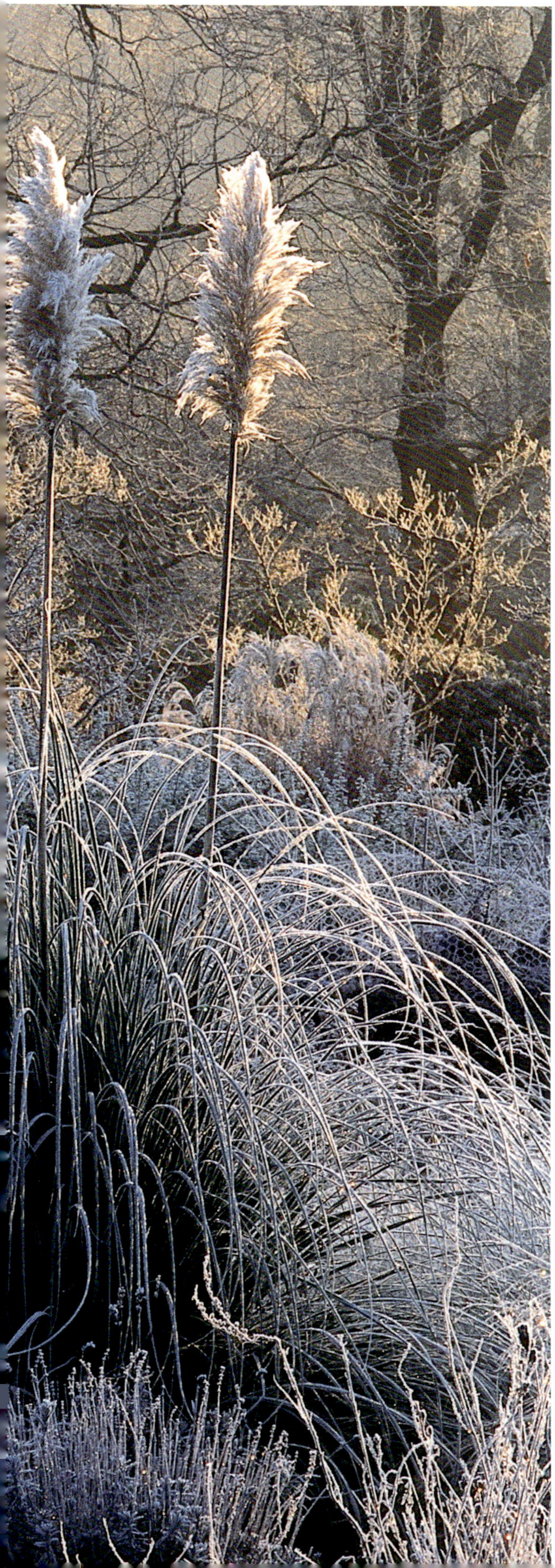

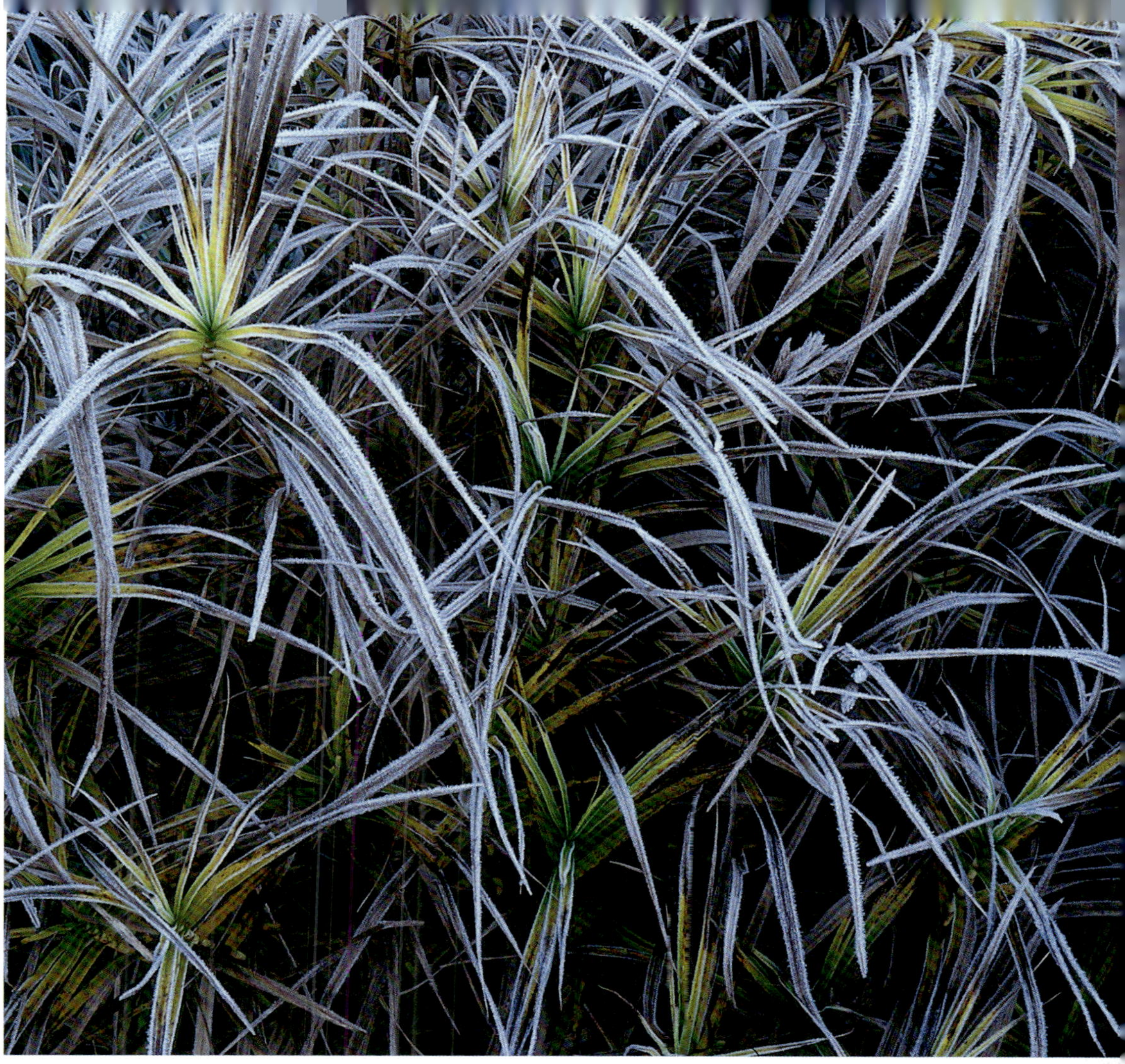

THE FIRST FROST

With the first night-time frost, the autumn bids us farewell, and in the pale morning light often only the outlines of the plants are visible. The freezing fog settles on the stems, leaves and flowers and accentuates every tiny detail. This amazing sight clearly demonstrates why it is worth leaving the faded flower heads on the plants as long as possible. And even the filigree structures of the grass flower and seed heads look as if they are made of lace.

Palm sedge (above)
The palm sedge *(Carex muskingumensis)* remains attractive all year round.

Impressions of autumn
In a frost the colours in the garden favour the shapes and structures in the background.

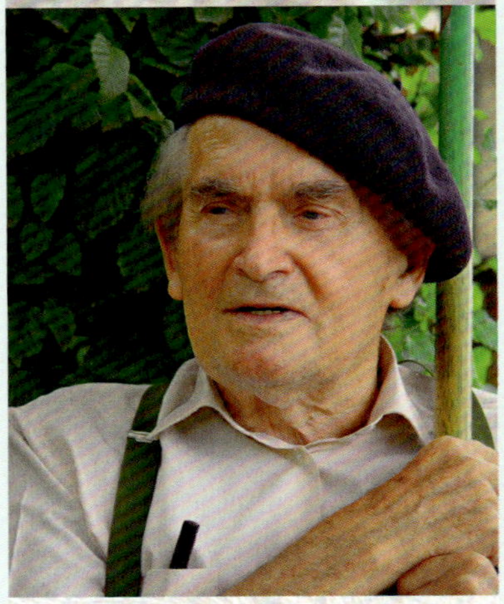

Ernst Pagels

Many of Ernst Pagels' cultivars are now even more established mainstays of the grass and shrub collection.

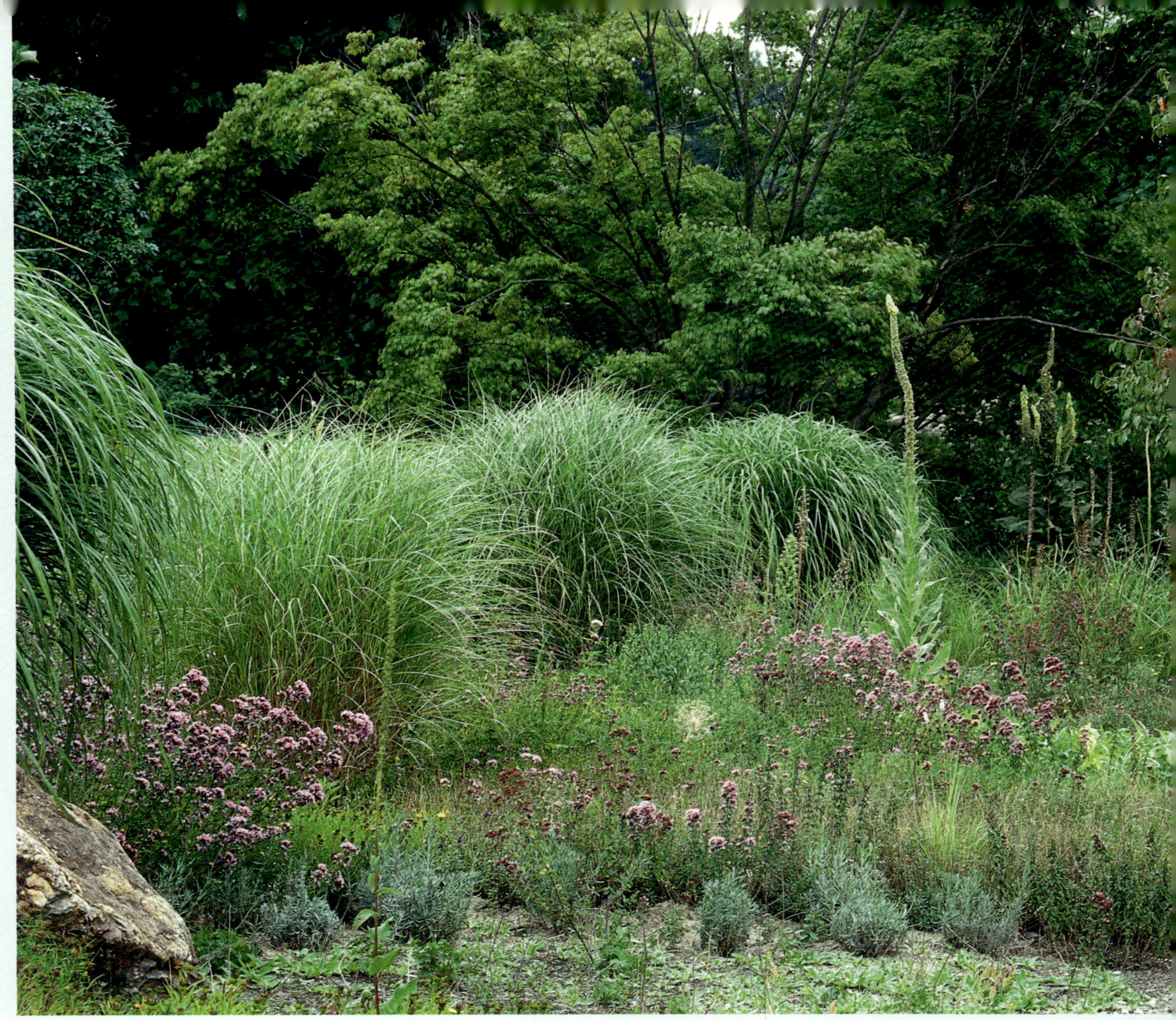

From 'little silver spiders' and 'flamingoes'

The legacy of Ernst Pagels.

Ernst Pagels was born in 1913 in East Friesland in Germany and was, alongside Karl Foerster, one of the most important shrub breeders in Germany and one of the greatest grass breeders of our time.

As a young gardener and garden architect, he first of all worked in the nursery of Karl Foerster, who was an enduring influence on his subsequent life and work. In his nursery in Leer, Ernst Pagels created about 130 different breeds of shrubs

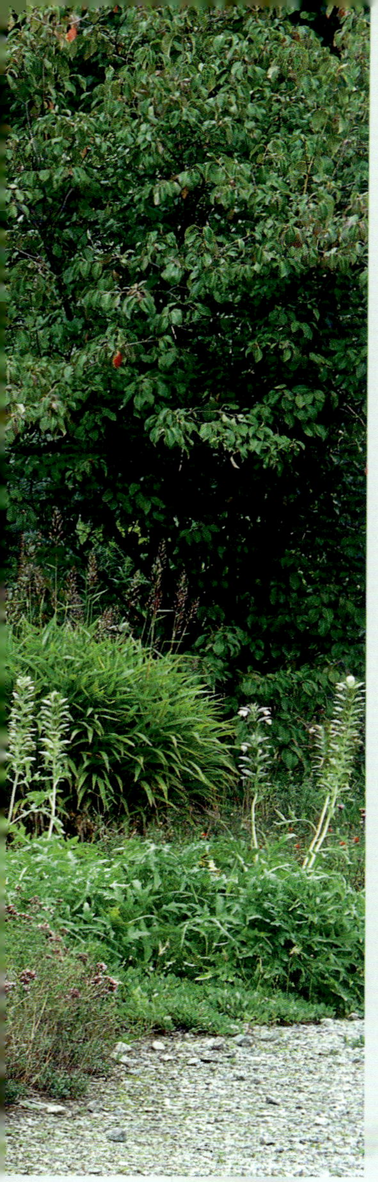

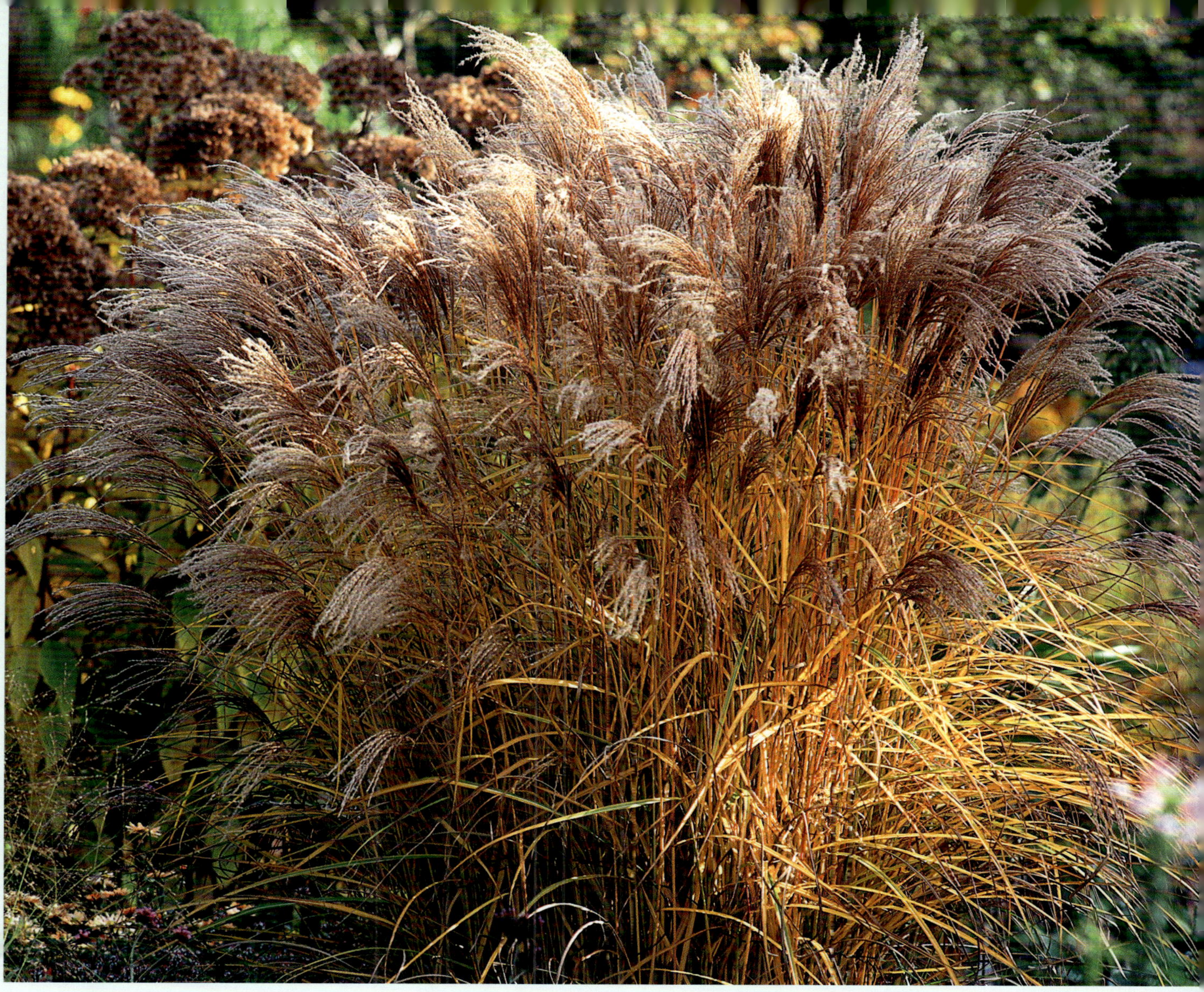

and grasses. Many of these can be described as groundbreaking, as seventy of his varieties still form an integral part of the modern collection of shrubs. Apart from an extensive collection of *Salvia-nemerosa,* it was above all grasses, in particular the genus *Miscanthus*, that made the name of this passionate gardener. His blooming miscanthus breeds revolutionised the world of grasses. Among them are the 'Malepartus', with its reddish blooms and red autumn colouring, 'Graziella', with silvery flower heads, 'Kleine Silberspinne' (lit. 'little silver spider'), with a silvery middle strip, and 'Flamingo', with pink-tinged flower heads. The early-blooming *Miscanthus oligostachys* 'Ghana' grows upright and in autumn turns a beautiful chocolate brown. *Miscanthus* 'Morning Light' has a white strip in the middle of its leaves and looks almost silvery – simply fantastic in front of a dark-green yew hedge.

But also moor grass *(Molinia)*, with the variants 'Windspiel' and 'Edith Duzus', forms part of his collection.

The modern world of plants is unimaginable without the cultivars of Ernst Pagels. All well-known plants people return again and again to his collection.

Some time ago an 'Ernst Pagels themed garden' was created in the 'Park of Gardens' in Bad Zwischenahn to commemorate the plant cultivator's life's work. Here all his essential cultivars are planted and combined in beautiful garden vistas. The garden was laid out by Anke Mattern, a garden designer and former colleague of Pagels.

Pagels received several German and international awards for his achievements, among them the highest honour of the Perennial Plant Association of America. Ernst Pagels died in 2007 at the age of ninety-three.

Miscanthus 'Flamingo' (above)
Many of the finest variants of miscanthus are a result of the cultivation work of Ernst Pagels.

Height gradation in the border (above left)
The tall miscanthus stands in the background. Through direct comparison, the differences in the growth habits of the different types can be clearly seen.

Dancing silhouettes (right)
A summer border with hare's tail grass *(Lagurus ovatus)* and cornflowers *(Centaurea).*

Contrasts in the summer border (opposite, top)
Difficult to combine, plants such as Indian shot plant (*Canna indica* 'Schwabenstolz') and ninebark (*Physocarpus opulifolius* 'Diabolo') have found a perfect accompaniment in Chinese silver grass *(Miscanthus sinensis).*

Feathery flower details (opposite, bottom)
The Chinese silver grass *(Miscanthus sinensis)* reveals its true beauty when backlit.

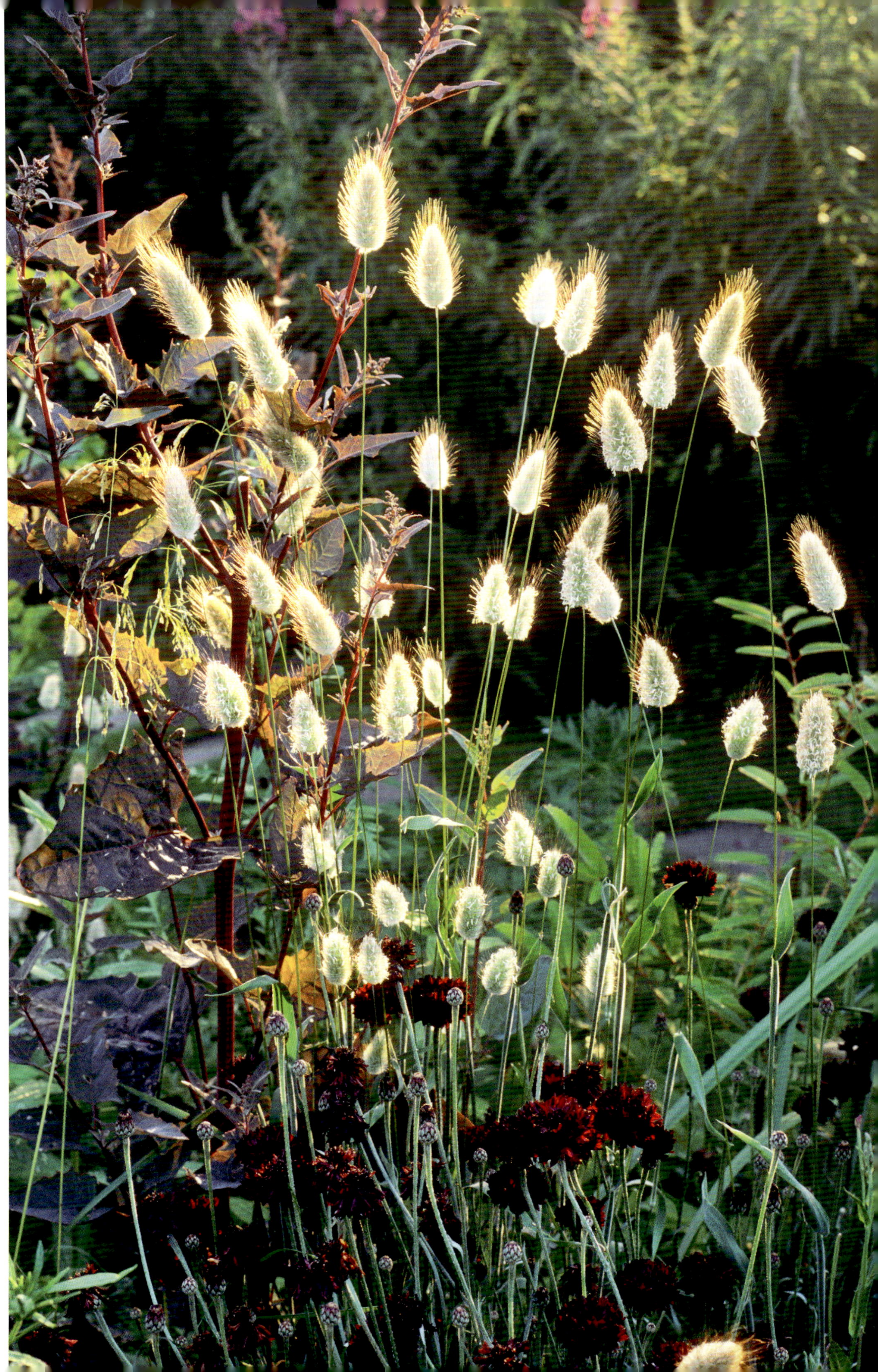

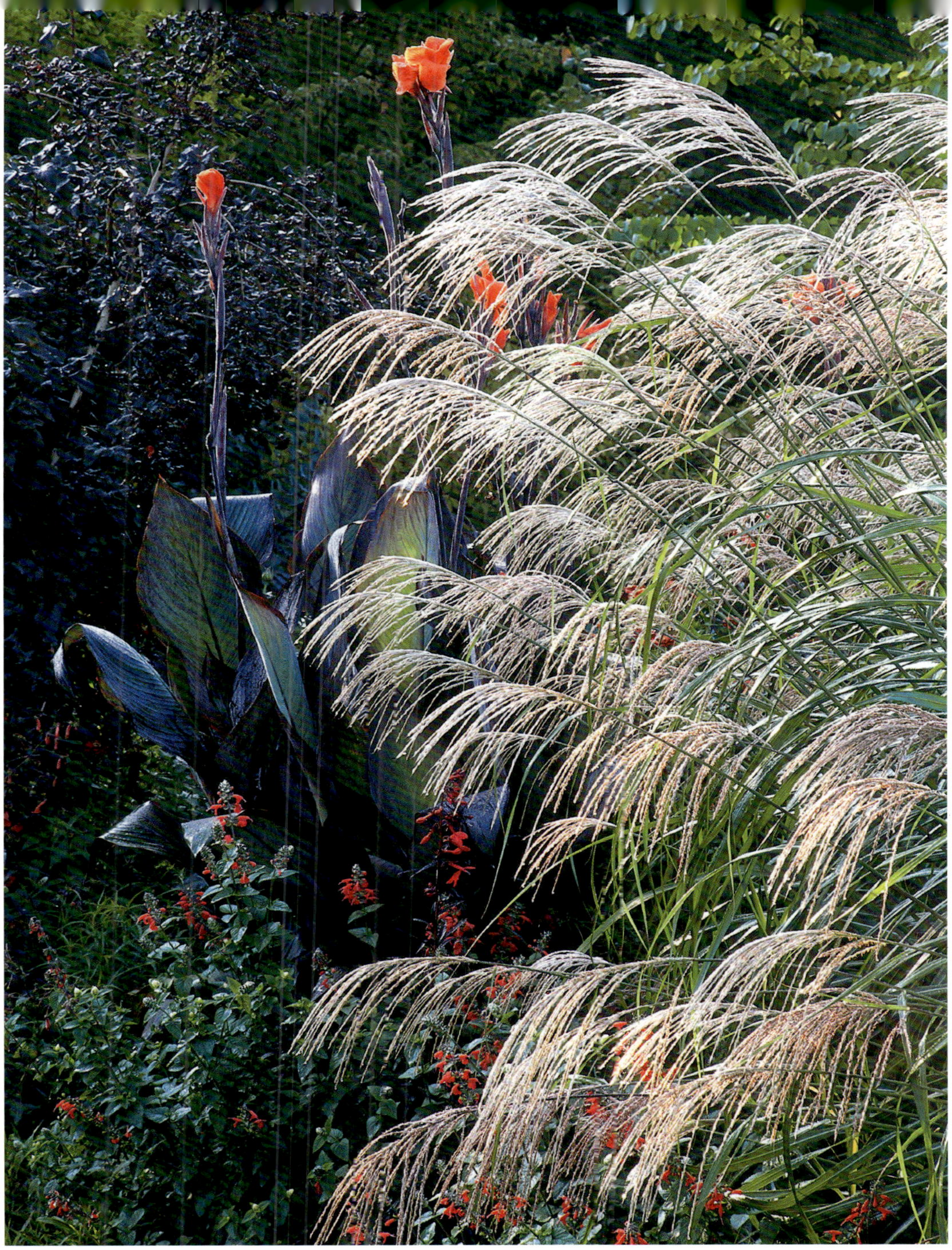

Light and Shade

Flowers and seed heads are shown at their best when backlit.

Often their contours first become visible when the sun shines. In this respect, nature has been very consistent – most of the blooms, especially of the taller grasses, develop in late summer and continue to decorate the plants right through into winter. At this time of year the sun is not as high in the sky, which creates beautiful backlighting effects in the garden. Also, after a foggy morning in autumn, when the sun finally breaks through, the effect can be quite breathtaking. When the sun quickly melts the frost, the grasses glisten for a short time as if adorned by a thousand diamonds. And then, a mere half hour later, the fascinating spectacle is over.

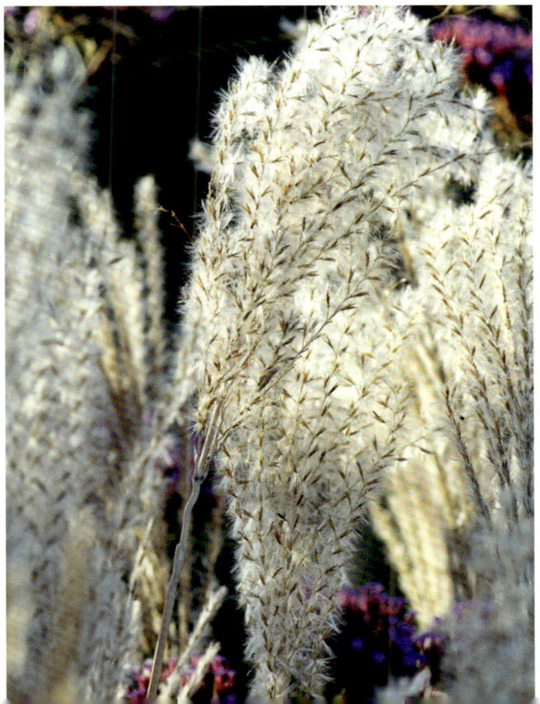

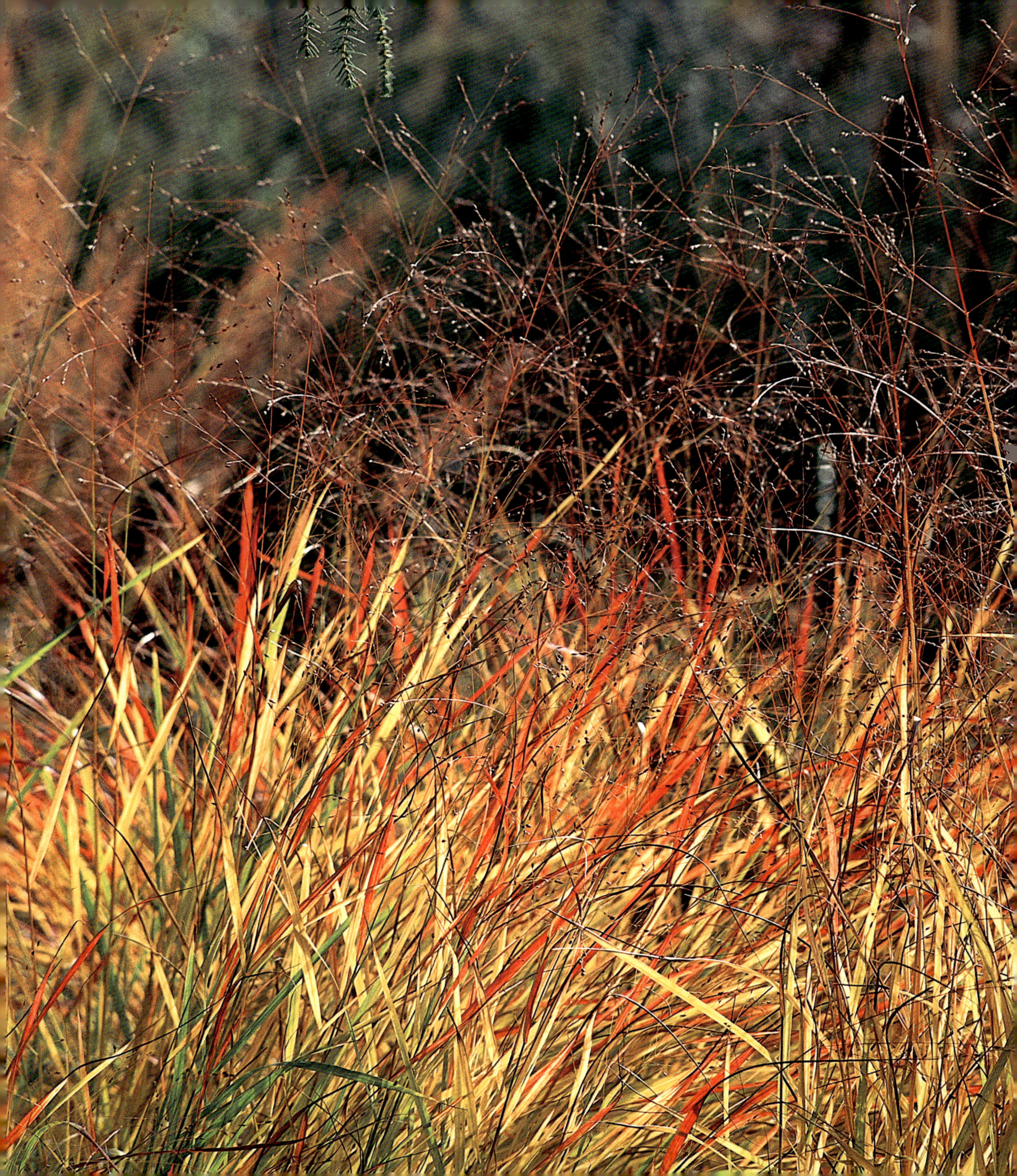

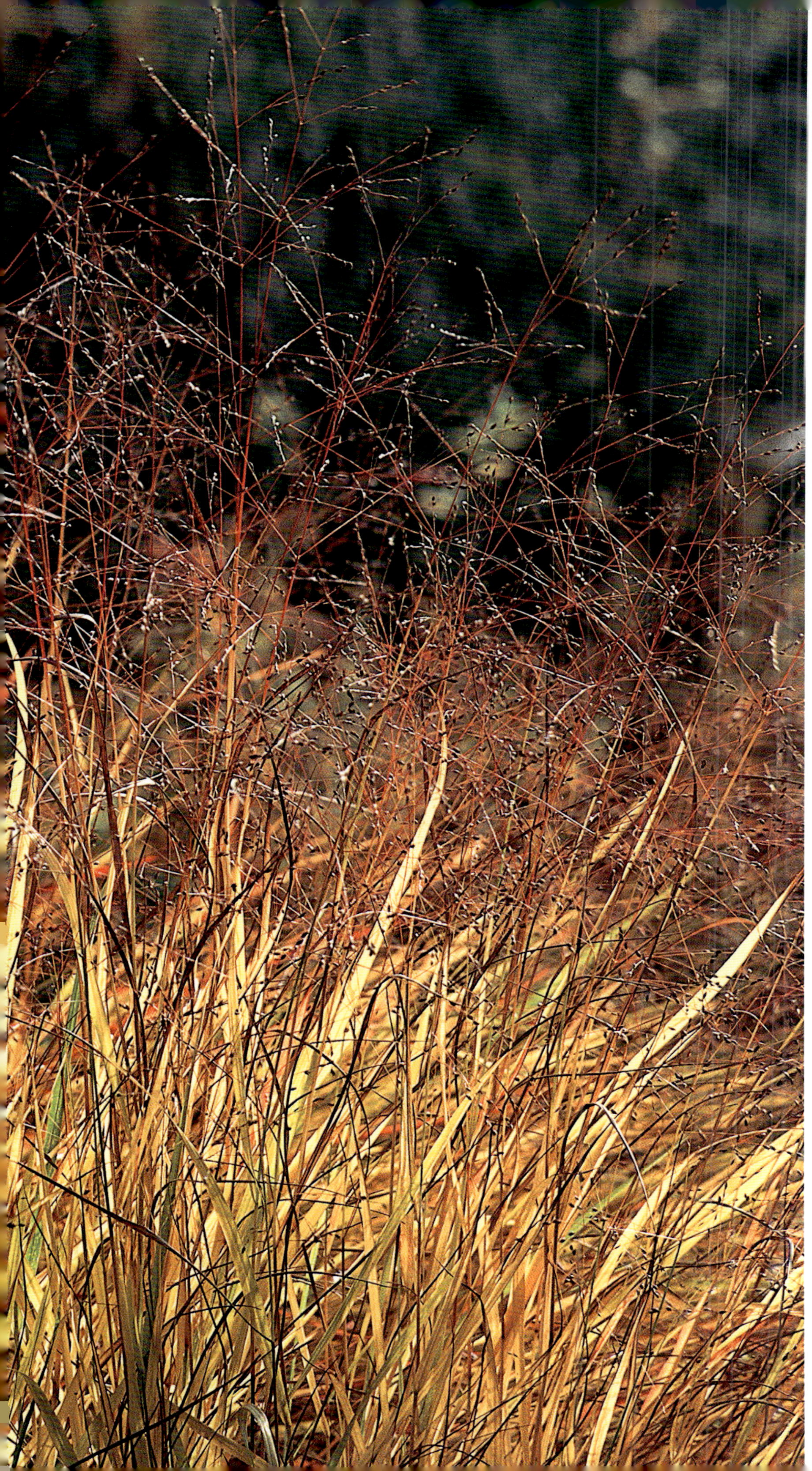

Switch grass

The flower heads of switch grass (Panicum virgatum) are as fine as hair and show themselves to best effect against a dark background.

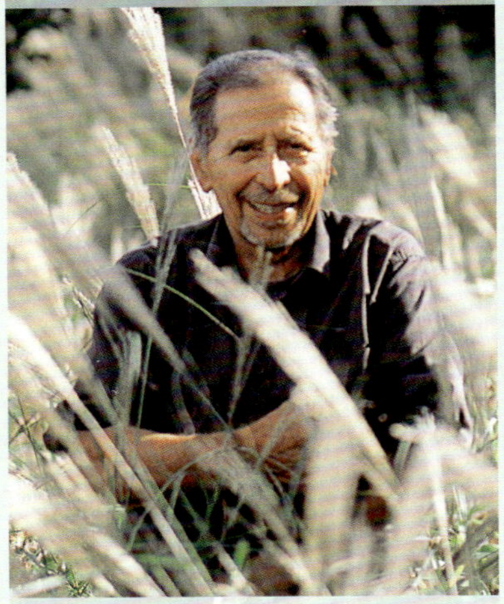

Wolfgang Oehme

Wolfgang Oehme is known for his massive, large-scale planting schemes using shrubs and grasses.

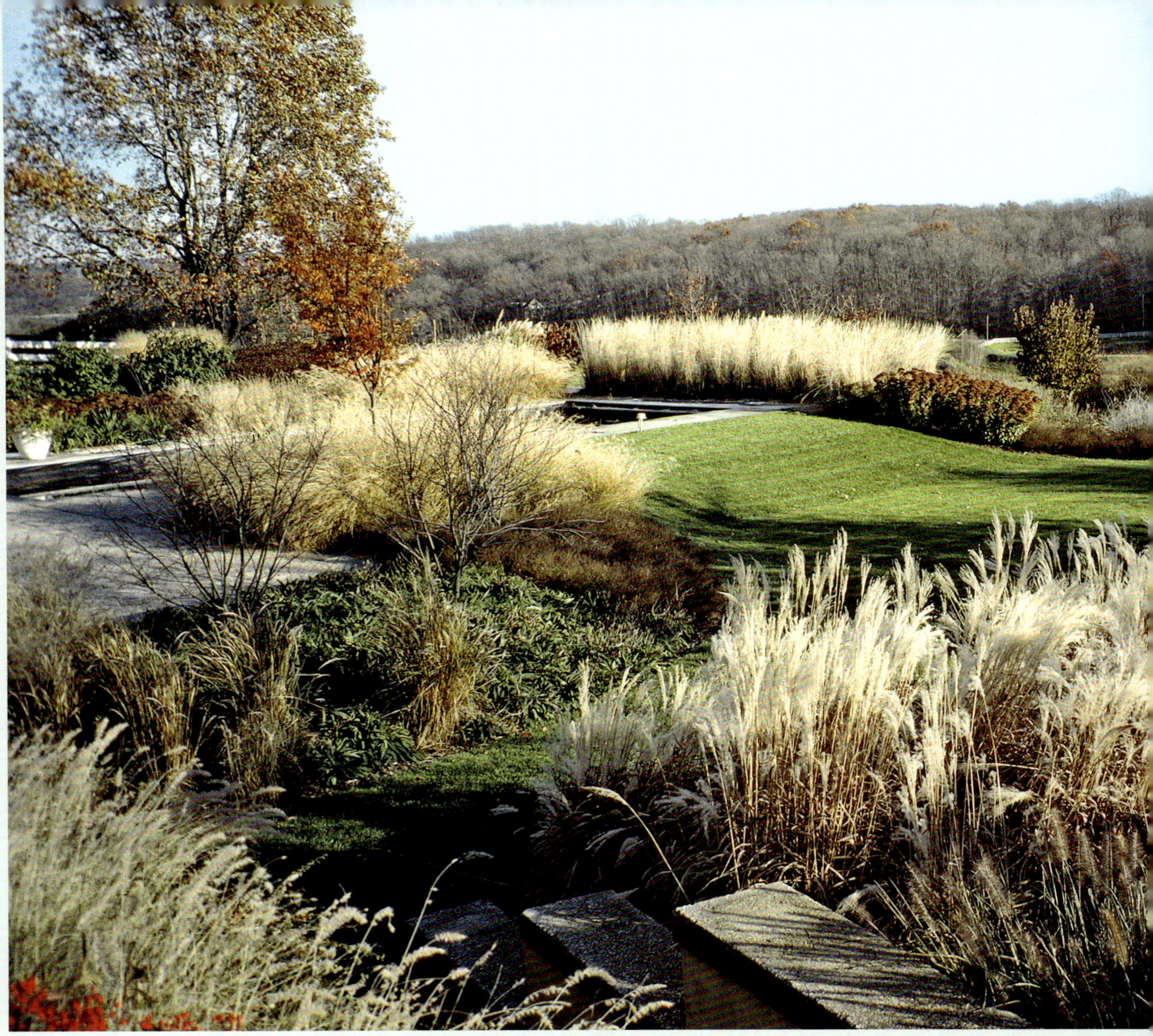

New Landscapes to Replace Monotonous Lawns

The design concept of Wolfgang Oehme

Wolfgang Oehme was born in 1930 in the town of Chemnitz in Saxony. In 1957, after graduating from horticultural college in Berlin-Dahlem, he emigrated to the USA. There he developed his own distinctive, spacious garden style in opposition to the predominant garden fashion and revolutionised the American garden scene, which until then had been dominated by large, mown lawns. His style is characterised by a

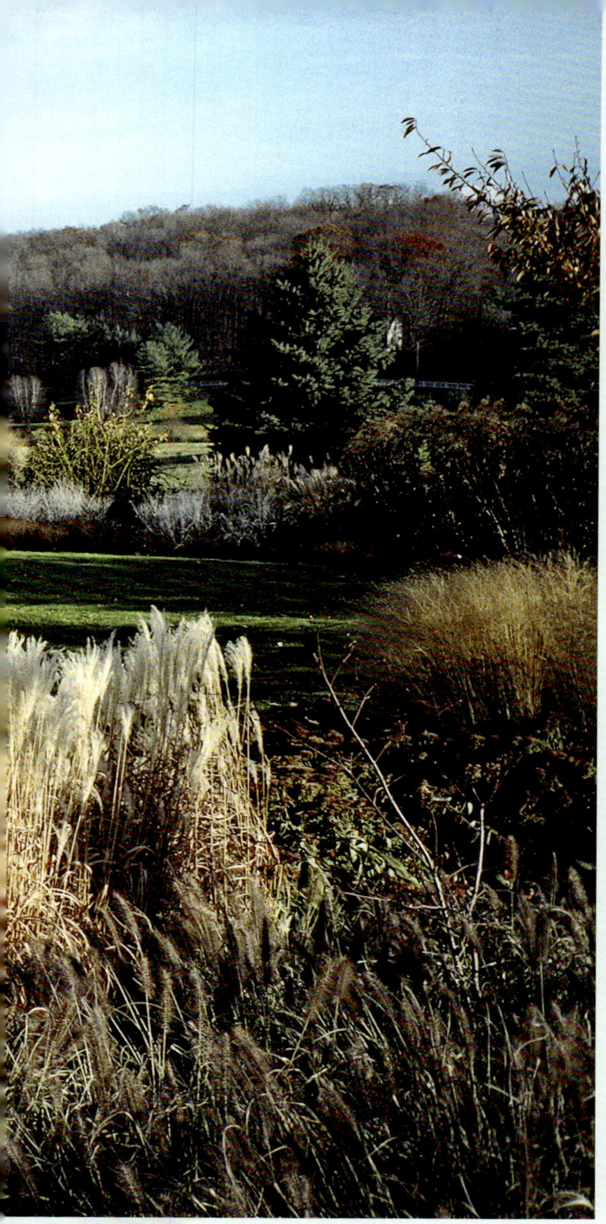

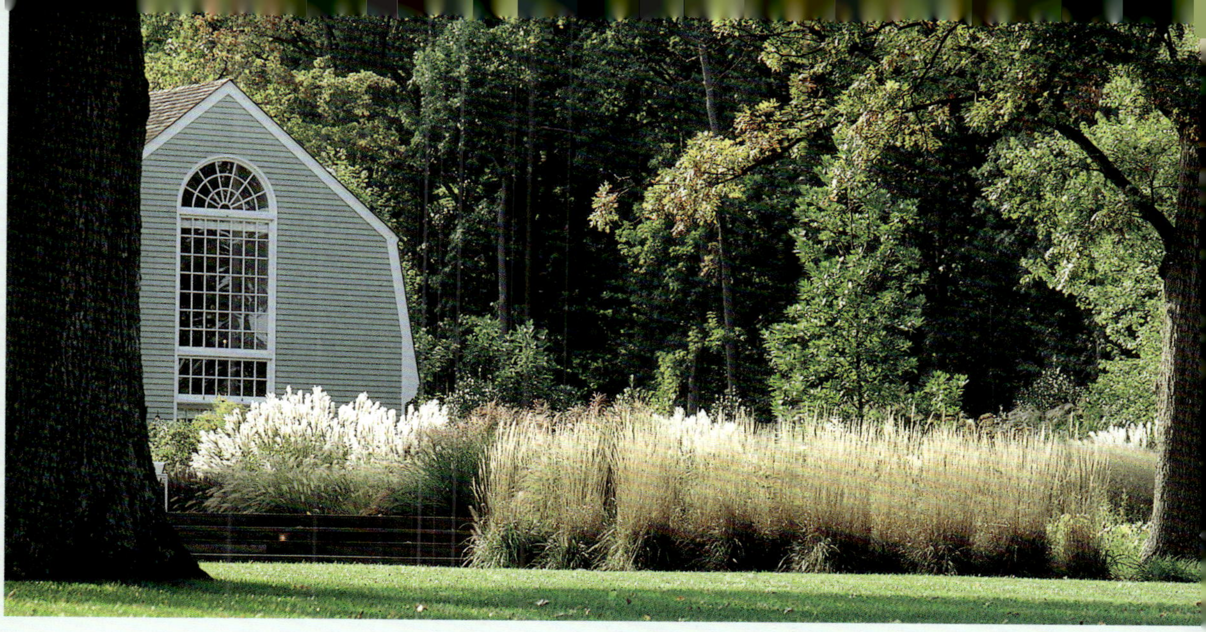

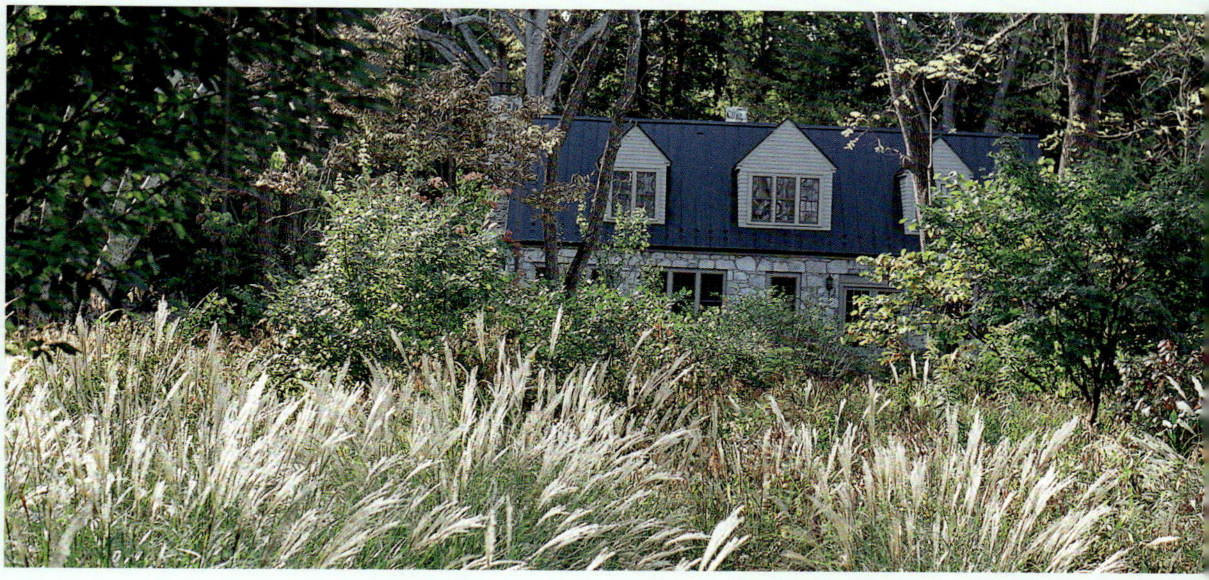

massive, large-scale use of robust, long-lived plants – shrubs as well as grasses, bold planting schemes and strong accents in an often expansive landscape or corresponding environment.

The plants employed for this must be carefully selected, because, due to the large-scale design, they have to be attractive year round, robust and long-living.

In particular, the use of combinations of fountain grass *(Pennisetum alopecuroides)*, stonecrop (*Sedum* 'Herbstfreude') and coneflower (*Rudbeckia fulgida* var. *sullivantii* 'Goldsturm') over large areas became almost a signature design of Wolfgang Oehme.

That several large shrubs and grasses such as boneset *(Eupatorium)*, miscanthus and reed grass *(Calamagrostis)* all came to be used extensively in modern garden design is primarily down to his ideas.

Oehme found his inspiration during his spell as a gardener in Germany, especially in the work of Karl Foerster and Karl Plomin.

His travels brought him home to Germany on an annual basis, where he perpetually discovered new plants in nurseries and botanical gardens that he then used in America – and conversely introduced new varieties into Germany or fostered their use there, such as *Persicaria polymorpha, Pycnanthemum muticum* or *Tanacetum macrophyllum*. These all have one thing in common: they are robust, long-living and attractive all year round.

Wolfgang Oehme currently lives in Baltimore and has been running a landscape architectural practice in partnership with James van Sweden for more than thirty years.

Garden scene in late summer (top)
Feather reed grass *(Calamagrostis x acutiflora)* and Chinese silver grass *(Miscanthus sinensis)* capture the last of the sun's rays.

Chinese silver grass beneath trees (bottom)
The combination of grasses and trees looks as if it is staged by nature itself.

Landscapes with grasses (opposite)
Wolfgang Oehme consistently manages to stage magnificent landscapes.

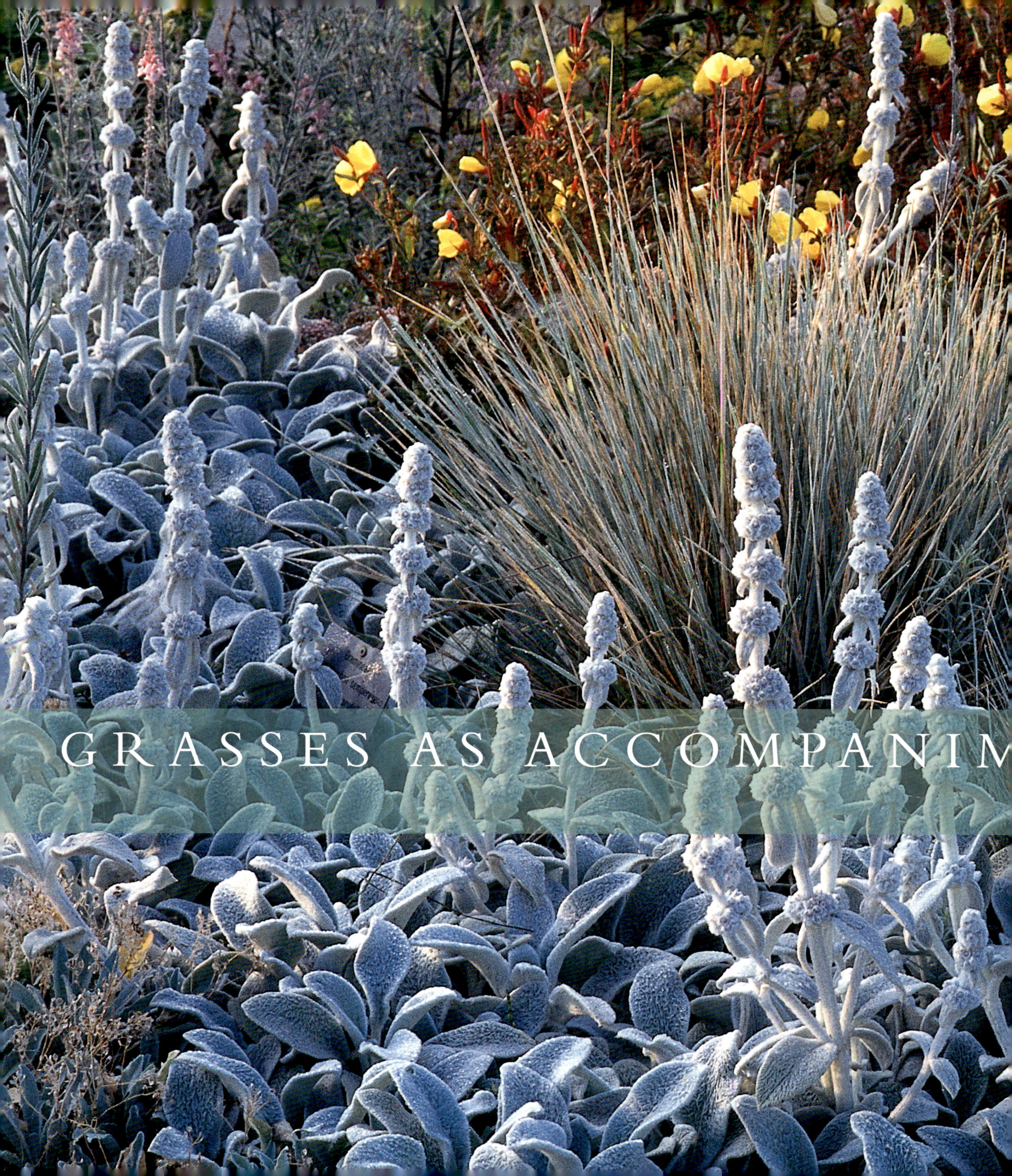

GRASSES AS ACCOMPANIM

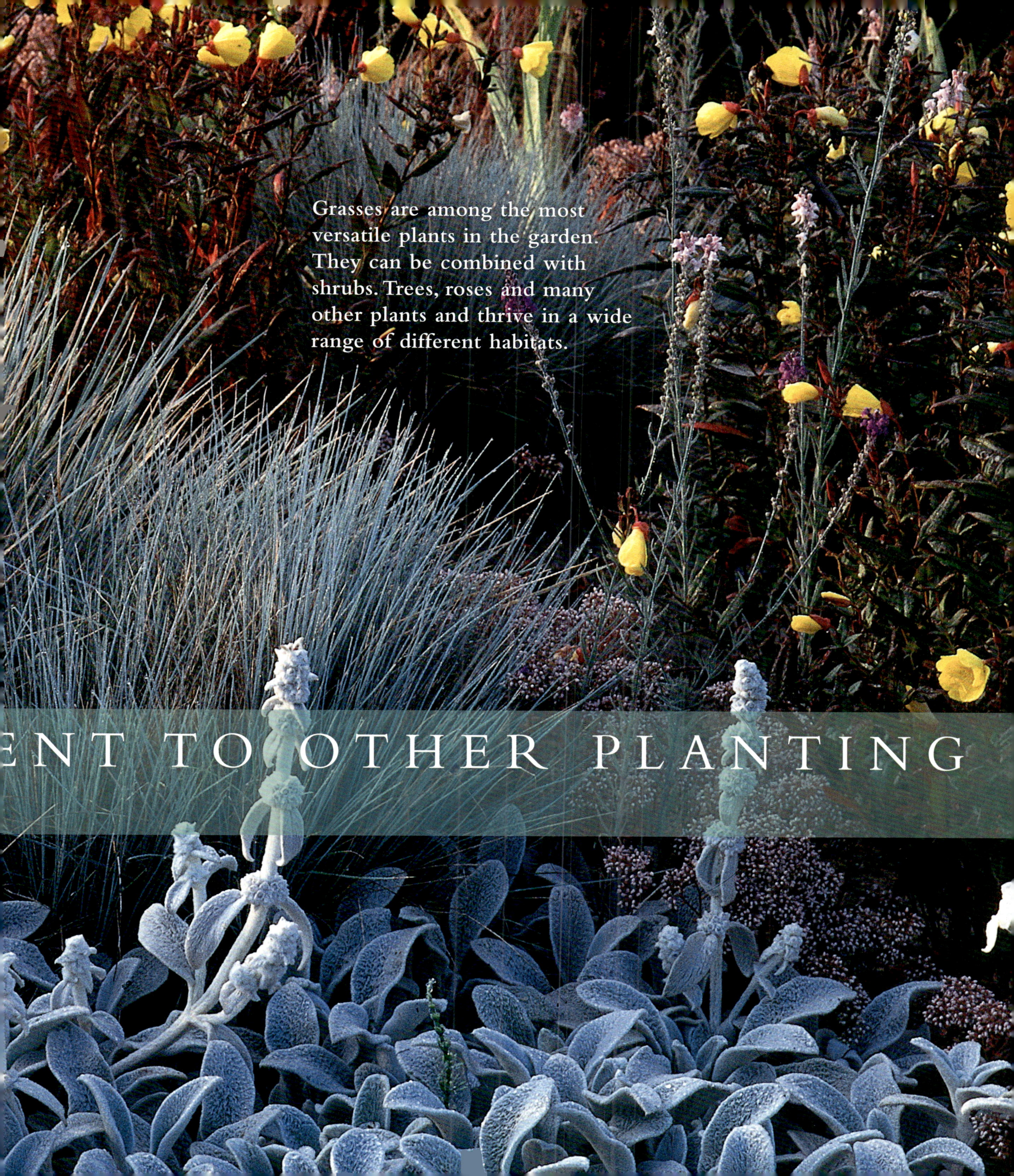

Grasses are among the most versatile plants in the garden. They can be combined with shrubs. Trees, roses and many other plants and thrive in a wide range of different habitats.

ENT TO OTHER PLANTING

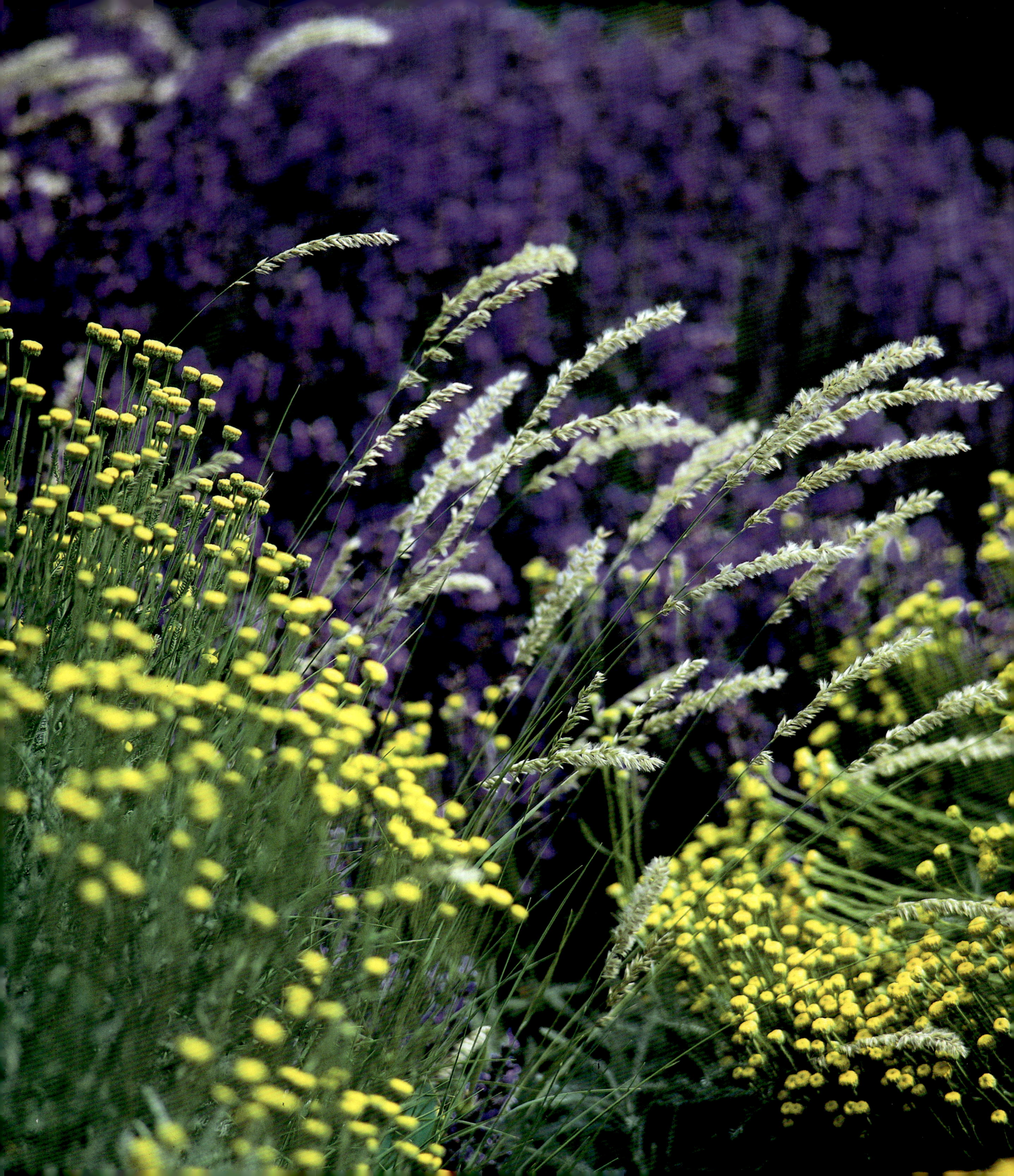

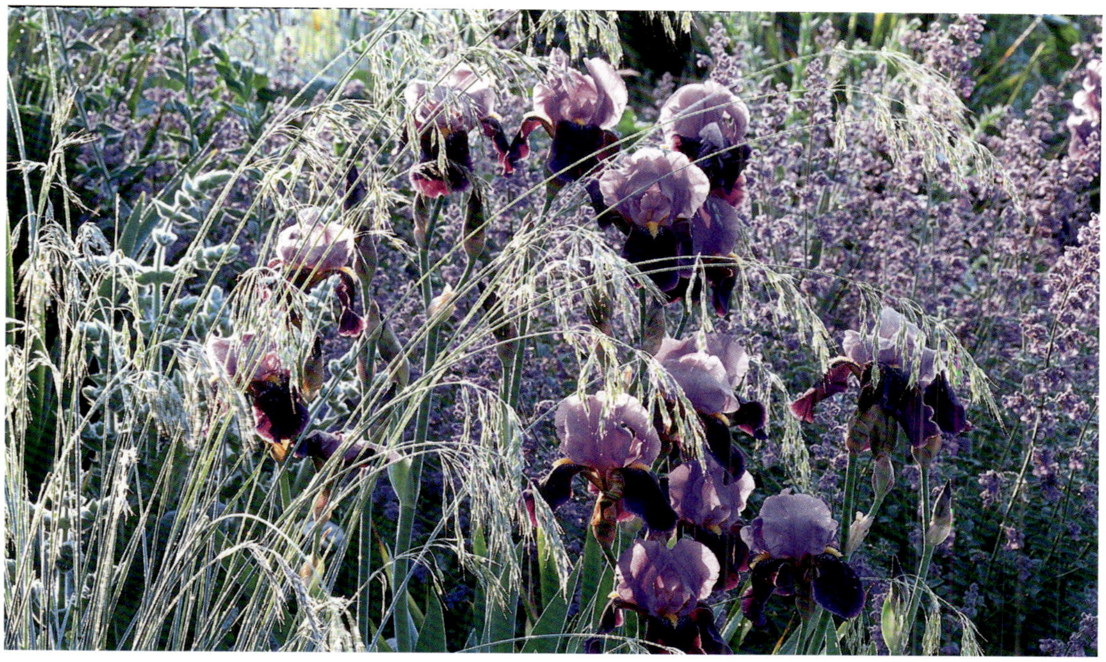

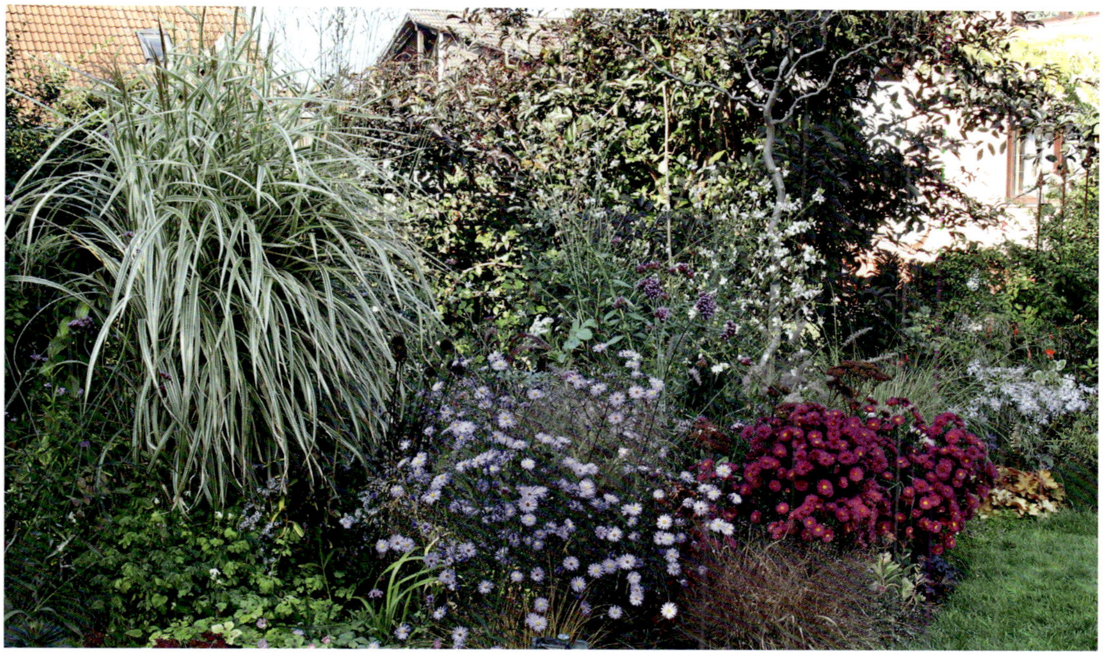

A Mediterranean mood (opposite)
Melic grass has the same soil requirements as, and thus makes an attractive accompaniment to, Mediterranean herbs such as lavender and lavender cotton *(Santolina)*.

A Mediterranean mood (left, top)
Sapphire blue oat grass (*Helictotrichon sempervirens* 'Sapphire Fountain' intermingles with the tall bearded iris (*Iris barbata elatior* 'Sharkskin').

Grasses and shrubs (left, bottom)
White-striped miscanthus creates a striking accent in the border, and asters provide some autumn colouring.

Grasses and Shrubs

Grasses without shrubs, shrubs without grasses – inconceivable in the garden.

Grasses combine well with other plants in all parts of the garden. Sunny locations with dry soil can be earmarked as 'sunny open steppeland areas'. They are characterised by free-draining soils with a high sand content, often in areas with low rainfall. The conditions that create a problem for most cultivated shrubs are perfect for other species. Many of them originated in the sun-baked plains of North America. But even some plants from southern Europe can work well in such steppe-like plantations in local gardens.

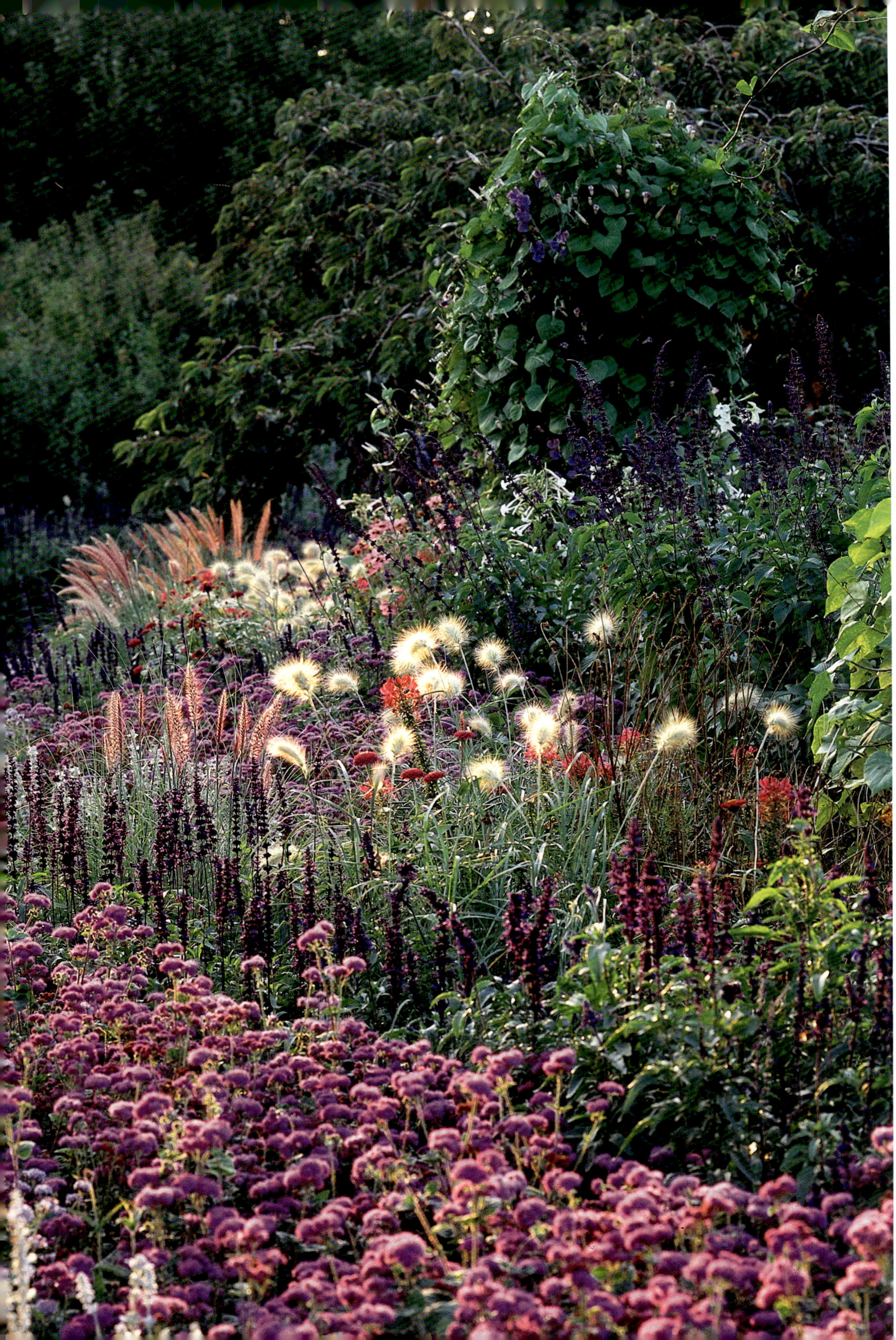
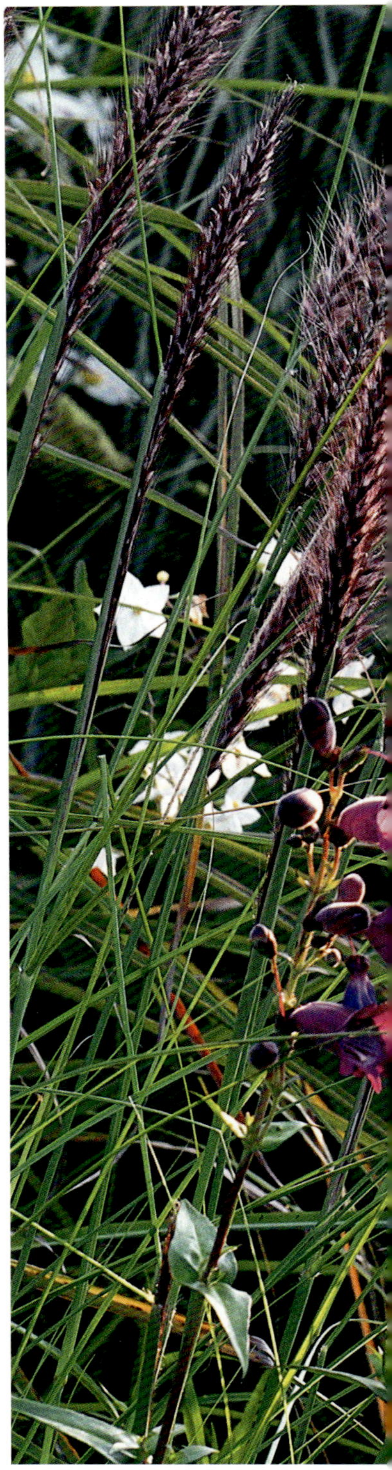

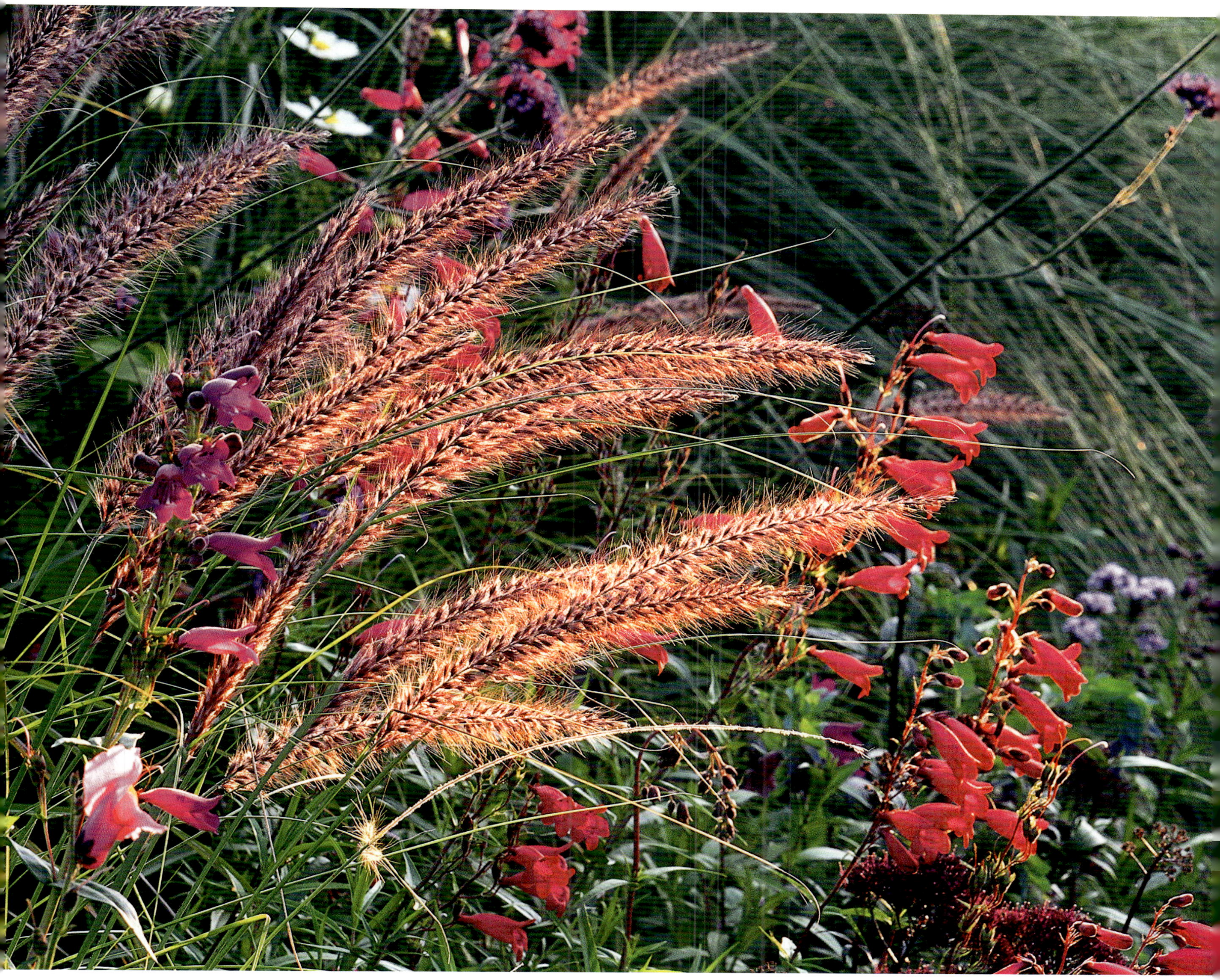

GRASSES AND SHRUBS

Shrubs can be supplemented by a large number of grasses as well as by tubers and bulbs. In the early part of the year there are already various kinds of crocuses, especially *Crocus sieberi*, followed by wild tulips, which in turn are supplanted around the end of April by the low-growing bearded iris *(Iris barbata nana)*. In between, the summer-flowering shrubs and grasses are starting to grow, such as the rock rose (*Helianthemum* hybrids), blue or yellow flax (*Linum perenne* and *L. flavum*), the highly adaptable valerian *(Centranthus ruber)*, catmint *(Nepeta x faassenii)* and king's spear *(Asphodeline lutea)*. Among the early summer-flowering grasses

Grasses and shrubs (above)
Pennisetum alopecuroides var. *viridescens* has long flower spikes in a soft violet. Here seen with Penstemon 'Andenken an Hahn' and 'Sour Grapes'.

Dream border in violet (opposite)
Annual grasses and summer flowers.

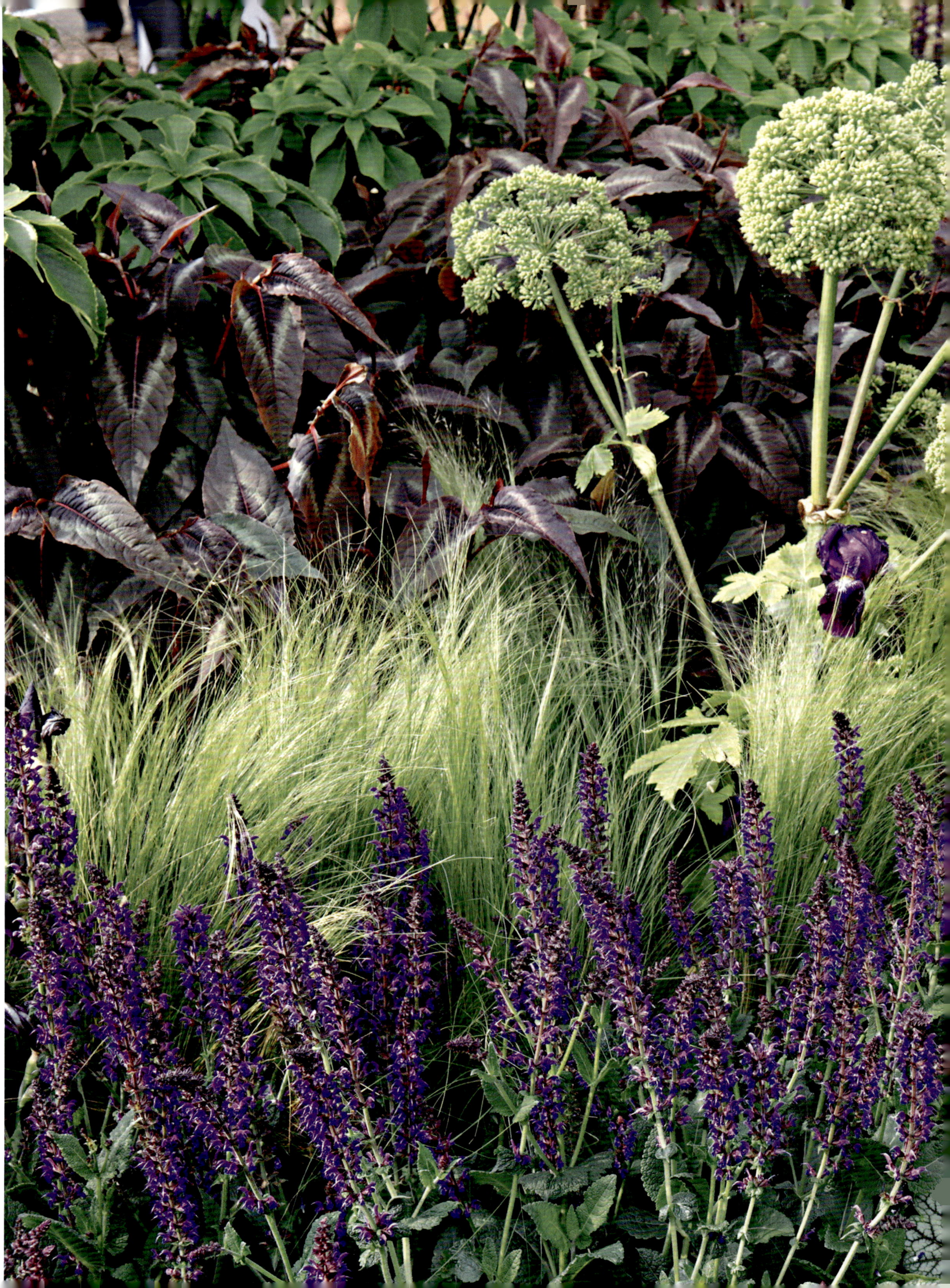

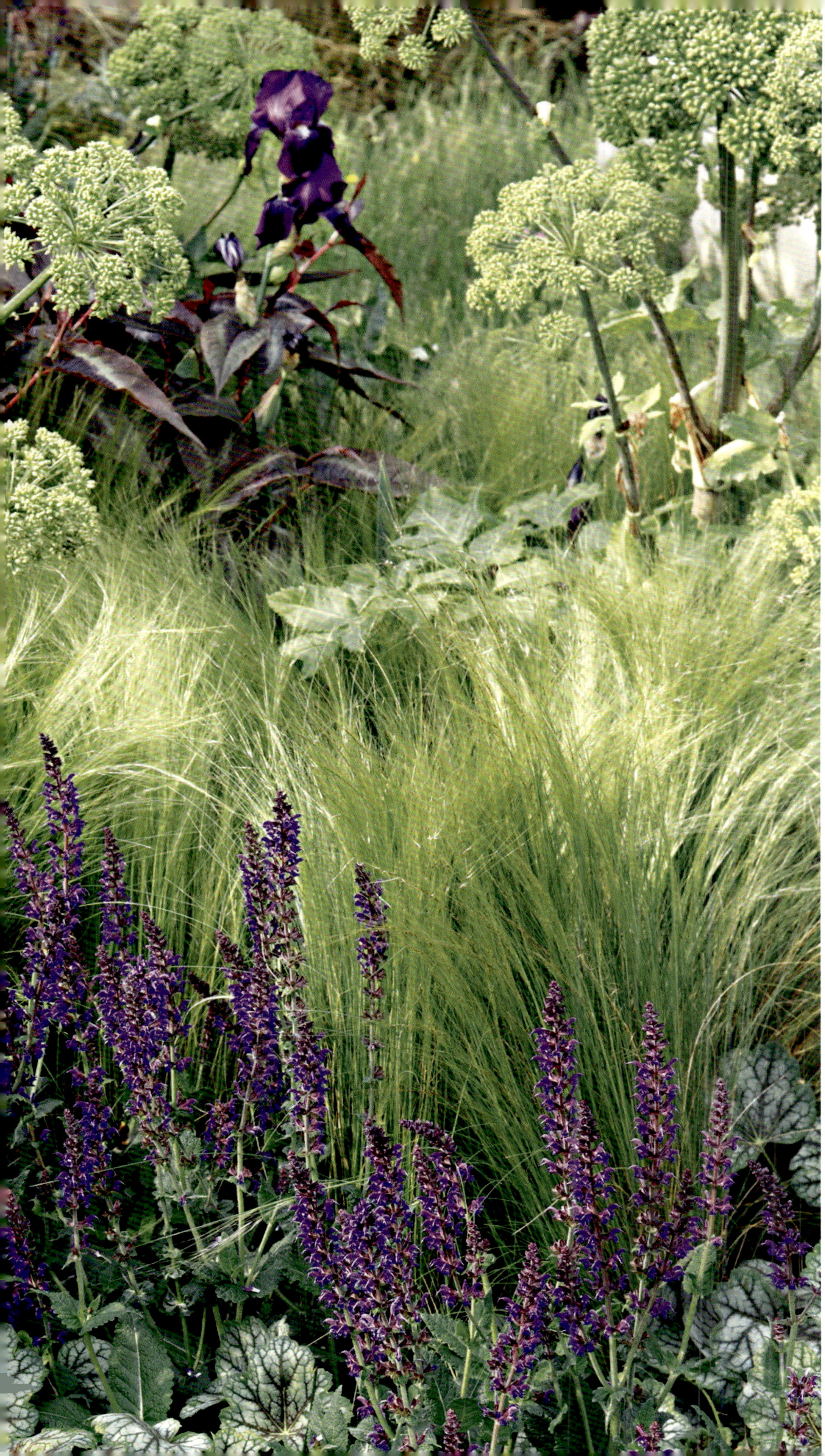

are quaking grass *(Briza media)* and the various types of blue fescue (*Festuca-Cinerea* hybrids). The drier the location, the stronger the blue colouring of the blue fescue's foliage.

Many shrubs that thrive in the steppeland border have silver-coloured or hairy leaves, which means that evaporation is kept to a minimum, and thus the plants need less watering. In mid-summer the spherical flower heads of the alliums stand tall on their wiry stems, while the inflorescences of the foxtail lilies *(Eremurus)* and red hot pokers *(Kniphofia)* blaze like torches above the other plants. They are best complemented by delicate grasses, which bloom only gradually. In late summer we reach the grand finale with Michaelmas daisies *(Aster amellus)*, stonecrop *(Sedum telephium)* and goldilocks aster *(Aster linosyris)*, which blooms well into the autumn. There is an almost unlimited choice of grasses to draw on: fountain grass (*Pennisetum orientale* and *P. alopecuroides*), with its bottlebrush flower heads, Indian grass *(Sorghastrum nutans)*, which grows to 1.8 metres tall and whose seed heads glow an especially beautiful gold colour, or the various sorts of feather grass (*Stipa gigantea* and *S. tenuifolia*) are worthy of note here. Most types of *Miscanthus sinenesis* are too massive, so delicate varieties such as 'Yakushima Dwarf' fit in very well. One shrub that has become very popular in recent years and seems predestined to be combined with grasses, is the Lindheimer's Beeblossom *(Gaura lindheimeri)*; its name tells you a lot about its appearance. It rarely survives hard

Exciting combinations
Massive and fine plant forms: maynight salvia (*Salvia nemorosa* 'Mainacht'), garden angelica *(Angelica archangelica)* and Mexican feather grass *(Nasella tenuissima)* are planted one behind the other in spacious strips.

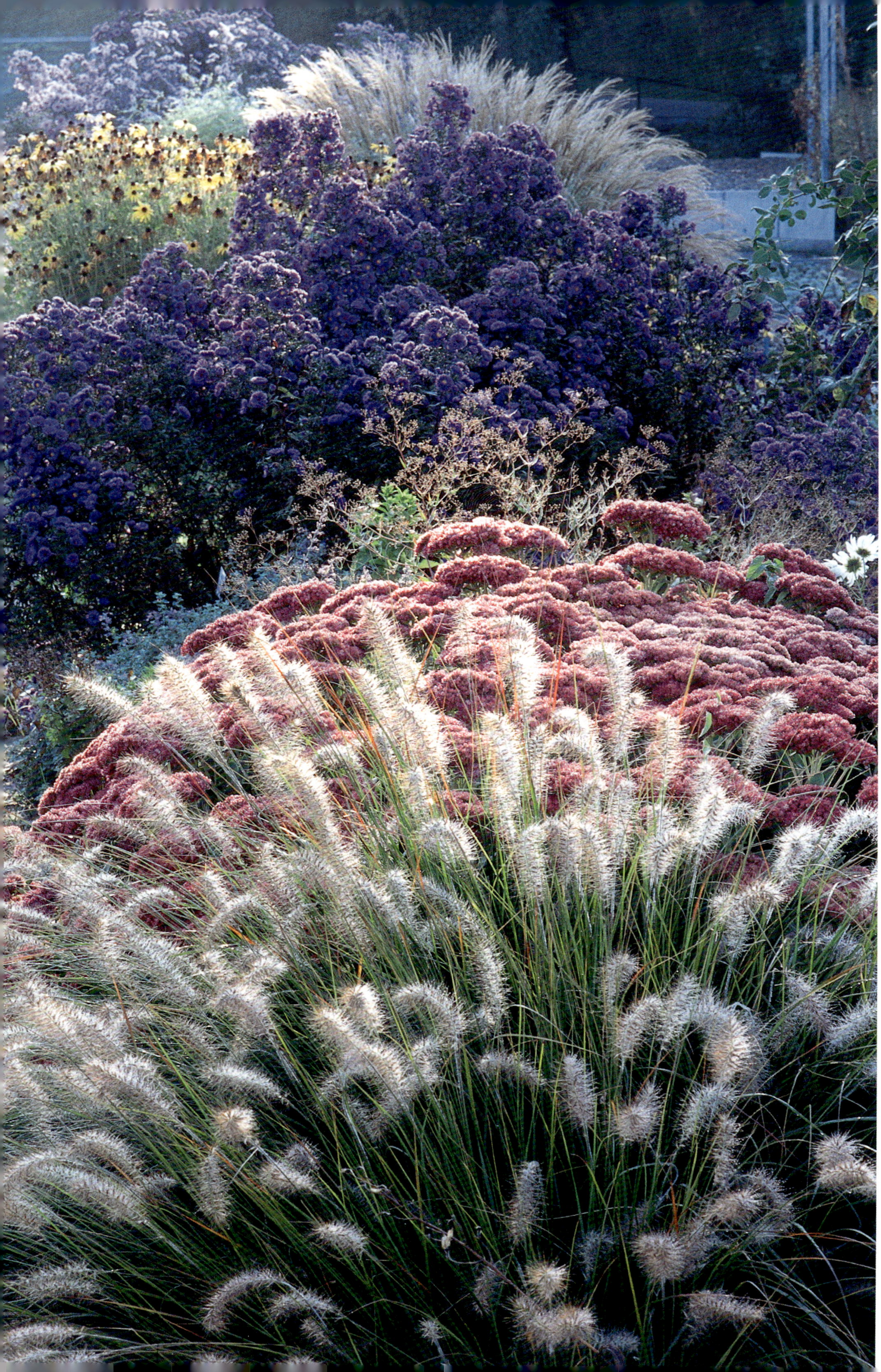

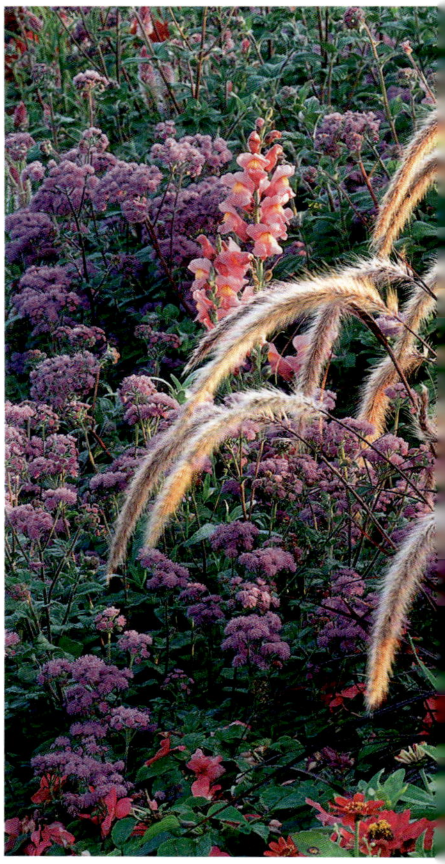

Grasses and summer flowers (above)
Red fountain grass (*Pennisetum setaceum* 'Rubrum') is not winter hardy and combines well with summer flowers such as snapdragon (*Antirrhinum majus* 'Rocket Orchid'), zinnia (*Zinnia elegans* 'Profusion Cherry'), *Ageratum houstonianum* 'Schnittwunder' and black kale (*Brassica oleracea* 'Nero Toscana').

Grasses and shrubs (left)
Various shrubs, including sedum, coneflowers *(Rudbeckia)* and asters (*Aster novi-belgii* 'Schöne von Dietlikon') pick up the fan shape of the fountain grass *(Pennisetum alopecuroides)* in the foreground.

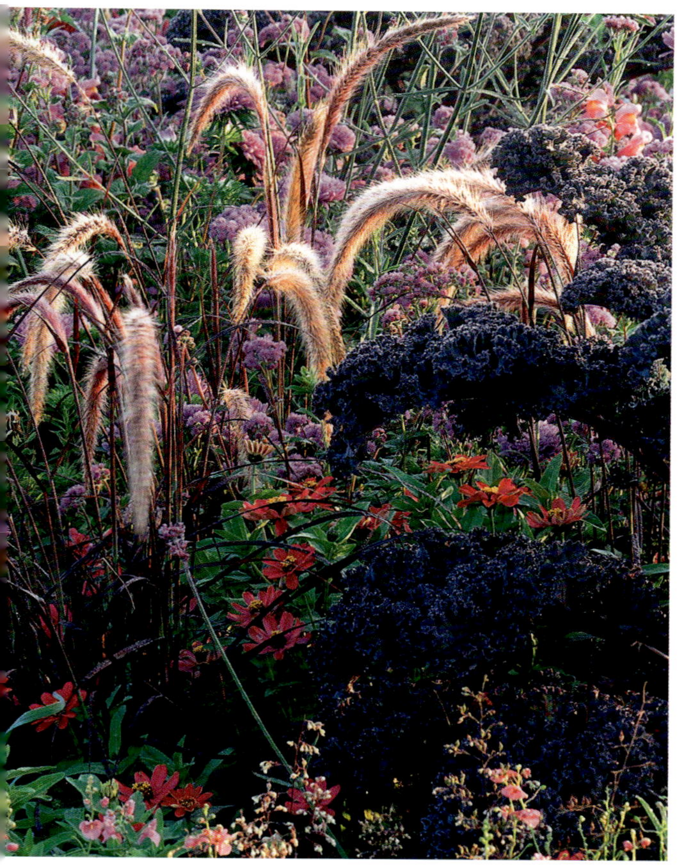

winters with heavy precipitation, but can quickly and easily be grown again from seed.

On slightly richer soil you can also combine cultivated shrubs and grasses in such a way that the planting has a steppeland quality, for example coneflower *(Rudbeckia)*, ironweed *(Vernonia crinita)* and New York Aster *(Aster novi-belgii)* with grasses such as switchgrass *(Panicum virgatum)*, which don't especially like lighter soils.

The rock steppe is a transition between steppe and rock garden, and incorporates larger flat stones and stepping stones as naturalistically as possible, integrating them in such a way that mound-forming plants can grow between them. Here vigorously growing shrubs are needed in order to harmonise visually with the steppeland planting, for example the Serbian bellflower *(Campanula poscharskyana)*, lemon thyme *(Thymus x citriodorus)* and Missouri evening primrose *(Oenothera macrocarpa)*, but also the perennial candytuft *(Iberis sempervirens)*, which has evergreen foliage. Bearded irises grow between the mound-forming plants, with their eye-catching, colourful,

Grasses and bulbs

By the time that the round-headed leek *(Allium sphaero-cephalum)* blooms, the quaking grass *(Briza media)* is already starting to seed.

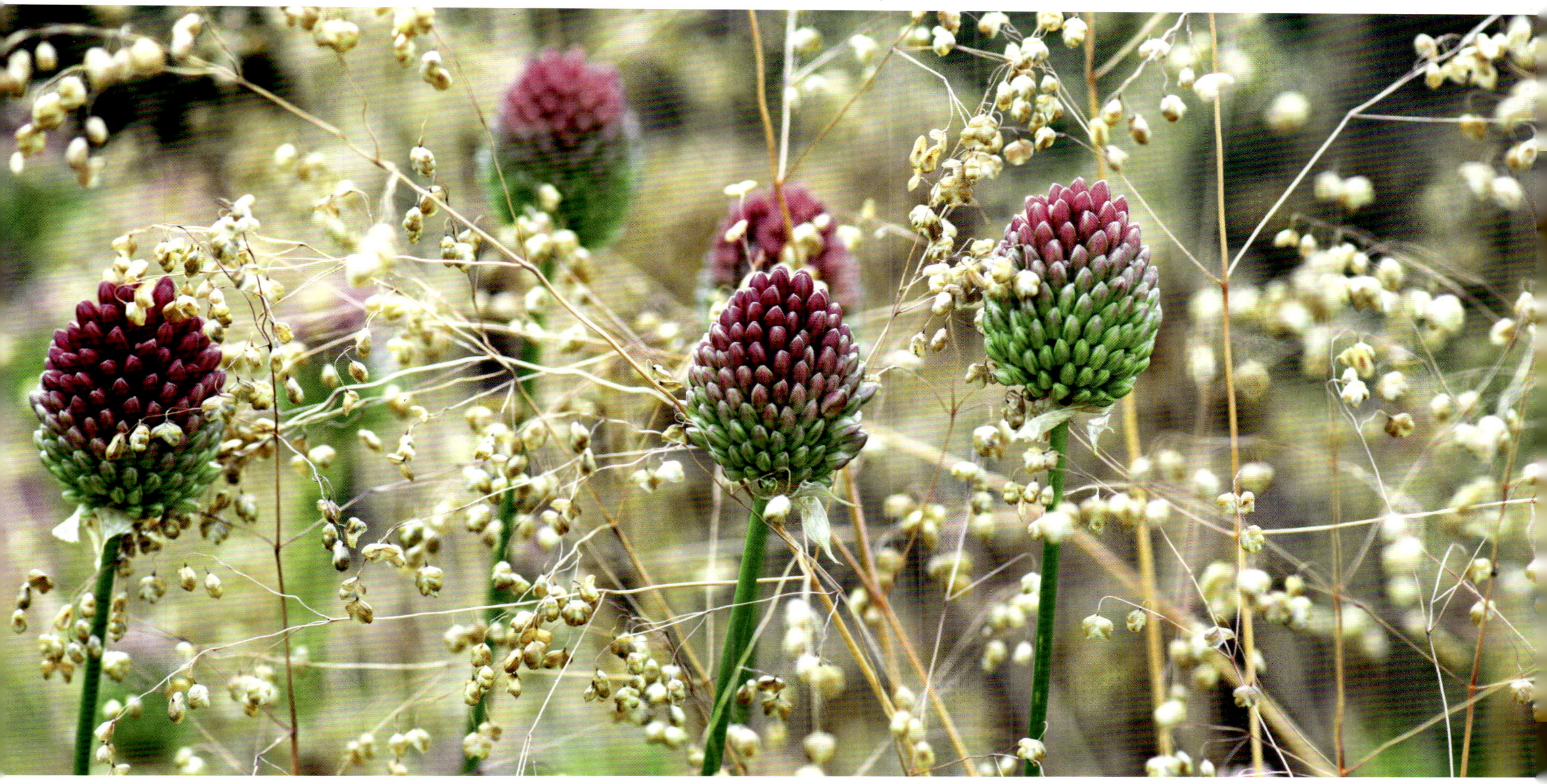

jewel-like blooms in the months of April and May. Widely distributed English lavenders *(Lavandula angustifolia)* and garden sage *(Salvia officinalis)* grow behind, complemented by the rounded hillocks of the stonecrop *(Sedum telephium)*.

Valerian *(Centranthus ruber)* may sow itself and weave its way through the bed without getting in the way of anything. And any number of bulbs can fit this scheme, from early-blooming crocuses *(Crocus sieberi)* to summer-blooming ornamental onion bulbs (*Allium sphaerocephalum* and *A.* 'Globemaster'), whose ball-shaped flower heads tower over the other plants. The dwarf *Miscanthus sinensis* 'Yakushima Dwarf', at 80cm, however, does not tower over the other planting and remains attractive well into the winter.

Grasses can also cut a fine figure in classical shrub borders. Tall grasses such as miscanthus or giant feather grass *(Stipa gigantea)* may be used at the back of the border. Pampas grass *(Cortaderia selloana)* is fairly difficult to combine and is mainly used as a stand-alone plant, although the dwarf variety 'Pumila' grows only 120cm high and cuts a good figure between shrubs.

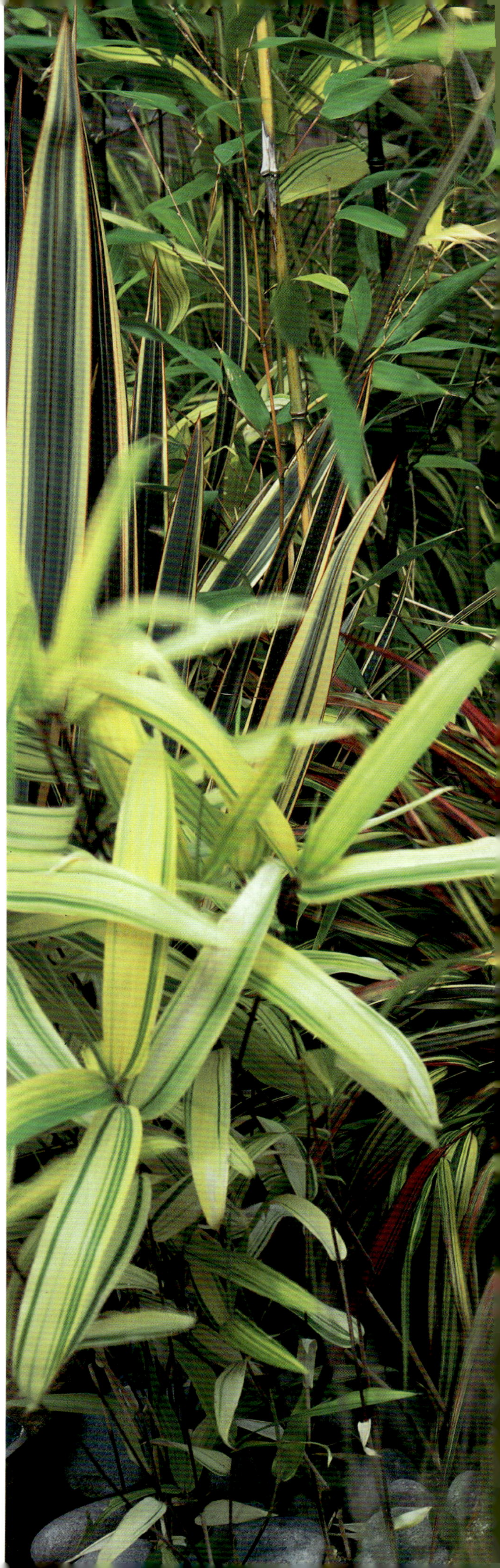

Planting at the water's edge

Japanese forest grass (*Hakonechlosa macra* 'Aureola') and dwarf bamboos.

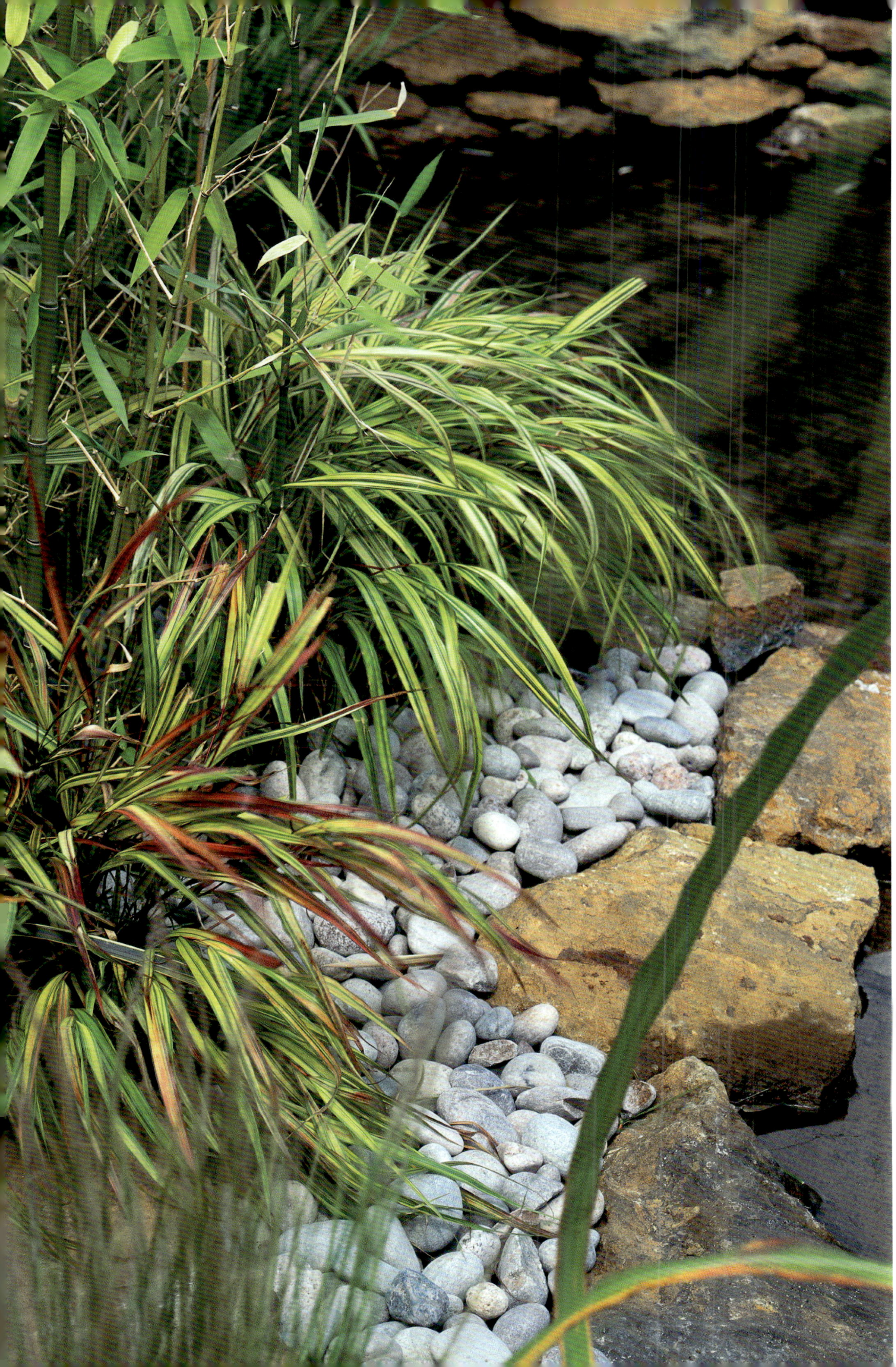

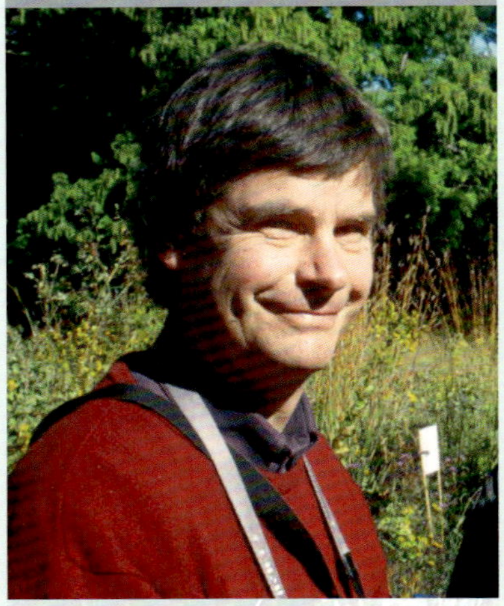

Noel Kingsbury

Noel Kingsbury champions the reintroduction of naturalism in garden design.

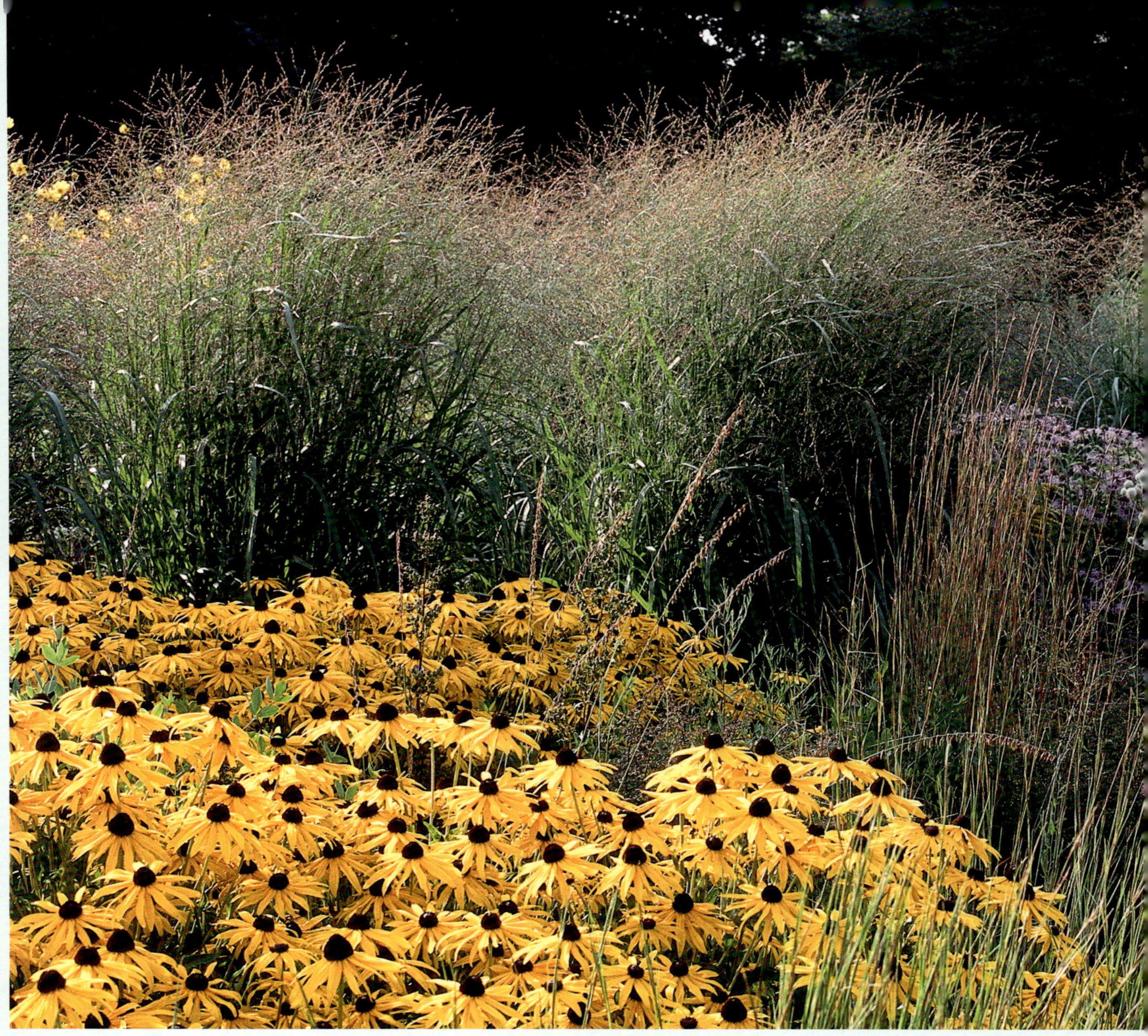

The Introduction of Naturalism to the Garden

Noel Kingsbury's continuation of the wild garden movement.

Noel Kingsbury favours a very naturalistic garden style. His interest lies in native, but garden-friendly, shrubs and grasses, which he combines with native plants. So he draws his inspiration from meadows and pastures and is impressed by how much diversity they contain, even within a single square metre. In his eyes,

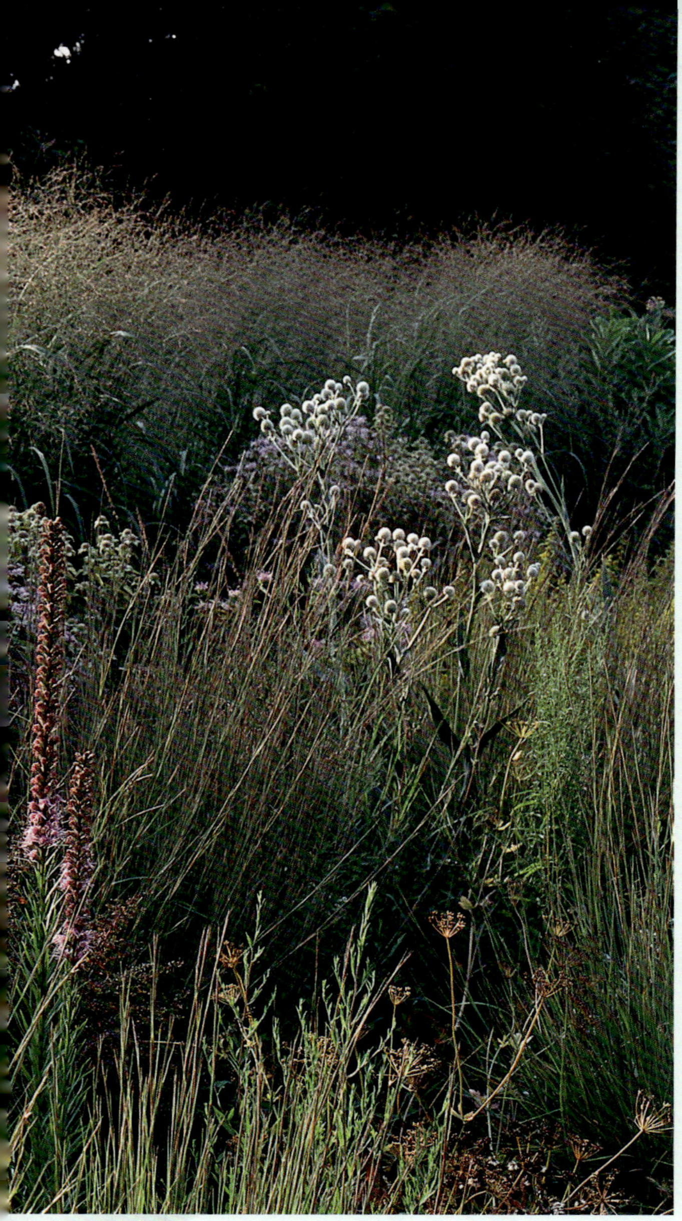

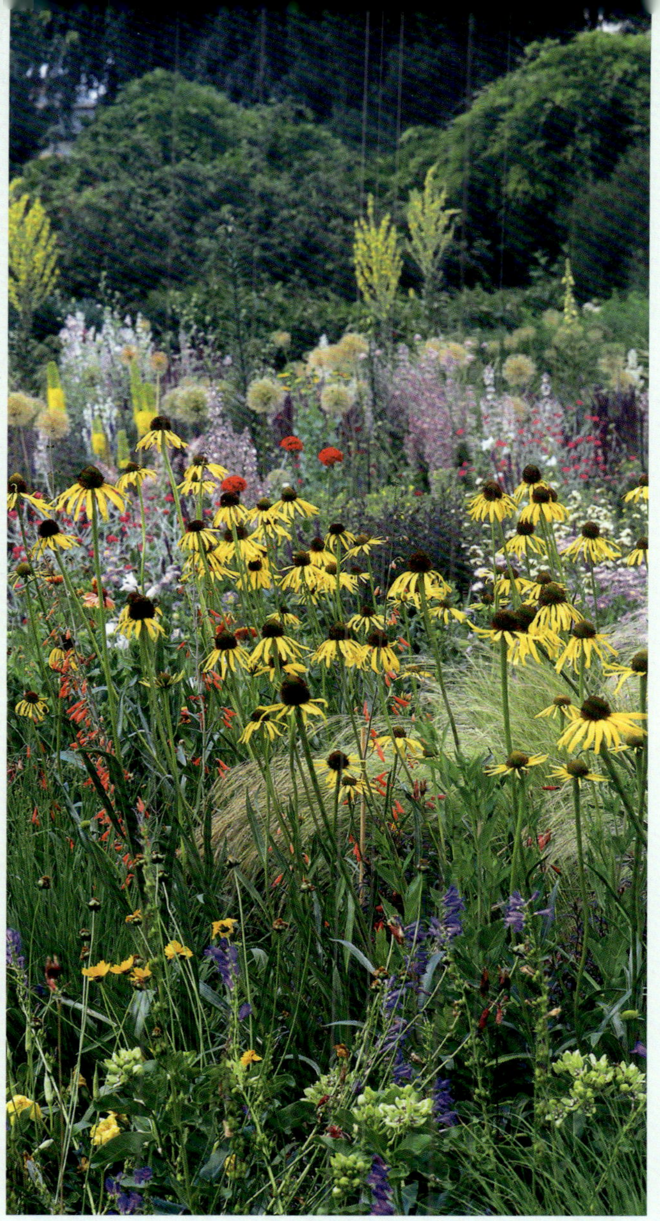

Naturalistic shrub border (far left)
Noel Kingsbury's spacious planting schemes appear very natural.

Prairie shrubs (left)
Various prairie shrubs such as coneflowers *(Rudbeckia)*, salvias, alliums and mullein *(Verbascum)* with grasses, including Mexican feather grass *(Nassella tenuissima)*.

working with these plants is a good opportunity to be close to nature and to bring a piece of that nature into the garden.

His real forebear is William Robinson, a pioneer of the wild garden movement of the nineteenth century who studied wild flower meadows and brought native flora into the spotlight.

Noel Kingsbury also looked overseas, however, and met the famous Brazilian painter and garden architect Roberto Burle Marx and made friends with James van Sweden, with whom he worked on a number of projects.

The use of plants in Germany was a revelation for him. He was influenced by the rich tradition of phytosociology practised by Richard Hansen.

He was very fascinated by places such as Munich's Westpark. And his friendship with Piet Oudolf has also left its mark on his own work: he admired his very clear, architectural designs paired with an immense passion for plants.

Noel Kingsbury currently works as a local authority consultant and holds a teaching post at the University of Sheffield. He conducts experiments in meadow-like mixed planting for public green spaces that will remain attractive all year round and require little maintenance. He is the author of numerous gardening books and writes for various gardening magazines.

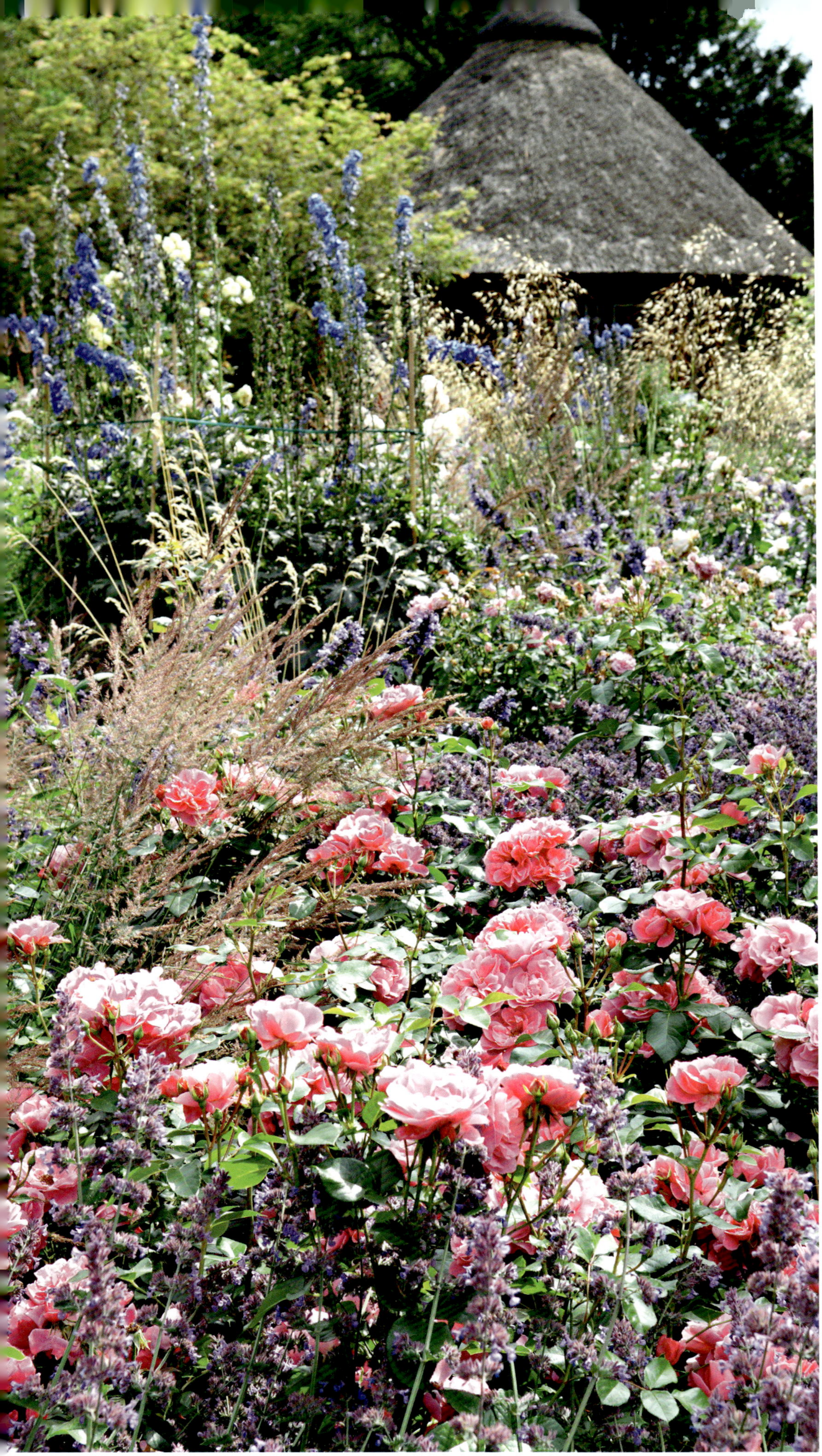

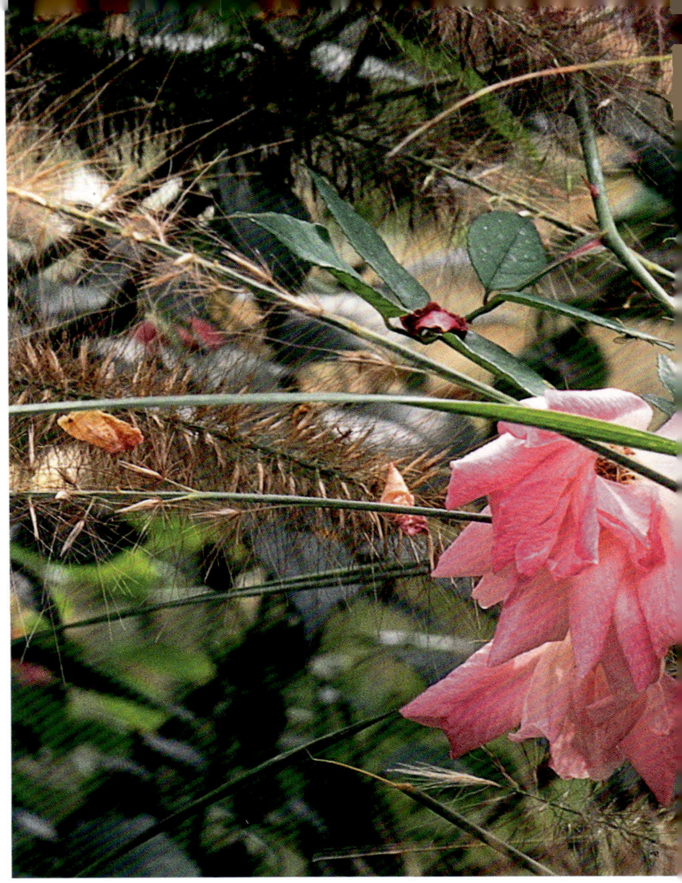

Roses were once planted in uniform groups. Today, people try to combine them with shrubs, grasses and trees. This has led to a shift in the range available. Upright hybrid teas and knee-high floribunda roses in bright colours are not so sought after now; instead, many new varieties, so-called shrub roses, have come on to the market.

We are not talking about a homogeneous group, but rather roses with very distinctive growing characteristics. Growth can be upright, overhanging or even almost low-lying. The latter in particular are used in flatter planting schemes, above all in public green spaces. The first two forms, on the other hand, lend themselves exceptionally well to combinations with shrubs and grasses. With a height of 1 to 1.2 metres, they act as a transition to classical shrub roses. But even the taller shrub roses combine well with shrubs and grasses when planted in the background.

When socialising roses in beds with other plants, one thing must be remembered: roses, even wild roses such as *Rosa spinosissima* or *R. rugosa*, need a lot of nutrients and feel most at home in heavy clay soils. The accompanying plants should have similar requirements. This rules out grasses that need dry locations and poor soil as accompaniments to roses. Besides, roses should not be crowded by neighbouring plants.

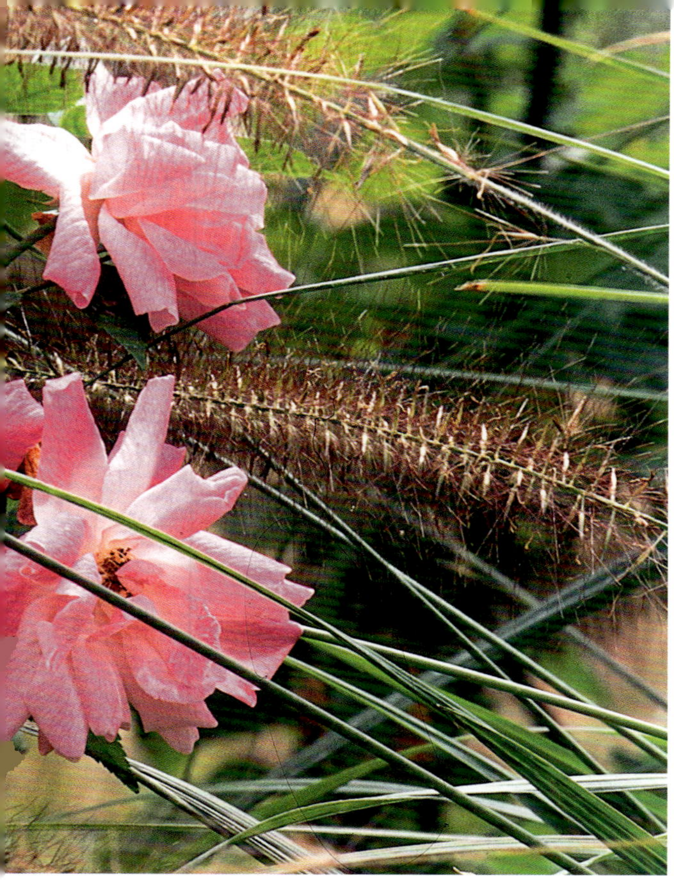

Grasses and Roses

Like much else in garden culture, the use of roses is also subject to constant change.

When planting, a sufficiently wide gap should be maintained. Grasses that spread vigorously through root runners would soon invade the rose's space and so do not make ideal partner plants.

There are many types of grass that do harmonise with roses, for example wood oats *(Chasmanthium latifolium)*, switchgrass *(Panicum virgatum)*, which turns red in autumn, or yellow Indiangrass *(Sorghastrum nutans)*. They are all characterised by moderate height and acceptable growth properties. Flower heads and autumn colouring harmonise exceptionally well with rose blooms of all colours. Korean feather reed grass *(Calamagrostis brachytricha)* has a splendidly long flowering season from June to September, grows to around 1.2-1.5 metres high and especially flatters small shrub roses with somewhat projecting growth. Purple moor grass *(Molinia arundinacea)* too lends itself to being combined with roses, even though it is strictly a heath- and moorland grass. Thanks to its broad range of habitats it copes best with well-maintained garden soils. Its flower stalks grow as high as a man, but because of their transparent appearance it is not too domineering. *Molinia caerulea* 'Edith Dudzus' also provides a lower-growing, very reliable variety and keeps its beautiful brown autumn colouring well into the winter.

TALL GRASSES IN THE BACKGROUND

If one doesn't wish to omit the giant grasses from the rose bed then they should be planted at the back with enough space around them to allow them to develop, over the course of a couple of years, into large clumps. In front of them, shrub roses of various heights, for example, can put on a show. Modern shrub roses often flower right through to November. The tall grasses correspond best with seemingly wild single and semi-double types. Suitable varieties include, for example, 'Pink Meidiland', 'Pretty Snow', the old but still unsurpassed 'Golden Wings' or the semi-double bright red 'Triade'. In addition to miscanthus varieties we have mentioned more than once, frost grass *(Spodiopogon sibiricus)* also comes into this category; its autumn colouring covers all shades of red and brown.

Grasses and old roses (above left)
Fountain grass *(Pennisetum)* and the historical rose 'Old Blush'.

Symphony in pink (opposite)
Grasses such as feather grass *(Stipa calamagrostis* and *S. gigantea)* enrich this mixed border of roses and shrubs.

Grasses and Trees

Not only among grasses, but among trees too there are many species and varieties that have magnificent autumn colouring. So it stands to reason that a skilful combination of the two groups can enhance the effect.

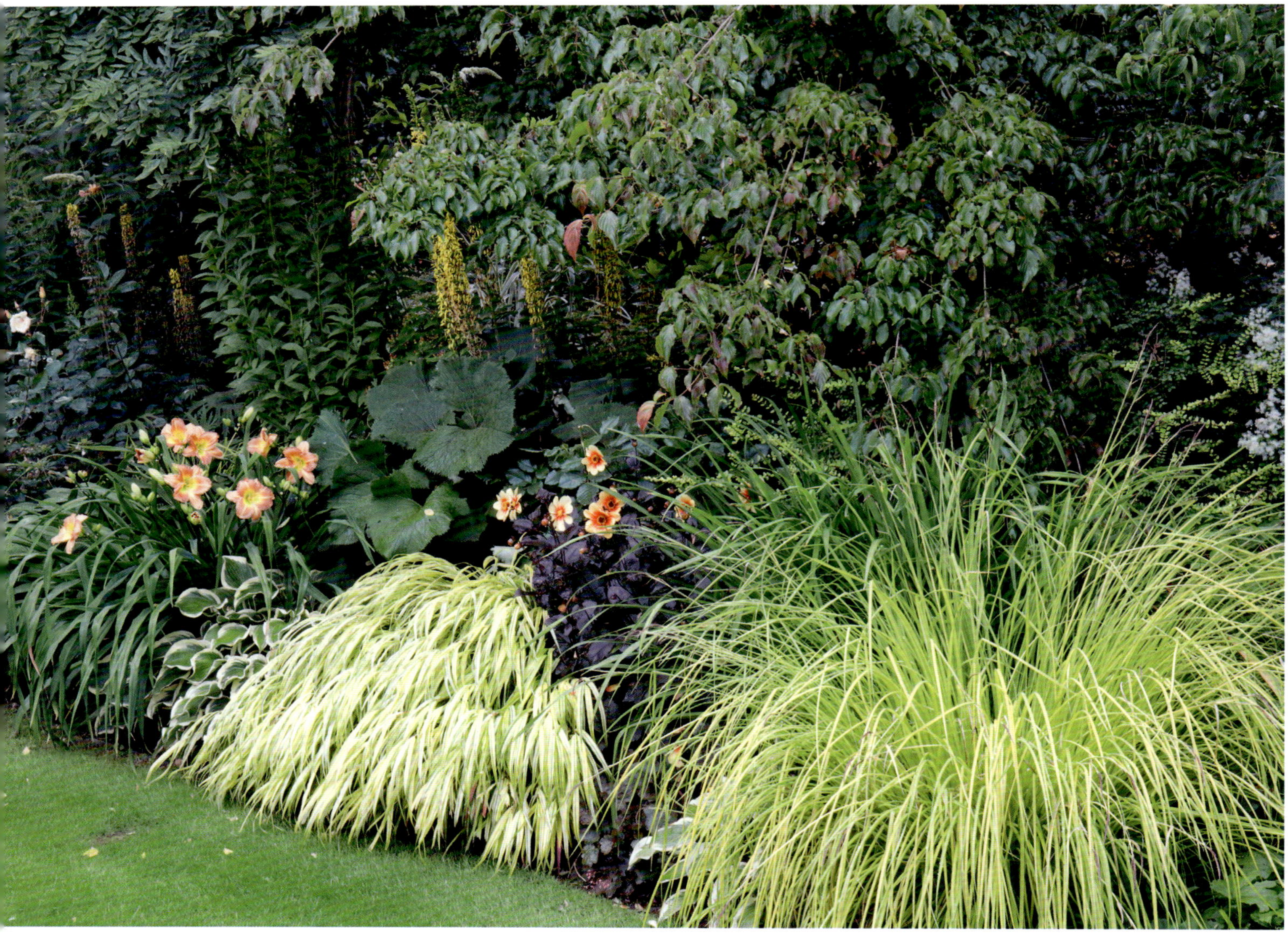

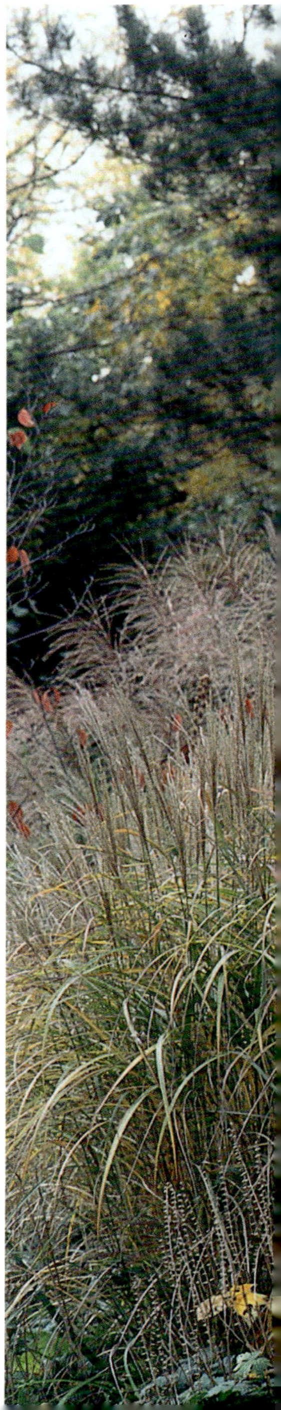

Light-green grasses in front of a dark wooded backdrop

Japanese forest grass *(Hakonechloa macra)*, gold-edged prairie cord grass (*Spartina pectinata* 'Aureomarginata') and shrubs at a woodland edge.

Autumn fireworks (right)

Low-growing miscanthus accompanies winged spindle *(Euonymus alatus)*, without crowding out the foreground.

The leaves of most types of dogwood *(cornus)* turn spectacular shades of orange and red in autumn. The varieties of *Cornus kousa* merit particular mention here. Switchgrass *(Panicum virgatum)* picks up these colours and together with small-leaved wild asters creates a wonderful planting scheme.

Many grasses, including for example rushes *(Luzula)*, many sedges *(Carex)* and also Japanese forest grass *(Hakonechloa macra)* thrive best in half shade and light shade, so are tailor-made for under-planting around trees. Especially among the sedges there are numerous varieties with variegated or yellow foliage. They effectively brighten up dark areas of the border or the garden and extend lines of sight. *Hakonechloa macra* 'Aureola' or the stripey form 'Albostriata' are suitable; the latter is the more vigorous grower. If you are seeking an effective grass for spring one need look no further than Bowles' golden grass (*Milium effesum* 'Aureum'), which has a golden yellow colour early in the air, which turns to a pleasing light green over the course of the summer.

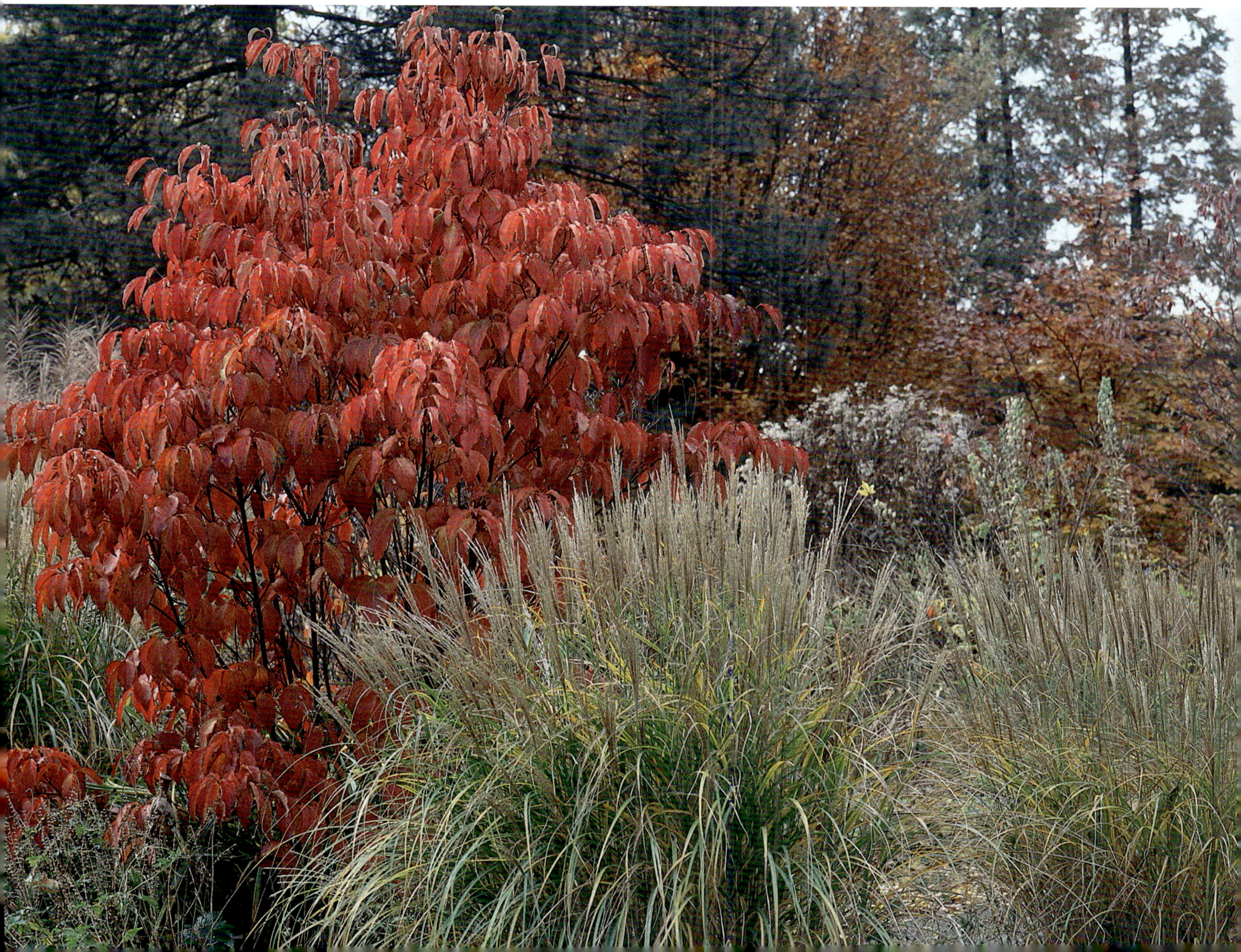

Grass drifts

Tall yew hedges frame this planting scheme and provide a visual limit. In between shrubs and grasses are planted in wide drifts.

When low-maintenance plant combinations are sought for public areas and private gardens, prairie gardens and steppeland planting are the first-choice design forms. Moreover, a new trend has become established whereby plants are whenever possible used in a way that matches the way they grow in the wild: in other words, not formally layered and arranged, but gathered together in strong groupings and flowing in and out of one another. The high grass steppe includes shrubs and grasses that prefer a nutrient-rich, fresh soil.

Contrary to popular opinion, the prairie and the steppe are not interchangeable, although most plants survive occasional dry spells quite well. Typical shrubs for this habitat include coneflower *(Rudbeckia)*, sneezeweed *(Helenium)* and *Echinacea*,

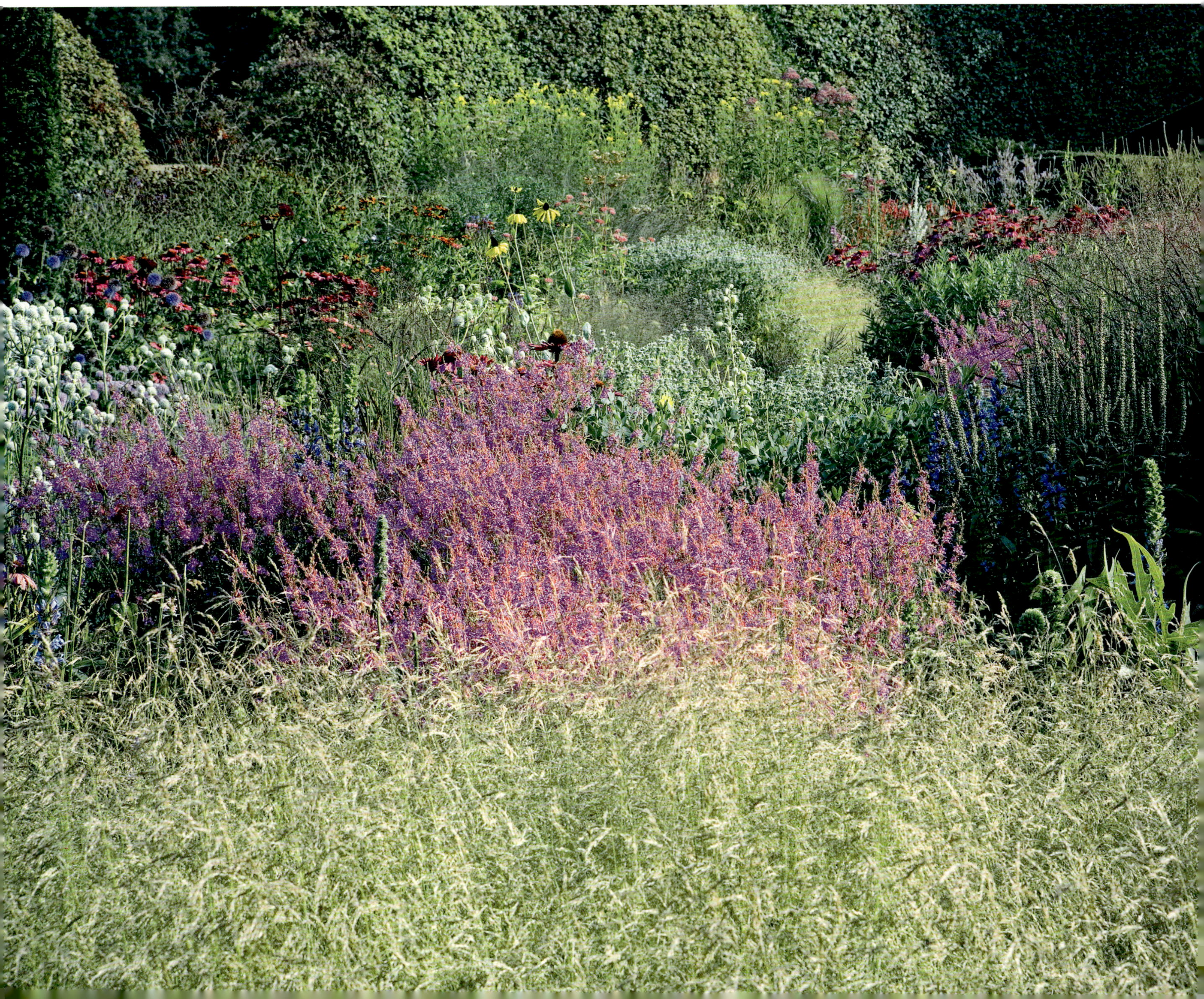

and among the grasses, big blue stem *(Andropogon gerardii)*, Indiangrass *(Sorghastrum nutans)* and blue stem *(Schizachyrium scoparium)*.

The short grass prairie is drier and poorer in nutrients. It is home to, for example, blue grama grass *(Bouteloua gracilis)* and prairie dropseed *(Sporobolus heterolepis)*. Elk grass *(Xerophyllum tenax)* is called a grass but is in fact a shrub with flower heads resembling those of the grass lily and thin, grass-like foliage. In the typical garden, fortunately, there is no compulsion to stick slavishly to geographical-botanical classifications; you can, for example, combine according to your taste European and Asian shrubs with North American grasses, so long as their requirements and characteristics are in harmony.

Prairie planting
Typical of prairie planting are numerous different flowers such as coneflower *(Rudbeckia)* and *Helenium*. But this border needs grasses to make it a proper prairie plantation.

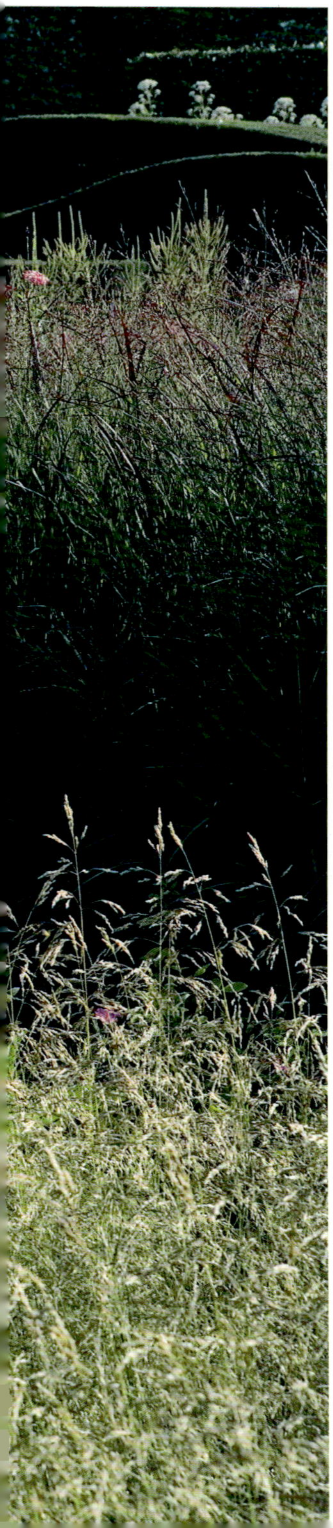

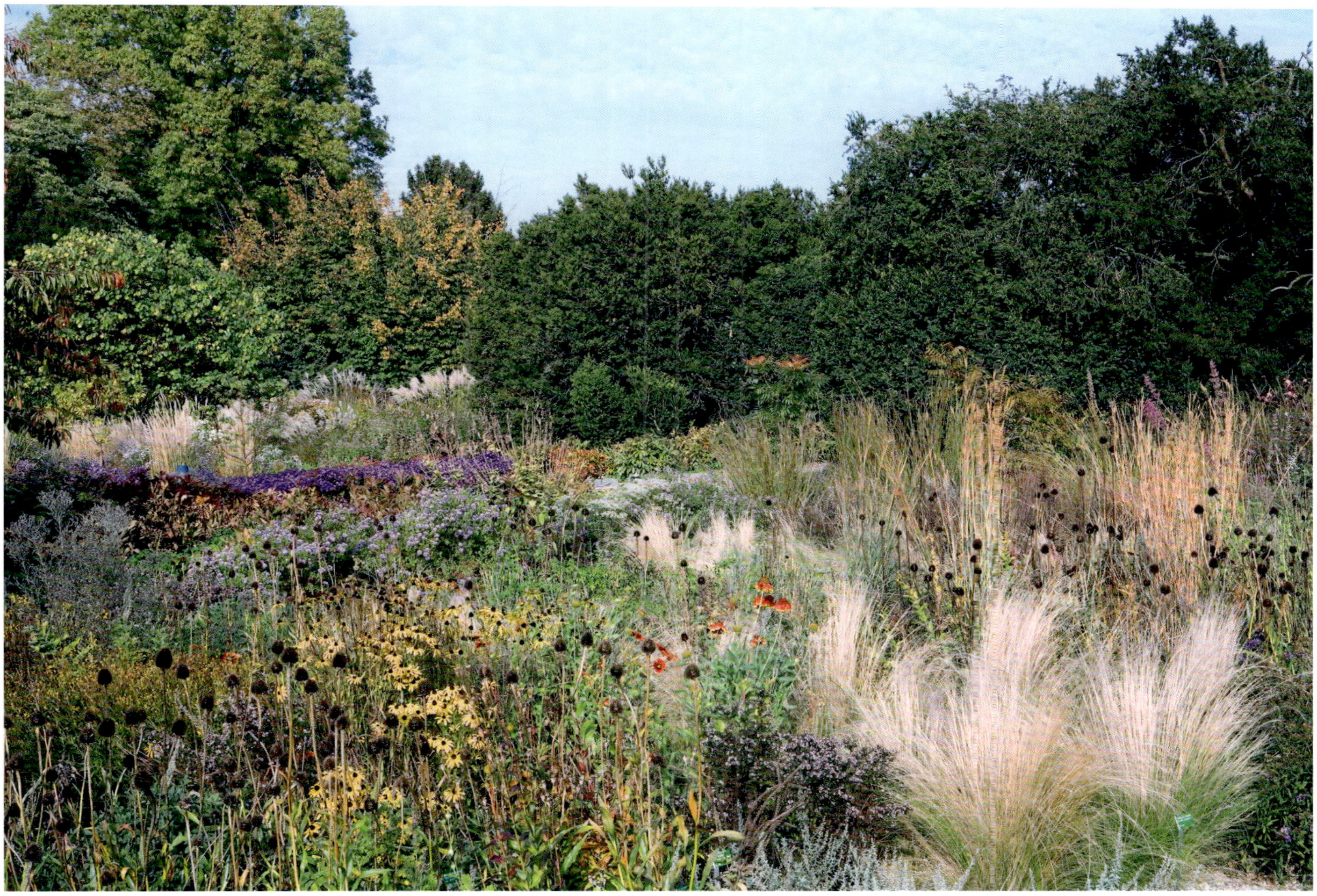

Prairie Gardens

Many plants from the North American prairies have been part of garden design for a long time, but people are largely unaware of their origin.

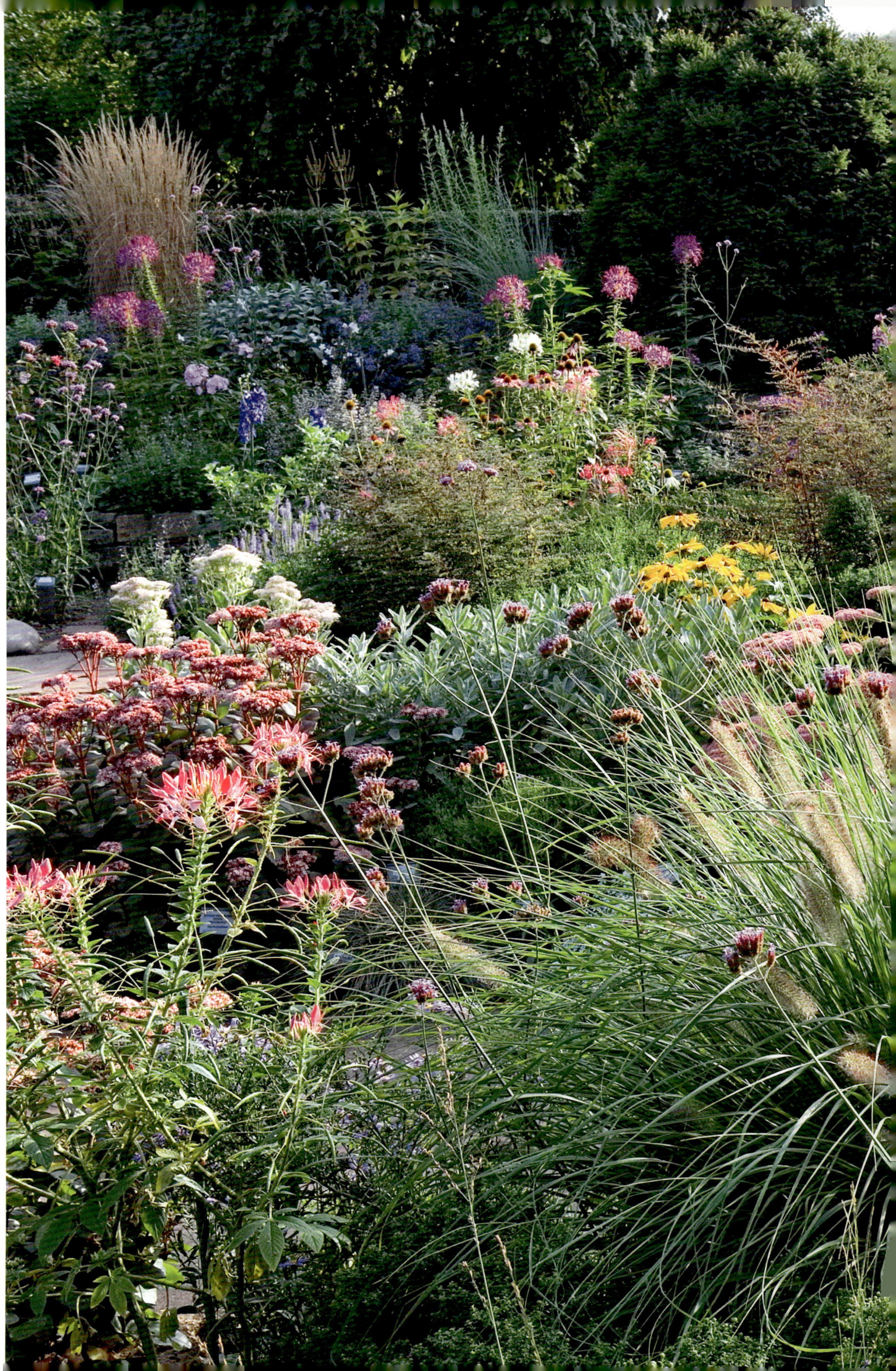

Structural grasses
Grasses create the basic framework of this planting scheme. Summer blooms and short-lived shrubs spread out in between.

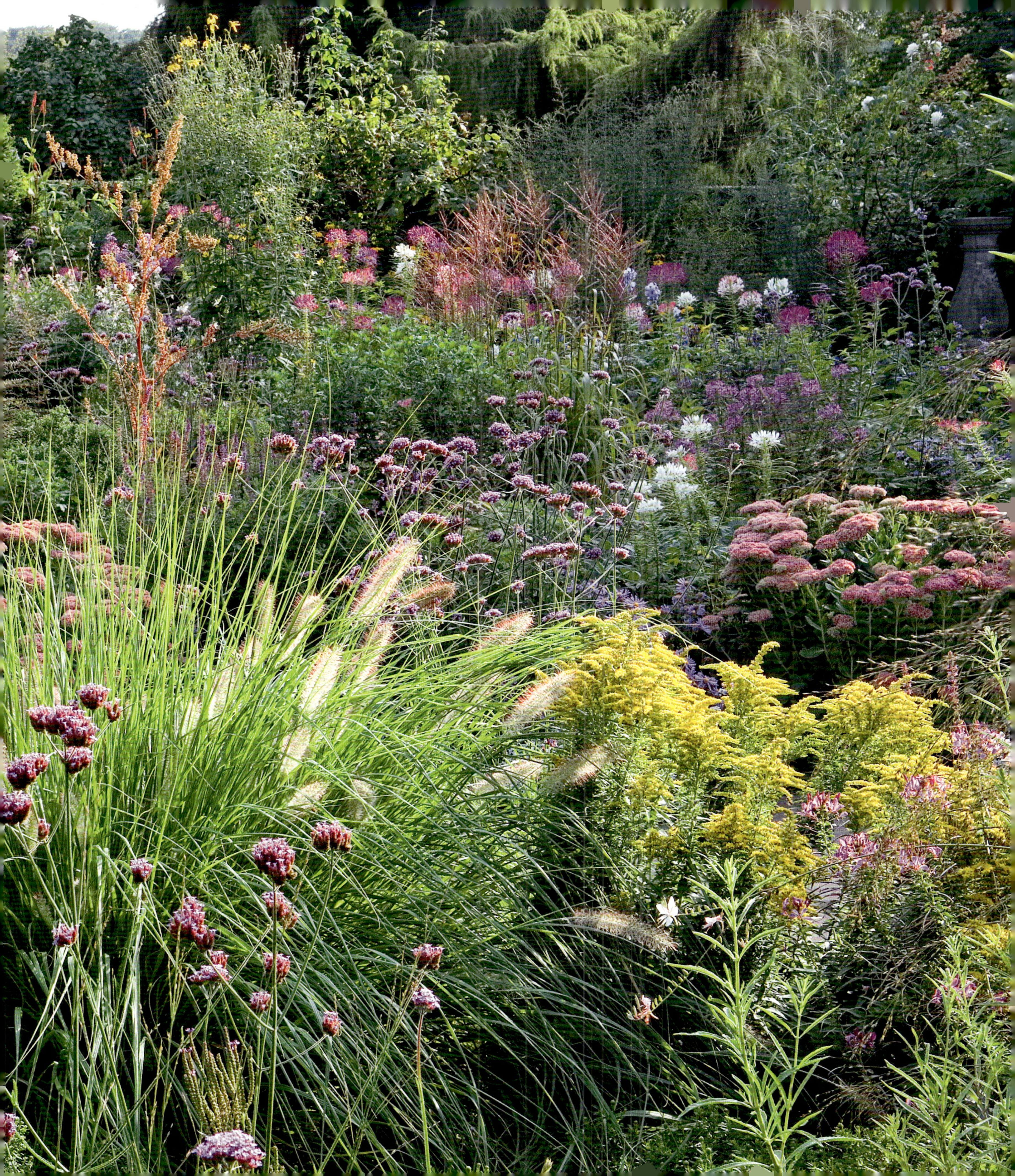

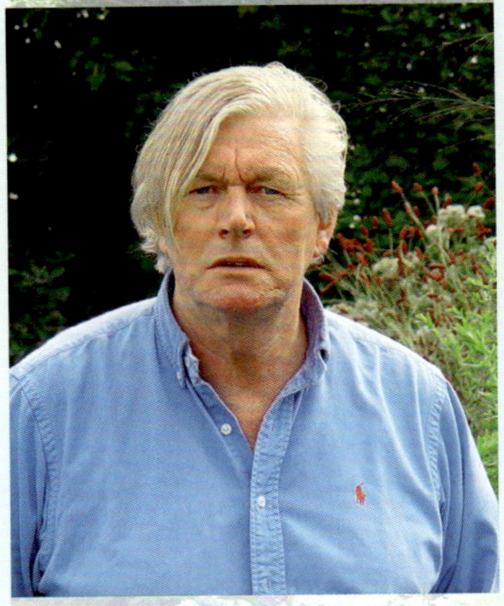

Piet Oudolf

Piet Oudolf is renowned for his combinations of ornamental grasses and sculptural shrubs.

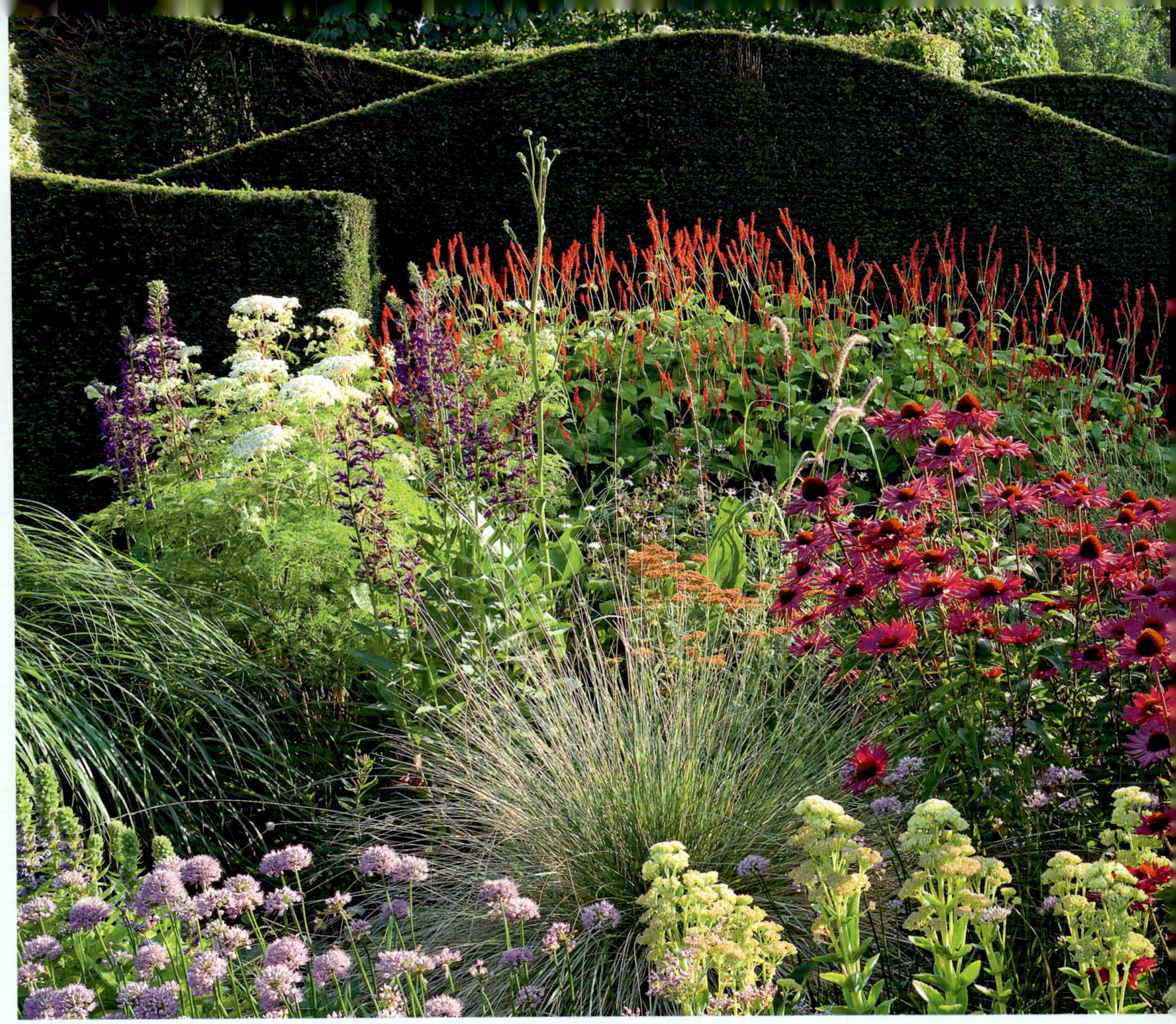

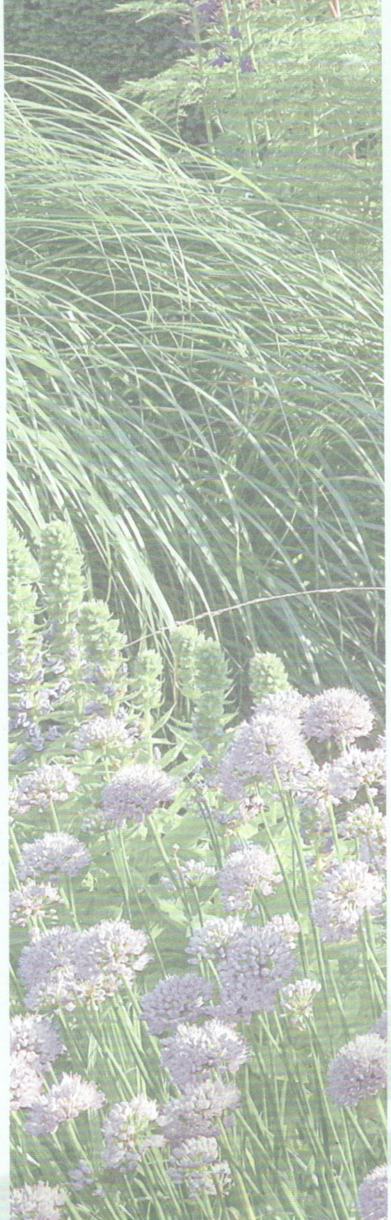

Prairie Planting and Grass Meadows

Piet Oudolf – the creator of enchanting combinations of topiary shrubs and grass planting schemes.

Piet Oudolf is one of the most successful and innovative garden designers of our time. He is especially known for using filigree plants such as ornamental grasses with sculptural shrubs in meadow-like combinations. In the parks and gardens he has designed, plants interweave with each other and plant groupings are repeated to create an enchanting roughly or densely textured

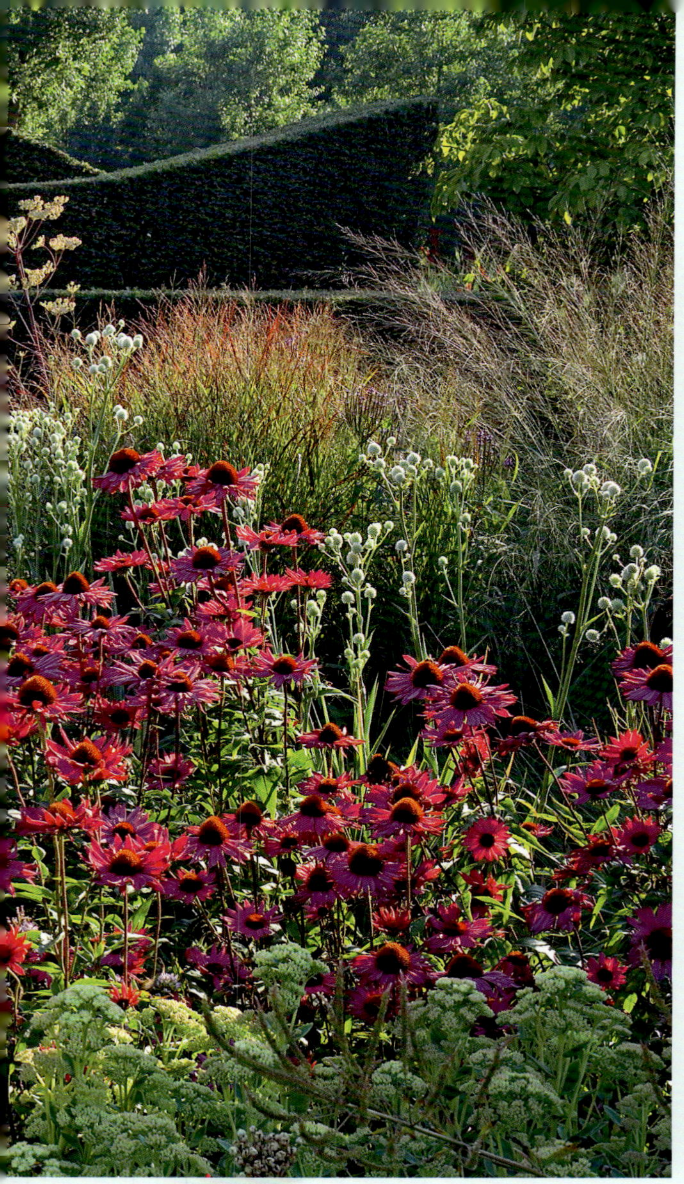

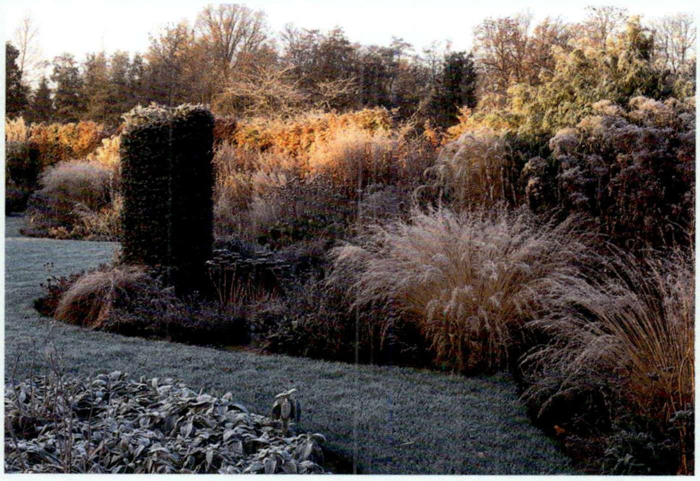

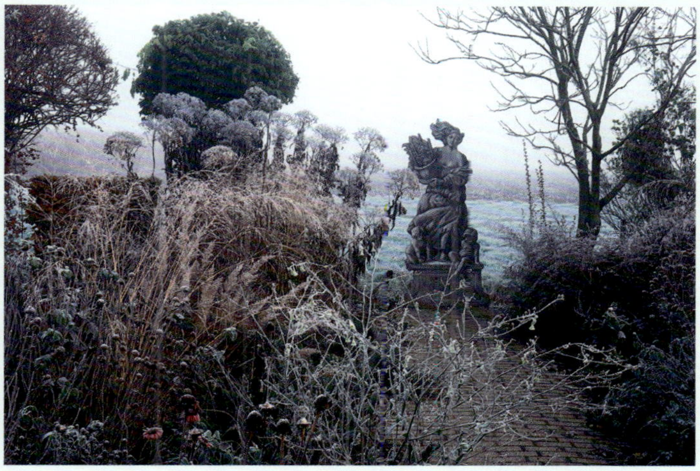

Curved lines (above left)
In the show gardens at Hummelo there are many pure grass borders. In autumn and winter they form a spectacular sight.

Grasses and sculptures (below left)
Combinations of tall umbellifers and giant grasses are a trademark of Oudolf's garden designs.

Hedges and prairie shrubs
A typical Oudolf design with yew topiary. Various grasses are complemented by spacious shrub planting.

pattern. Piet Oudolf prioritises shrubs with a natural, wild character in his plant compositions.

In his nursery in Hummelo, which he runs together with his wife Anja, he propogates and breeds mainly shrubs and grasses, which he then uses in his planting schemes. He has created many new varieties. In his show gardens, shaped hedges of box and yew create an enticing contrast with his artistic planting compositions. He sets great store by schemes that look attractive in all seasons, including winter. He enjoys the whole cycle from first shoots to die-back, the cycle of birth and death.

He is greatly in favour of exploiting the potential of dead growth in winter, when frost and snow can add magic to garden plants. His schemes emphasise the play of light and movement. In selecting plants he concentrates on their shapes, rather than the colours of their flowers, dividing them into various groupings, such as umbels, spikes, panicles or small heads. He also selects plants on the basis of characteristics such as durability, robustness and length of flowering.

He doesn't copy nature so much as try to impart a feeling of nature; you could say that he transforms nature artistically.

Piet Oudolf currently works internationally and has designed public and private gardens in places as far afield as Holland, Sweden, Great Britain and the USA.

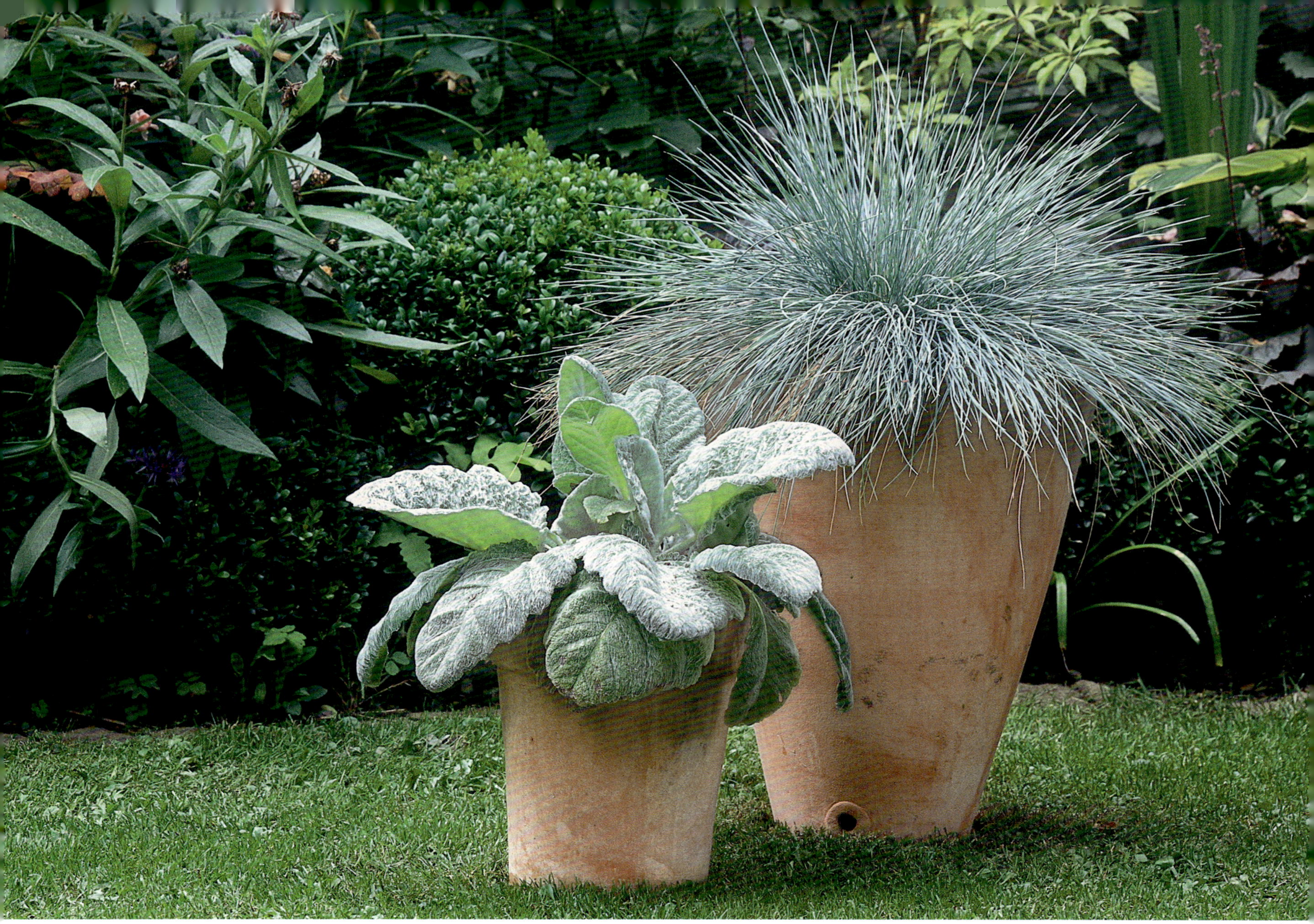

Grasses as Container Plants

Plants can be tended in pots for any number of reasons. On a terrace or balcony, summer flowers, shrubs, trees – and grasses – can all be grown in this way.

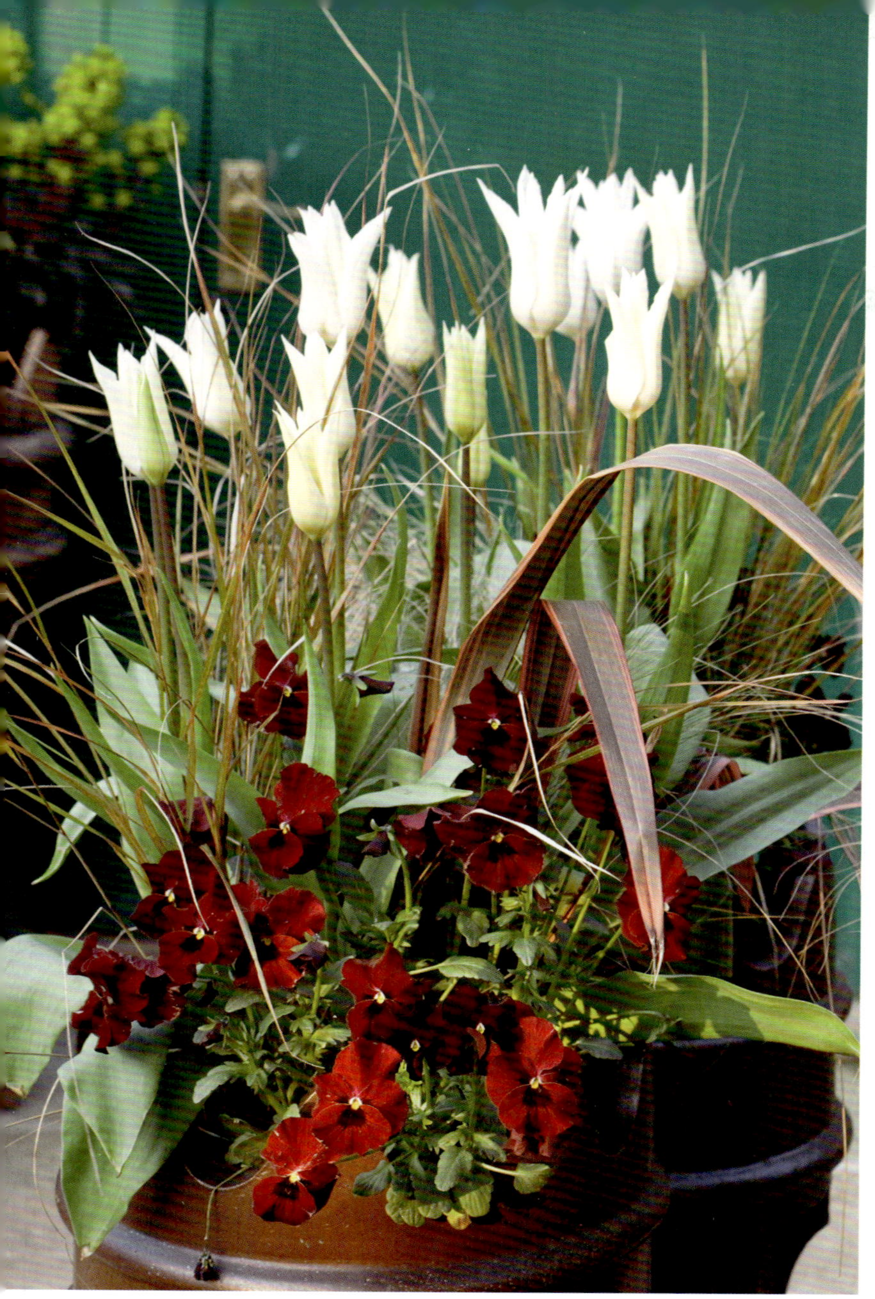

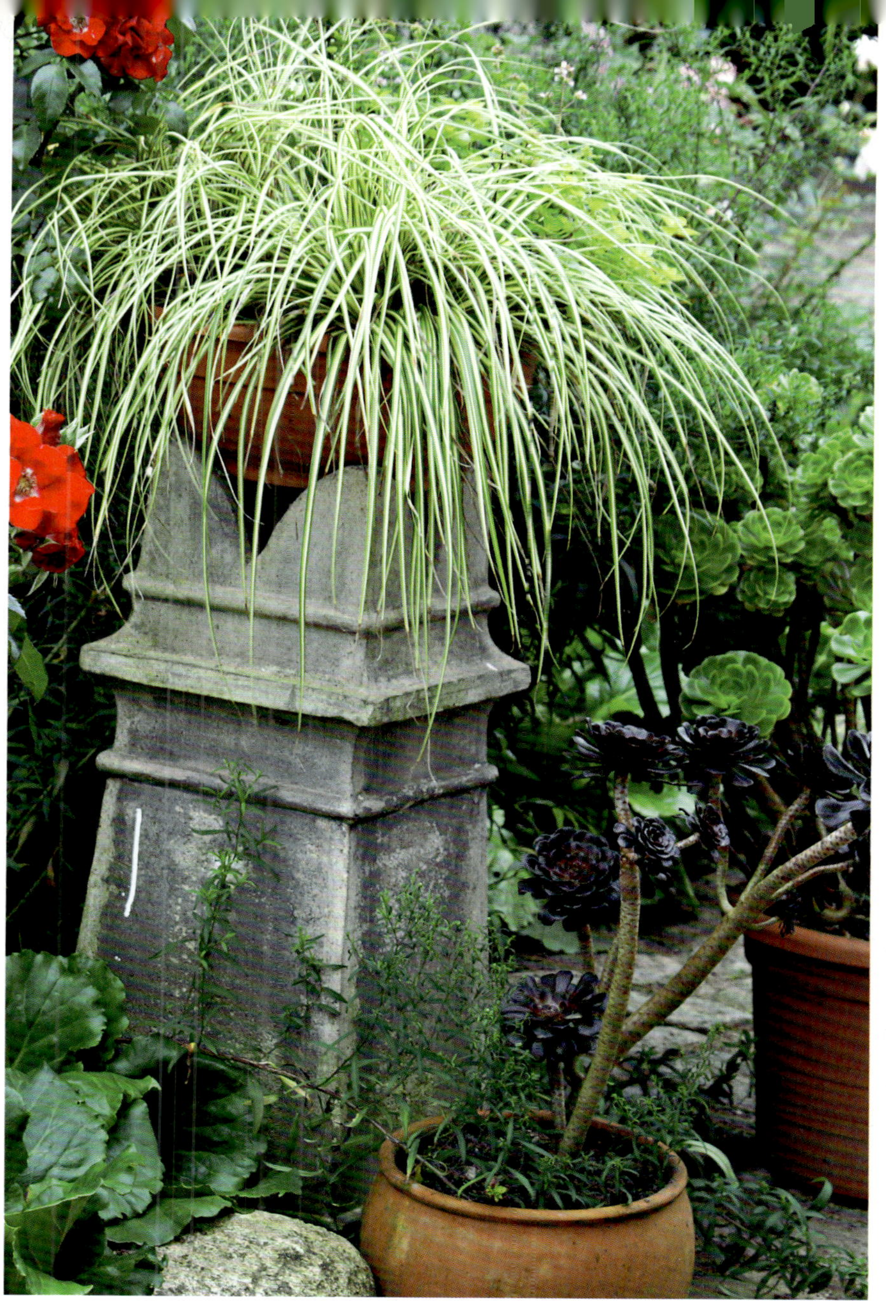

Particularly attractive grasses can be planted on their own in decorative containers to create accents and draw the eye. Also, certain plants can be so delicate that they need to be specially monitored, or their requirements are hard to meet when they are planted in a border, when the ground is too wet, too dry or too chalky.

In the garden, accents can be created using plants and of course grasses too. Overhanging grasses, such as many species of *Carex*, are set off much better when their shock of leaves can dangle over the side of a container. They work best when raised to eye level, for example on a pedestal, so that the fine tracery of their leaves or other ornamental details can be observed at close hand. Many people think that grasses can look very attractive in pots. Some types of Mexican feather grass *(Nassella tenuissima)* planted together in a long trug, for example, can look good on top of a wall on the terrace or can provide a filigree supplement to mixed container plantings.

Elegant silver-grey (left)
The contrast between the fine blue fescue *(Festuca cinerea)* and the felt-like leaves of the mullein *(verbascum)* lend these plant pots a special elegance.

Spring combination (centre)
White lily-tulips with wine-red pansies and fresh grass blades.

On a pedestal (right)
Japanese sedge (*Carex oshimensis* 'Evergold) presents its overhanging striped foliage at eye level.

Behind man-sized stems of miscanthus and the like you can sunbathe in peace; and even though the foliage and stems are cut back at the start of the year, the screening effect lasts all through the winter. Then everything grows back by the summer. As well as the tall miscanthus varieties, other species lend themselves for use as sightscreens. The giant reed *(Arundo donax)* grows up to 4 metres tall and spreads slowly and in a non-invasive way through short rhizomes. This grass has to be pruned in spring, so it is not until early summer that it grows high enough to block prying eyes. It is worth noting that the giant reed is not terribly winter hardy and its use is best restricted to milder climates.

Bamboos are exceptionally good for use as screens. All types are evergreen and are attractive the year round. Above all, species and varieties that are clump-forming can be cultivated in pots, as long as these are large enough and the plants get enough water and nutrients, especially in winter. If the screen is along a property boundary, it will need to include a rhizome block at the boundary line, except for bamboos of the genus *Fargesia*. Almost all the other species spread in an unrestricted manner through rhizomes, which is undesirable, and not only on your neighbour's property: you should also restrict spread on your own property by means of a rhizome block. Within the blocked area, the bamboos will soon grow into a thick forest of stems. Medium-height bamboos are most suitable as screens, for example *Fargesia murielae* 'Jumbo' and 'Dragon', *Fargesia* 'Jiuzhigou', *Phyllostachys humilis* and also

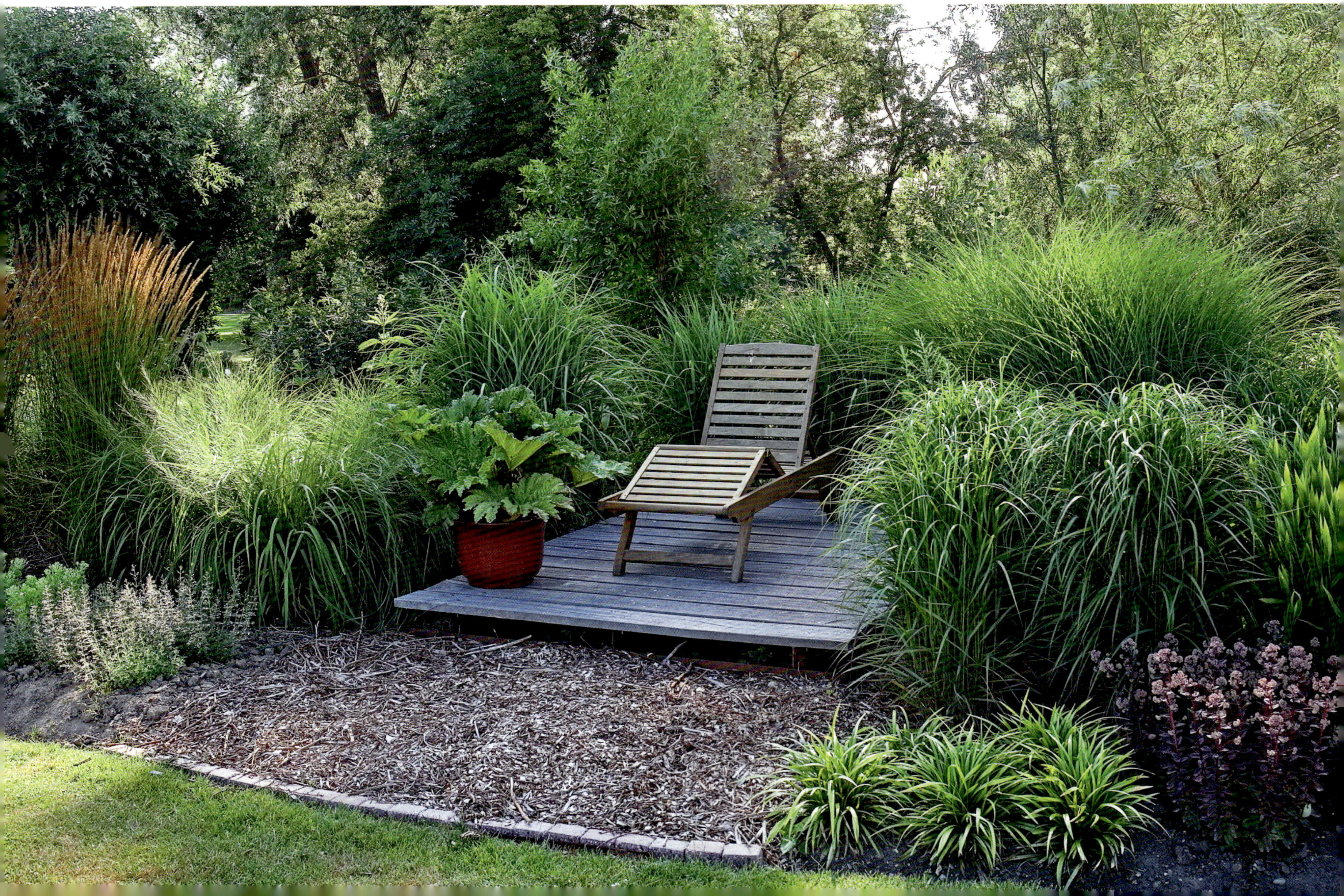

A feeling of wellbeing in the garden
Thanks to a surround of tall grasses you can relax on a reclining chair hidden from prying eyes.

Pseudosasa japonica. Only fargesias don't need a rhizome block, as they are clump forming. Nevertheless, mature plants will require several square metres of space! All the above varieties do not grow taller than 3-4 metres in Europe.

However, any types that proliferate through rhizomes can be sustainably cultivated in large containers. They may end up weaker, but their exuberant proliferation is kept in check. Growing bamboos in containers also has the advantage that they can be moved to wherever a screen is needed. When choosing a container, bear in mind the strong growth of the rhizome spikes – the pot must be made of sturdy material.

Bamboos can also be used to make screen walls. For this purpose you will need a frame of thick, sturdy stems, while thin, pliable stems can be used for the infilling. Depending on your skill, you can choose a simpler or more complicated weave pattern – the imagination has no limits. The weaving techniques used for willows work just as well for bamboos.

A Pergola with Asiatic charm
A bamboo hedge is just as thick as the classical *Thuja* hedge, and just as evergreen, but is much fresher and more attractive.

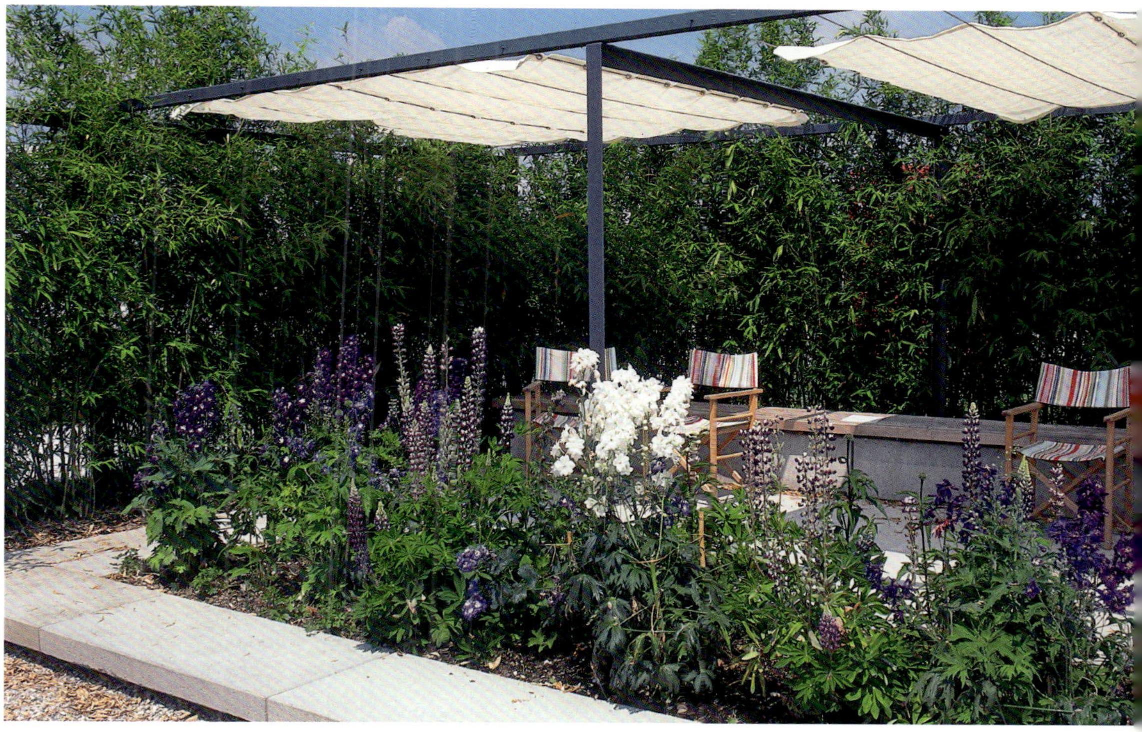

Grasses as Screens

Grasses grow quickly and their rustling stems make perfect screens.

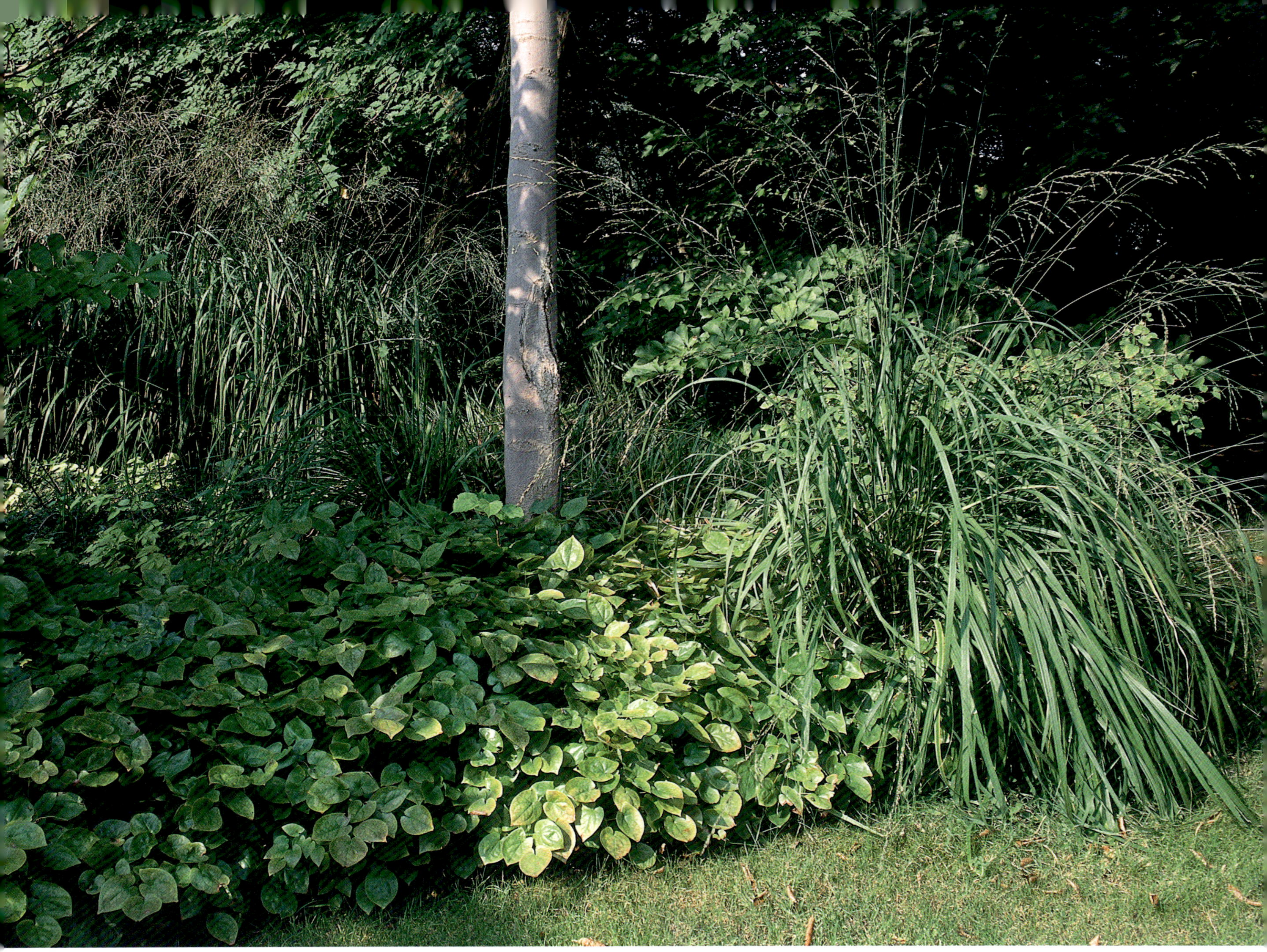

The Woodland Garden

At the edge of woods, beneath trees and bushes and in shady areas of the garden near buildings, grasses come into their own.

In woods, hence under tall trees, the soil is mostly fresh humus, the humidity is higher than in open spaces and the temperature is more consistent and usually on the cool side. There are rarely large fluctuations between day and night. In deciduous forests, the ground receives a significant amount of light only in the winter months, when the trees have lost their leaves. The rest of the time, the location is in light to full shade. For many shrubs, ferns and grasses these are perfect living conditions. In the garden, too, there can often be shady spots, mainly under single mature trees or next to high buildings.

The woodland edge, on the other hand, is mostly half shade, that is, for at least several hours a day the location receives direct sunlight. Many grasses of the open plain can handle temporary shade, and equally typical shade-loving grasses can easily tolerate occasional direct sunlight.

SHADE

Anyone looking for attractive and low-maintenance grasses for shady areas in the garden should always consider the sedges *(Carex)*. There are a number of variegated forms, mostly striped white or yellow. They are a good way to inject colour into the undergrowth. Sedges can be grouped together between ground-cover plants and shrubs, but can also be planted en masse as ground cover themselves. Several species are evergreen and, therefore, especially valuable. Several varieties can also cope with damp locations, for example the Gray's sedge *(Carex grayi)*. The range of its habitat extends as far as the shallows of lakes and streams. The blooms work well as cut flowers in arrangements.

Among the 'striped' grasses the following are particularly worthy of note: *Carex conica* 'Snowline', which throws out short runners and thus is non-invasive; Japanese sedge (*Carex morrowii* 'Aureomarginata' und 'Gilt'), both with very conspicuous edging; bird's foot sedge (*Carex ornithopoda* 'Variegata') and the yellow- and white-striped *Carex oshimensis* 'Evergold'. *Carex* 'Silver Sceptre' is a hybrid; with its abundant runners it can, over time, form thick ground cover.

Even among that other major group of shade-loving grasses, wood-rush *(Luzula)*, you can find variegated or yellow-leafed varieties, which conjure up an effect of brightness and dappled light on the woodland floor. Foerster's evergreen great wood-rush *(Luzula sylvatica)* variety 'Marginata' is still a stock plant. 'Aurea' is distinguished by its broad yellow leaf fringes. 'Tauernpass', on the other hand, is a product of chance, and is characterised by its light-green foliage and strong growth. These grasses are best grouped with low-growing shade-loving shrubs. The foamflower *(Tiarella cordifolia)* spreads quickly to carpet small areas. Its white flowers are like candles, and in addition the foliage of this 20cm-high plant displays brown markings. It is ideal for the foreground and can also be used as ground

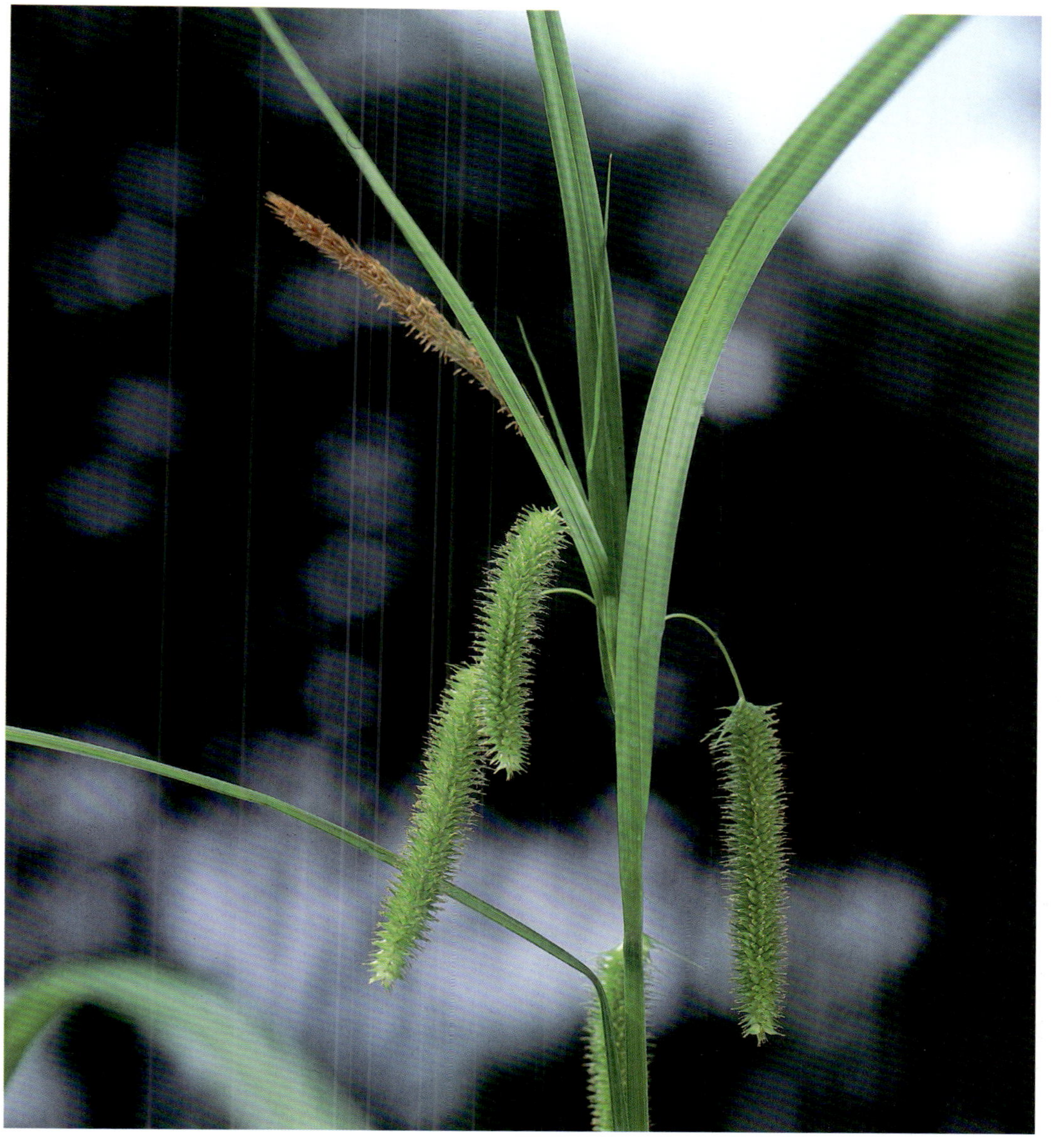

Cyperus sedge (above)
Carex pseudocyperus has elegant nodding flower and seed heads.

Woodland edge planting (opposite)
Tall moor grass *(Molinia arundinacea)* feels at home at the edge of woods.

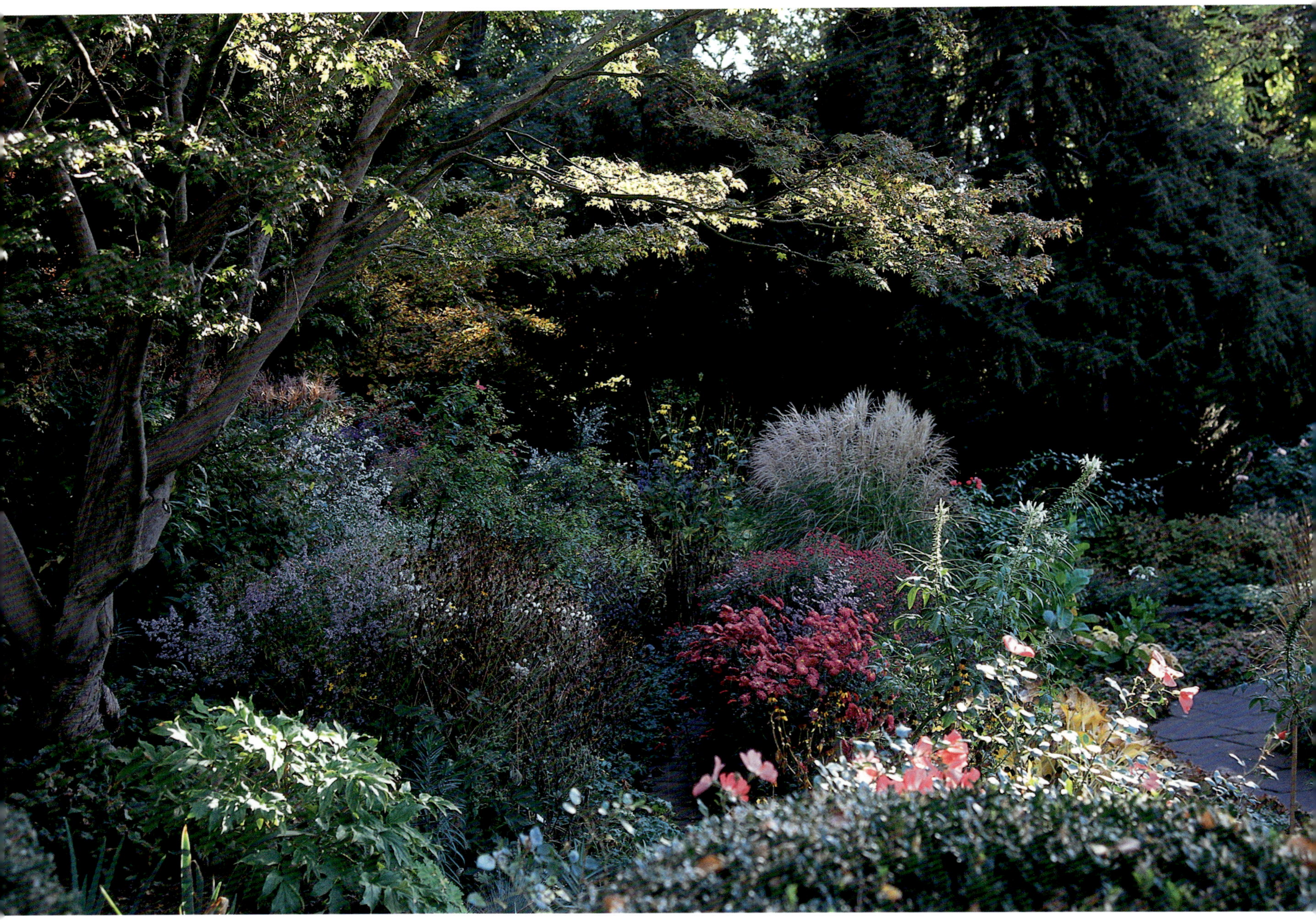

Light shade at the edge of a wood
Even mixed with classical woodland edge shrubs, *Miscanthus sinensis* cuts a fine figure.

cover. Further, the various types of alumroot (*Heuchera* and *Heucherella*) as well as the diverse forms of hostas and ferns in all their shapes and forms should also be mentioned.

For the foreground, the filigree shade-loving saxifrages (for example *Saxifraga x urbium*, *S. trifurcata* or *S. geum*) are well suited. Prettily marked foliage and small white flowers are two of the special features of these small gems.

The Japanese, or forest poppy *(Hylomecon japonica)* is a rarity. However, its merits are unmissable: strong yellow poppy flowers, thick, compact growth and an early blooming season in April. It grows up to 20-30 cm and combines well with cowslips *(Primula veris)* and bitter vetch *(Lathyrus vernus)*.

PARTIAL SHADE

Japanese forest grass *(Hakonechloa macra)* is perfect for partial shade at woodland edges or in clearings. With its overhanging, waterfall-like growth it is an ideal foreground plant for the fullmoon maple *(Acer japonicum)* and other trees that have strong autumn colouring. The contrast

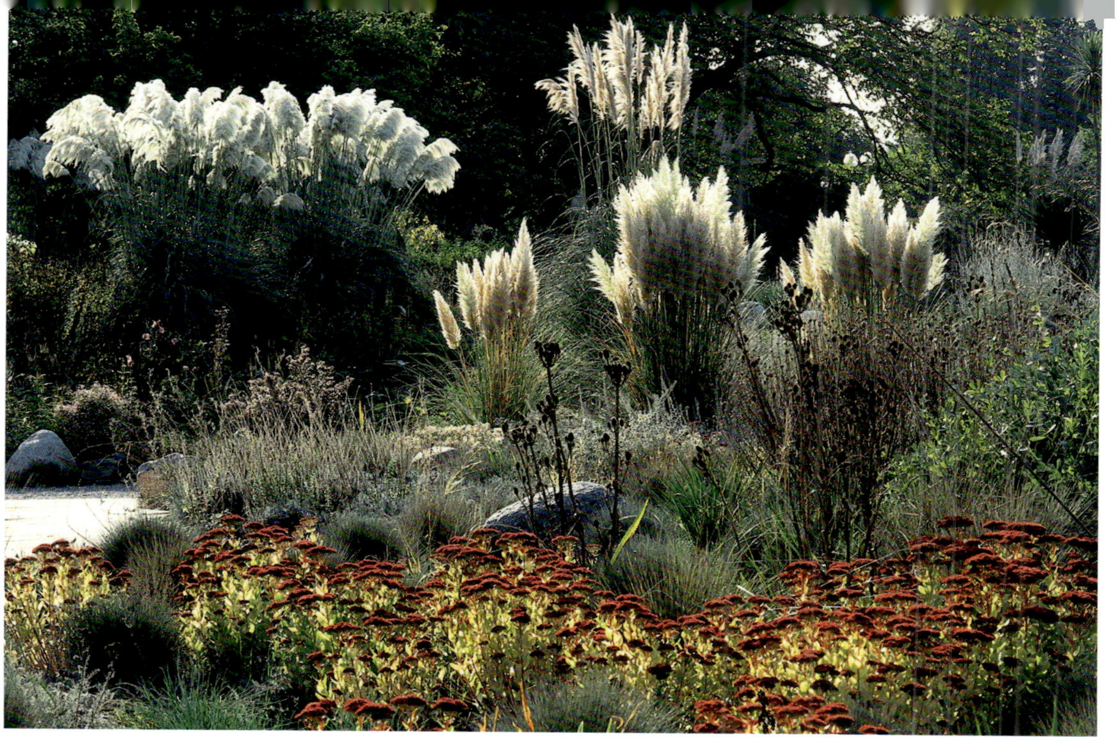

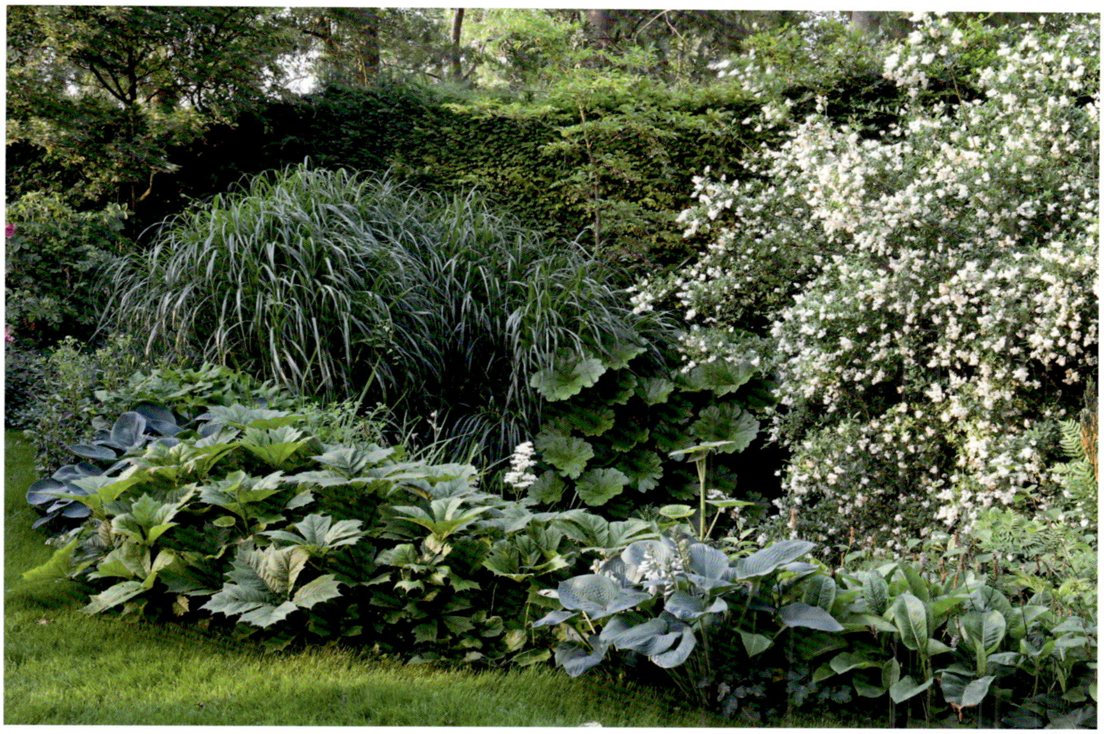

Steppeland at the edge of a wood (top)
Steppeland planting is especially effective against a backdrop of a dark wood.

Playing with forms (bottom)
Exciting garden images can be created with just leaf and plant forms. Large-leafed shrubs such as Indian rhubarb (*Darmera*), rodgersia and hostas provide a counterpart to fine grass foliage.

between the red autumn leaves and the still fresh light-green or green- and yellow-striped foliage of the 'Aureola' variety makes for a stunning sight. At 1.2 metres Bowles' golden grass (*Milium effesum* 'Aureum') grows even higher, and it combines well with woodland edge shrubs. Weeping sedge (*Carex pendula*) also grows to a tall height and moreover forms into attractive clumps.

For accompanying shrubs we should turn to black cohosh (*Cimicifuga racemosa* var. *cordifolia, C. ramosa* and *C. simplex*), which bloom from July to October. They can reach impressive heights of up to 2 metres and are adorned all over with creamy white filigree flower candles. If the soil is sufficiently humus-rich and fresh, black cohosh can stay in the same location in the border all year round without special care or transplantation.

Aconite or monkshood (*Aconitum carmichaelii* and *A. napellus*) is known as a reliable autumn-flowering shade-loving shrub. The white-flowered *A. lycotonum* ssp. *lycotonum* 'Ivorine' and the early-flowering pale-yellow-flowered *A. lycotonum* ssp. *Vulparia*, which blooms early in the year, however, have yet to break through. With their light-coloured foliage they bring flashes of light to dark corners.

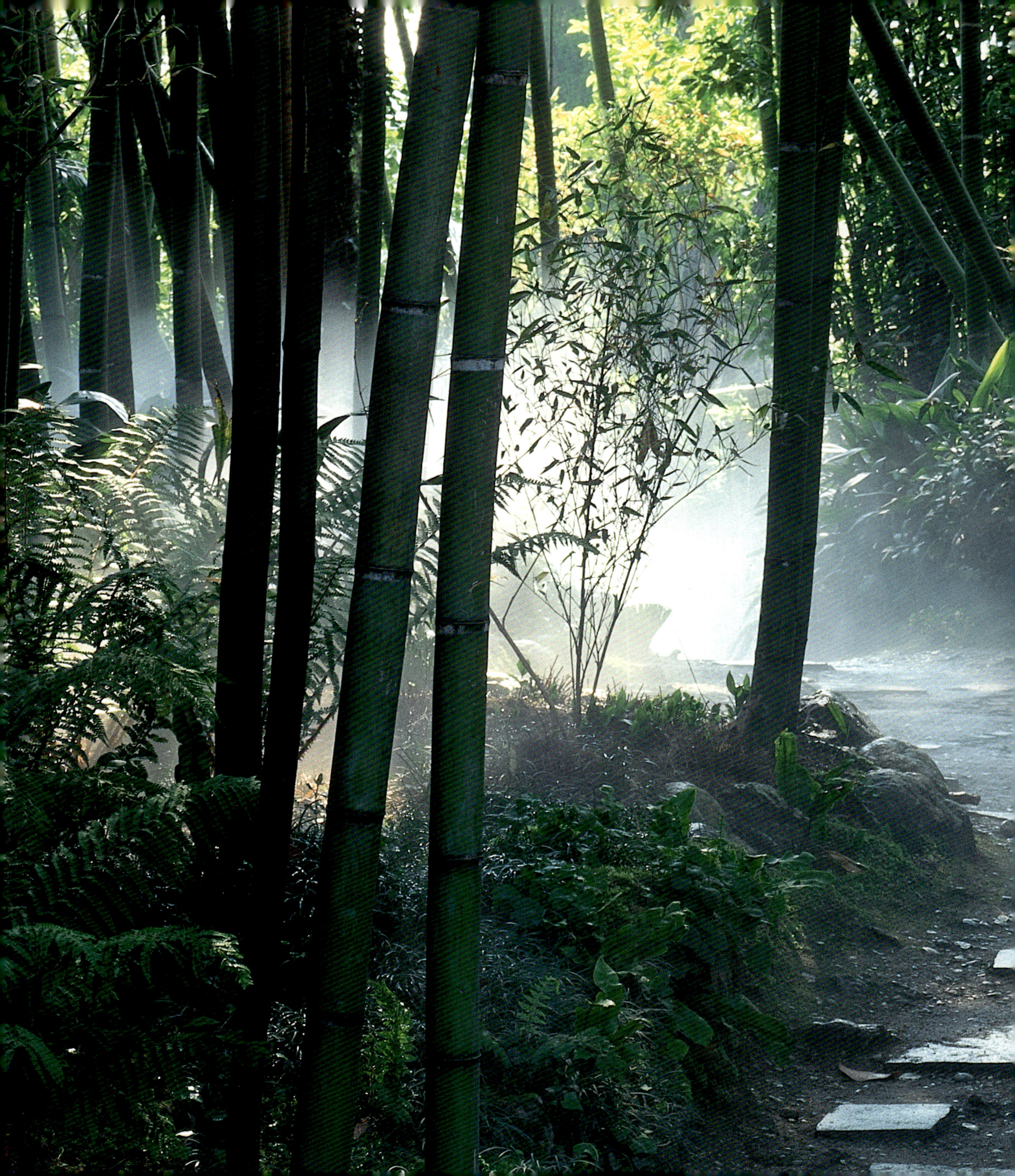

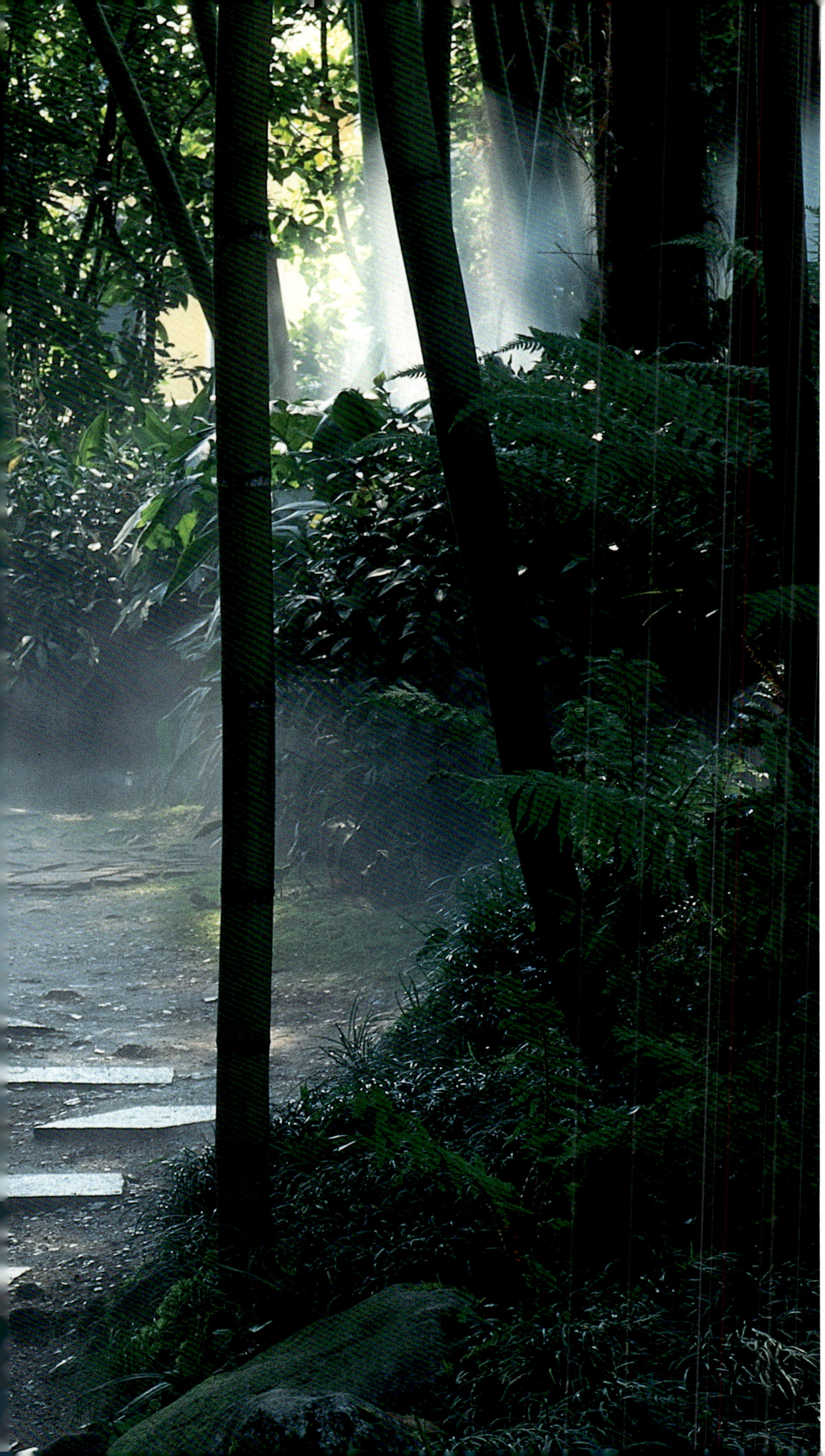

Bowman's root *(Gillenia trifoliata)* is a wonderful shade-loving plant with a delicate beauty that unfortunately is not as well known as it should be. Its small light-pink flowers dance like butterflies above its delicate dark foliage. It blooms in June/July and grows to about 70cm.

Yellow wax-bells *(Kirengeshoma palmata)* are an interesting visitor from Asia. As well as are maple-shaped leaves, the plants also have satisfying delicate yellow bell-shaped flowers, which bloom from July onwards atop 80cm stems.

The Japanese orchid lily, or toad lily *(Tricyrtis hirta)*, which also originates in Asia, has a strange beauty. Its flowers have a fascinating spotted pattern in pink and lilac. Despite its fragile appearance, it is a robust plant and grows on humus-rich, loose soils and forms magnificent clumps.

The flower candles of the white gooseneck loosestrife *(Lysimachia clethroides)* appear in late summer on plants around 60cm tall. They tend to grow in an arc and their shape is evocative of a duck's bill. These shrubs work best in large stands. Their flower stems work well in flower arrangements.

An attractive early summer bloomer is meadow rue *(Thalictrum aquilegifolium)*, with its pink or white flower heads, which look like small powder puffs. They grow to 1.2 metres high and require an acidic soil.

An exotic bamboo grove

Tall bamboo stems provide shade in the garden. The woodland floor is planted with various ferns.

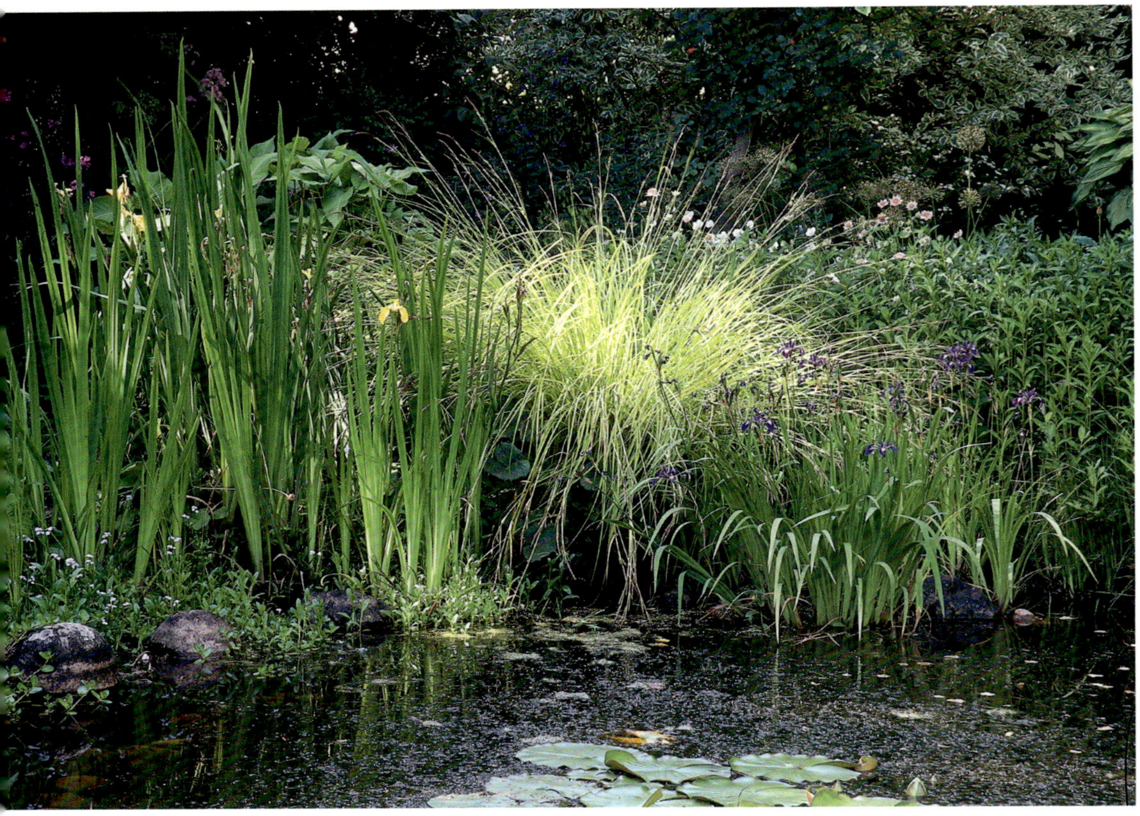

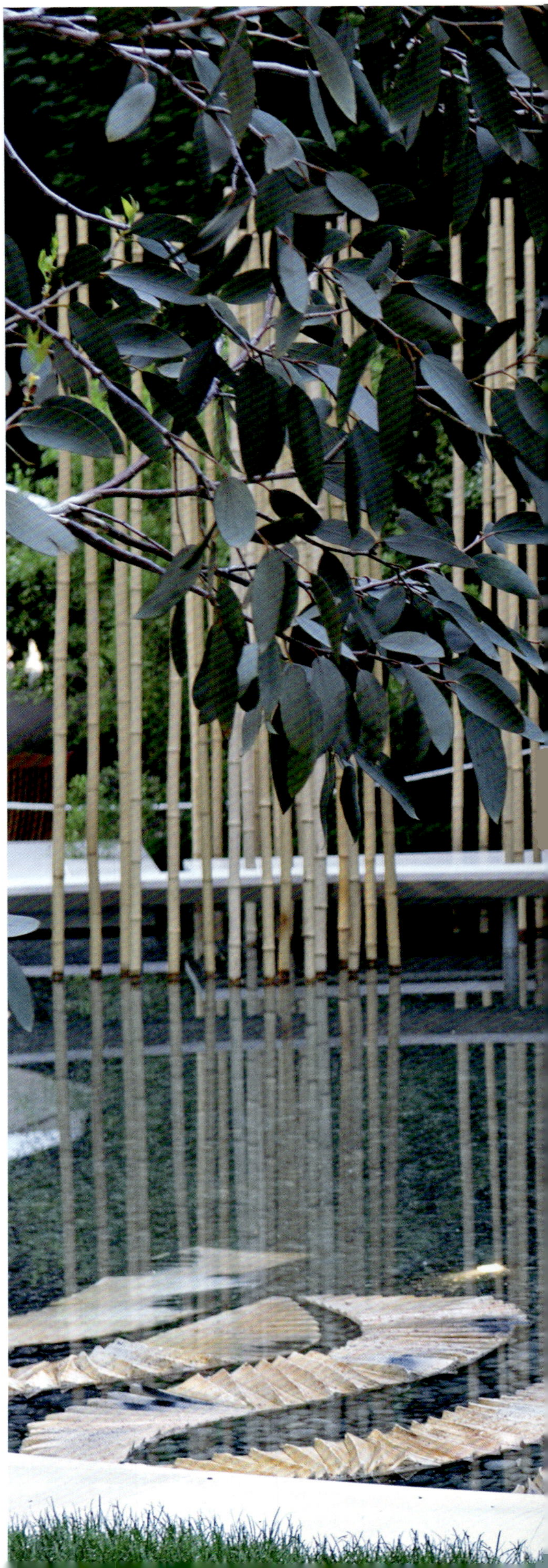

Pond Planting

In the wild, you never see a pond without grasses. There are always reeds growing round the edges, where ducks and other wildfowl can find shelter and lay their eggs.

Planting around a pond (above)
Grasses and shrubs with similar leaf forms.

A formal pond (opposite)
Bamboo stems as works of art. In the foreground, in the dry zone, is Mexican feather grass *(Nassella tenuissima)*.

A garden pond only really blends in naturally with its surroundings when it is planted with typical waterside shrubs and grasses. One shouldn't use man-sized plants, which would easily visually overwhelm a small pond. There are weak-growing varieties even of the reed mace, and instead of reeds, reed canary grass *(Phalaris arundinacea)* can be used; the colourful-leafed 'Mervin Freesey' variety is not only especially graceful, but is less rampant than the rest of the species and grows no higher than 150cm. Another

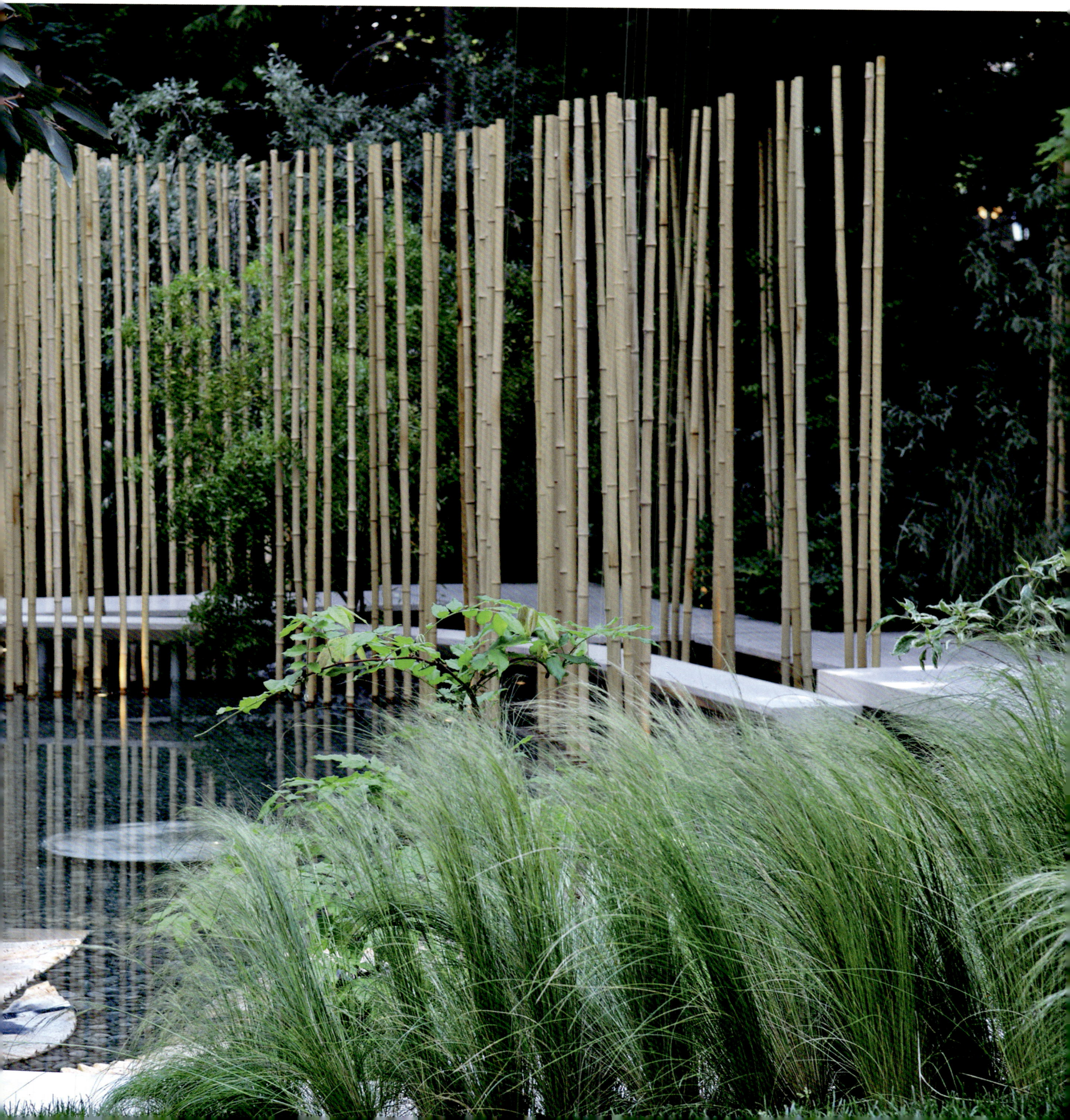

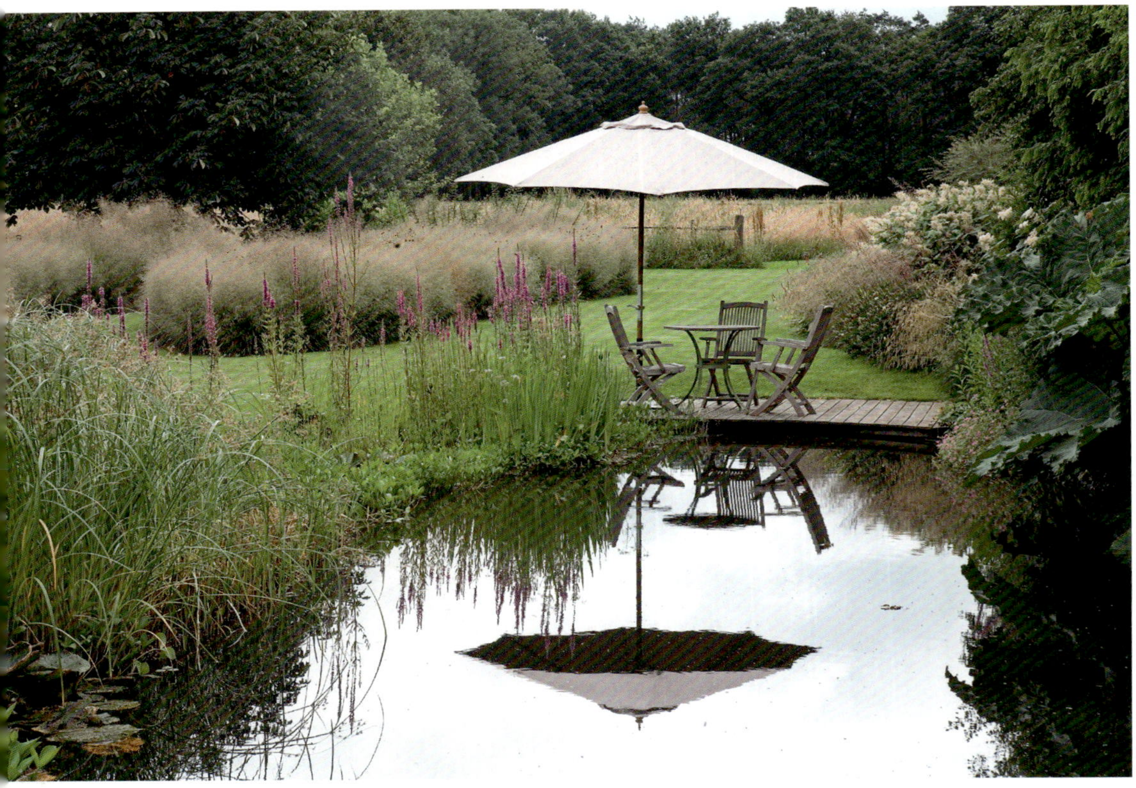

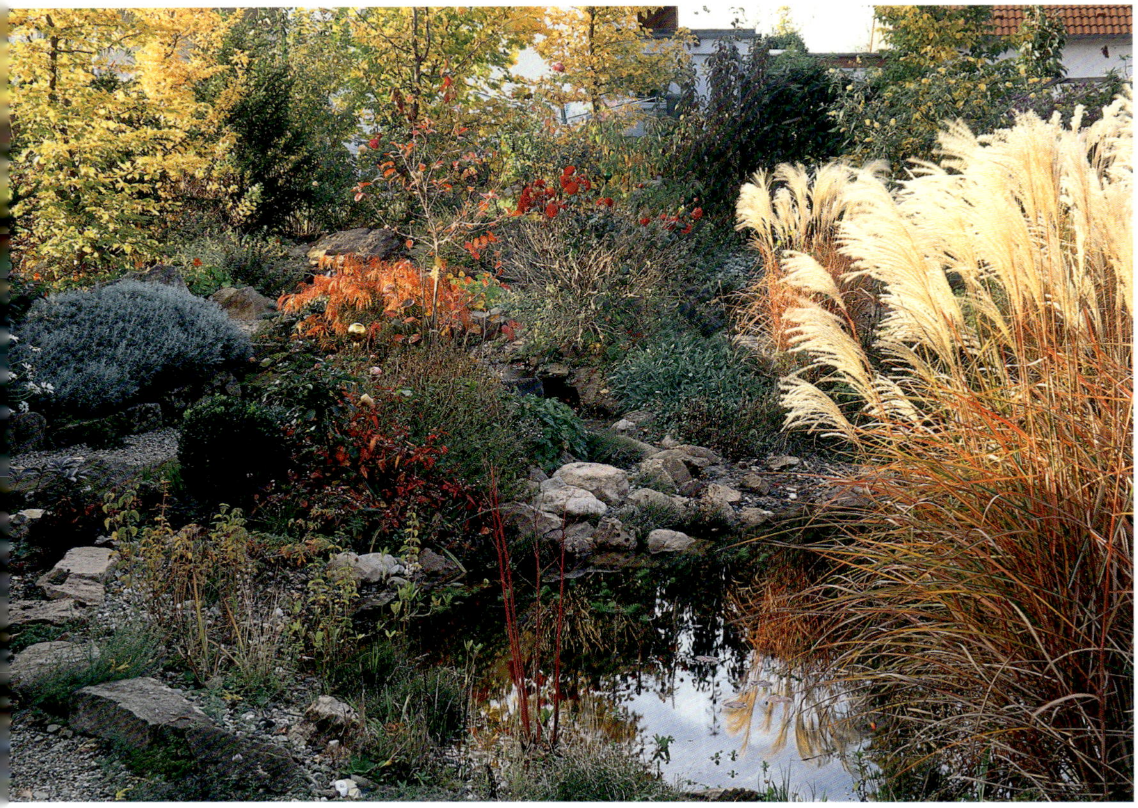

Sitting place by the pond
Grasses and purple loosestrife *(Lythrum Salicaria)* complement each other perfectly.

Small pond (below)
An eclectic design incorporating grasses and various shrubs.

important group of grasses for the water's edge are rushes *(Juncus)*, but even some sedges feel most at home in the vicinity of water.

POND AND BANKSIDE

When planting round the edge of a pond it is important to observe a few basic principles. The transition from water to dry land consists of three zones, which have different degrees of dampness. In the marsh zone the water is consistently several centimetres deep, which means that the plants that will be happy here are those that like having 'wet feet'.

In the damp zone the ground never dries out, but the water level can vary, according to the amount of rainfall, between 0 and 5 cm. The width of the damp zone can depend on where the pond liner is laid and how steep or flat the bank is.

In the dry or pondside zone one generally finds fresh soil conditions that are not substantially different from those elsewhere in the garden. All garden shrubs that prefer fresh, strong soils are suitable for this area.

When selecting shrubs and grasses for the dry zone, design criteria can be uppermost. The best plants for this area are those that give the impression of meadow flowers.

The hard rush *(Juncus inflexus)* needs to have its feet wet; at 50cm it is not too tall for small ponds. Cyperus sedge *(Carex pseudocyperus)* has really beautiful flowers but has a tendency to proliferate, it is best to put it in a planting basket and sink it near the bank. The common club-rush *(Scirpus lacustris)* also tends to spread and should be controlled by use of a basket. The softstem bulrush (*Scirpus tabernaemontani* 'Zebrinus'), with its colourful foliage, does not spread so vigorously and in larger ponds can be planted straight into the plant substratum. A dwarf version of the native reed is the dwarf bulrush *(Typha minima)*, which, at 60cm tall, is especially suited to miniature ponds. The brown cylindrical bulbs are likewise smaller, but just as ornamental. They last all winter and look good cut for flower vases.

In the damp zone, with its fresh to damp soil, almost all types of grass that favour such

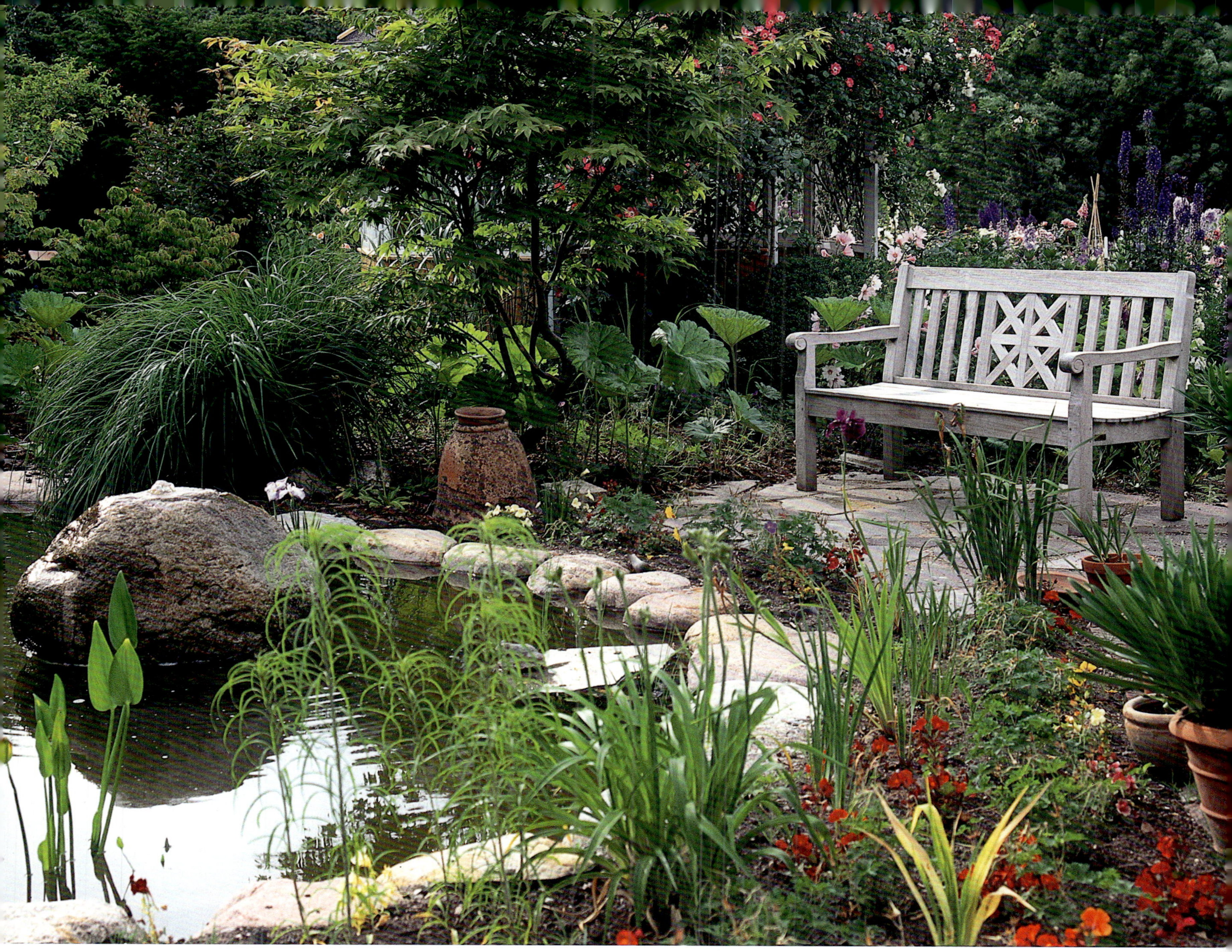

conditions can be used. Palm sedge *(Carex muskingumensis)* can replace reeds in smaller ponds. Bowles' golden sedge *(Carex elata 'Aurea')* is adorned with thick dark-brown flowers/spikes from early in the year and stands out due to its yellow-green leaves.

In a normal dry zone, *Carex pendula*, all types of miscanthus, frost grass *(Spodiopogon sibiricus)* and also some of the smaller species of bamboo can be used. Siberian iris *(Iris sibirica)*, day lily *(hemerocallis)*, *Astilbe* and loosestrife (*Lysimachia ciliata* and *L. clethroides*) also work here. *Bergenias* flower very early in the year, but their strong foliage is attractive all year round. Brightly coloured primulas (*Primula japonica* and *P.* x *bullesiana*) look very beautiful at the edge of a pond. They need a humus-based, consistently damp soil.

If the pond is large enough, ornamental leaf shrubs such as gunnera, willow-leaved sunflower *(Helianthus salicifolius)*, boneset *(Eupatorium)* or plume poppy *(Macleaya cordata)* can be included as well.

Sitting place by the pond
Eulalia *(Miscanthus sinensis)* in the background harmonises perfectly with water feature boulder.

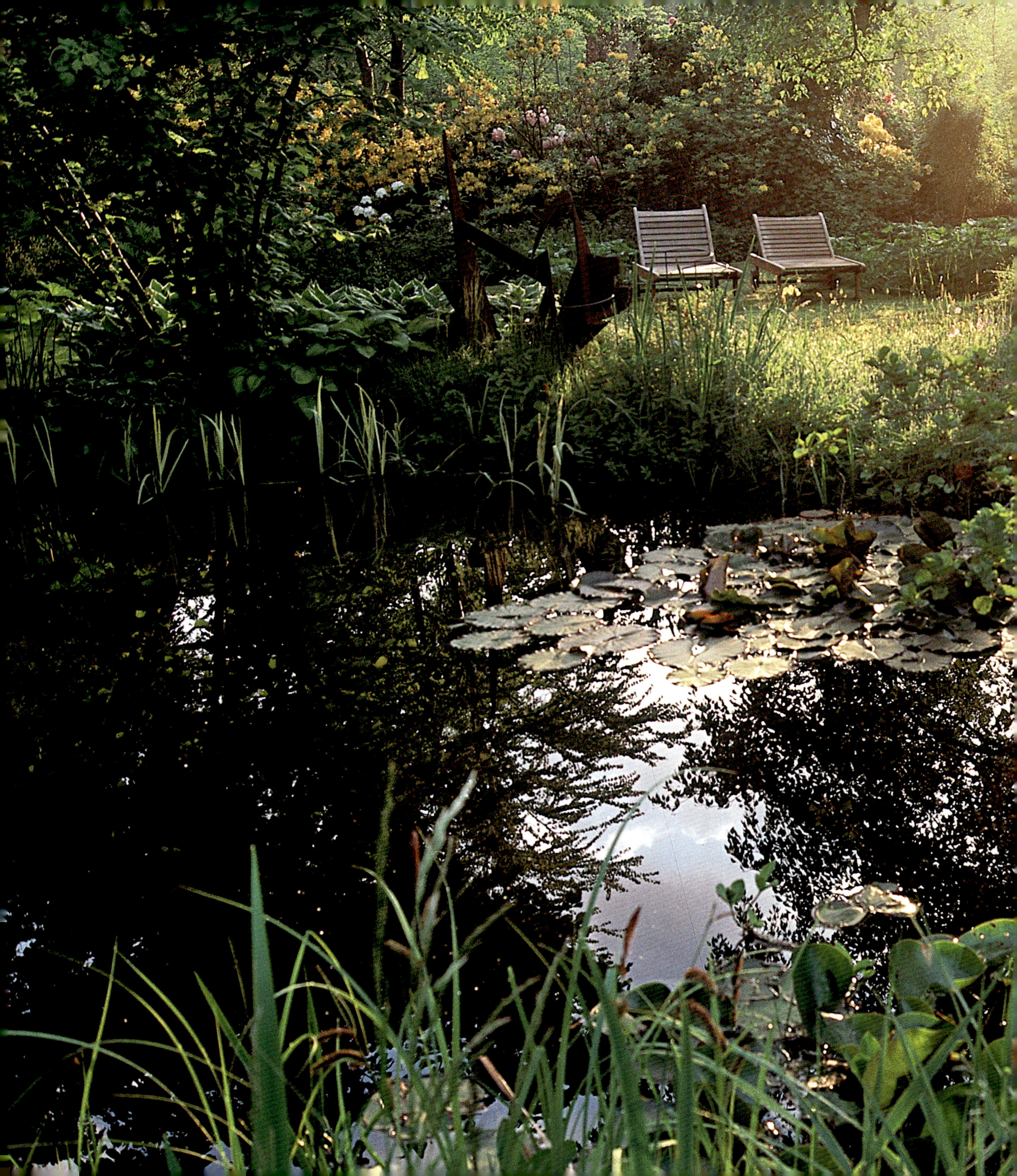

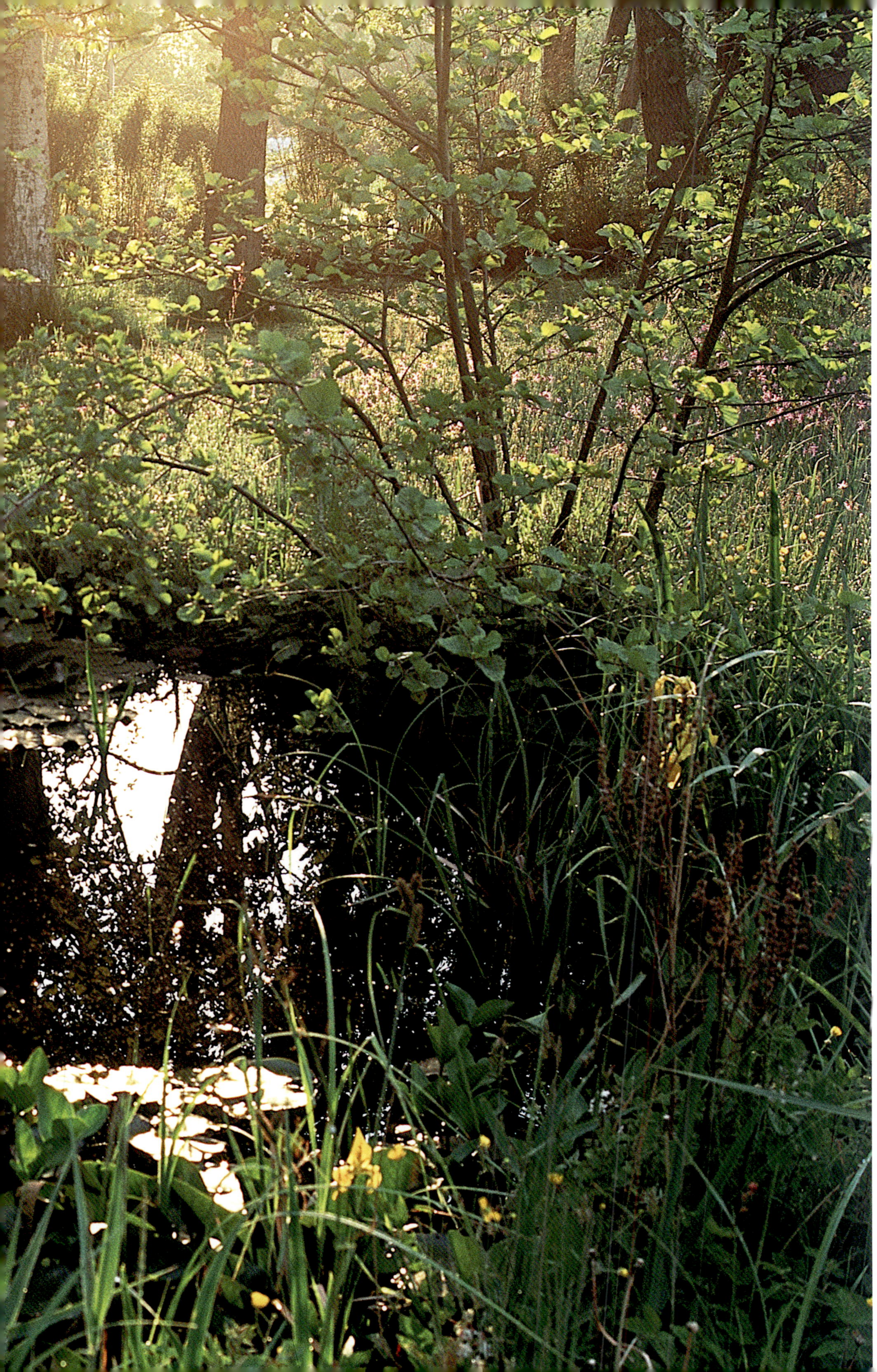

Enchanted forest clearing
You can use the prolific reed sweet grass (*Glyceria maxima* 'Variegata') for a natural-looking garden design.

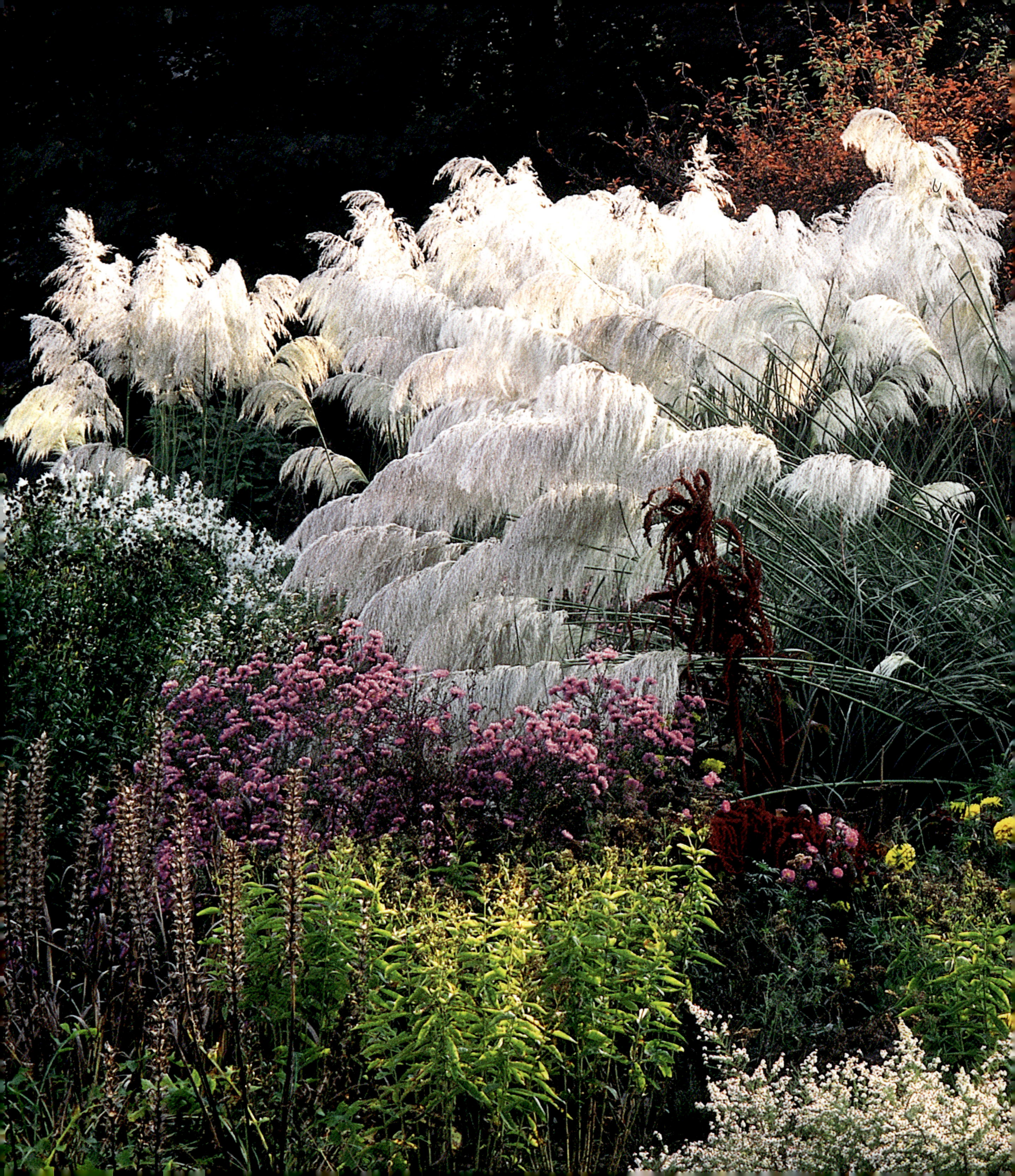

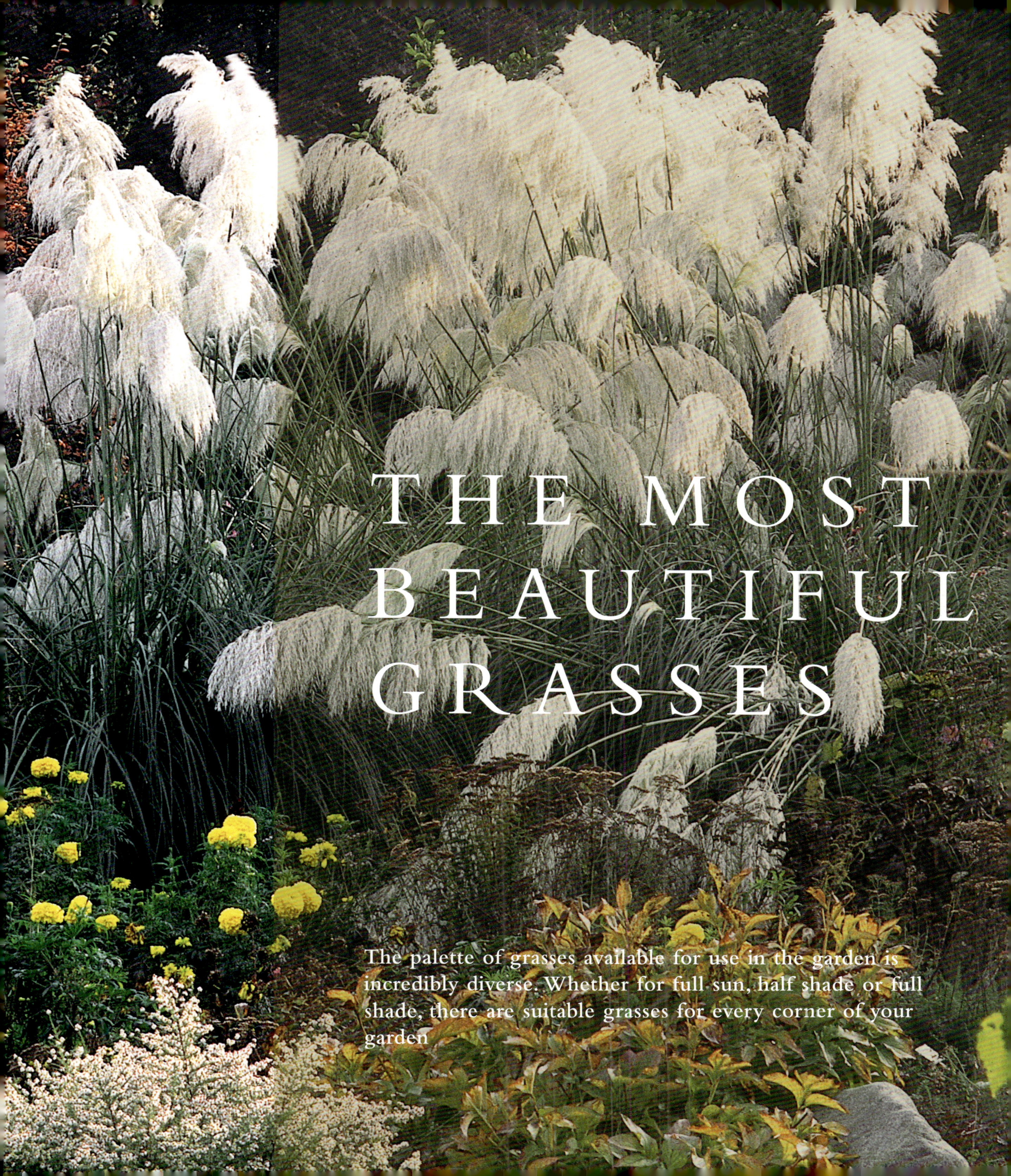

THE MOST BEAUTIFUL GRASSES

The palette of grasses available for use in the garden is incredibly diverse. Whether for full sun, half shade or full shade, there are suitable grasses for every corner of your garden

System and Classification

Grasses are divided into three groups: true grasses, sedges and rushes.

As the name implies, only true grasses *(Poaceae)* can properly be designated as grasses. From the gardening point of view, however, other plants that grow in a similar way to grasses are usually lumped into the same category.

TRUE GRASSES

True grasses belong to the botanical order of Poales, which consists of only one family, namely *Poaceae*. The family of true grasses, with around 700 genera and 10,000 species is one of the largest, and it is distributed over the entire globe. True grasses provide one of the most important sources of nutrition for humans and animals alike. Usually true grasses possess hermaphrodite flowers (i.e. the male and female components in one flower); pollination is wind-borne. The individual

Carex montana (right)
Mountain sedge, or soft-leaved sedge is a typical example of the sedge family (Cyperaceae).

Miscanthus sinensis 'Strictus' (opposite, top)
Miscanthus, in this case a type with striated leaves, is an example of a true grass *(Poaceae)*.

Juncus glaucus (opposite, bottom)
Rushes *(Juncacae)* have typical flowers arranged in inflorescences and round stems.

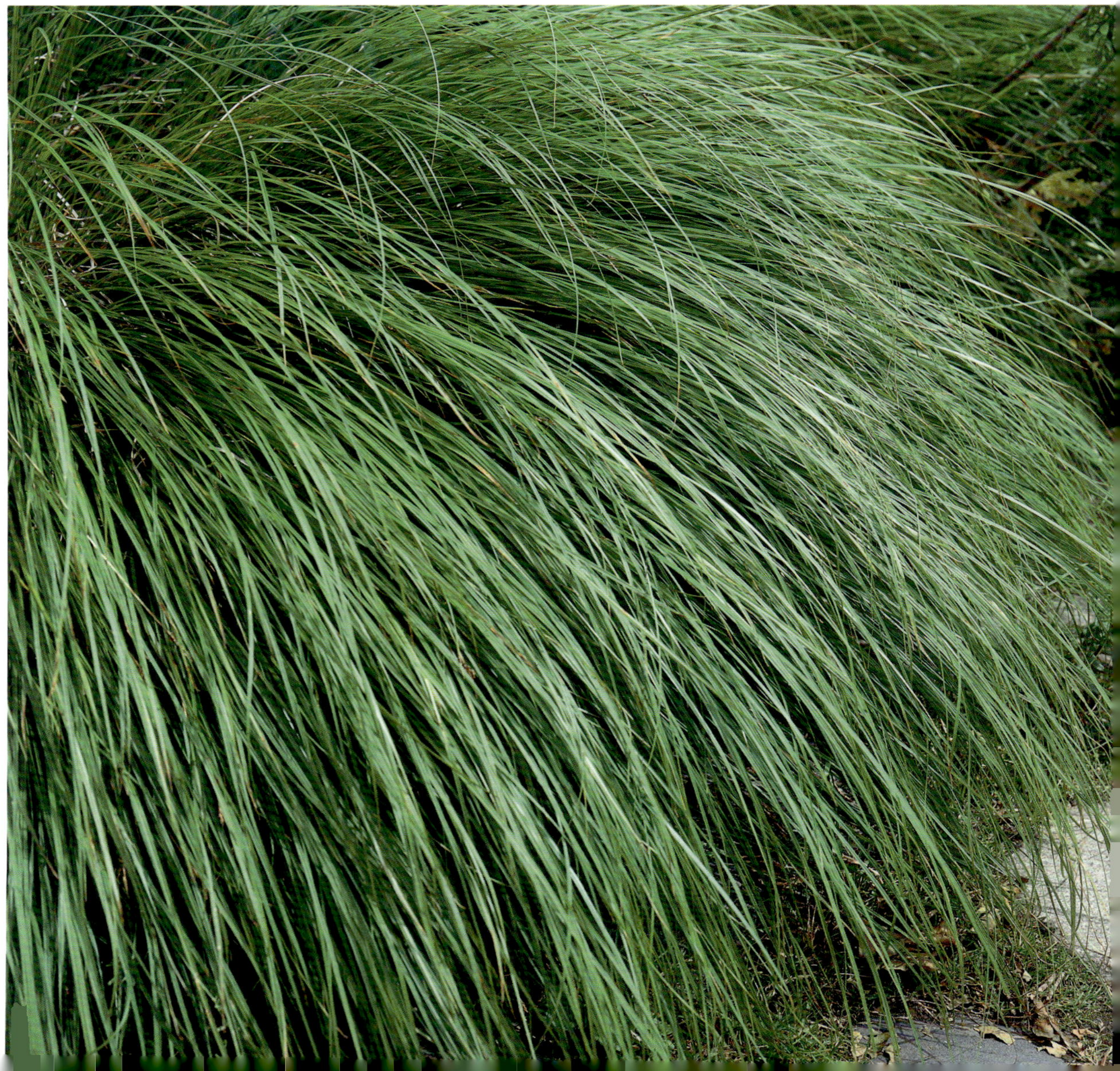

flowers are grouped into so-called spikelets, these in turn to all inflorescences (spikes). The individual flowers are enveloped by glumes, and the lemma is often provided with a bristle-like awn. The stems have a round cross section and nodular swellings (nodes) spaced at intervals. Bamboo is also one of the true grasses.

SEDGES

The sedges belong to an order *(Cyperrales)* that has only one family, the botanical *Cyperaceae*. Appearance-wise they are very similar to the true grasses; however, unlike them, they usually have trihedral stems and mostly no nodular thickening. The stems are not hollow, like those of the sweet grasses, but are filled with marrow. Historically, sedges are much older than true grasses, and they have significantly fewer species. Its flowers may be unisexual or hermaphrodite, and the individual flowers are usually arranged in spikes. They too rely on the wind for pollination. Many sedges populate damp to wet, shady locations.

RUSHES

Like the other two families, rushes *(Juncaceae)* are the sole family belonging to the order Juncales. They are the smallest of the three families, with only nine genera. Rushes have a round stem cross-section, and the stems are always filled with marrow and not divided by nodes. The flowers, which are also pollinated by the wind, are arranged in the form of inflorescences. Also, the marginal individual blooms have longer stalks, resulting in a sort of funnel-shaped umbel. Rushes are evergreen and, like the sedges, live mainly in damp or wet locations, often on acidic soil. Rushes have been used for millennia for weaving, as they are very flexible. Baskets, bags and shoes can be made from them, as can fish traps. Even thatched roofs are often made out of rushes.

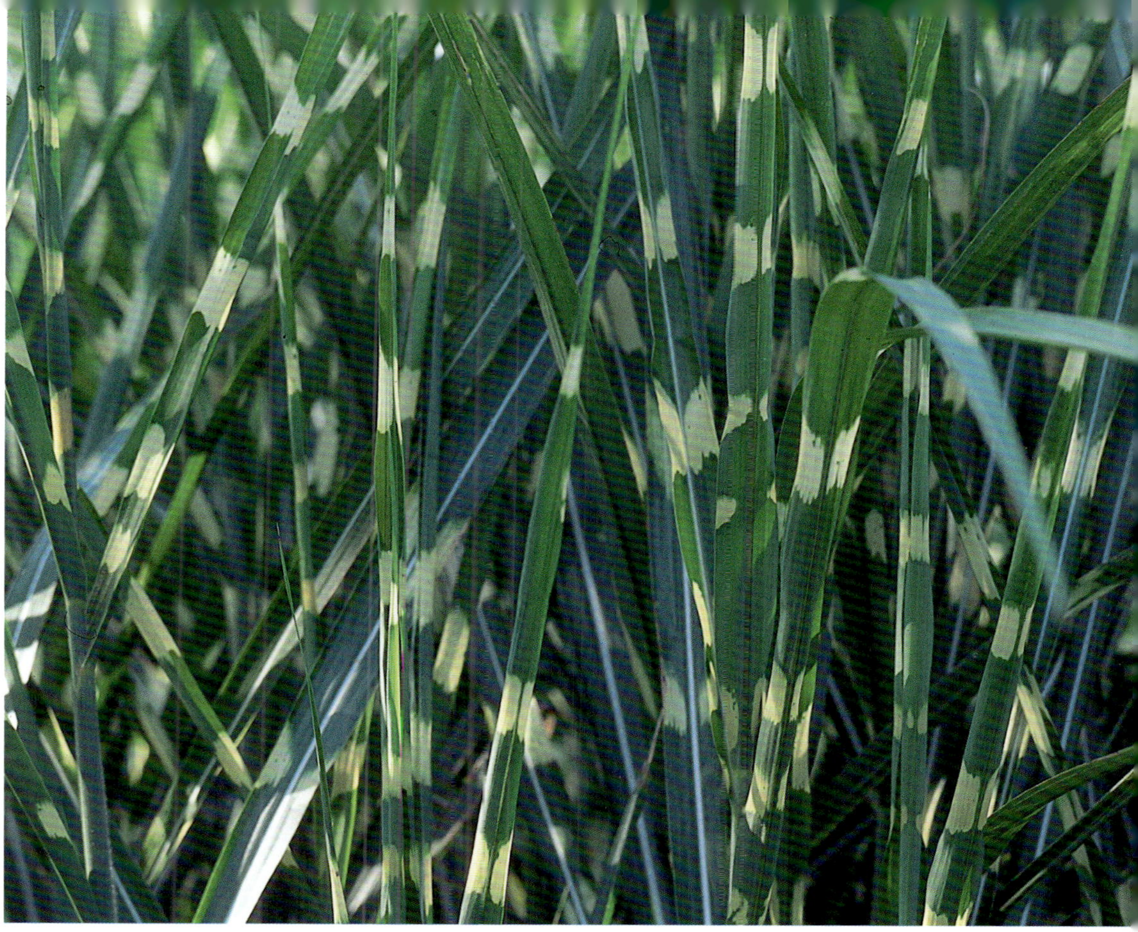

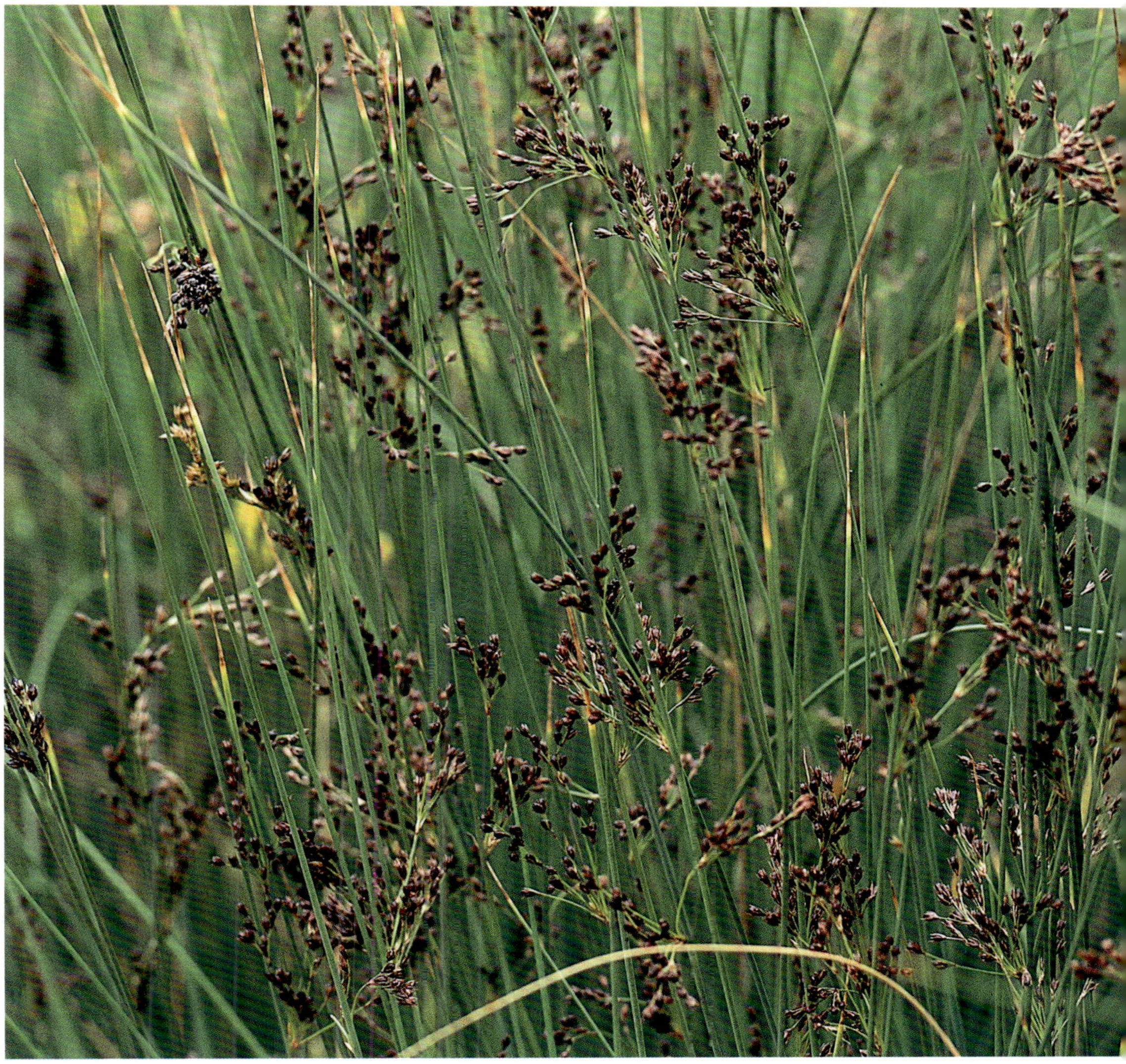

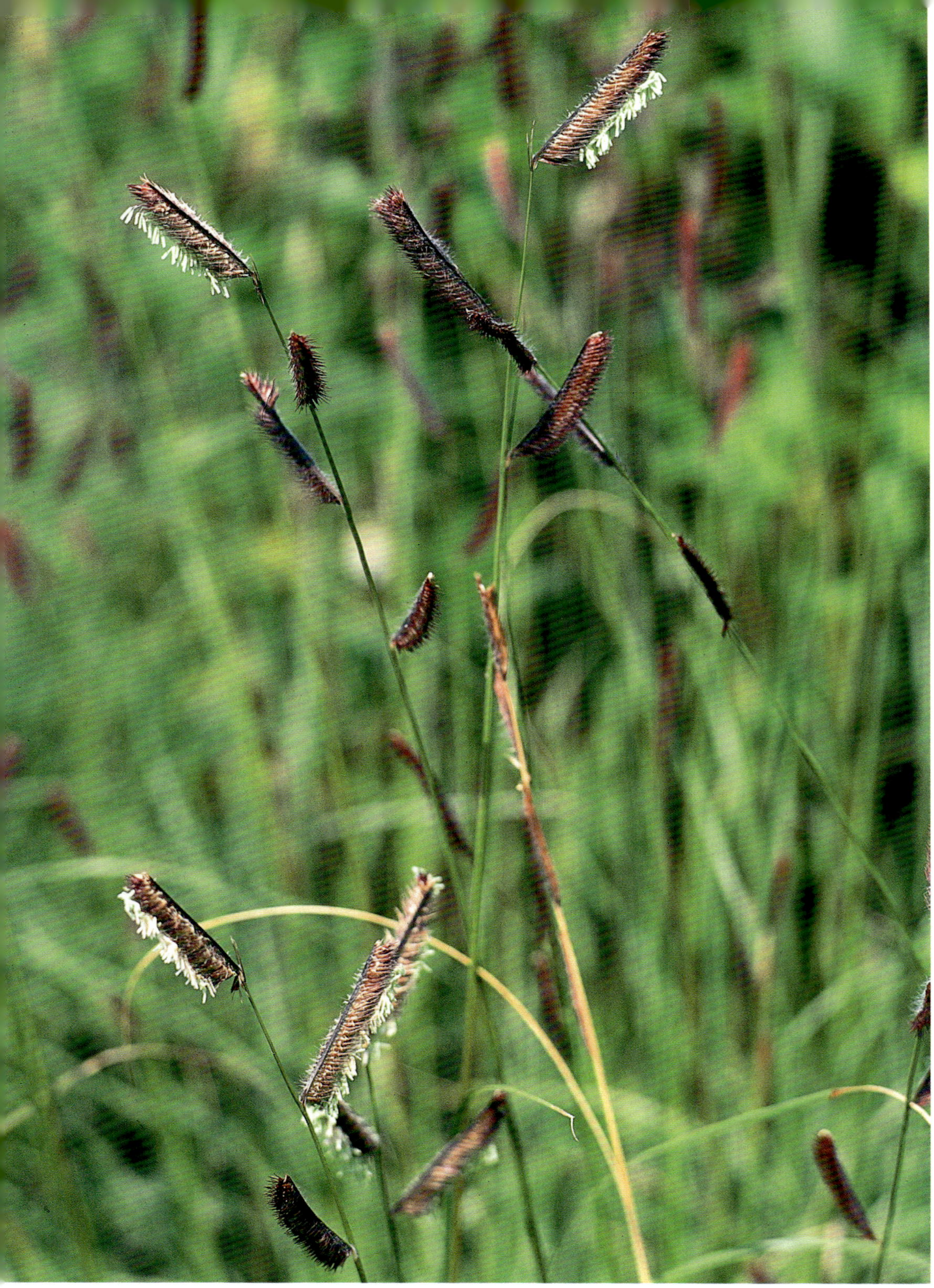

ANEMANTHELE LESSONIANA
syn. Stipa arundinacea
Pheasant's tail grass
Height: 70–100cm, **width:** 90cm
Growth: dense clump-forming, fine stems, elegantly overhanging.
Leaves: blue-green; yellow, orange or red in autumn. Sometimes evergreen.
Flowers: loose, overhanging panicles from August to September.
Location: sunny to shaded, prefers rich soil. Not reliably winter hardy, winter protection recommended.
Use: accent plant in borders, winter interest due to its long-lasting autumn colouring.
Recommended varieties: 'Autumn Tints' has a pronounced red autumn colouring. 'Golden Hue' has golden-yellow autumn colouring.

ARUNDO DONAX
Giant reed or Spanish reed
Height: up to 400cm, **width:** 150cm
Growth: upright, with strong stems, shape a little reminiscent of tropical reeds.
Leaves: dark-green, wide, bending over.
Flowers: light panicles, most hidden by foliage, from September to October, though rarely blooms in Europe.
Location: sunny, sheltered, as warm as possible.
Use: as a solitary plant, planting in front of walls, and also very effective at edges of ponds. Needs a lot of water and must be well soaked in dry spells. Feed regularly.
Recommended varieties: 'Versicolor' has yellowish white striped leaves and is sensitive to frost and so is better suited for use as a container plant.

Sunny Locations

Sunny locations are defined as those parts of the garden that receive full sunlight almost all day long. This is home to many prairie and steppe grasses as well as other species that, in the wild, grow on open plains.

BOUTELOUA GRACILIS

Blue grama grass

Height: 40cm, **width:** 30cm

Growth: Loose clump-forming, delicate, with wiry stems.

Leaves: blue-green, very slender.

Flowers: dark-brown, thick spikes that grow almost horizontally from the stems, from July to September.

Location: sunny, warm. Prefers loose, well-drained soil, and copes well with few nutrients.

Use: in rock gardens, on dry walls, and also in steppe planting schemes; very attractive with wild flowers. Most effective in places where it can be observed from close up.

CALAMAGROSTIS X ACUTIFLORA

Feather reed grass

Height: 150–180cm, **width:** 50cm

Growth: straight upright, the flower stems are several times taller than the foliage. Forms slender clumps; does not send out runners.

Leaves: mid-green, slender; the new leaves appear very early in the year. The early flower stems are a bright straw-yellow. Attractive through to mid-winter.

Flowers: lightly fan-shaped flower panicles, from June to August. Seed heads slimmer. Keeps its shape in winter. Attractive straw-yellow colour especially in late autumn and winter.

Location: sunny, not very sturdy in half shade. Tolerates dry to moderately damp soil.

Use: in herbaceous borders, in small groups, but also extensively with prairie shrubs, as in countless planting schemes by Wolfgang Oehme. Also effective as solitary plants.

Recommended varieties: 'Karl Foerster' is the most popular type and is very sturdy and vigorous. 'Overdam' has pale-yellow leaf fringes, which turn white over the course of time. Overall, they are more delicate and weak-growing. 'Waldenbuch' is more compact, somewhat lower-growing and has especially attractive flowers.

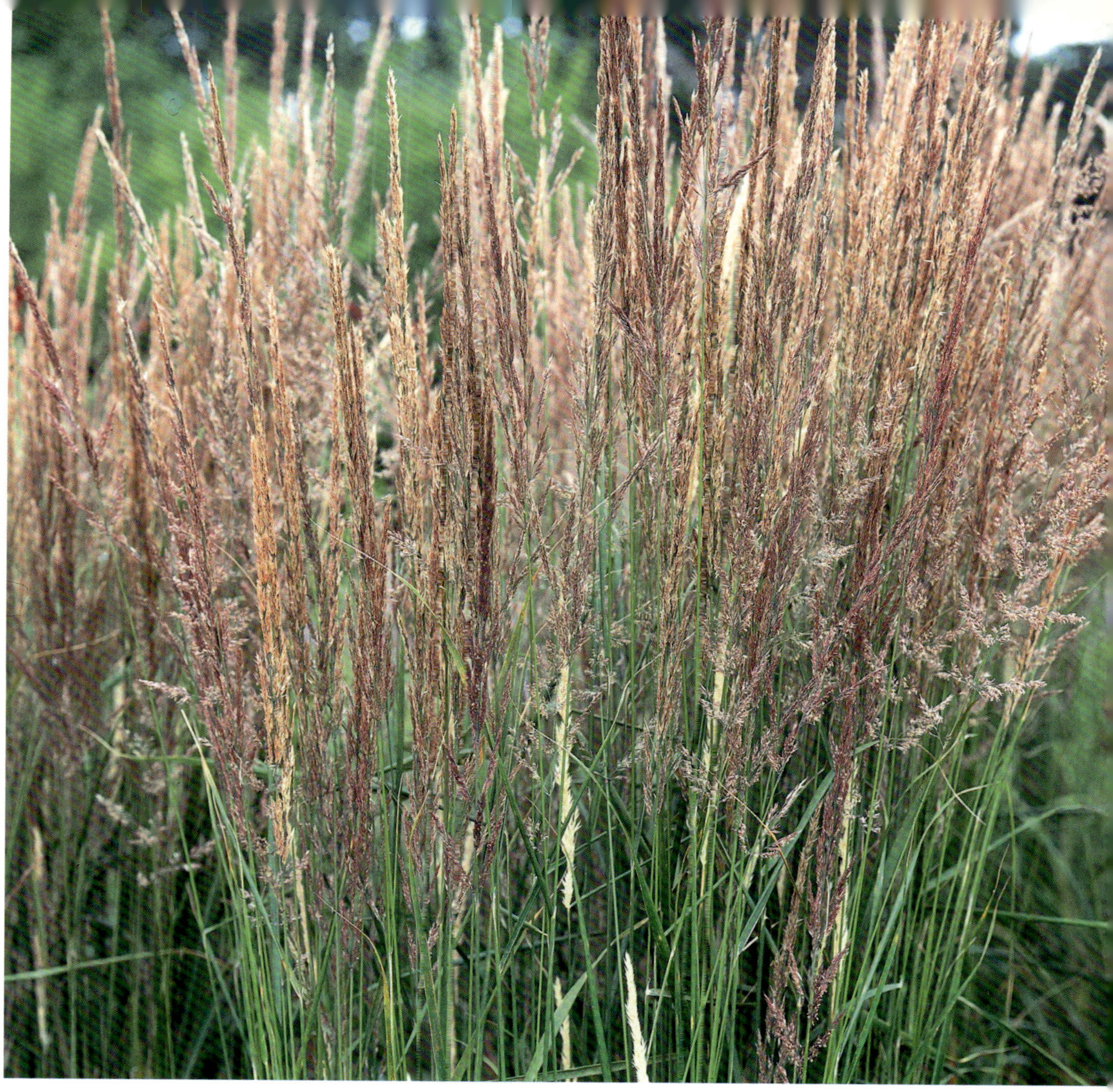

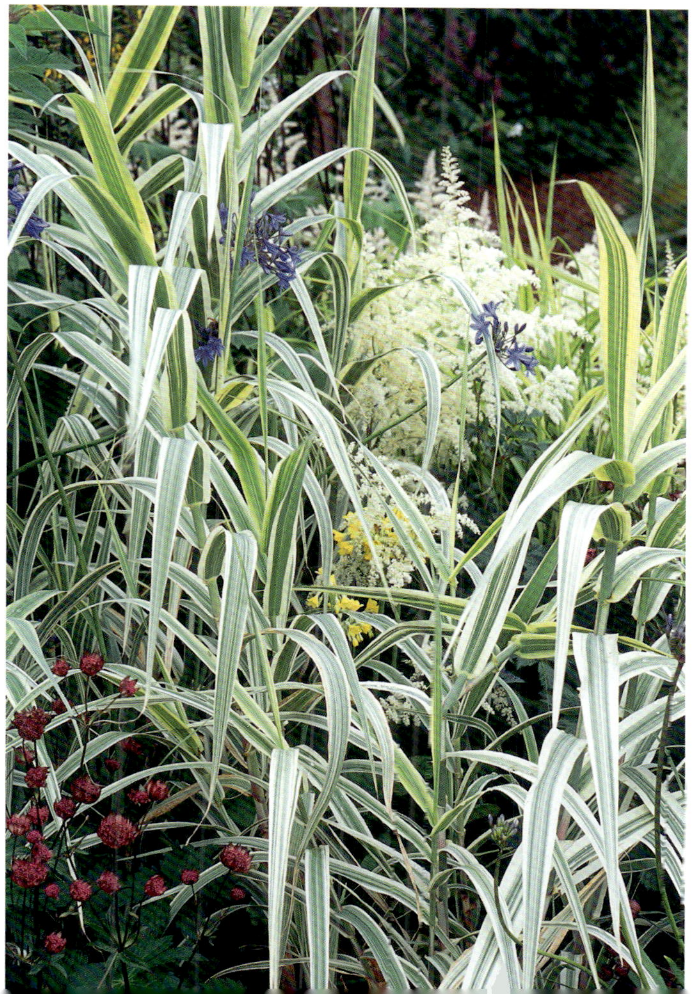

Calamagrostis x acutiflorus 'Karl Foerster' (above) Feather reed grass is one of Karl Foerster's best selections.

Arundo donax 'Versicolor' (left) The stripy-leafed form of the variegated giant reed is somewhat more frost-sensitive than the rest of the species.

Bouteloua gracilis (opposite) Like tiny insects, the flowers of the blue grama grass dance above their stems.

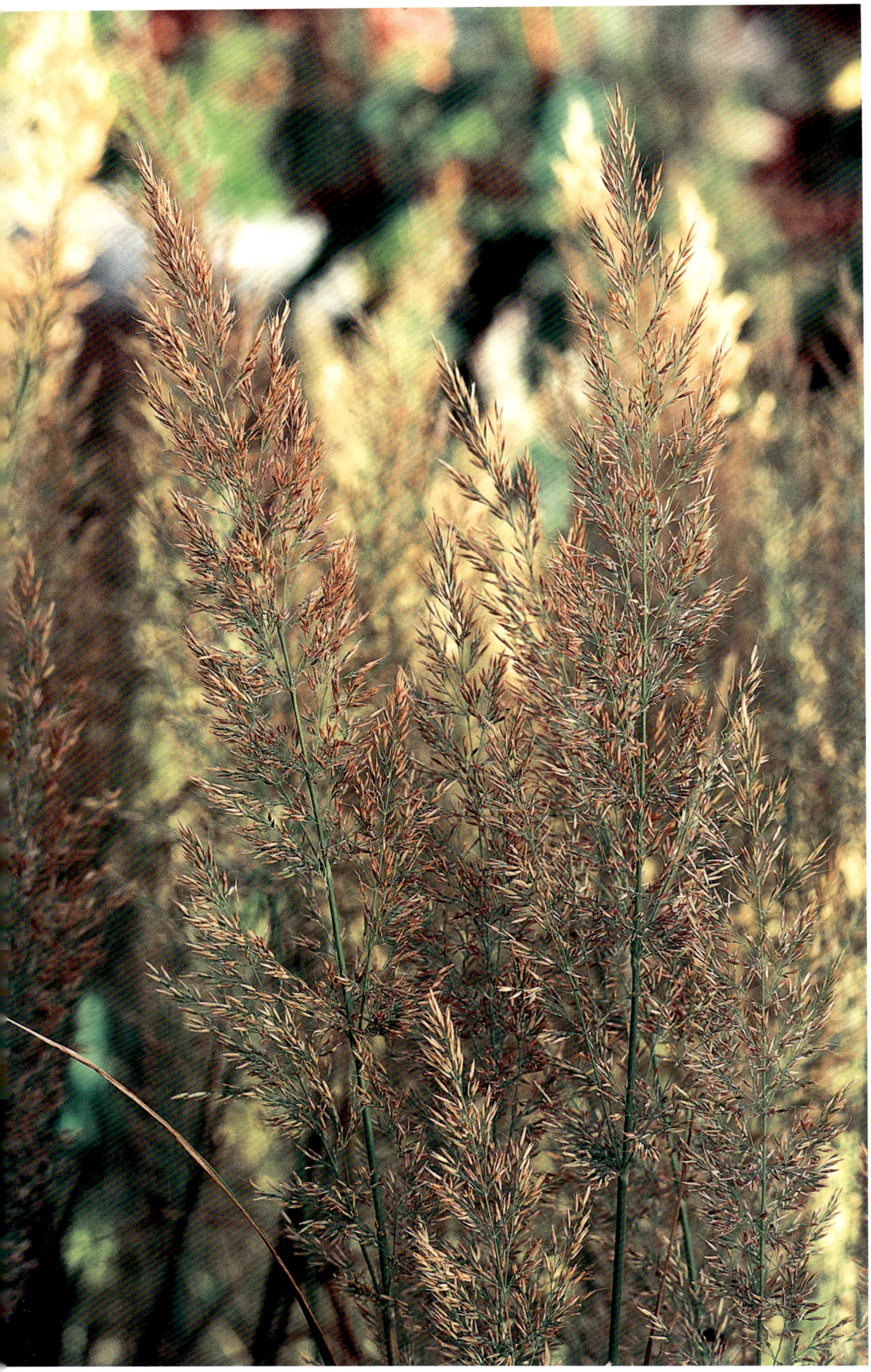

CALAMAGROSTIS BRACHYTRICHA

syn. *Achnatherum brachytricha*

Diamond grass or Korean feather reed grass

Height: 120cm, **width:** 80-100cm

Growth: loose, often somewhat irregular clumps, the foliage appears early in the year. Flower heads stand well above the leaves. Forms no runners, so is not invasive.

Leaves: feathery overhanging panicles, from June to September. Very attractive and conspicuous, changing to pink tones when in full bloom, later turning yellow. Maintains its colour until winter.

Location: sunny to light shade, prefers warm, sheltered spots. Thrives in all not too heavy soils.

Use: as an accent plant, in small groups in borders. Very nice-looking at the front of steppe borders.

CAREX BUCHANANII

Leatherleaf sedge

Height: 150-180cm , **width:** 50cm

Growth: stiff, upright, the flower stems are several times higher than the foliage. Forms narrow clumps, does not form runners.

Leaves: mid-green, slender, the new foliage appears very early in the year, when the leaf stems are a bright straw-yellow. Attractive through until mid winter, wintergreen.

Flowers: slightly fanned flower panicles, from June to August. The seed heads are more slender. Keep their shape until winter. An attractive straw-yellow colour especially in late autumn and winter.

Location: sunny, less sturdy in half shade. Tolerates dry to moderately damp soil.

Use: in borders, in small groups, but also extensively with prairie shrubs, as in countless designs by Wolfgang Oehme. Can also be used as solitary plants.

CAREX COMANS

New Zealand sedge

Height: 40cm, **width:** 60cm

Growth: clump-forming, with a broad spread. The tips lie on the ground.

Leaves: pale-green, very slender, turning yellow at the tip.

Flowers: somewhat unremarkable brown panicles, from April to May.

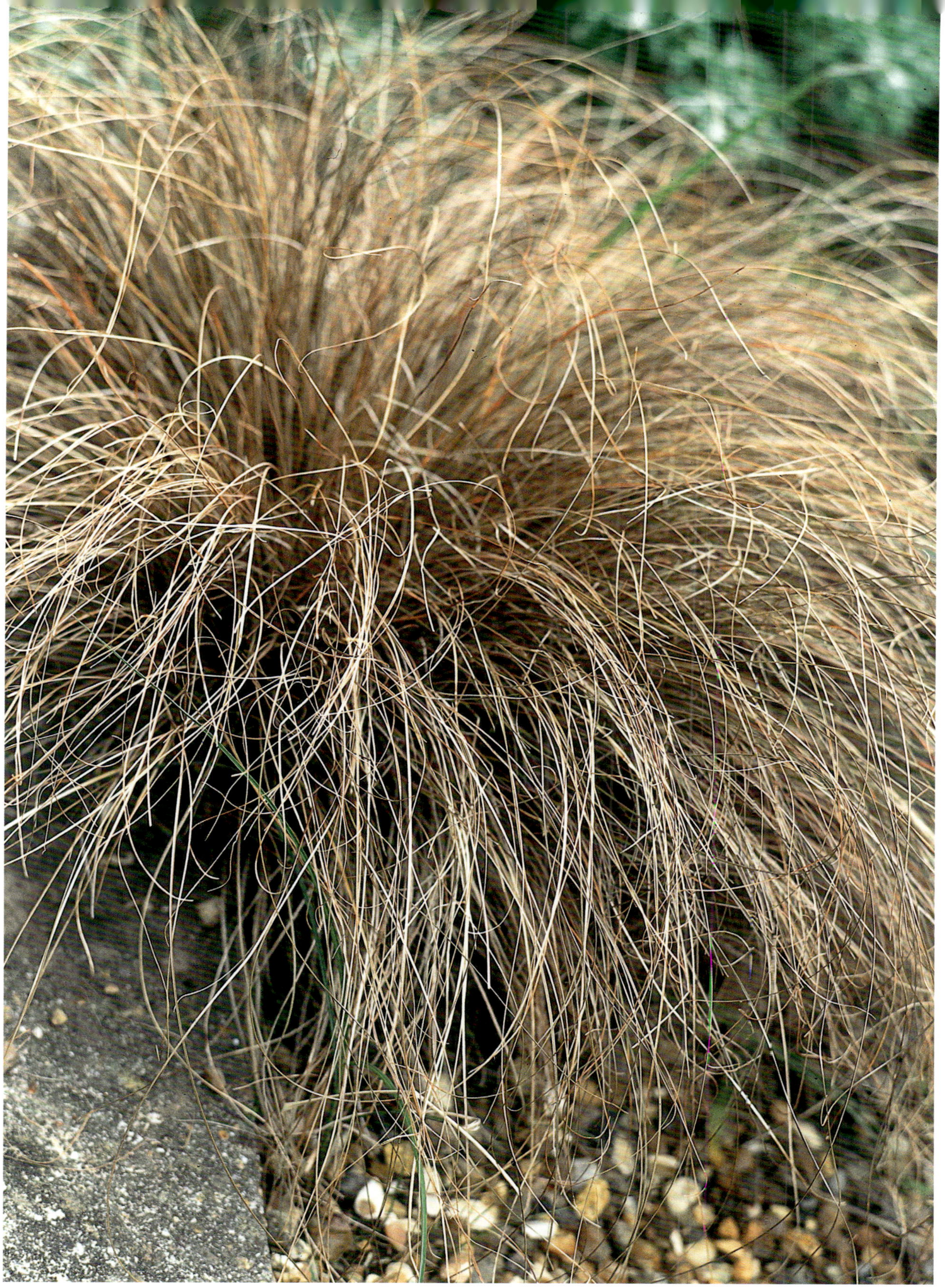

Carex comans 'Bronze' (left)
The dark-leafed form of the New Zealand hair sedge has the fine leaves that are typical of the species.

Calamagrostis brachytricha (opposite)
Korean feather reed grass has fine panicles, which gather the early-morning dew.

Location: sunny, prefers damp soil, but copes with fresh soils.
Use: as a solitary or accent plant in the foreground. Very beautiful next to water, where the tufts of leaves can elegantly bend down towards the surface of the water.

Recommended varieties: 'Bronze' or 'Bronze Form' has pale-yellow leaves. Because of their leaf colouring, the plants can sometimes have a withered appearance.

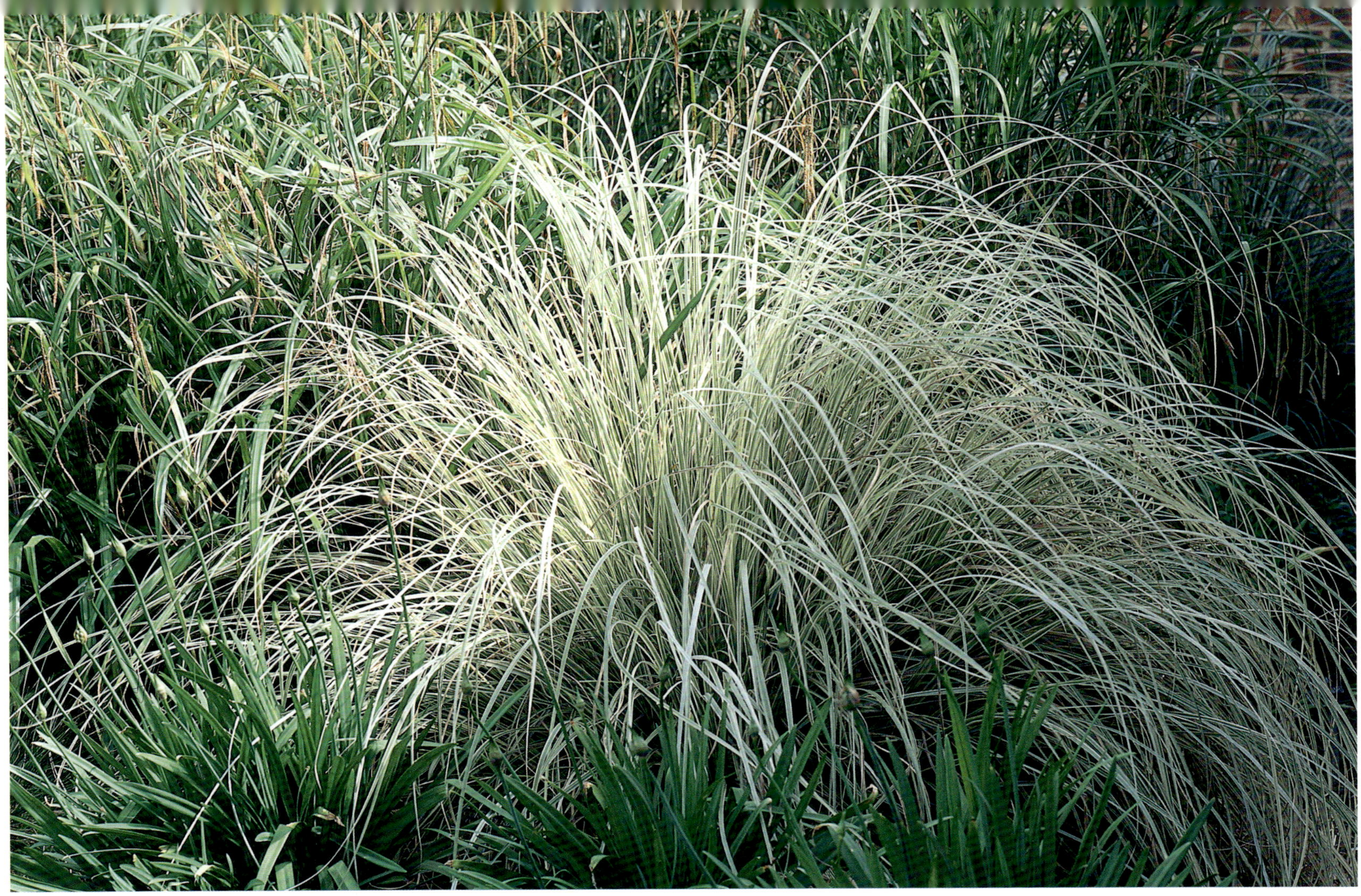

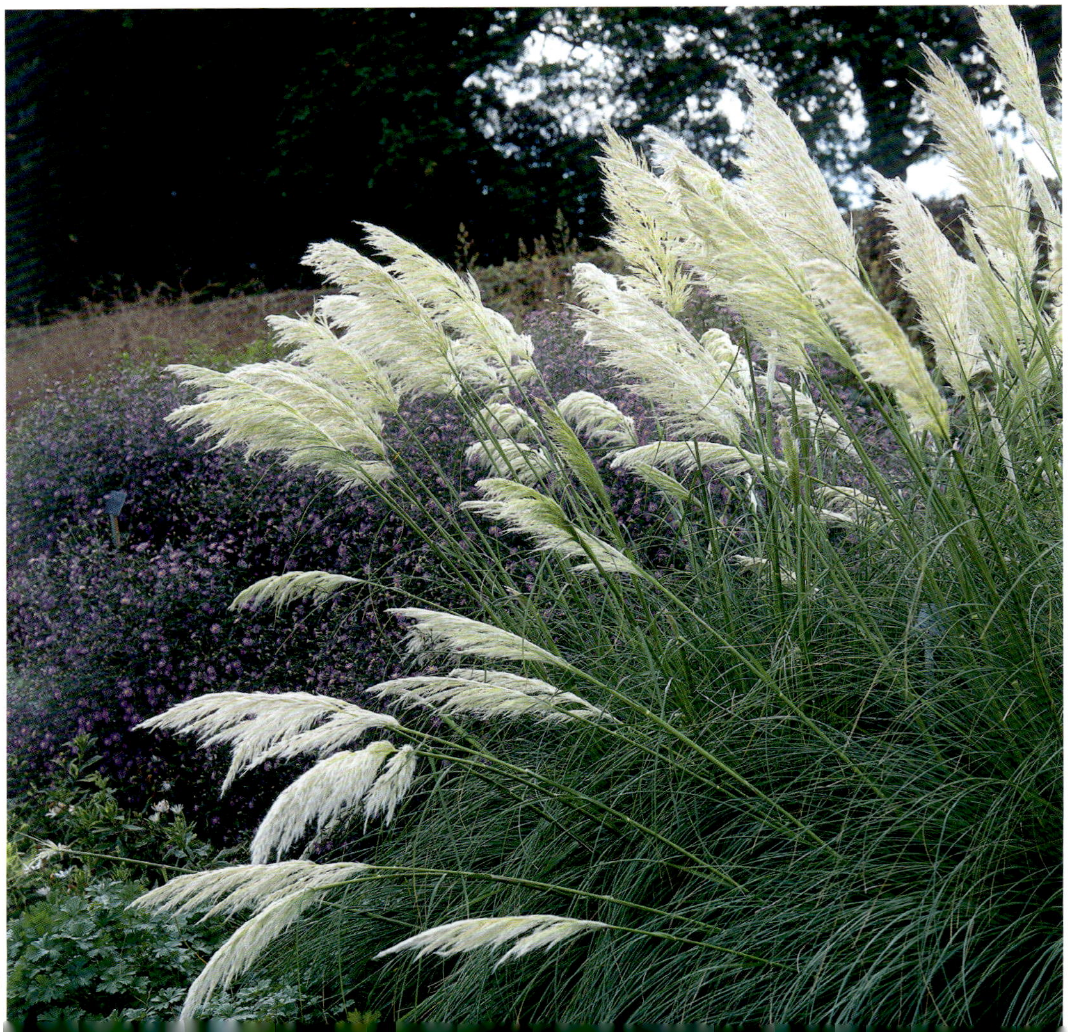

CHRYSOPOGON GRYLLUS

Scented grass

Height: 180cm, **width:** 80cm

Growth: clump-forming, fairly flat. The flower stems are much taller than the foliage.

Leaves: slender, grey-green.

Flowers: loose ears, overhanging; violet with yellow awns, from July to August. Good filigree effect when grouped together.

Location: sunny, prefers dry soils and needs a warm summer to bloom. Otherwise low-maintenance.

Use: as a solitary or accent plant in steppe and gravel beds.

CORTADERIA SELLOANA

Pampas grass

Height: 250cm, **width:** 200cm

Growth: clump-forming, with stiff flower stems.

Leaves: slender, dark-green, overhanging.

Flowers: remarkable white panicles that look like thick plumes, from September to October.

Location: sunny and warm, requires fresh, fertile but free-draining soil. Winter protection is needed in cold regions.
Use: as a solitary plant, the background of mixed borders, and also in pure grass borders with other tall grasses.
Recommended varieties: 'Sunningdale Silver' has loose silvery flower panicles with a generally more transparent appearance. The low-growing 'Pumila' reaches only 1.2 metres in height and grows in a more compact shape. 'Variegata' has green and white striped (variegated) leaves.

FESTUCA AMETHYSTINA
Tufted fescue
Height: 40–50cm, **width:** 30cm
Growth: clump-forming, almost semi-spherical, with wiry, lightly bending flower stems.
Leaves: very slender, blue-green, shimmering in many colours in autumn. Wintergreen.
Flowers: filigree, overhanging ears that become brightly coloured in the summer. Blooms June to July.
Location: sunny, needs free-draining, ideally dry, but never damp soil.
Use: in steppe and gravel beds, in small groups or singly as accent plants.

FESTUCA CINEREA
syn. *Festuca glauca*
Blue fescue
Height: 30cm, **width:** 20cm
Growth: semi-spherical, compact clumps.
Leaves: slender, blue-green, very fine.
Flowers: small flower panicles on thin, wiry stems above the foliage, from May to June.
Location: sunny, warm places, needs free-draining, soil with not too many nutrients.
Use: in steppe borders, in rock gardens, on tops of walls. Also works well as container planting. In general, the varieties with blue or silvery leaves are more sensitive to damp than those with green leaves.
Recommended varieties: 'Azurit' has especially pleasing blue foliage. 'Harz' has blue foliage with reddish tips. 'Silbersee' produces more compact and weaker silver-blue foliage. The clump-forming 'Blauglut' has deep-blue stems, which are strongly frosted.

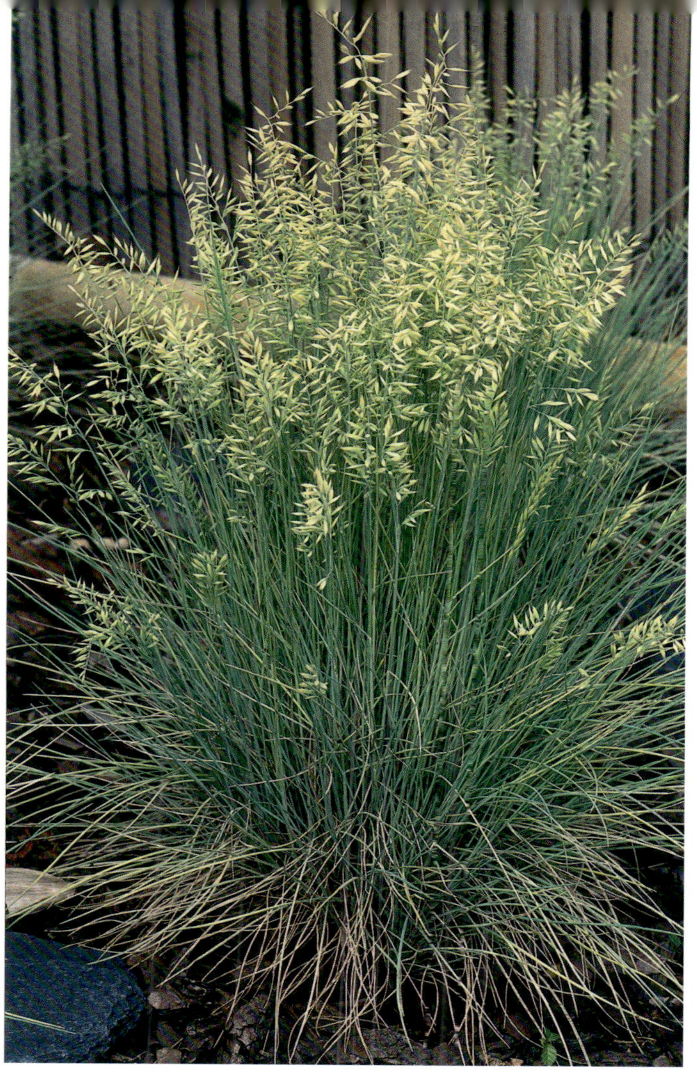

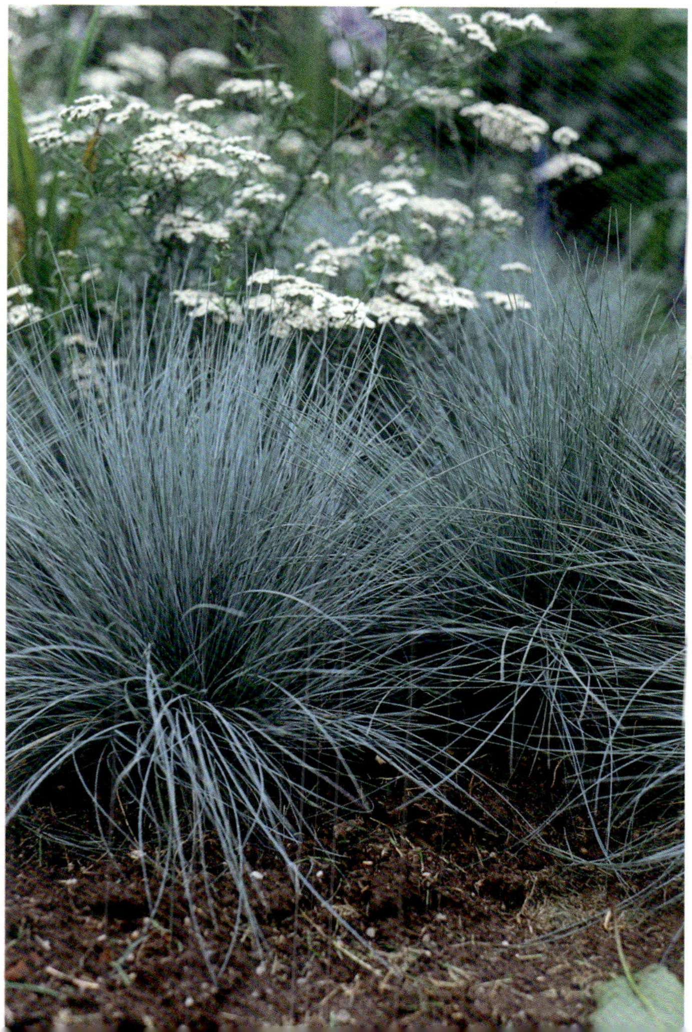

Cortaderia selloana 'Variegata' (above opposite)
The stripy leaves of this variety of pampas grass look white from a distance.

Cortaderia selloana 'Sunningdale Silver' (below opposite)
The flower panicles of this variety are looser and appear transparent.

Festuca cinerea 'Golden Toupee' (above left)
The leaf colouring of this variety of blue fescue is more green.

Festuca cinerea 'Blauglut' (below left)
The prickly pin cushion of the blue fescue is ideal for dry beds and planting areas.

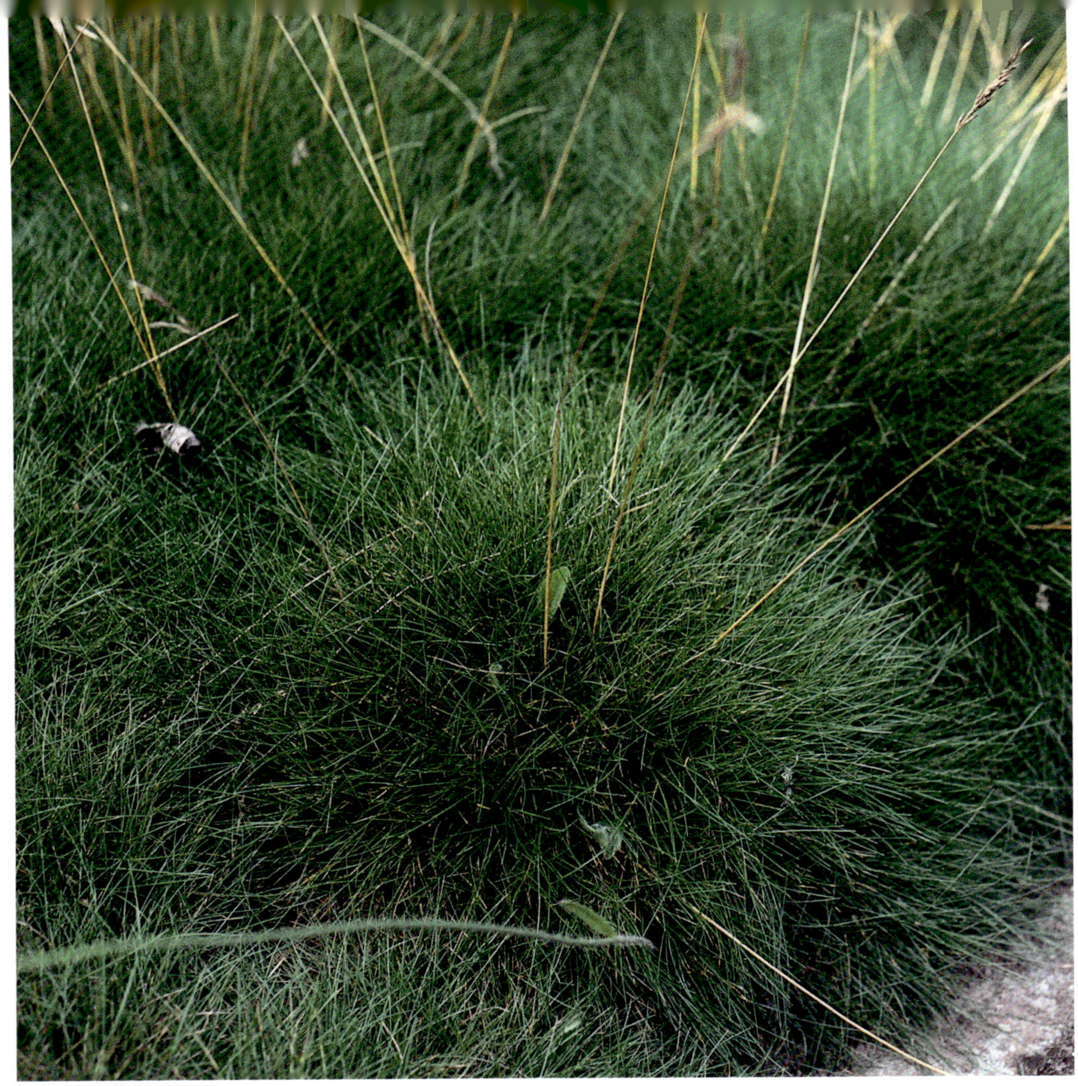

FESTUCA GAUTIERI

syn. ***Festuca scoparia***

Bearskin fescue

Height: 30cm, **width:** 40cm.

Growth: mound-forming to cushion-domed, compact.

Leaves: fresh green, very fine leaves, wintergreen.

Flowers: yellow-green, very fine panicles on thin, wiry stems, from June to July.

Location: sunny to light shade, needs free-draining, not too fertile soil. Protect from strong sunlight in winter.

Use: singly or in small groups, in heath or steppe borders, also effective as a container plant.

Recommended varieties: 'Pit Carlit' is even more compact and has somewhat darker leaves.

FESTUCA MAIREI

Atlas fescue

Height: 80-100cm, **width:** 80cm

Growth: clump-forming, very regular, almost semi-spherical.

Leaves: light-green, slender, elegantly overhanging.

Flowers: delicate panicles on thin, wiry stems. Stems turn yellow early, from June to July.

Location: sunny, grows on all fertile, not too damp soils, but flourishes best on free-draining loam soils.

Use: in shrub borders, singly or in groups. A good partner for roses.

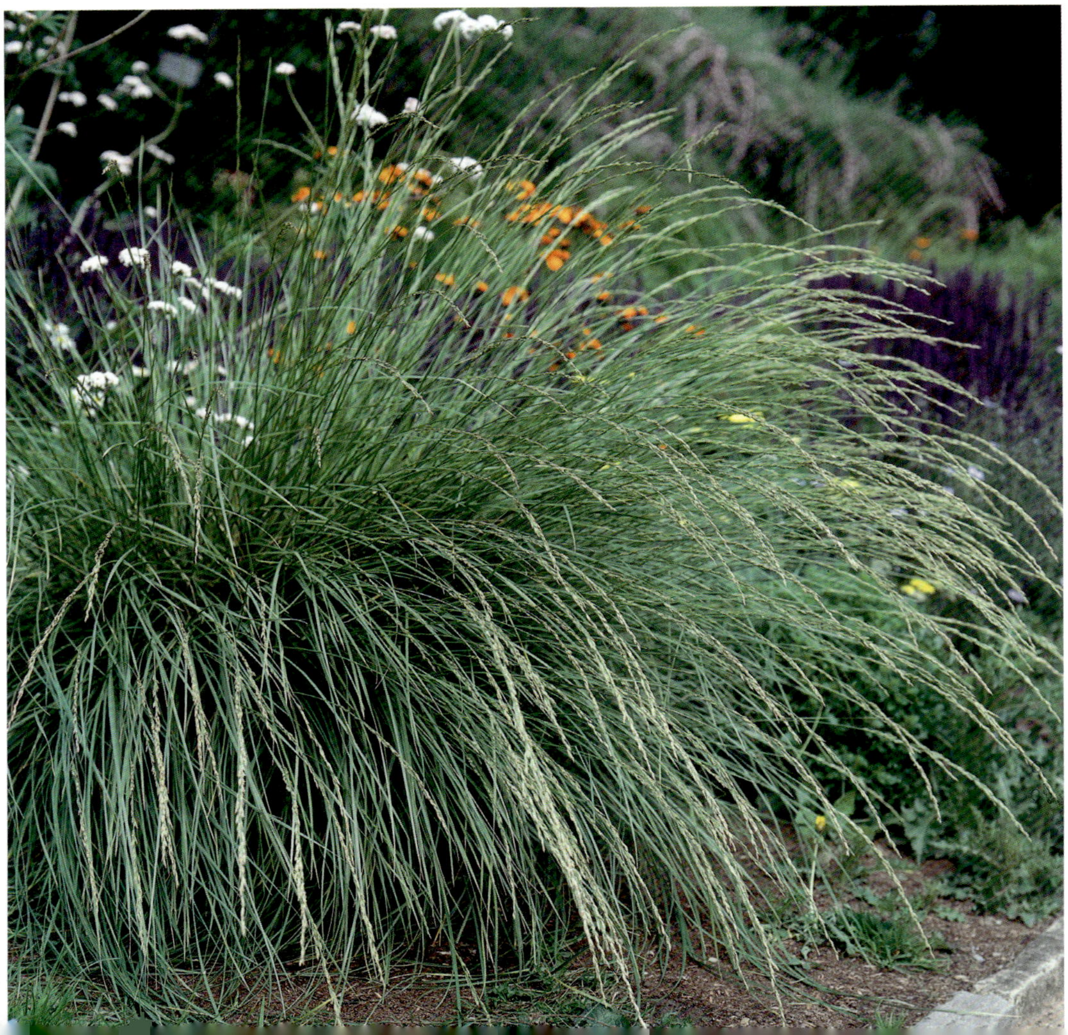

Festuca gautieri (top)
The bearskin fescue has characteristic thick green cushions.

Festuca mairei (bottom)
The atlas fescue is an ideal accompaniment to roses.

HELICTOTRICHON SEMPERVIRENS

Blue oat grass

Height: 120cm, **width:** 60cm

Growth: semi-spherical clump-forming.

Leaves: slender, blue-green, stiff. Wintergreen.

Flowers: yellow, arching, overhanging, delicate panicles on stiff stems. Blooms July to August.

Location: sunny, needs a warm location with free-draining soil poor in nutrients. Short-lived on damp soil.

Use: singly or in small groups, in steppe borders, on dry walls.

Recommended varieties: 'Saphirsprudel', or 'Sapphire Fountain', is an especially robust selection.

IMPERATA CYLINDRICA 'RUBRA'

syn. *Imperata* **Red 'Baron'**

Japanese blood grass or Cogon grass

Height: 40cm, **width:** 30cm

Growth: stiff upright, forming dense clumps.

Leaves: fresh green, turning a glowing red as early as the summer.

Flowers: does not flower in Europe.

Location: sunny, needs fresh, fertile soil, but a warm location. Winter protection is advisable.

Use: in shrub borders, singly or in small groups. A pleasing accent plant, also at sunny woodland edges.

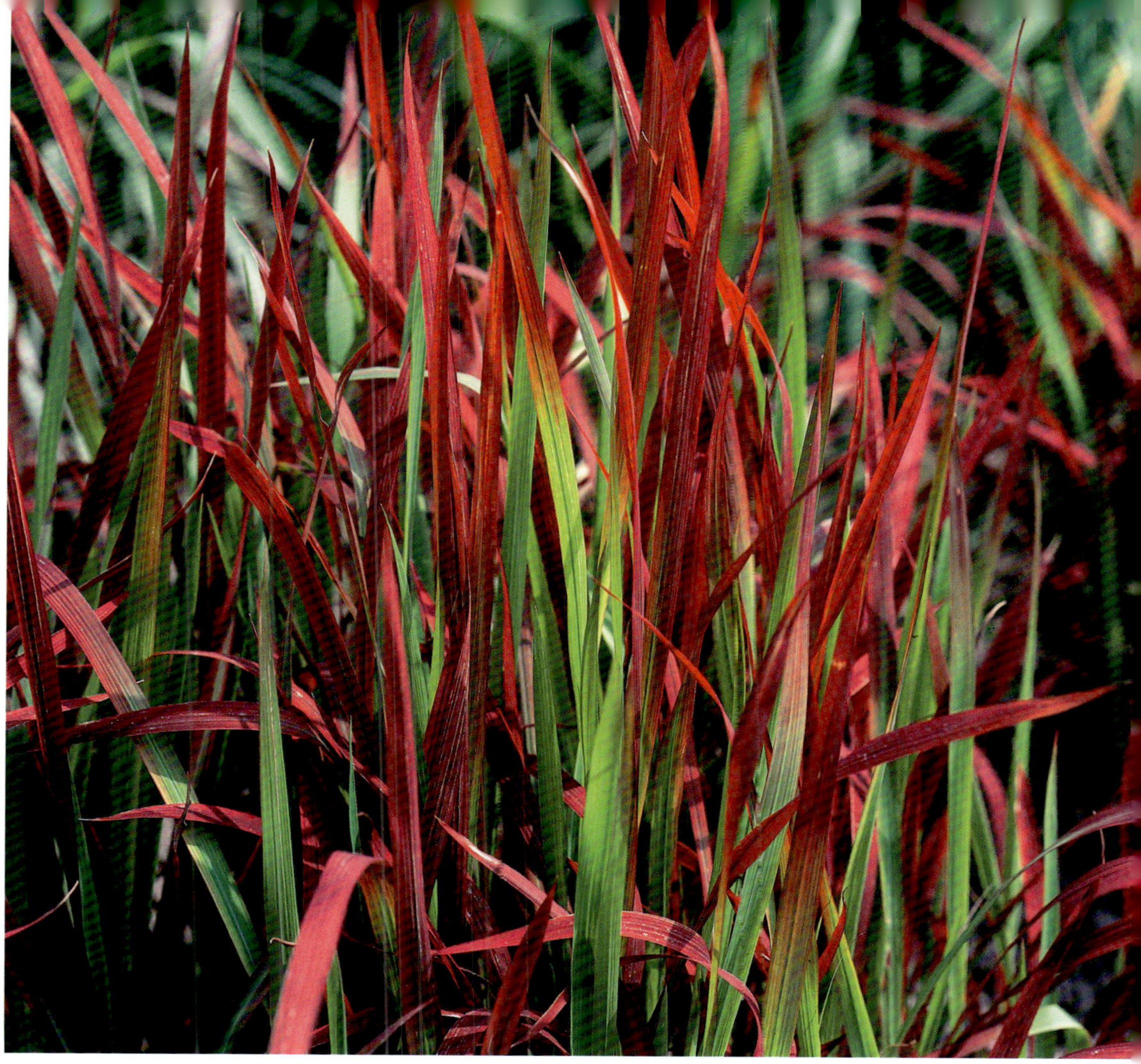

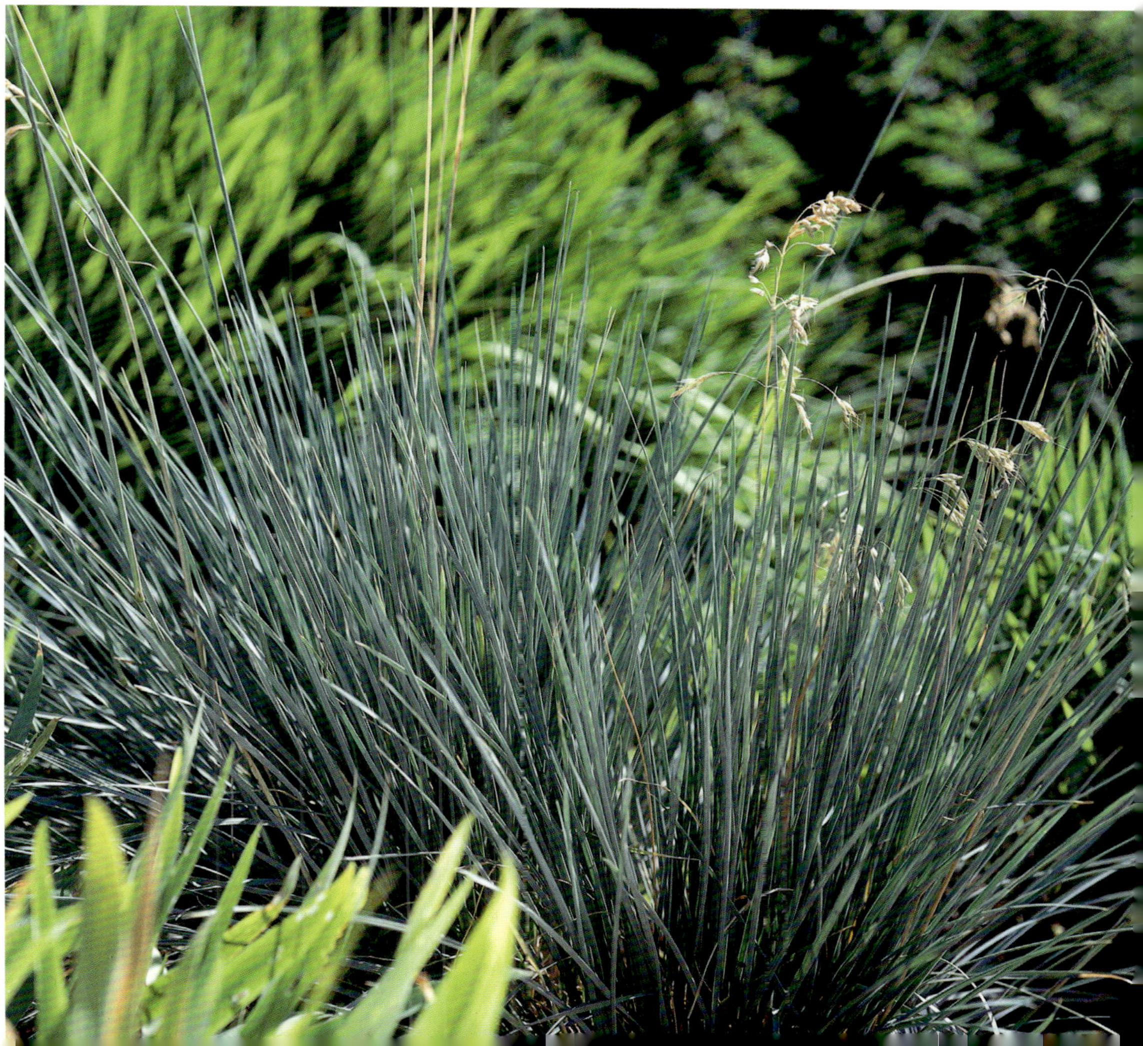

Imperata cylindrica 'Rubra' (top)

Very few grasses possess as intensive a leaf colouring as blood grass.

Helictotrichon sempervirens (bottom)

Blue oat grass is ideal for dry locations in the garden.

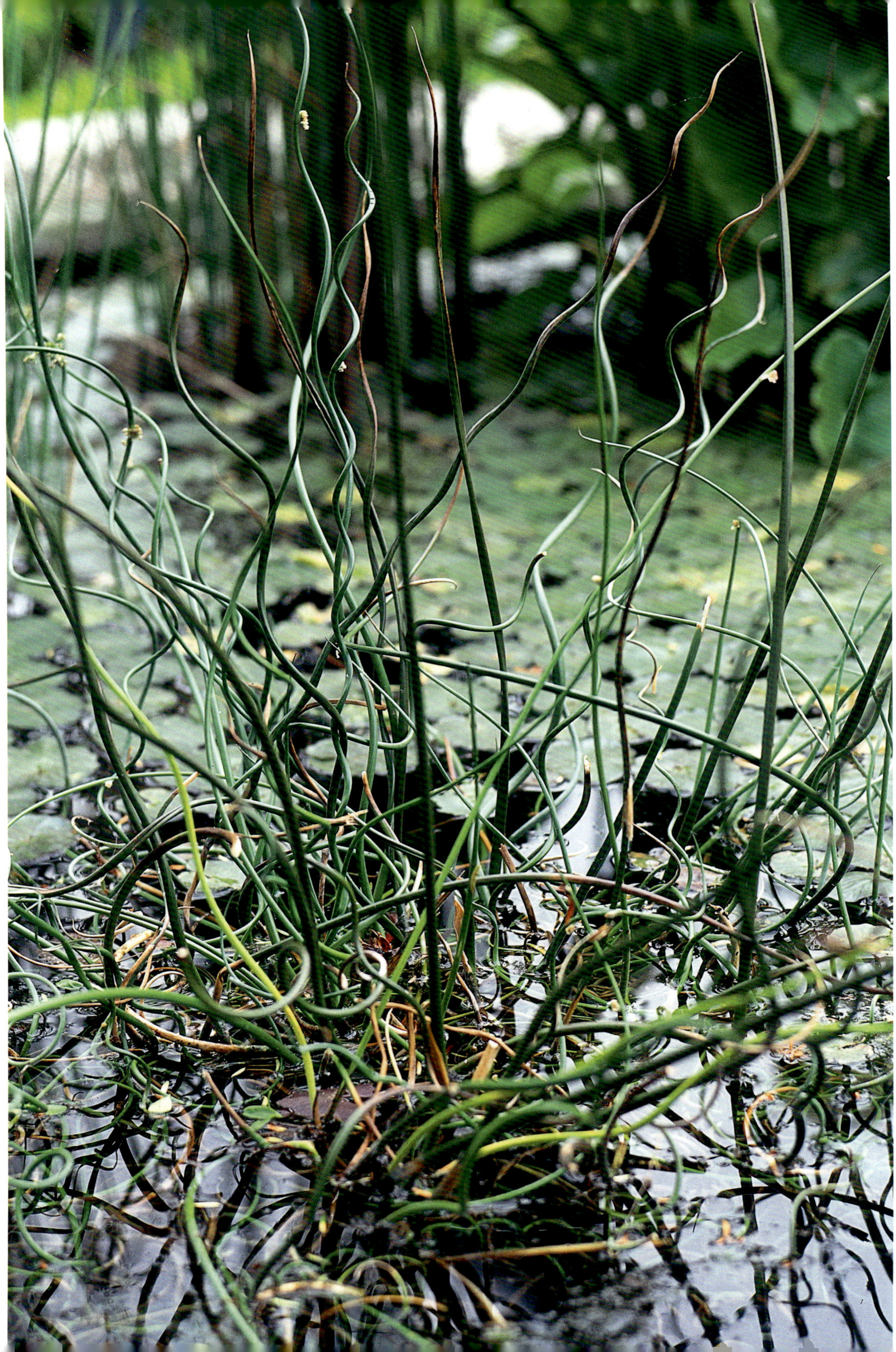

JUNCUS EFFUSUS

Soft rush or common rush

Height: 50cm, **width:** 80cm

Growth: clump-forming, firmly upright, spreads through runners. Wintergreen.

Leaves: slender, with a round cross section, light green.

Flowers: small brown spikes, growing sideways from the stem, from June to August.

Location: sunny, moist to damp, can also stand in water.

Use: singly or in groups, at the edge of ponds, can spread prolifically.

Recommended varieties: 'Spiralis' is a curious variety with corkscrew-shaped stems and a loose growth habit.

LEYMUS ARENARIUS

Sea lime grass or blue grass

Height: 100cm, **width:** 80–100cm

Growth: powerful clumps, quickly establishes itself through runners.

Leaves: broad, spiky blue-green that roll together in extreme dry spells.

Flowers: slender spikes reminiscent of wheat, from July to August.

Location: a native grass of sand dunes – its creeping roots contribute significantly to coastal protection.

Use: can only be kept under control in larger gardens. For sunny and warm locations – ideally on sandy soil. Containers. In combination with other coastal plants such as Oleaster *(Elaeagnus)*, rugosa rose *(Rosa rugosa)* and also sea holly *(Eryngium maritimum)*.

MELICA ALTISSIMA

Siberian melic grass

Height: 100cm, **width:** 60cm

Growth: loose clumps.

Leaves: slender, dull green, bending and overhanging.

Flowers: loose spikes on inclined stems. Black seeds, from May to June.

Location: sunny to half shade, flourishes on any not too moist soil.

Use: in borders, as accent plants singly or in small groups.

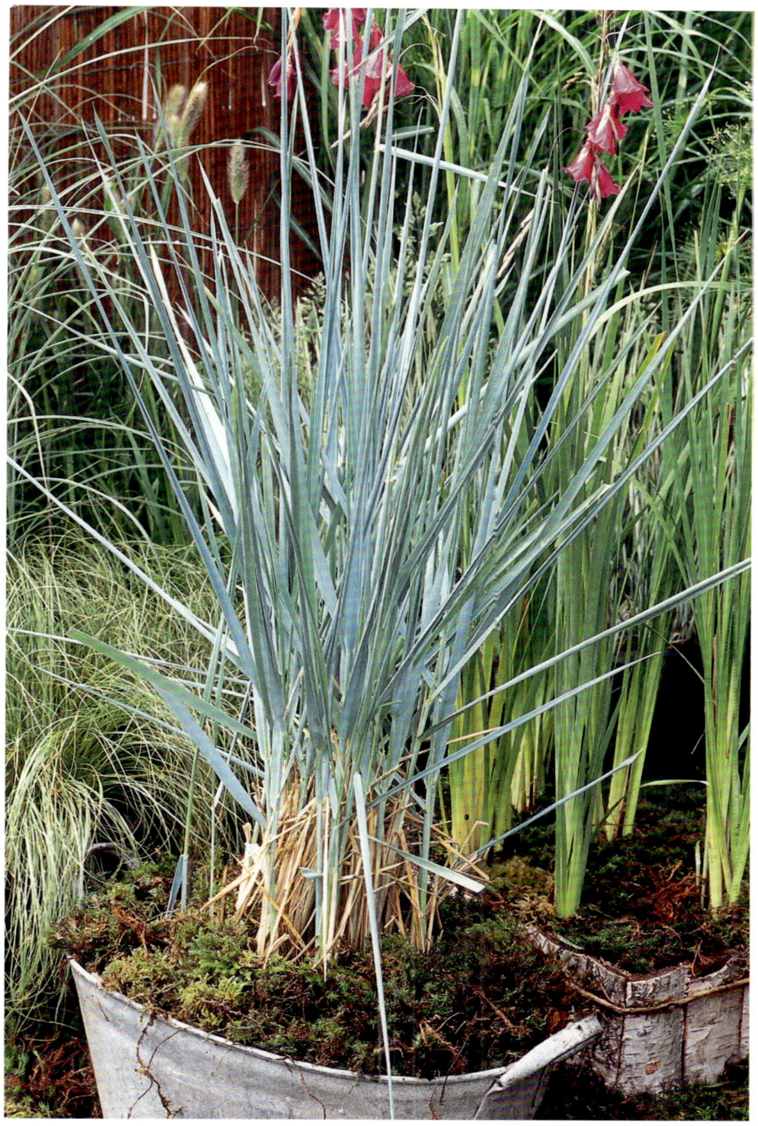

Leymus arenarius (left)
Sea lime grass is suitable for containers and has steel-blue stems.

Juncus effusus 'Spiralis' (opposite)
The corkscrew rush is a variant of the soft rush.

Recommended varieties: 'Atropurpurea' has purple-coloured flower spikes.

MELICIA CILIATA

Hairy melic or silky spike melic

Height: 60cm, **width:** 40cm

Growth: loose, overhanging clumps.

Leaves: slender, grey-green, stiff upright.

Flowers: thick, cylindrical spikes on wiry stems, from May to June. Turn pale-yellow after blooming, and are long-lasting and decorative.

Location: sunny, warm and sheltered. Prefers dry, chalky soil. In heavy ground weak growing and short-lived.

Use: in steppe borders and larger rock gardens, also grown amongst heather.

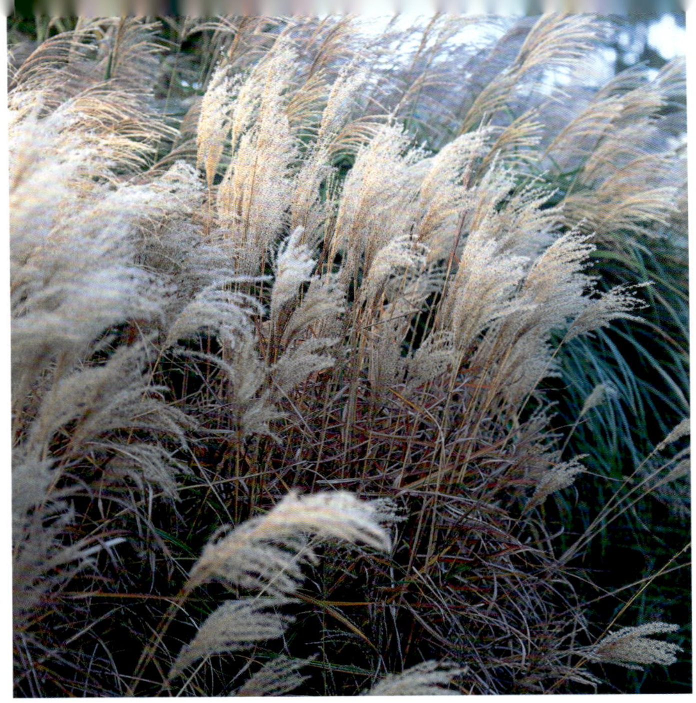

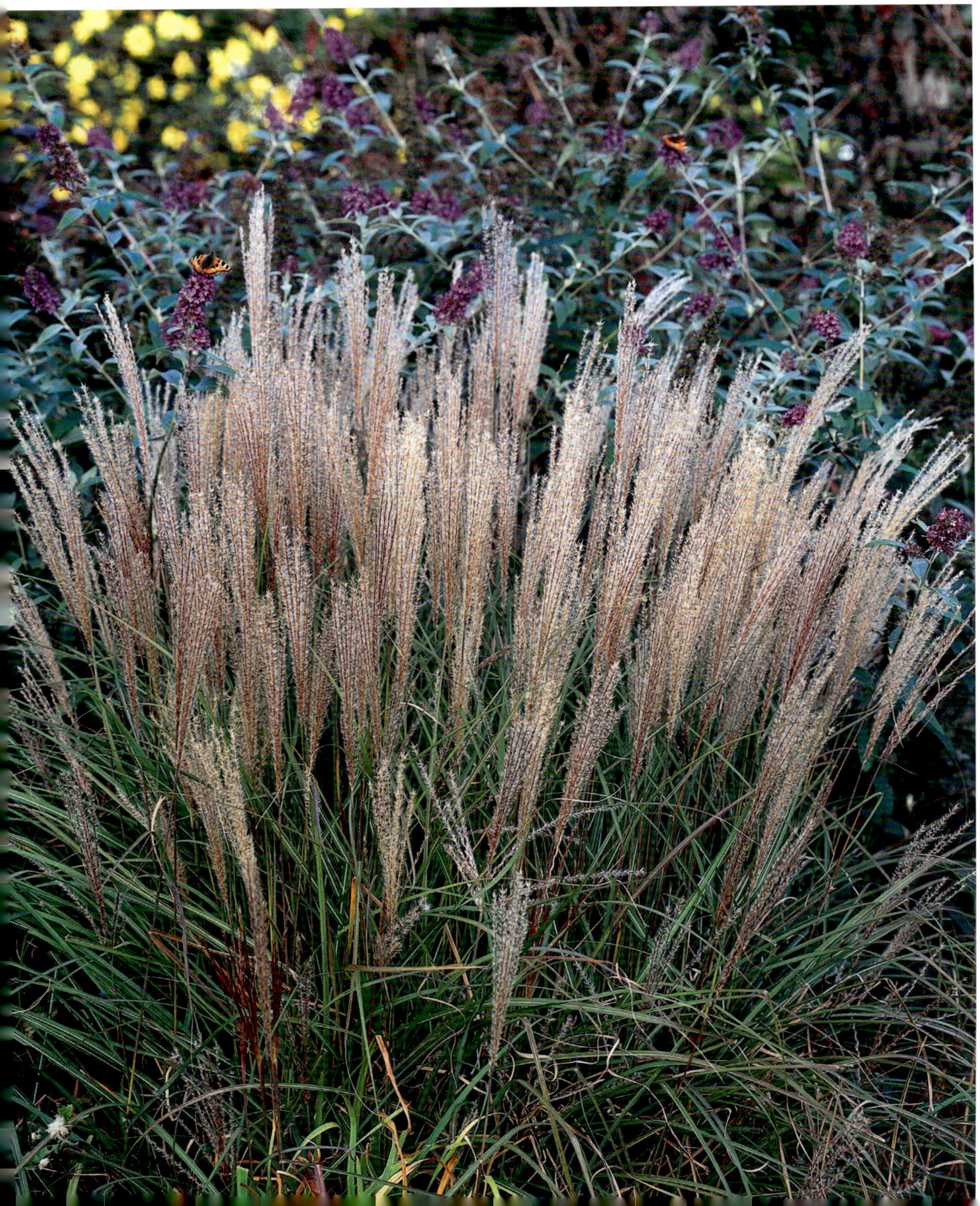

MISCANTHUS SINENSIS

Chinese silver grass

Height: 150–300cm, depending on the variety, **width:** 150–200cm

Growth: forms powerful clumps and spreads widely through short runners.

Leaves: broad spiky, fresh green, elegantly overhangng. Turn yellow in autumn – some varieties also have red autumn colouring.

Flowers: feathery panicles, at first upright and spreading, then bending and overhanging, from August to October. Silver-white, often also reddish. Very graceful and long-lasting.

Location: sunny, prefers strong, fresh, fertile soil.

Use: as a solitary plant or in groups, as background planting in beds, in front of trees and also at the edge of ponds. A spectacular giant grass that is also an important provider of structure in winter.

Recommended varieties: from a wide palette the following are especially recommended: 'China' by Ernst Pagels, which grows 180cm high and has large flower heads. The slender olive-green leaves turn red in autumn. 'Gnom', a new variety, grows only to 120cm. 'Graziella' is also relatively low-growing at 150cm and flowers particularly early. 'Flamingo' is one of Ernst Pagel's best varieties. It has light-pink flowers and has a pinkish-red autumn colouring. 'Giraffe' reaches a height of 250cm, the leaves are striped yellow-green. 'Kaskade' has a pleasing overhanging growth habit and has large flower panicles. 'Malepartus' is an old but outstanding variety with magnificent autumn colouring. 'Nishidake' grows 250cm high, but has a transparent appearance. Very sturdy!

Miscanthus sinensis 'Nippon' (top)
The flower panicles of the 'Nippon' variety are more upright than the many other sorts of Chinese silver grass.

Miscanthus sinensis 'Kleine Silberspinne' (bottom)
This variety is part of the legacy of the shrub breeder Ernst Pagel.

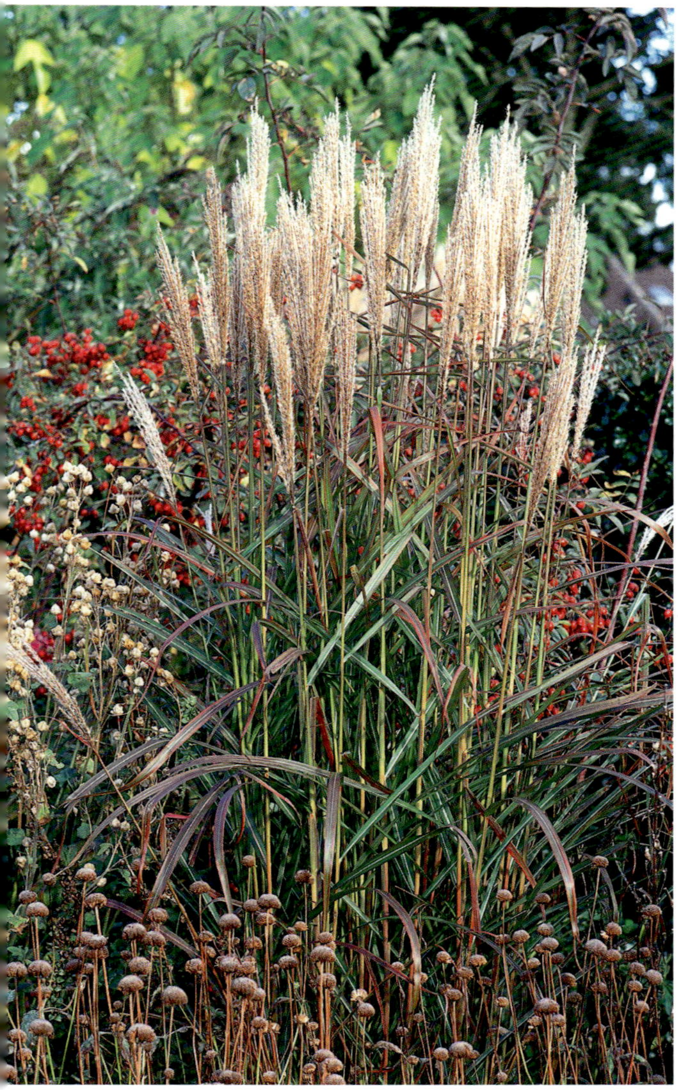

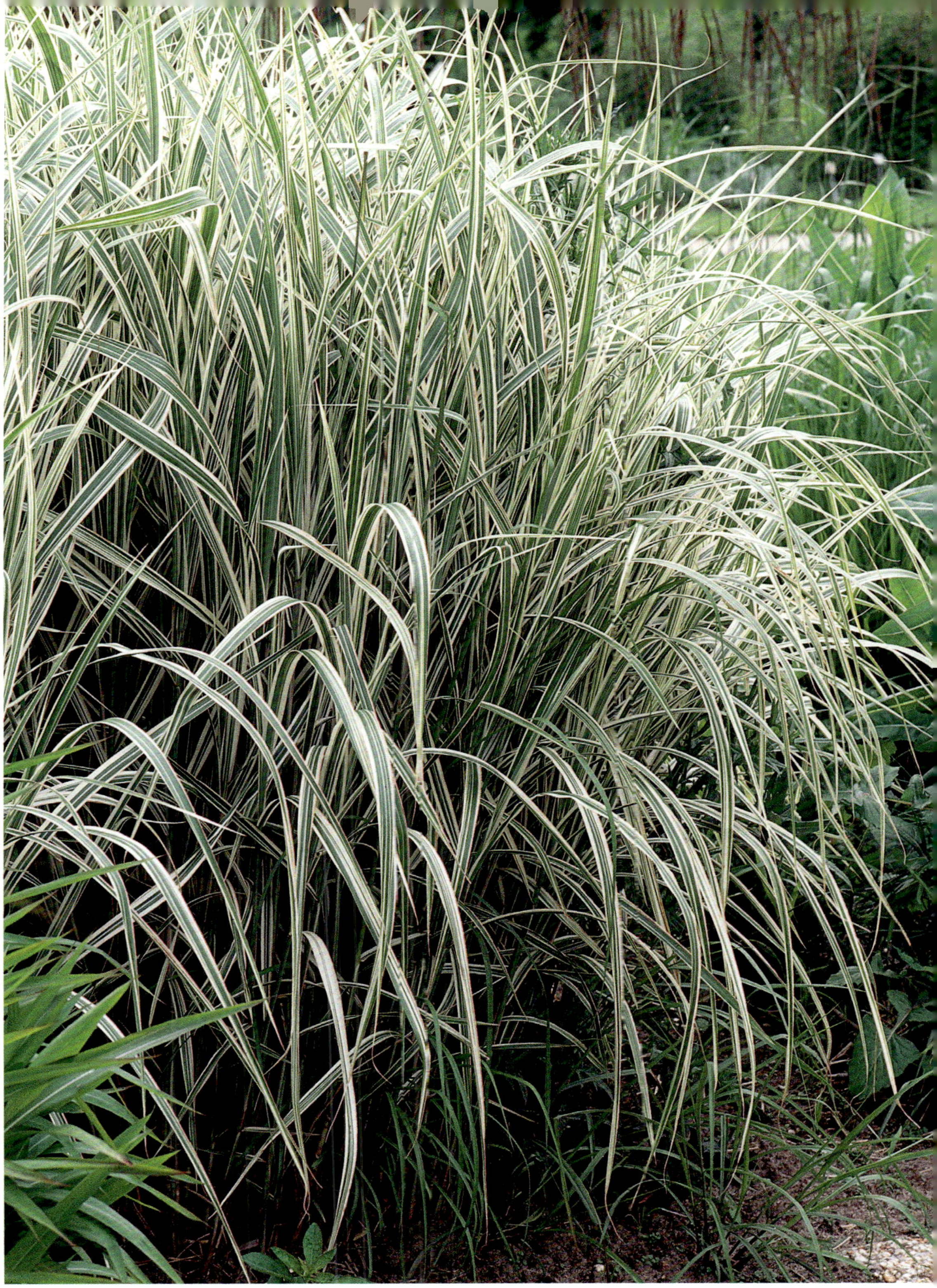

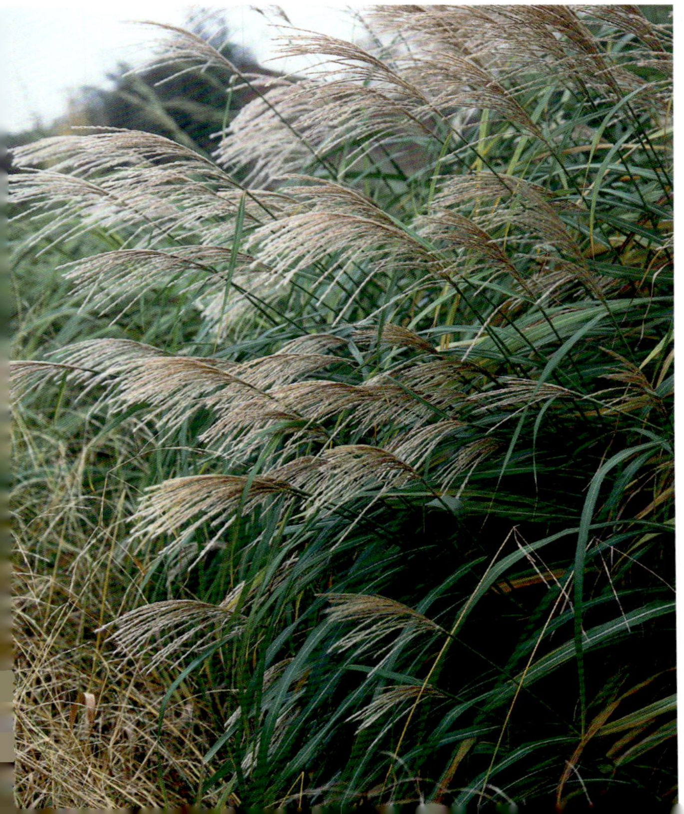

Miscanthus sinensis 'Roter Pfeil' (above left)
The reddish-tinged leaves and stems are typical of this variety.

Miscanthus sinensis 'Variegatus' (above right)
In contrast to 'Strictus' (see p. 107) the leaves of 'Variegatus' are striped lengthwise.

Miscanthus sinensis 'Silberfeder' (left)
Elegant flower panicles are characteristic of the 'Silberfeder'.

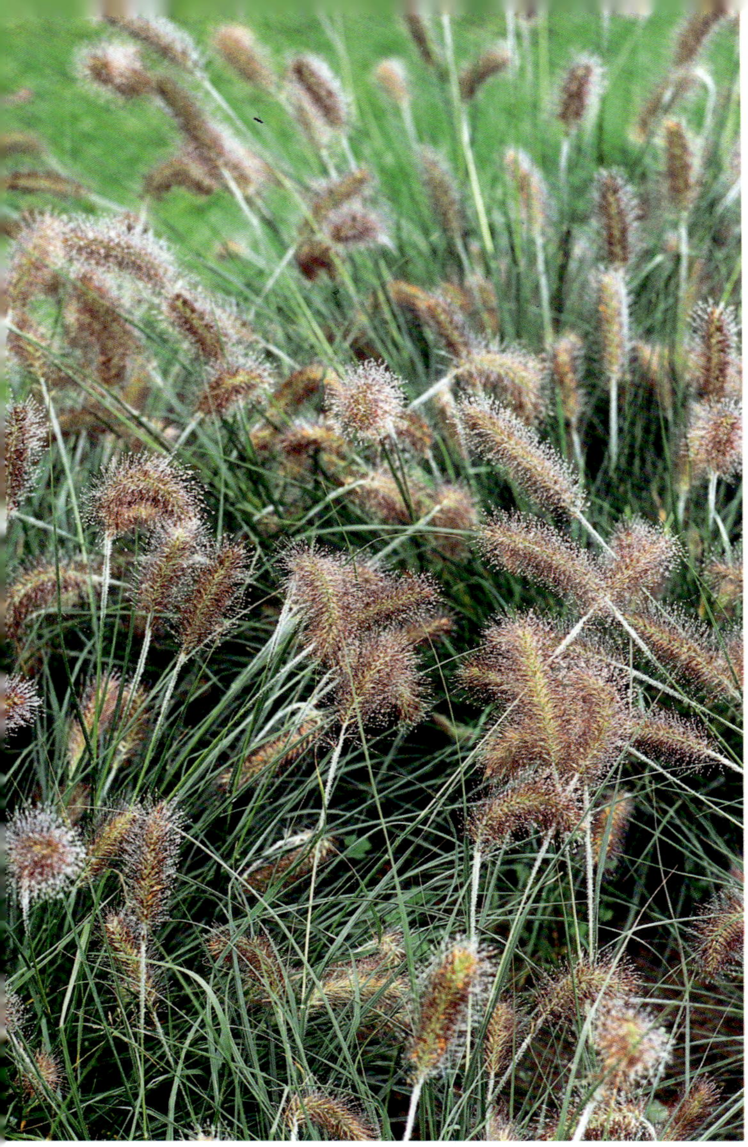

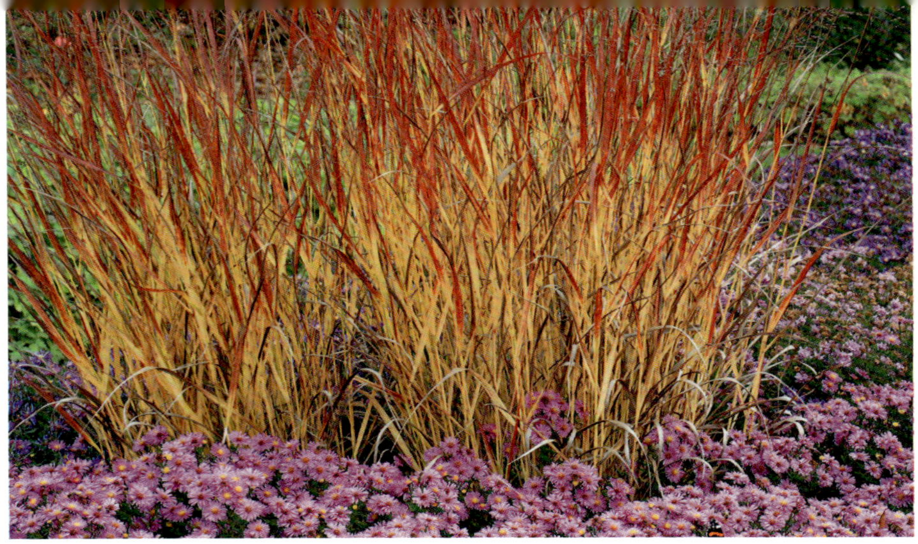

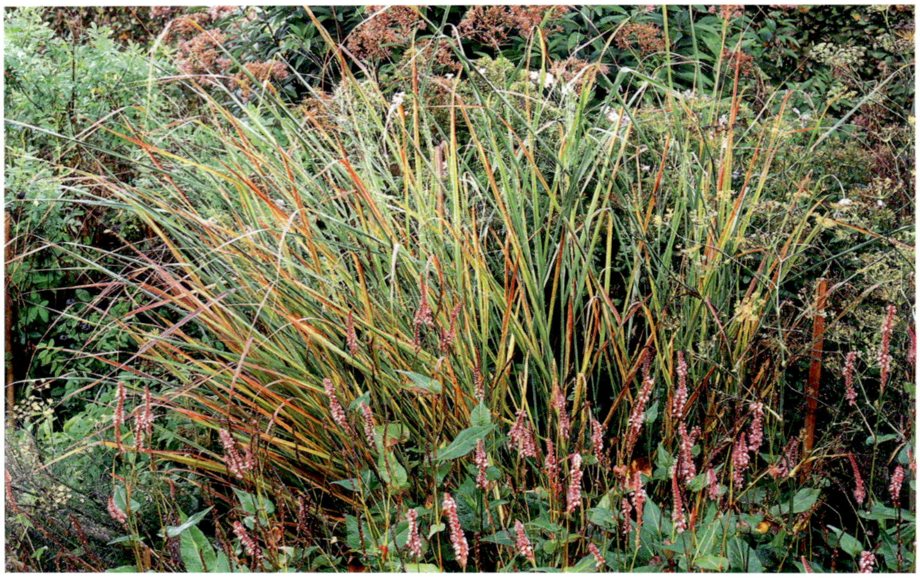

Pennisetum alopecuroides 'Weserbergland' (left)
This variety is one of the lowest-growing of the fountain grasses.

Panicum virgatum 'Hänse Herms' (right, top)
Switchgrass has some of the finest late-summer colouring of all the grasses.

Panicum virgatum 'Cloud Nine' (right, bottom)
The leaf colouring on this variety appears in lengthwise stripes.

NASSELLA TENUISSIMA

syn. *Stipa tenuissima*
Mexican feathergrass
Height: 60cm, **width:** 60cm
Growth: dense, upright clumps.
Leaves: upright, very slender, turn to a pale, almost white, straw-yellow in late summer.
Flowers: arching, silky flower heads, with a structure a bit like hair, from May to June.
Location: sunny, prefers warm locations with free-draining soil. Needs winter protection in cold regions.
Use: in sunny borders, gravel beds and steppe planting schemes. Also attractive in large groups. Suitable for container planting. The filigree, feathery flower heads are quite eye-catching in the border. As it spreads only modestly, Mexican feathergrass is well suited to dense borders and as an accompaniment to roses.

PANICUM VIRGATUM

Switchgrass
Height: 100cm, **width:** 50cm
Growth: upright, thick clumps, fan-shaped.
Leaves: slender, tapering, tips slightly overhanging. Red colouring in late summer. Late sprouting.
Flowers: filigree spikes, dangling above the foliage, from August to September.
Location: sunny, prefers free-draining, reasonably fertile soil, otherwise grows weakly.
Use: in beds and borders, between autumn-flowering shrubs. Works singly or in small groups.
Recommended varieties: 'Hänse Herms', with glowing brown-red autumn colouring. 'Heavy Metal' is significantly taller at 150cm, blue-green foliage, barely any autumn colouring. 'Shenandoah' has the most magnificent autumn colouring and has red leaf tips even when sprouting. 'Strictum' grows straight upright and turns a glowing yellow in autumn.

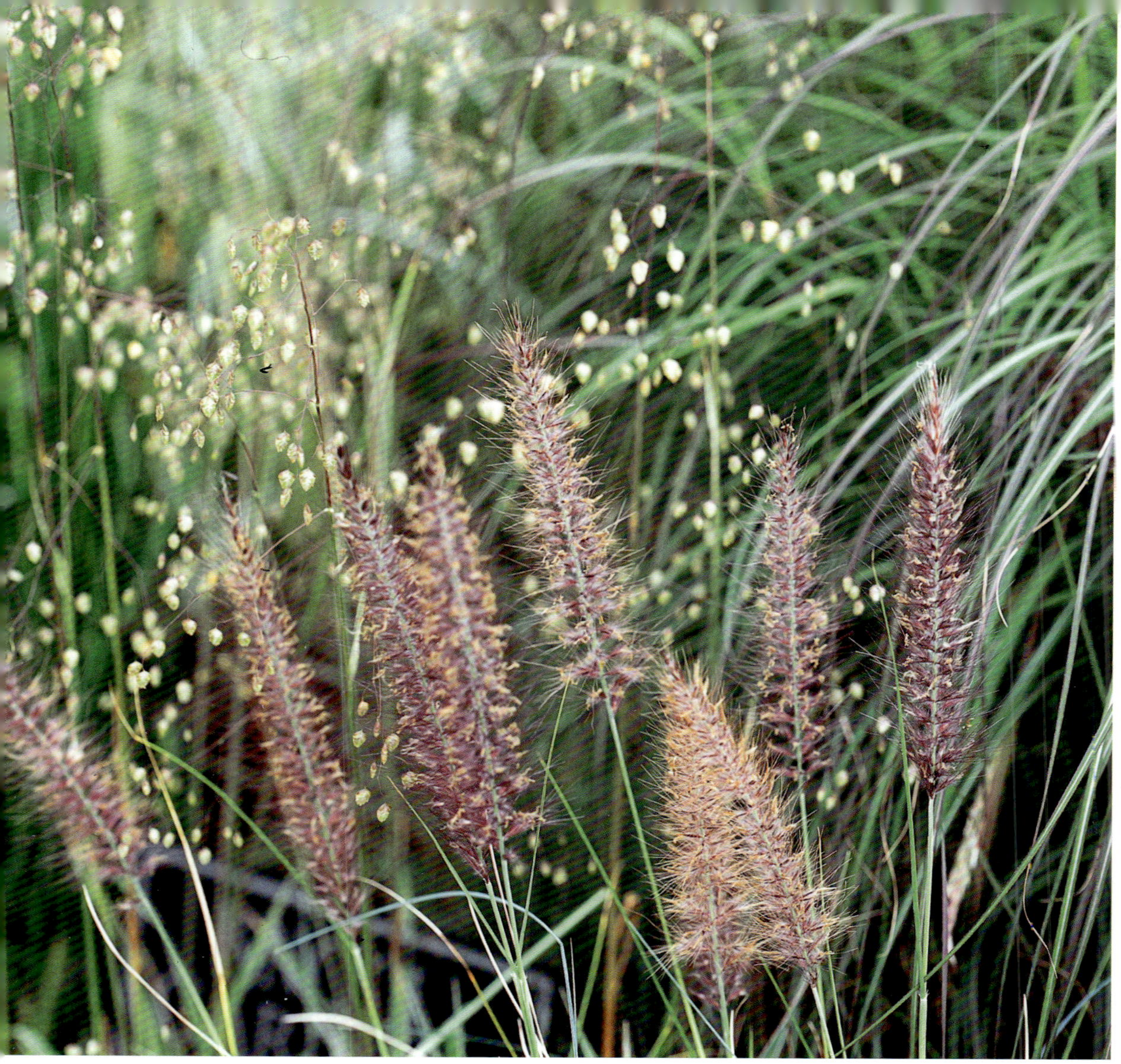

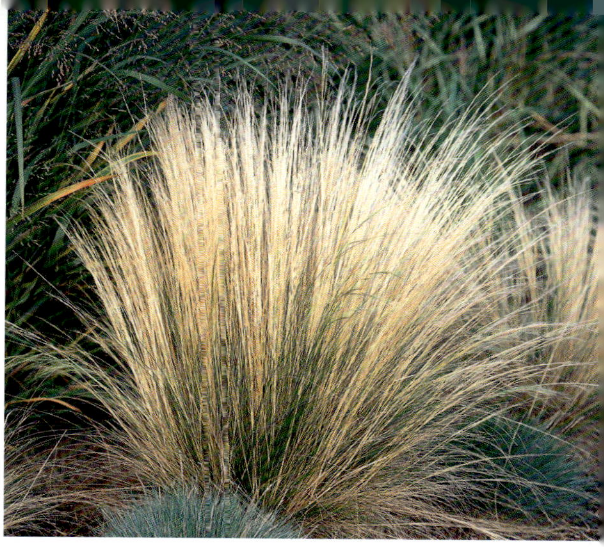

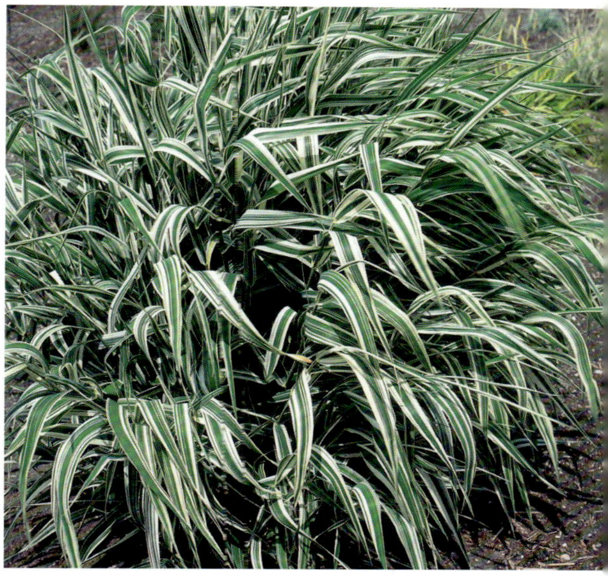

Pennisetum alopecuroides var. *viridescens* (left)

The flower panicles of this variety of fountain grass are especially long and intensively coloured.

Nasella tenuissima (right, top)

Mexican feather grass is indispensable in dry locations.

Phalaris arundinacea 'Picta' (right, bottom)

The white variegated form of reed canary has lengthwise striped foliage reminiscent of bamboo leaves.

PENNISETUM ALOPECUROIDES

Fountain grass

Height: 80cm, **width:** 70cm

Growth: dense clumps, spherical, overhanging, very regular.

Leaves: dark-green, slender, leaning over. Late sprouting, yellow autumn colouring.

Flowers: cylindrical spikes on the ends of the stems evoke bottlebrushes, from September to October.

Location: sunny, prefers free-draining but fertile soil, which should not be allowed to dry out.

Use: in beds and borders, singly or in small groups, also beautiful at sunny woodland edges.

Recommended varieties: 'Hameln' distinguishes itself from the species by its more compact growth, and it blooms somewhat earlier. *Pennisetum alopecuroides* var. *viridescens* has darker foliage and especially pleasing dark and thick spikes. This variety can be propagated from seed.

PHALARIS ARUNDINACEA

Reed canary grass

Height: 120cm, **width:** 80cm

Growth: stiff upright, spreads through rhizome runners.

Leaves: slender, stiff, the upper third kinked.

Flowers: slender panicles, unremarkable, from June to July.

Location: sunny to half-shade, prefers loamy, fresh to moist soil. In dry weather the leaves quickly show signs of damage.

Use: in natural-looking planting schemes in combination with shrubs that can hold their own, on the banks of large ponds.

Recommended varieties: 'Picta' is a white variegated, frequently planted form, which proliferates just like the rest of the species. 'Freesy's Form' is even more vividly marked and does not proliferate quite as profusely.

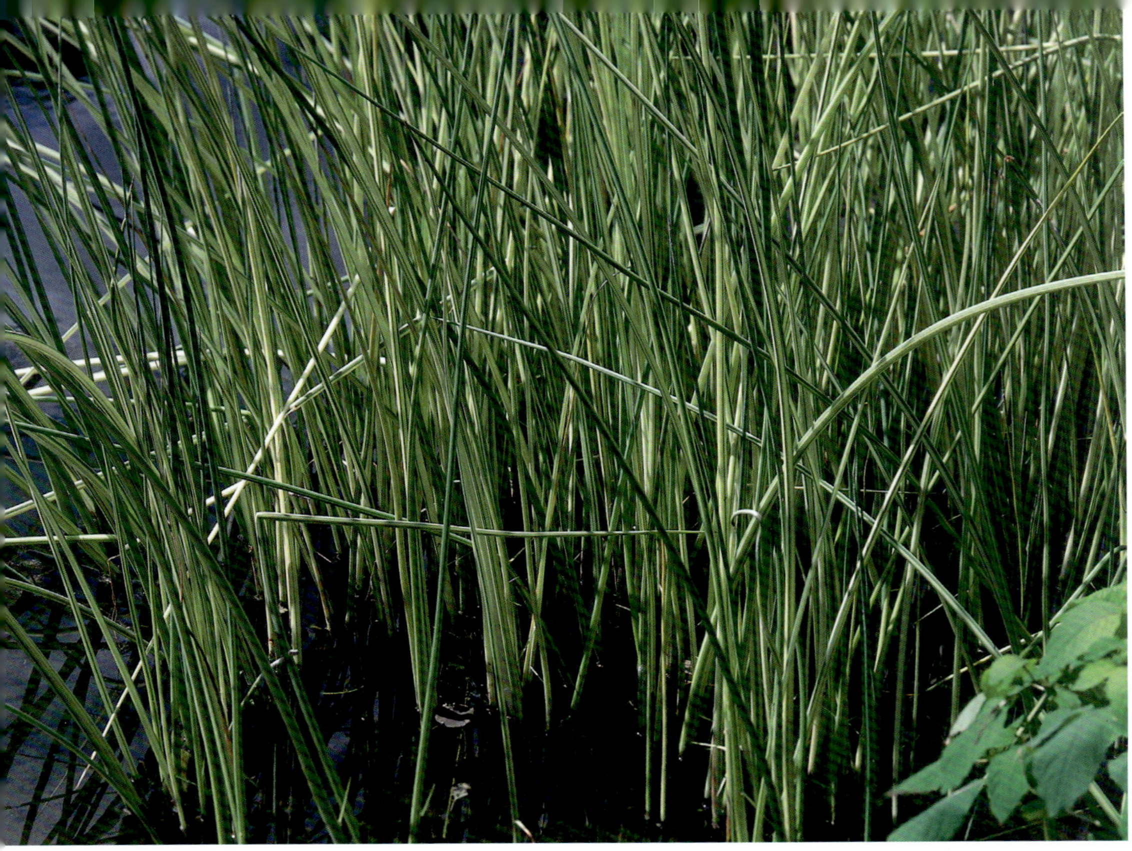

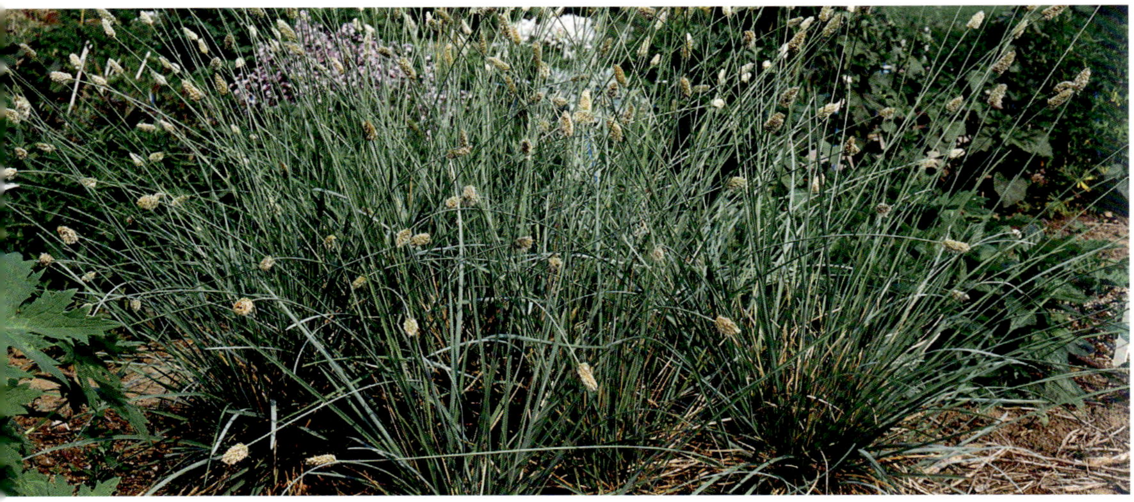

Schoenoplectus lacustris 'Albescens' (top)
The bulrush is one of the stock plants used in planting at the edges of ponds and in the marsh zone.

Sesleria nitida (bottom)
Nest moor grass is suitable for moorland beds and hedging.

SCHOENOPLECTUS LACUSTRIS

Common club rush or bulrush

Height: 100cm, **width:** 70cm
Growth: clump-forming, spreads rapidly through runners.
Leaves: leafless, with round stems becoming smaller towards the top.
Flowers: tufts with brown spikes growing directly out of the stem, from June to September.
Location: sunny, moist to damp soil, and can also stand in water.
Use: without a root barrier only next to large natural areas of water; otherwise in containers, which can also be submerged in the pond.
Recommended varieties: 'Albescens' has cross-stripes, white-green stems, though unfortunately it is as prolific as the rest of the species. Quite similar is the *Scirpus tabernaemontani* 'Zebrinus', with its green-white cross-striped stems, which is somewhat less rampant, but which nonetheless is suited only to larger areas of water or garden ponds.

SCHIZACHYRIUM SCOPARIUM

Little bluestem or beard grass

Height: 120cm, **width:** 50cm
Growth: erect and upright, dense clumps. The common name is misleading: the grass is not little but quite tall-growing.
Leaves: slender, blue-green, with pleasing red-brown autumn colouring.
Flowers: slender panicles, which turn from red-brown to silver, from August to October.
Location: sunny, prefers reasonably dry to fresh soil high in nutrients.
Use: as specimen and structural plants in borders, in combination with autumn-flowering shrubs.

SESLERIA NITIDA

Nest moor grass

Height: 40-80cm, **width:** 50cm
Growth: clump-forming, half-rounded, very regular.
Leaves: slender, silver-grey, somewhat stiff.
Flowers: white-grey thick spikes on partially leaved stems, from April to May.
Location: sunny, prefers mineral-rich, fresh to moist soil.
Use: at the edge of moorland borders, as hedging.

SORGHASTRUM NUTANS

Indiangrass

Height: 120-150cm, **width:** 50cm
Growth: erect, upright, slender clumps.
Leaves: slender, grey-green, erect and upright, late sprouting.
Flowers: feathery red-brown, lush panicles with golden stamens, blooms August to October.
Location: sunny, flourishes on any not too dry soil. Generally low maintenance.
Use: as an accent plant in beds and borders, in combination with autumn-flowering shrubs, attractive in steppe planting schemes.

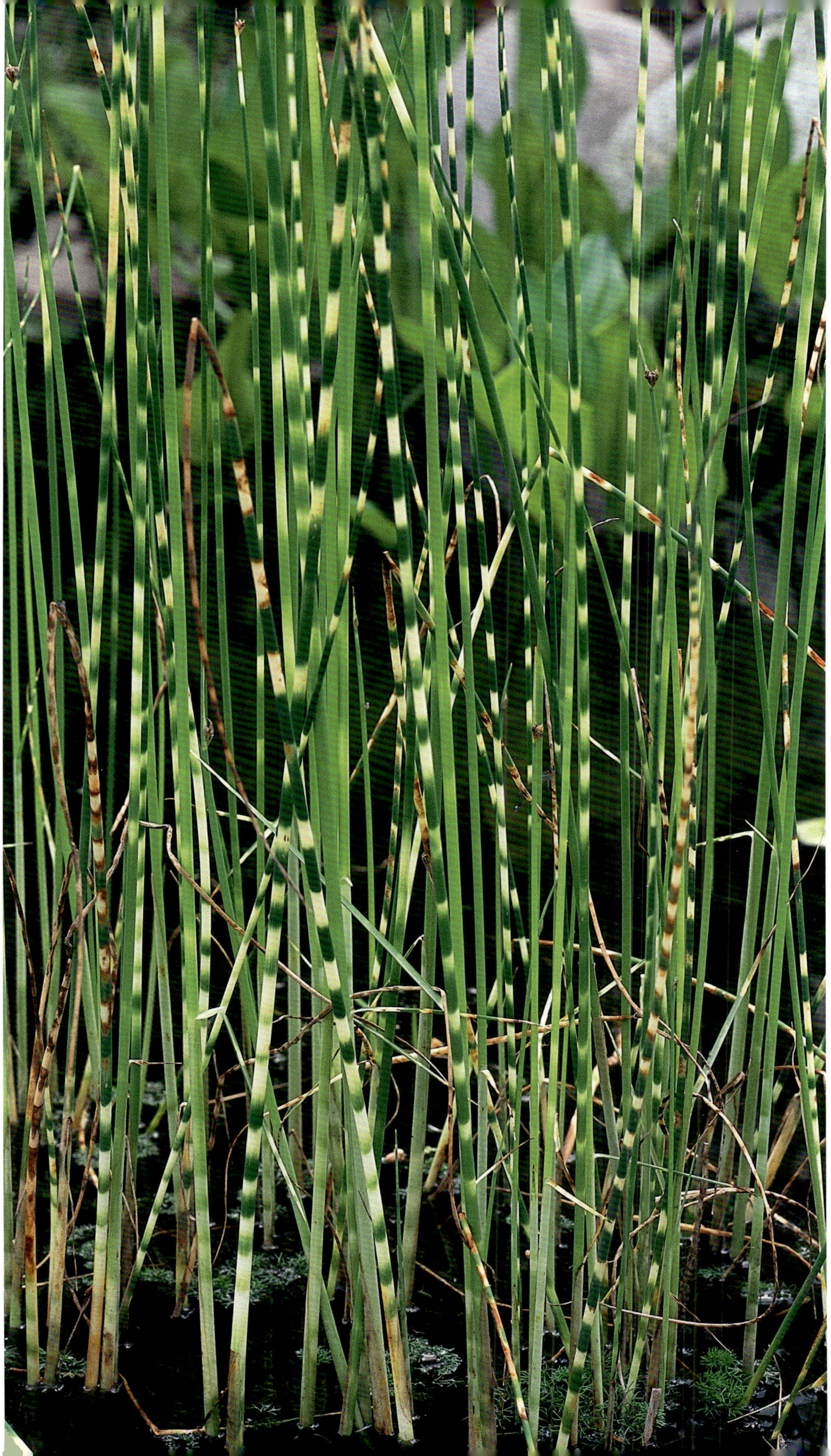

Schoenoplectus tabernaemontani 'Zebrinus'
The zebra rush has green and white cross-striped leaves.

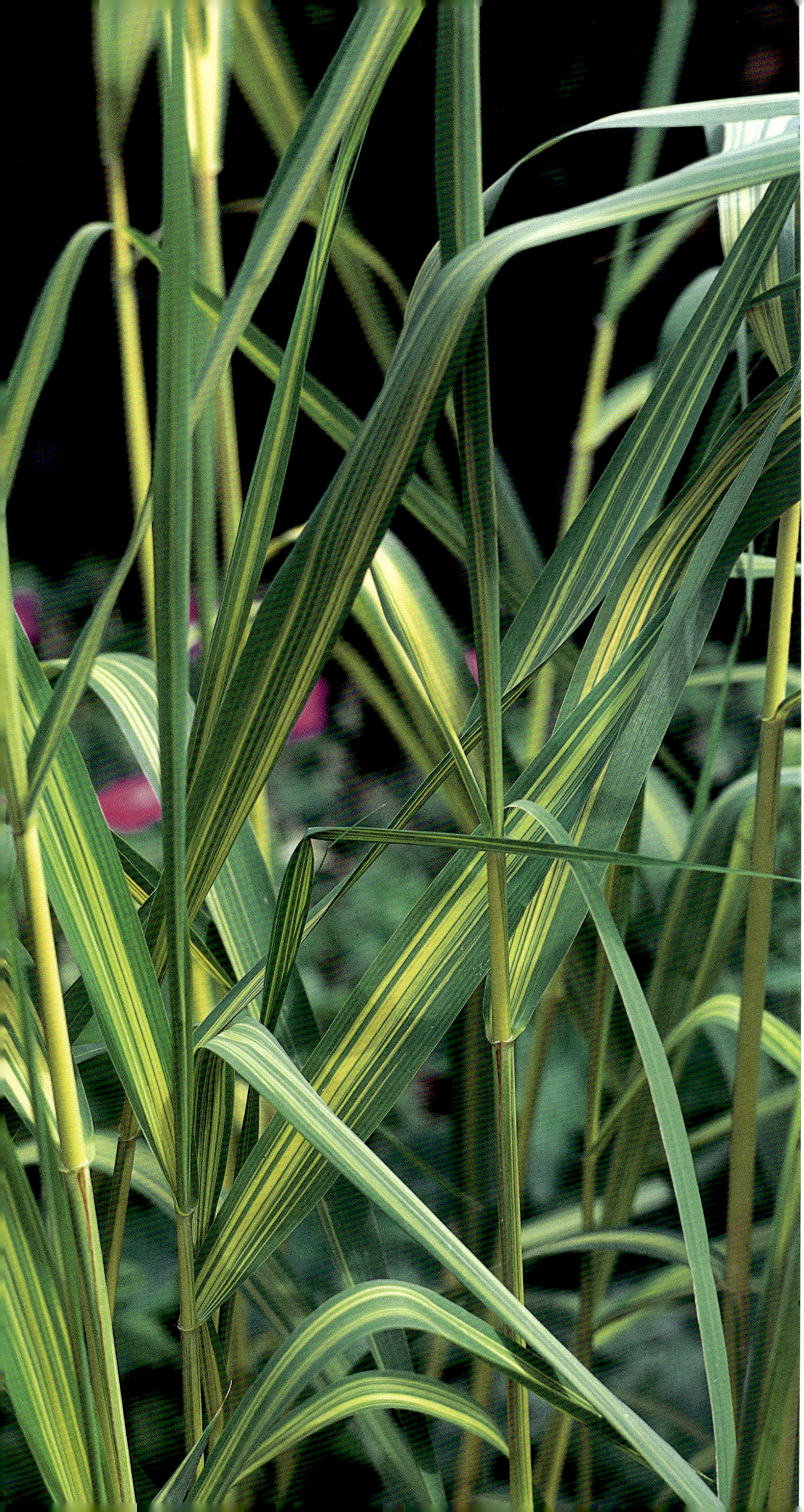

SPARTINA PECTINATA 'AUREOMARGINATA'
Gold-edged prairie cordgrass
Height: 150cm, **width:** 100cm
Growth: upright, with overhanging foliage. Spreads gradually through short runners.
Leaves: slender, pale-green with yellow stripes, elegantly inclined. Glowing yellow autumn colouring.
Flowers: August to September. Thick spikes, unremarkable.
Location: sunny to half shade, but does not flourish at all on dry soil.
Use: at edges of ponds, also in borders with moist soil, at sunny woodland edges.

STIPA CALAMAGROSTIS
Feather grass or pheasant grass
Height: 70-90cm, **width:** 80cm
Growth: dense, bushy clumps with inclining leaves.
Leaves: slender, grey-green, overhanging.
Flowers: silvery feathery panicles, elegantly overhanging, from June to September.
Location: sunny, prefers reasonably dry to fresh soil, chalk-loving, weak growing on heavy soil.
Use: singly or in groups in sunny beds, steppe borders. Well suited to natural-looking planting schemes.
Recommended varieties: 'Algäu' has an erect, upright growth habit and very beautiful flower panicles. 'Lemperg' is more compact and is very a prolific bloomer, with red autumn colouring.

STIPA CAPILLATA
Bridal veil
Height: 60-80cm, **width:** 50cm
Growth: erect, upright, fan-shaped near the top.
Leaves: very slender, hair-thin, dark-green.
Flowers: erect, upright flower panicles with thread-like awns, from July to September.
Location: sunny, requires a free-draining, preferably dry soil, chalk-loving.
Use: in steppe planting schemes, gravel beds, also suitable for containers. Seeds itself in favourable spots and becomes extensive, without, however, becoming a problem.

STIPA GIGANTEA

Giant feather grass or golden oats

Height: 200cm, **width:** 50cm

Growth: loose clumps with erect, upright tall flower stems.

Leaves: blue-green, slender, overhanging, wintergreen.

Flowers: loose panicles, reminiscent of oats, from June to August. On strong stems high above the foliage.

Location: sunny and warm, prefers free-draining soil not too rich in nutrients.

Use: in steppe borders, sunny beds, gravel beds. Combines beautifully with silver-leafed shrubs. Needs winter protection, especially from winter damp.

STIPA PULCHERRIMA SSP. NUDICOSTA

Height: 80–100cm, **width:** 50cm

Growth: upright with elegantly inclined stalk tips.

Leaves: very slender, hair-thin, grey-green.

Flowers: fine panicles with very long awns.

Location: sunny, requires free-draining, nutrient-poor soil, otherwise short-lived. Seeds itself frequently.

Use: in steppe borders, gravel beds, singly or in groups.

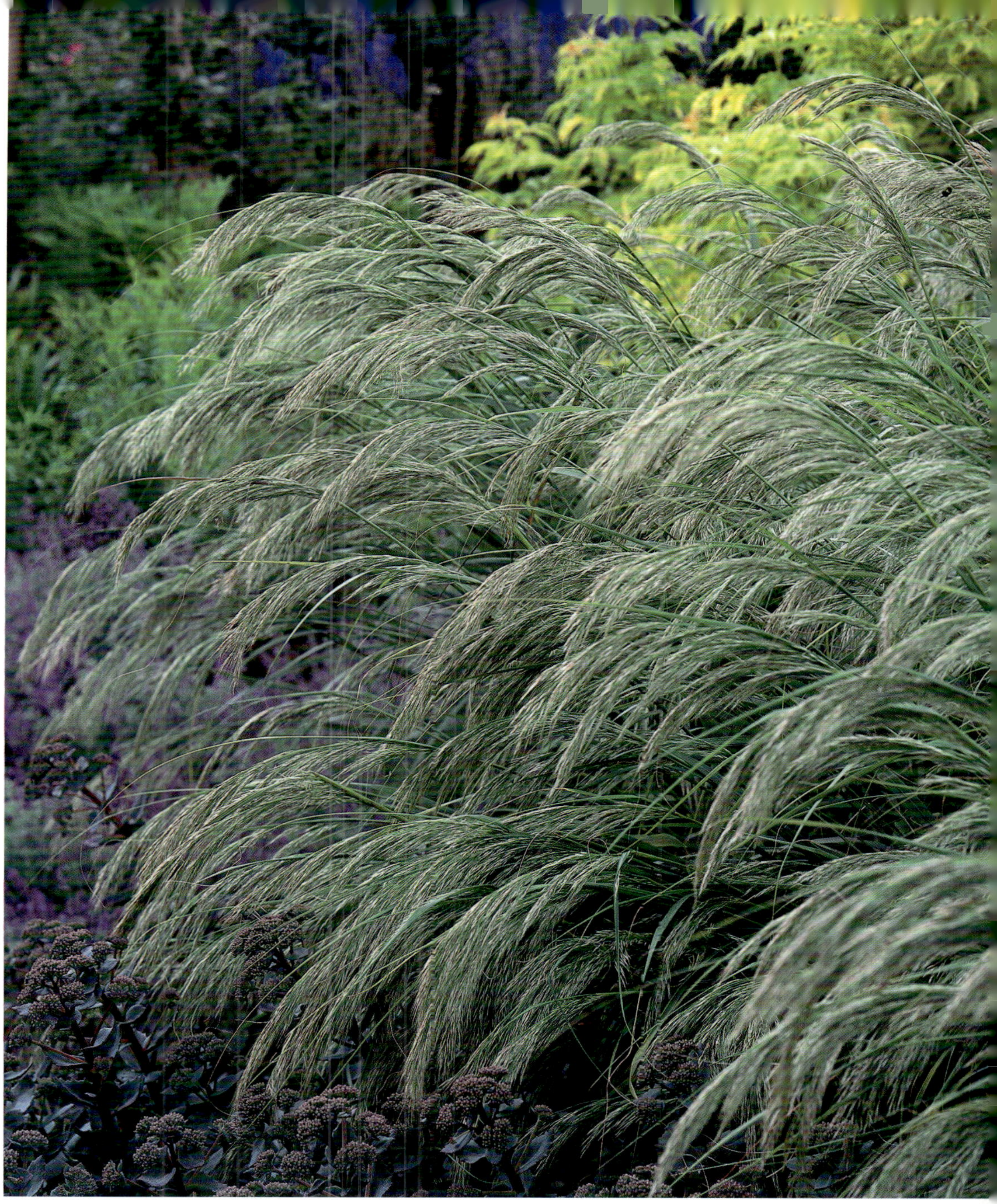

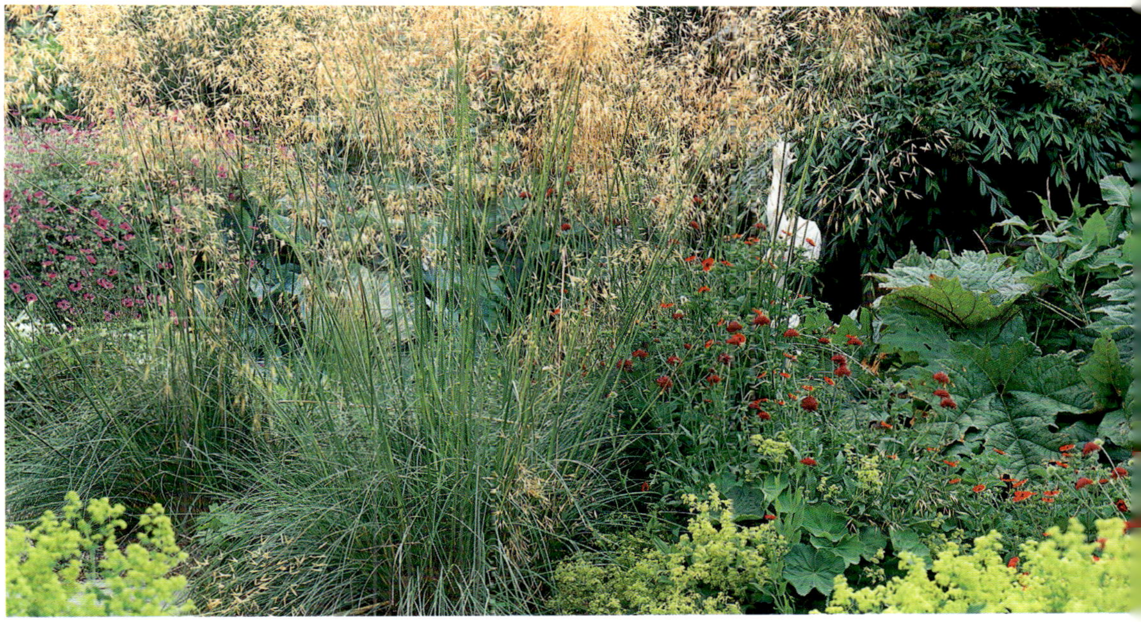

Stipa calamagrostis (top right)

Feather grass thrives on chalky soils and has elegantly overhanging panicles.

Stipa gigantea (bottom right)

With a height of 2 metres, the giant feather grass certainly lives up to its name.

Spartina pectinata 'Aureomarginata' (opposite)

Gold-edged prairie cordgrass makes an interesting substitute for reeds on a not too dry soil.

Half-shade

Half-shaded locations in the garden spend the majority of the day in shade or are in the light shade of trees. They should, however, receive around four to five hours of sun a day.

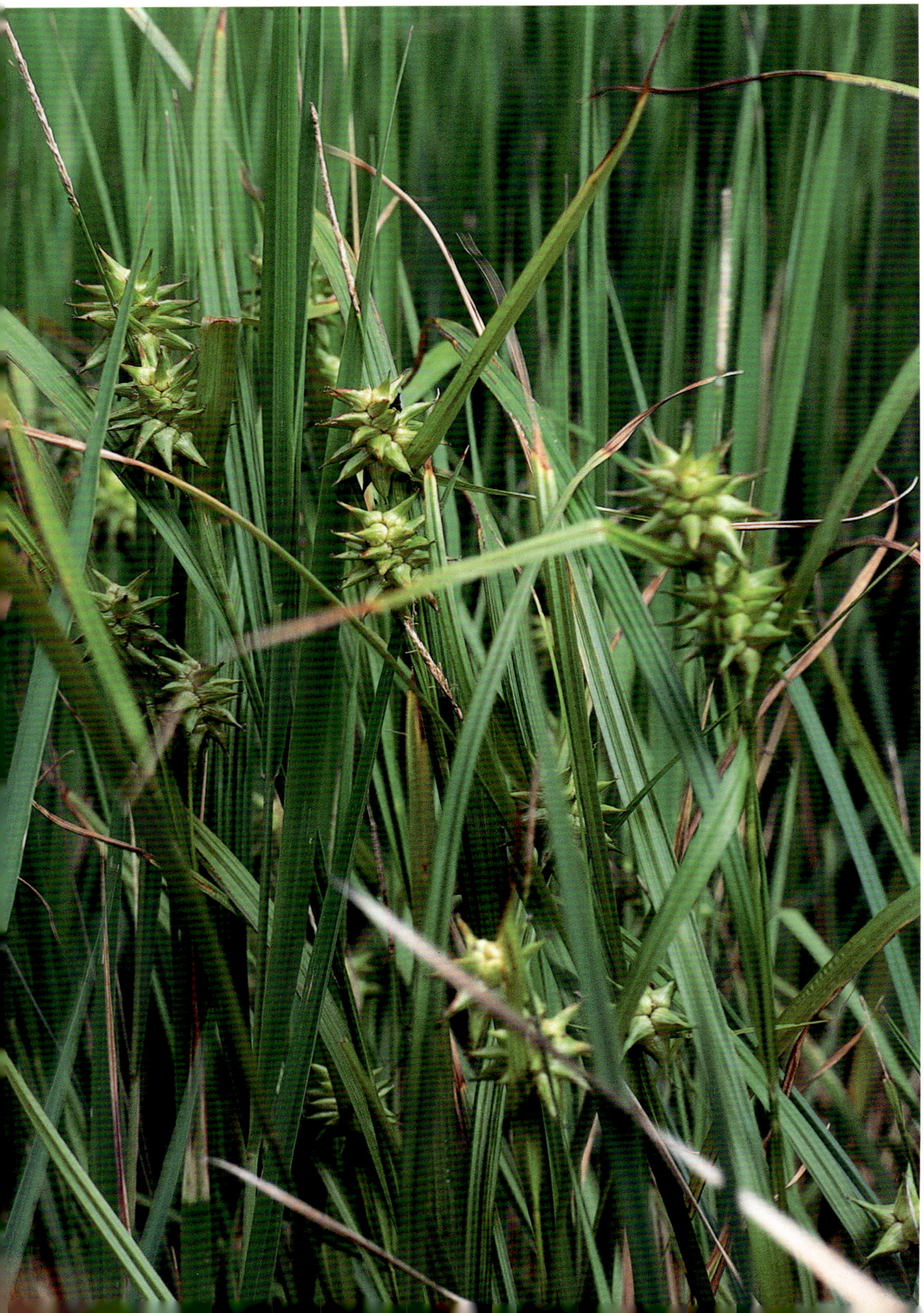

CAREX CARYOPHYLLACEA 'THE BEATLES'
syn. ***Carex-digitata*****-Hybride 'The Beatles'**
The Beatles spring or vernal sedge
Height: 25cm, **width:** 30cm
Growth: loose, broad clumps with overhanging leaves
Leaves: pale-green, slender, turned inwards. Predominantly evergreen.
Flowers: small brown panicles, unremarkable, from April to May.
Location: half shade, under trees; can withstand the root pressure of well-rooted trees.
Use: under trees in not too dark places, in large groups as ground cover.

CAREX ELATA 'AUREA' ('BOWLES GOLDEN')
Bowles' golden sedge
Height: 50-60cm, **width:** 60cm
Growth: clump-forming, dense, almost semi-spherical.
Leaves: slender, loosely overhanging. Early sprouting, glowing yellow-green with yellow tips, turning more green later; wintergreen.
Flowers: brown, thick spikes, from May to June.
Location: half shade to light shade, requires humus-rich, preferably moist soil. With sufficiently moist soil it can also manage a sunny location.
Use: very effective grass in combination with woodland edge shrubs. Looks good in front of a dark background. Can also be planted by the water's edge.
Recommended varieties: 'Knightshayes' has perfectly yellow foliage.

CAREX GRAYI
Gray's sedge
Height: 60cm, **width:** 40-50cm

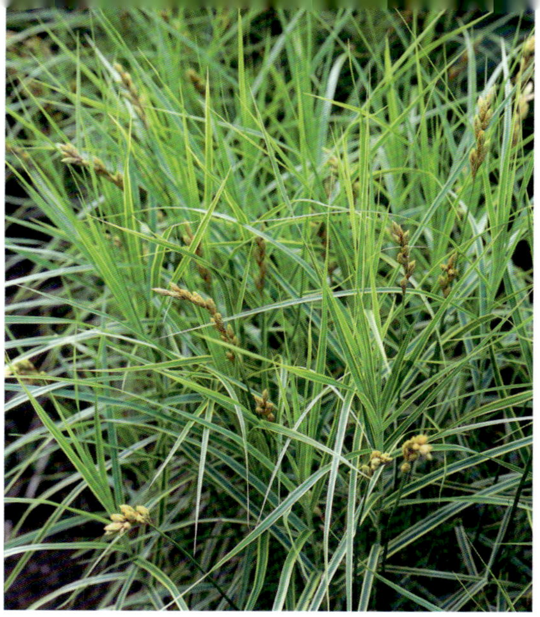

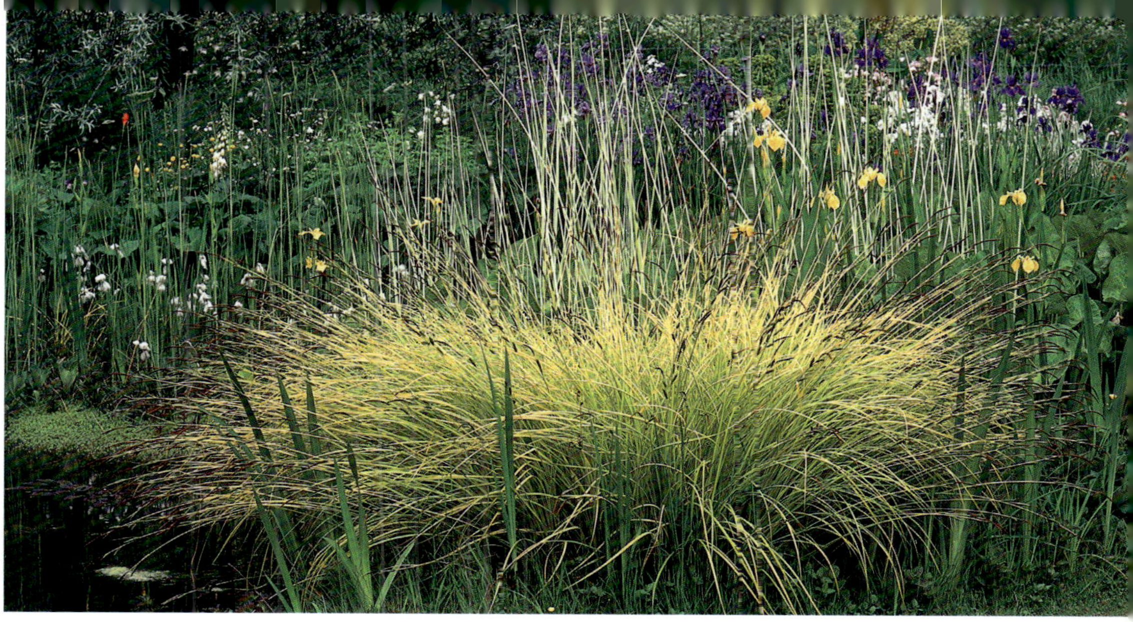

Growth: erect, upright with bent-over tips, forming slender clumps.
Leaves: mid green, early sprouting, keeps its colour well into autumn.
Flowers: unremarkable panicles, from June to August, and then decorative, long-lasting fruit, reminiscent in shape of morning stars.
Location: half shade, any fresh to moist soil. On moist soils can stand in sun.
Use: singly or in groups at the water's edge, in natural-looking planting schemes. The fruit heads look good in a vase.

CAREX MORROWII
Japanese sedge
Height: 40–50cm, **width:** 30cm
Growth: dense, half-rounded clumps, spread very wide over the course of the year.
Leaves: dark-green, stiff, with overhanging ends.
Flowers: yellow spikes in the leaf tufts, unremarkable, from April to May.
Location: half shade to shade, on humus-rich, ideally fresh soil. Hates dry locations and is sensitive to winter sun.
Use: in small groups as underplanting for trees, between shrubs with decorative leaves in the shade, works well in combination with rhododendrons.
Recommended varieties: 'Variegata' has slender white edging stripes. 'Gilt' has a pleasing deep variegation, but grows somewhat more weakly. *Carex morrowii* ssp. *foliosissima* 'Ice Dance' has pleasing creamy white stripes and spreads slowly though runners. Good ground cover.

CAREX MUSKINGUMENSIS
Palm sedge
Height: 70cm, **width:** 50cm
Growth: upright, forming dense, rigid clumps.
Leaves: light-green, slender, the foliage comes out of the stalks in whorls.
Flowers: brown-yellow, thick panicles at the upper ends of the stalks, from July to August.
Location: sunny to half shade, prefers fresh to moist, humus-rich soil. Cut back older clumps at the start of the year, so that they don't collapse.
Use: ideal grass for the water's edge.
Recommended varieties: 'Silberstreif' has a thin white central stripe on the leaves and is rather weak-growing. 'Wachtposten' is an especially sturdy variety with much better winter hardiness.

CAREX PENDULA
Weeping sedge
Height: 120cm, **width:** 80cm
Growth: clump-forming, overhanging flower stems.
Leaves: dark-green, erect, upright, overhanging in the upper third, wintergreen.
Flowers: cylindrical hanging 'catkins', yellow to brown, on powerful stems high above the foliage, from April to June.
Location: half shade to shade, prefers cool locations with humus-rich, fresh soil. Protect from winter sun to avoid damage to the foliage.
Use: as accompaniment to woodland-edge shrubs, under trees. Also very attractive in large groups with daylilies. Given the right conditions, it can self-seed.

Carex muskingumensis 'Oehme' (above left)
This variety of the palm sedge is especially sturdy.

Carex elcta 'Aurea' (above right)
Bowles' golden sedge grows into wide, flat clumps; it has fresh yellow inclined leaves.

Carex grayi (opposite)
The characteristic morning-star seedheads of the Gray's sedge.

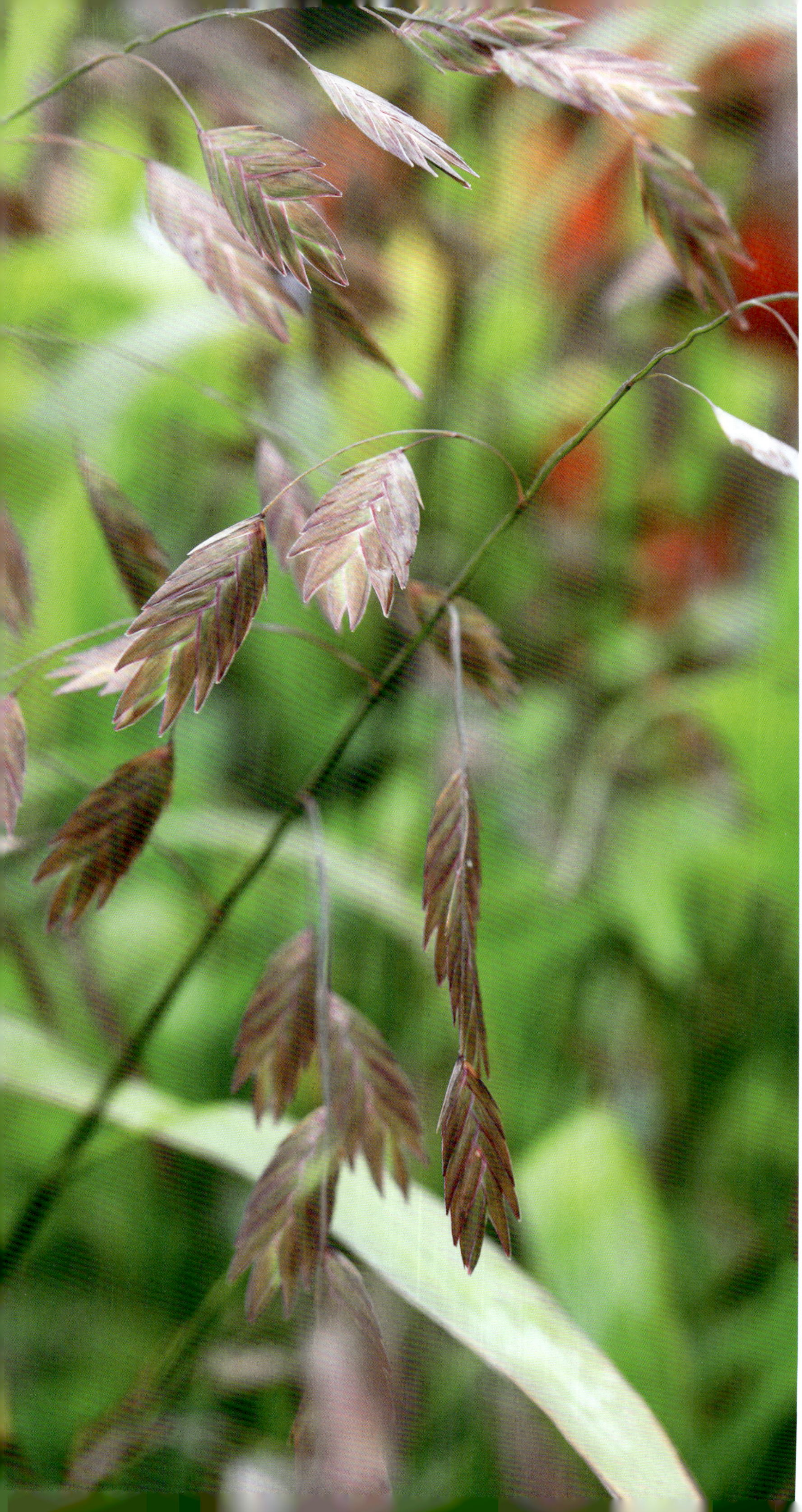

CHASMANTHIUM LATIFOLIUM

Spangle grass, wood oats, North American wild oats

Height: 100cm, **width:** 50cm

Growth: loose clump-forming, with upright flower stems.

Leaves: pale-green, broad, golden to red-brown colouring from late summer.

Flowers: teardrop-shaped, flattened spikes arranged along the stems, from August to October. Start out green, later turning russet.

Location: sunny to half shade, likes warmth, prefers fresh, fertile soil.

Use: in borders between autumn-flowering shrubs, planting areas at sunny or light-shaded woodland edges. Harmonises with autumn asters and autumn anemones.

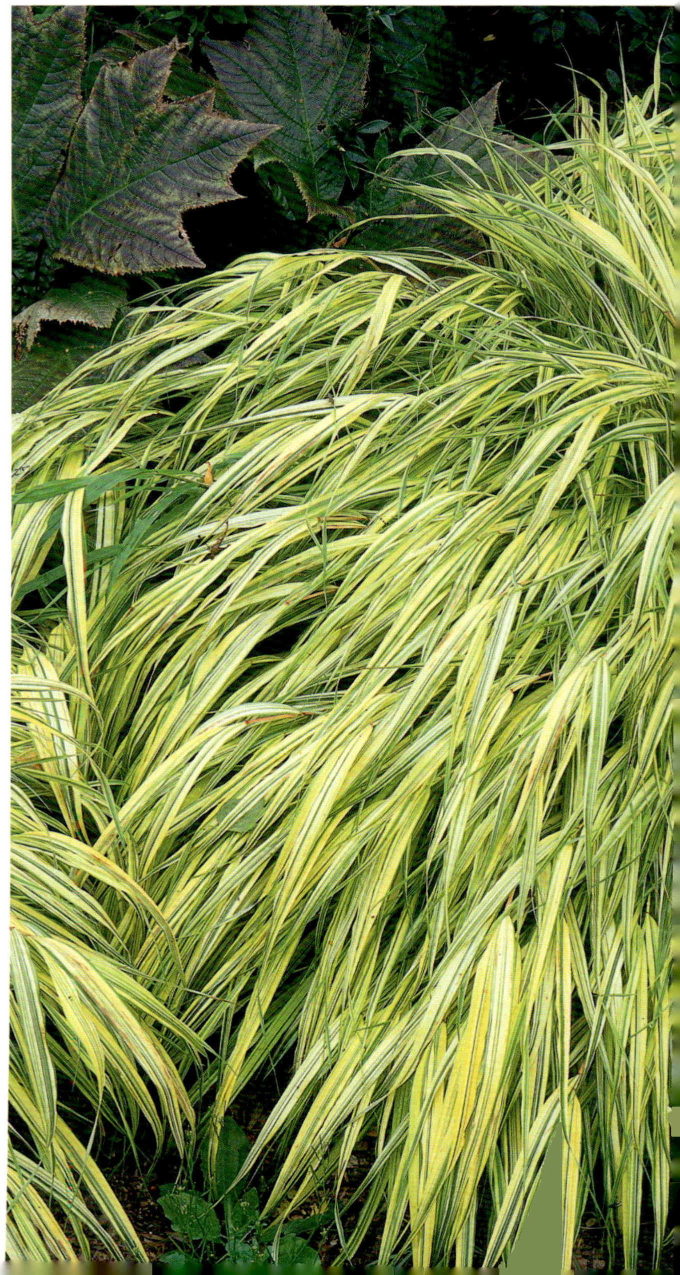

DESCHAMPSIA CAESPITOSA

Tufted hair grass or tussock grass

Height: 100cm, **width:** 80cm

Growth: clump-forming, dense, with compact leaf tufts. Tall straight stems.

Leaves: dark-green, slender, overhanging. Early sprouting.

Flowers: delicate, very long panicles, feathery, sticking out from the stems, from June to August. Transparent appearance.

Location: light shade to half shade, prefers humus-rich, fresh to moist soil.

Use: singly or in groups as an accompaniment to typical woodland-edge shrubs such as campanula, but also with ferns. Looks decorative in front of a dark background.

Recommended varieties: 'Bronzeschleier' has golden brown flower panicles and blooms as early as May. 'Goldgehänge' has slightly overhanging stems and golden yellow spikes. The appeal of 'Tauträger' is its long blooming period, which lasts well into the autumn.

HAKONECHLOA MACRA

Japanese forest grass

Height: 30cm, **width:** 30-50cm

Growth: wide and overhanging, forming mats through short runners.

Leaves: fresh green, elegantly overhanging, reddish autumn colouring.

Flowers: delicate flower panicles amongst the foliage, relatively unremarkable, from August to October.

Location: half shade to shade, prefers cool locations with humus-rich, fresh soil.

Use: underplanting for trees, also in combination with ferns and hostas. Singly, in groups or also as widely planted ground cover.

Recommended varieties: 'Aureola' has yellow and green striped foliage. 'Albostriata' grows more strongly and has green foliage with thin white stripes.

Chasmanthium latifolium (opposite)
The seedheads of the spangle grass turn a wonderful red in autumn.

Hakonechloa macra 'Aureola' (centre)
Like a golden yellow waterfall the leaves of the Japanese forest grass pour out of the shaded border.

Deschampsia caespitosa (right)
The tufted hair grass forms loose, fluffy clumps.

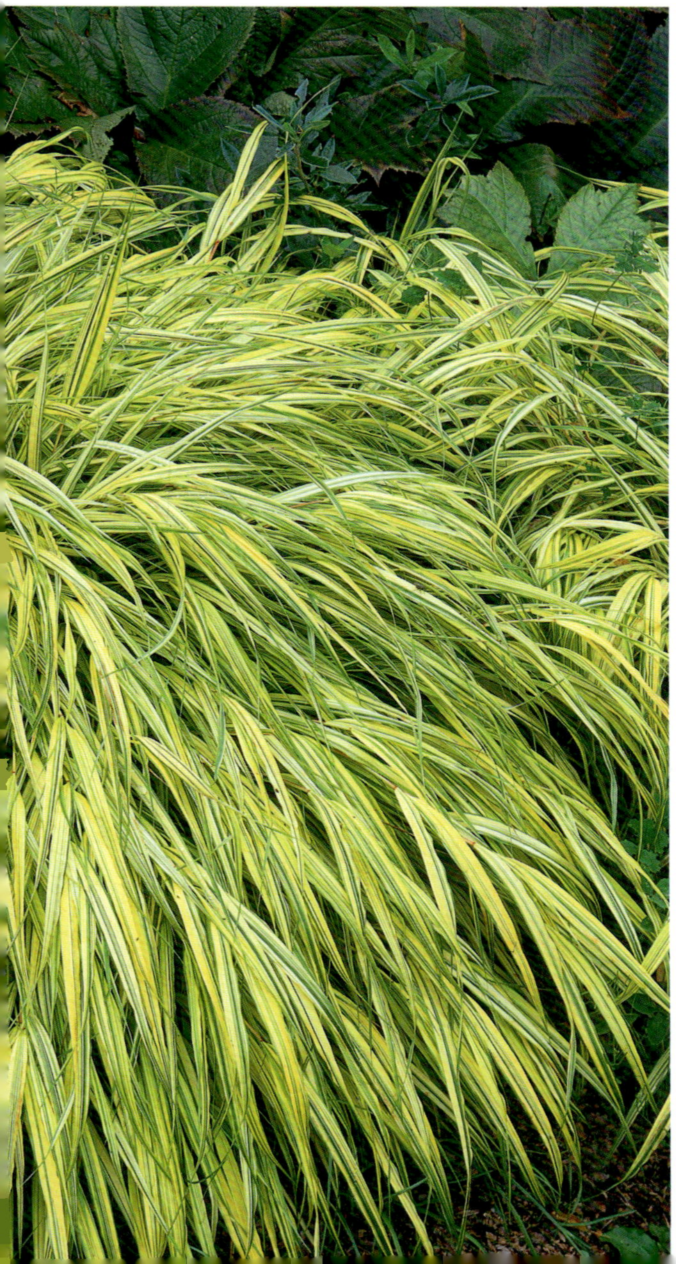

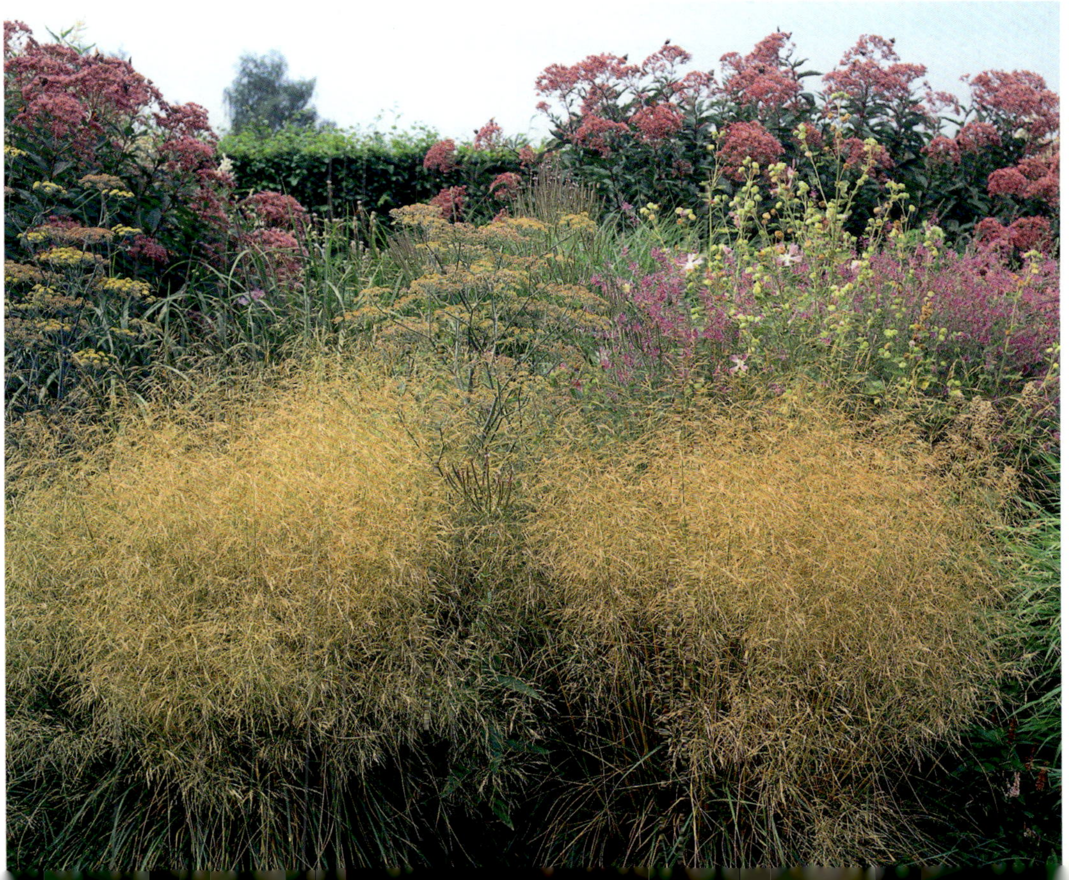

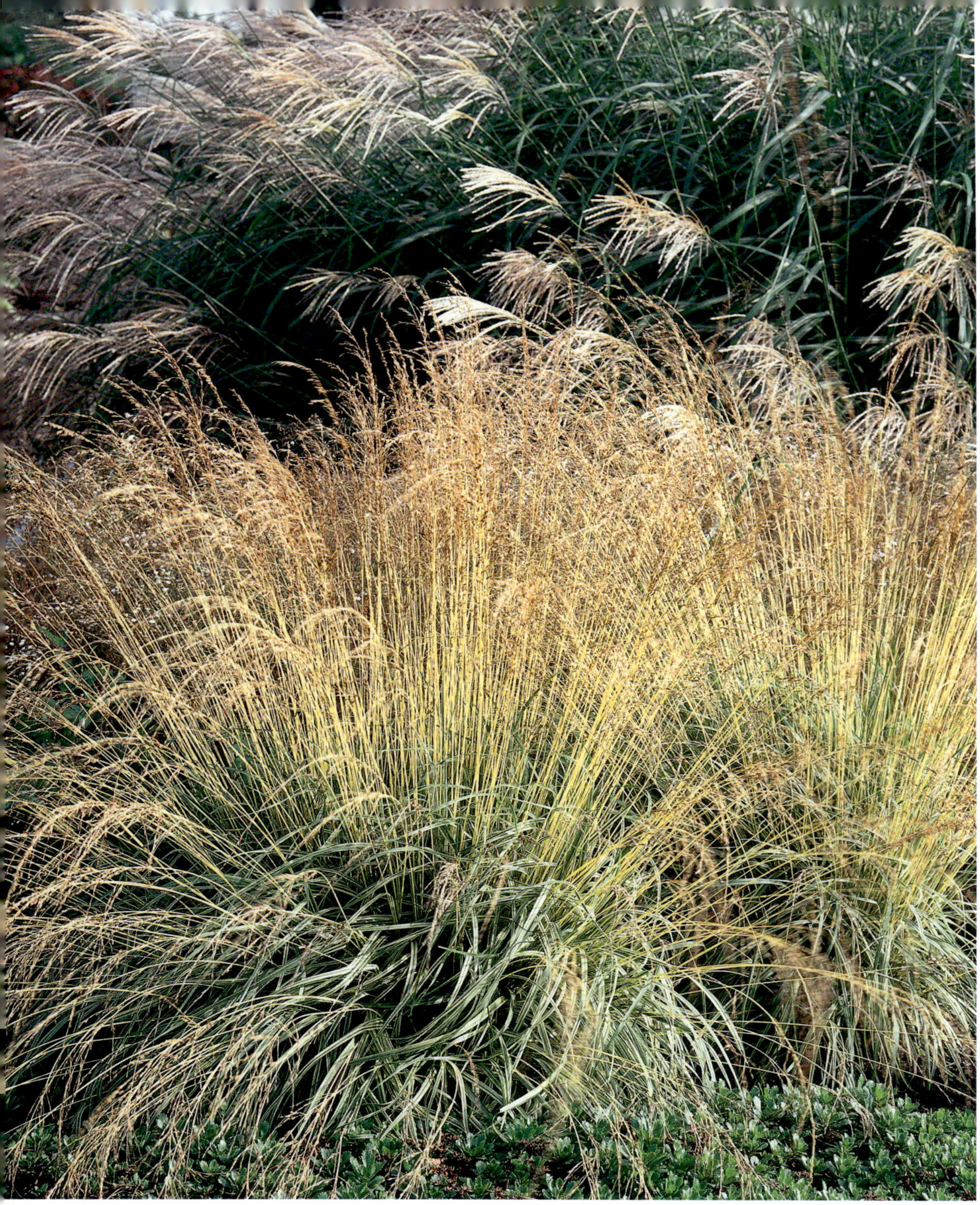

Molinia caerulea 'Variegata'
The white-striped foliage of this low-growing variety of the purple moor grass turns yellow-brown in autumn.

MILIUM EFFESUM 'AUREUM'
Bowles' golden grass
Height: 30–40cm, **width:** 40cm
Growth: upright with delicate, overhanging leaf ends
Leaves: yellow-green, glowing yellow when sprouting. Seedlings come true but green up a little over the summer.
Flowers: fine, transparent panicles, from June to July.
Location: half shade, prefers humus-rich but not too moist soil.
Use: as accent plants beneath trees. Very attractive when combined with spring blooms, especially bulbs. Creates glowing accents in the undergrowth.

MOLINIA CAERULEA
Purple moor grass
Height: 180–220cm, **width:** 70cm
Growth: clump-forming, with fan-shaped, tall flower stems high above the leaf tufts.
Leaves: slender, blue-green, with yellow autumn colouring. Die back completely in winter and sprout again in early spring.
Flowers: brownish spikes on strong stems, from August to October, which survive the winter.
Location: half shade to light shade, requires a chalk-free soil, reasonably fresh to moist.
Use: moorland borders, next to water, under light trees such as birch, in the heathland garden.
Recommended varieties: 'Edith Dudzas' has very sturdy flower stems and maintains its beautiful brown colouring deep into winter. 'Heidebraut' has decorative light-yellow spikes and is very sturdy. 'Strahlenquelle' has more widely fanned-out flower stems that overhang slightly. 'Moorhexe' grows up to 60cm high and has dark flower stems, and beautiful yellow-brown autumn colouring. 'Variegata' grows to only 50cm, has white-yellow variegated foliage and is especially suitable as hedging.

SESLERIA HEUFFLERIANA

Blue-green moor grass

Height: 40–60cm, **width:** 50cm

Growth: clump- to mound-forming.

Leaves: slender, blue-green, wintergreen and early sprouting.

Flowers: black-brown, thick spikes on stiff stems standing above the foliage, from March to April.

Location: half shade to light shade, prefers fresh to moist, humus-rich soil.

Use: in rock gardens on the side facing away from the sun, in light under-tree shade. Singly or in small groups.

SPODIOPOGON SIBIRICUS

Frost grass

Height: 150cm, **width:** 40cm

Growth: erect, upright clumps.

Leaves: layers of broad, horizontal leaves sticking out of the stems. Red-brown autumn colouring, at its best after warm summers.

Flowers: feathery, vertical spikes, from August to October.

Location: half shade, also sunny, prefers fresh, humus-rich soil.

Use: in mixed planting at woodland edges, at the water's edge in the drier zone, also as a solitary plant.

Recommended varieties: 'West Lake' has a distinctive reddish fresh growth and has very sturdy stems.

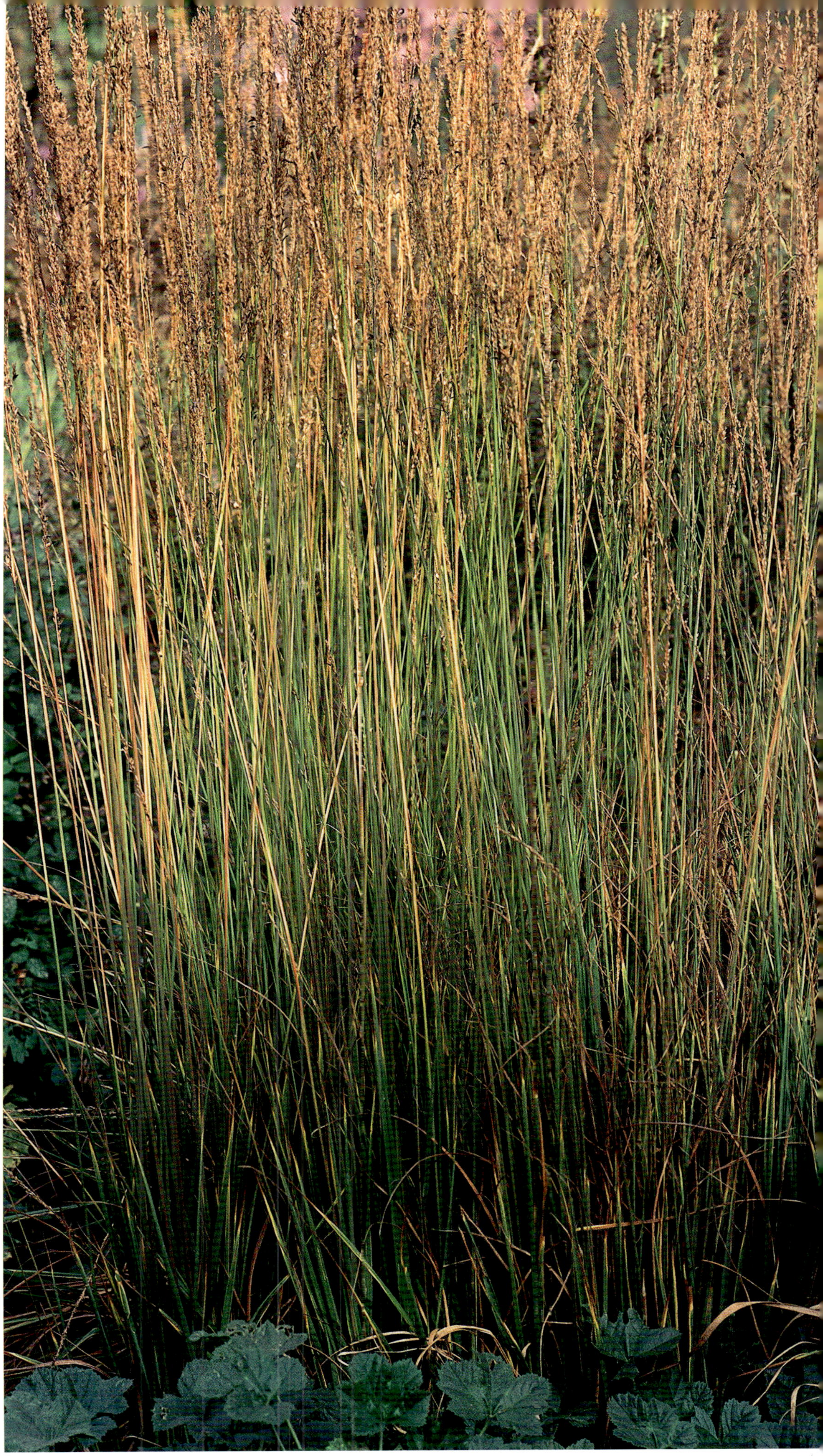

Molinia caerulea 'Moorhexe'
The flower stems of the purple moor grass 'Moorhexe' are darker than the leaves. The autumn colouring is yellow-brown.

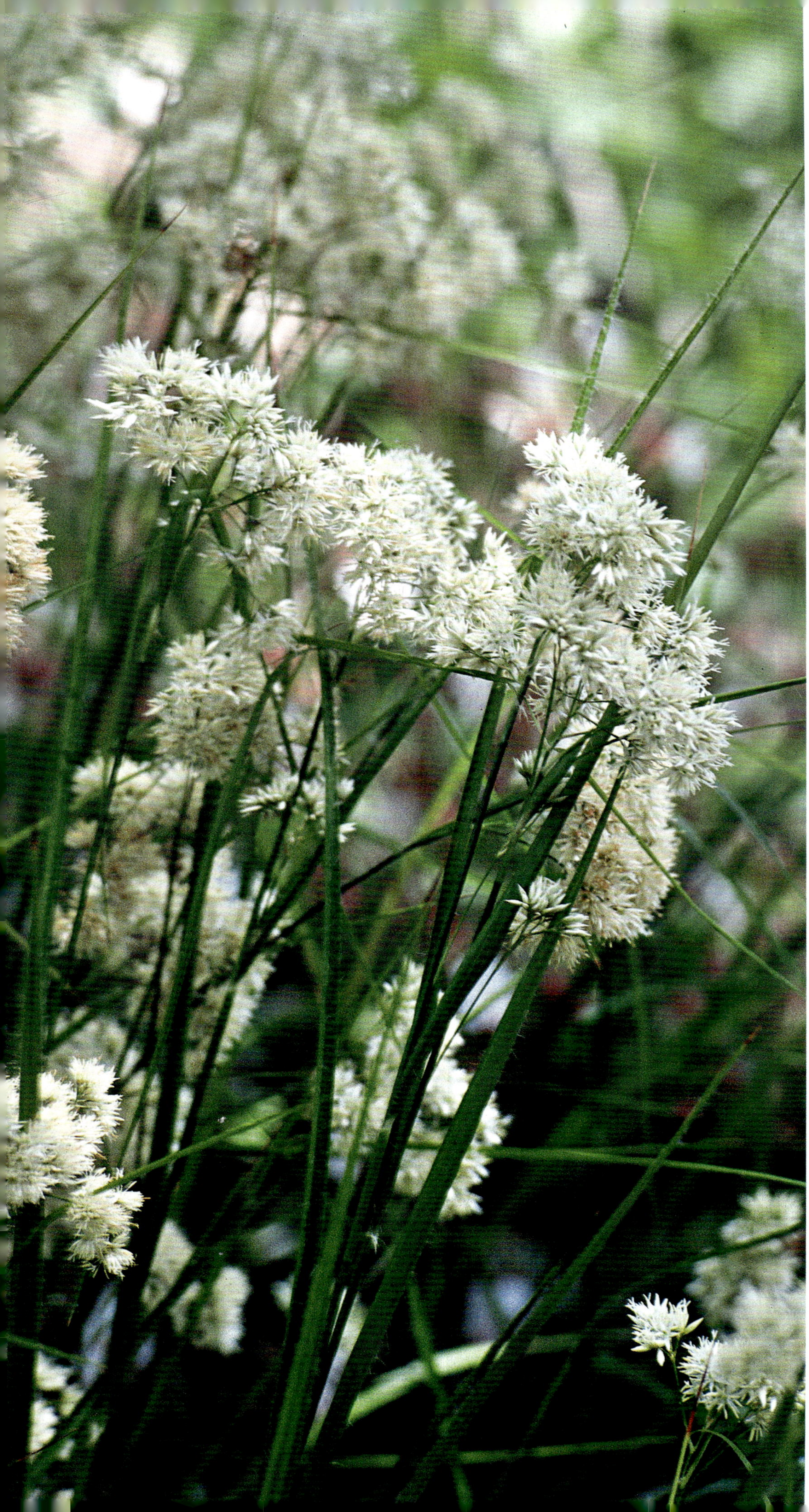

Shade

Shaded locations receive only a tiny amount of sunlight. Often they are fully shaded or in light shade next to trees and buildings.

CAREX OSHIMENSIS 'EVERGOLD'
Japanese sedge
Height: 25cm, **width:** 30-40cm
Growth: loose clump-forming, wider than it is high.
Leaves: slender, dark-green with distinctive yellow central stripes; evergreen.
Flowers: small unremarkable spikes, from April to May.
Location: shade, also half-shade, with fresh, humus-rich soil. Requires a sheltered spot in order to maintain its attractive foliage into the winter. Sensitive to winter sun.
Use: in small groups under trees, to lighten up shady parts of the garden.
Other recommended varieties: 'Variegata' has white-striped foliage, but otherwise has the same characteristics as the rest of the species. Similar is *Carex comans* 'Snowline', which grows to only 15-20cm and is used in the same way as *C. oshimensis*.

Luzula nivea
The flowerheads of the snowy wood rush evoke freshly fallen snowflakes.

CAREX PLANTAGINEA
Plantain-leaf sedge
Height: 20-30cm, **width:** 30cm
Growth: flat clumps, spreads slowly through short runners.
Leaves: fresh green, wide, with distinct lengthwise ribs. The surface is slightly wavy. Wintergreen.
Flowers: small yellow spikes, unremarkable, from May to June.
Location: shade, with fresh, humus-rich soil. Prefers cool, not too damp locations, does not tolerate accumulated dampness.
Use: in small groups beneath trees, attractive in winter. Among ground-cover plants such as lungwort and epimedium.

CAREX SIDEROSTICHA 'VARIEGATA'
Broad-leaved sedge
Height: 30cm, **width:** 30cm
Growth: clumping to spreading, slowly forming mats through runners. Dies back fully in winter.
Leaves: broad, dark-green with white edges. Decorative speckled bud.
Flowers: reddish spikes, unremarkable, from June to July.
Location: shade, prefers cool locations with humus-rich soil.
Use: as ground cover beneath trees, also tolerates leaf fall. Among other ground-cover plants and low-growing woodland shrubs.
Other recommended varieties: 'Island Brocade' has yellow leaf fringes. 'Kisukaido' grows in a flatter shape and does not spread out as far.

LUZULA NIVEA
Snowy wood-rush
Height: 40cm, **width:** 20cm
Growth: loose. Low-growing clumps.
Leaves: dark-green, strap-like, with overhanging tips.
Flowers: white, clustered panicles, from May to June.
Location: shade or half-shade, prefers humus-rich, fresh soil, but can handle reasonably dry locations.
Use: beneath trees, in shady spots in rock gardens.

LUZULA SYLVATICA
Great wood rush
Height: 40-80cm, **width:** 30cm
Growth: loose clump-forming, slowly spreading through short runners.
Leaves: fresh green, with soft hairs, wintergreen.
Flowers: brown clustered panicles, from May to June.
Location: shade, reasonably dry to fresh soil. Tolerates root pressure.
Use: as underplanting for trees, also in dark places as acceptable ground cover.
Recommended varieties: 'Aurea' has yellow-fringed foliage. 'Tauernpass' is cushion-shaped and spreads more strongly through runners.

Carex oshimensis 'Evergold'
The Japanese sedge is one of the best grasses for planting beneath trees.

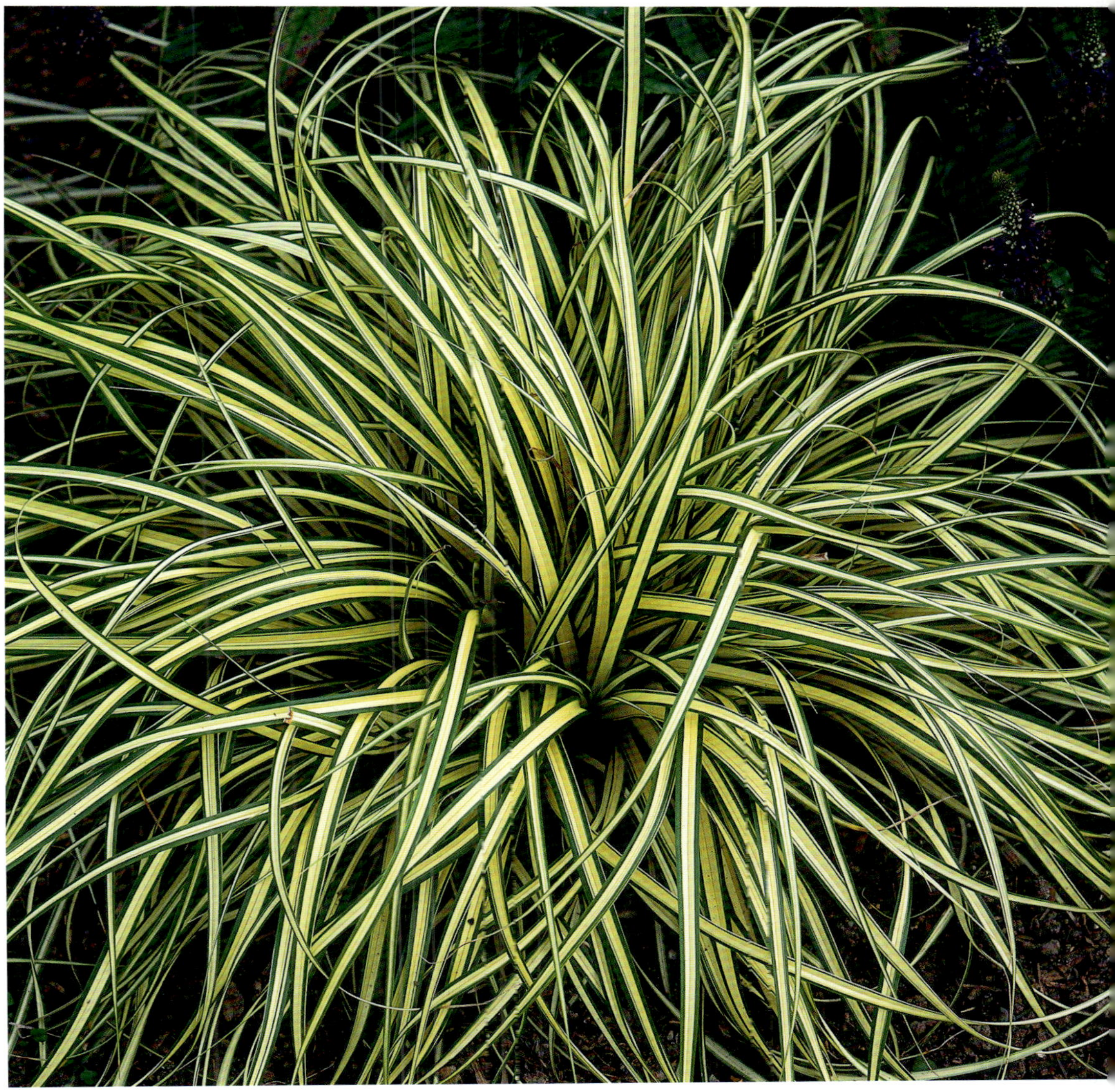

Annual Grasses

In contrast to the species and varieties described on previous pages, the following grasses complete their life cycle in the space of a single growing season and thus have to be grown afresh every year.

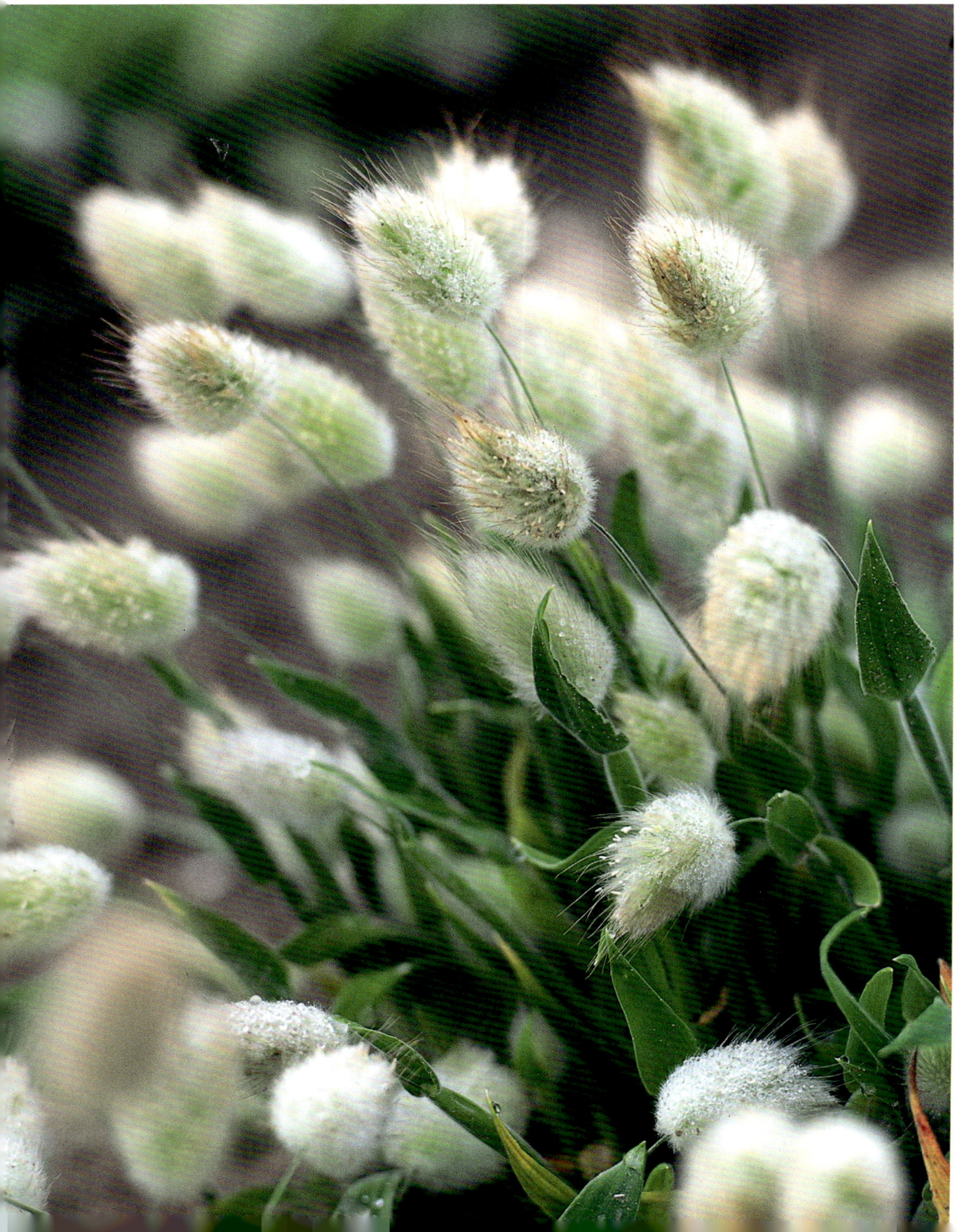

CYPERUS GLABER

Papyrus sedge

Height: 40-50cm, **width:** 30cm

Growth: loose clumps with stiff upright flower stems.

Leaves: light-green to fresh green, stiff, often with folded-over leaf tips.

Flowers: small green clustered flower heads on the ends of short stems, from July to September.

Location: sunny, thrives on all fertile and not too dry soils.

Use: in summer borders, as a filler in mixed borders. The flower heads can be used both fresh and dried in cut-flower displays.

HORDEUM JUBATUM

Foxtail barley

Height: 60-80cm, **width:** 30cm

Growth: loose clump-forming, like cereals.

Leaves: slender, fresh green.

Flowers: spikes with long awns, from June to July. When the seeds ripen the ears turn straw-yellow.

Location: sunny, on any fertile soil. Best sown directly into the border.

Use: in summer flower beds and flower meadows, pretty in flower bouquets. Can also be used dried.

LAGURUS OVATUS

Hare's tail grass

Height: 50cm, **width:** 30cm

Growth: loose clump-forming with wiry stems.

Leaves: slender, mid green.

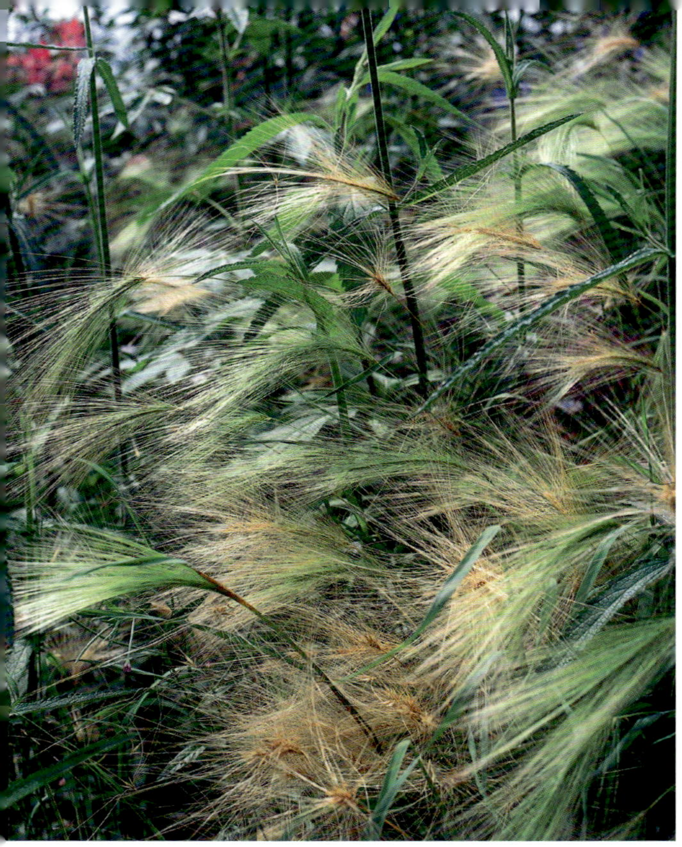

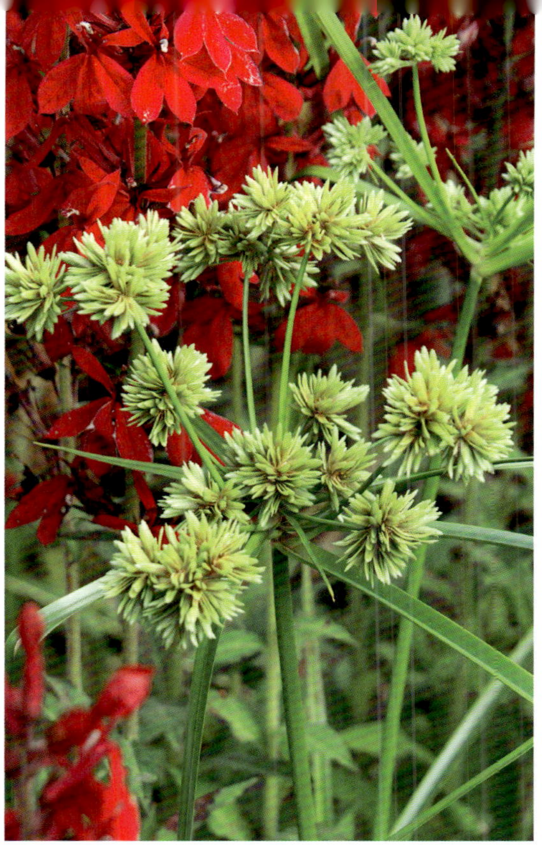

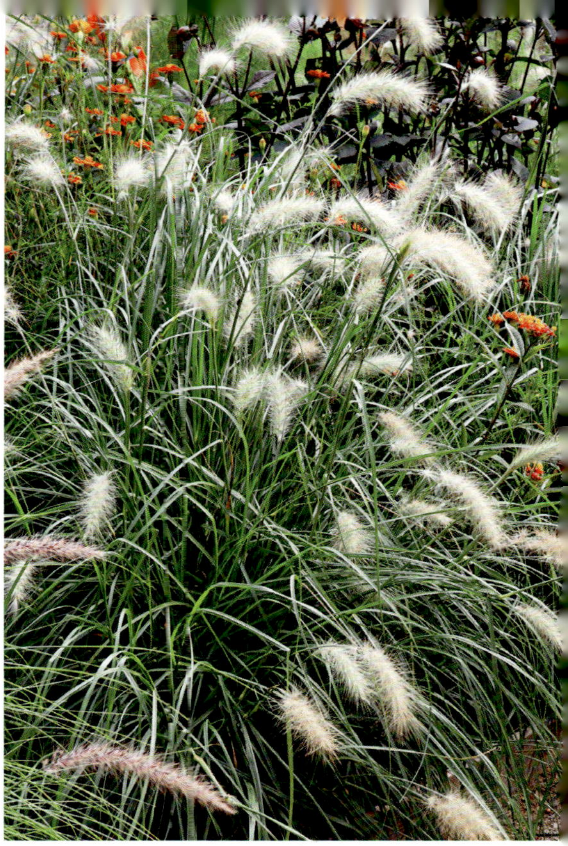

Flowers: woolly, oval flowerheads, reminiscent of rabbits' tails, from June to August.
Location: sunny, on any not too heavy soil. Direct sowing is advisable.
Use: among wild summer flowers, in brightly coloured beds, and as a gap filler in natural-looking shrub borders.

PANICUM MILIACEUM
Proso millet
Height: 100cm, **width:** 60cm
Growth: upright clumps with strong flower stems.
Leaves: slender, fresh green, even at the tops of the stems.
Flowers: overhanging, loose panicles, turning to brown seeds, from July to August.
Location: sunny, all free-draining, not too dry soils.
Use: in colourful summer flower beds, as gap fillers in shrub borders. Also good in floral displays.
Recommended varieties: 'Violaceum' has especially decorative purple-red flower panicles.

PENNISETUM SETACEUM
Red fountain grass
Height: 75cm, **width:** 60cm
Growth: upright, clump-forming with elegantly overhanging stems.
Leaves: slender, mid green.
Flowers: overhanging, feathery spikes, pink to violet from June to September.
Location: sunny, sheltered, all dry to reasonably fresh soils.
Use: as a filler plant in shrub borders, between summer flowers, also very effective as a solitary plant in a pot.
Recommended varieties: 'Rubrum' has purple-violet foliage.

PENNISETUM VILLOSUM
Feathertop
Height: 60cm, **width:** 50–60cm
Growth: loose-growing, with underground rhizomes. Actually a perennial grass, but in Europe is cultivated as an annual.
Leaves: fresh green, slender.
Flowers: roundish thick panicles that look like small silvery plumes; from August to September.
Location: sunny, all dry to reasonably fresh soils.
Use: in summer flower beds, in steppe borders among shrubs. Also good in cut flower displays.

Hordeum jubatum (above left)
Foxtail barley has initially fresh green, later straw-yellow, flowers with long awns.

Cyperus glaber (centre)
The annual papyrus sedge has clustered flowerheads, which appear at the ends of the stems.

Pennisetum villosum (above right)
This woolly fountain grass blooms from August to September.

Lagurus ovatus (opposite)
The furry flowers of the hare's tail grass look good in summer flower beds and are suitable as cut flowers in vases.

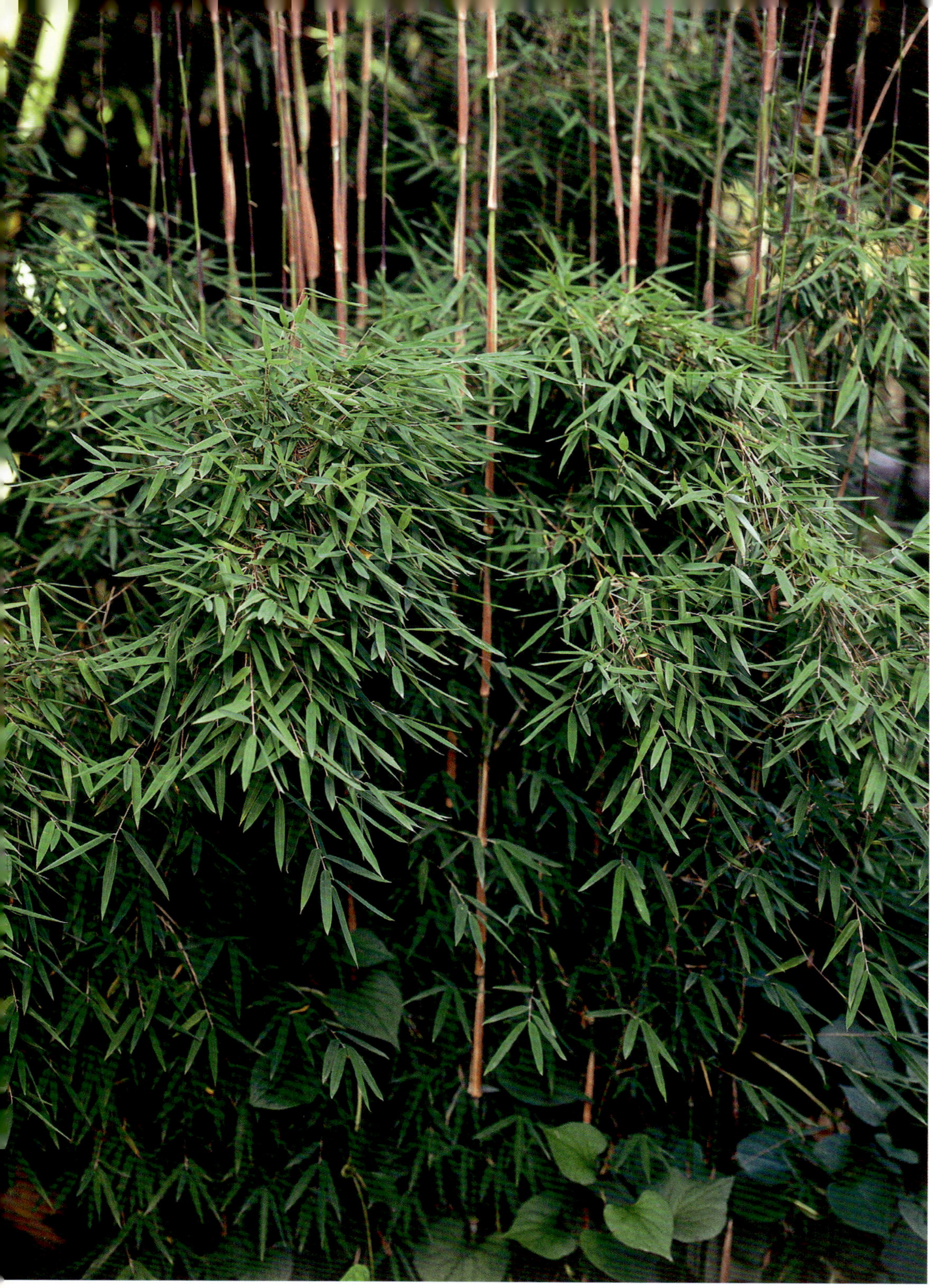

FARGESIA MURIELAE
Umbrella bamboo
Height: 3-4m
Growth: clump-forming, dense, overhanging tips.
Stems: sparse, green, fading to yellow, decoratively marked, dangling tips.
Leaves: small, mid green, dwarf, reddish branches.
Location: half-shade to sunny.
Winter hardiness: -18°C to -28°C.
Use: as large solitary plants, as hedges, screens, at the edge of ponds, takes well to cutting, good container plant.

FARGESIA NITIDA
Blue fountain bamboo
Height: 3-4m
Growth: clump-forming, straight, dense, compact; fine foliage.
Stems: green, dusted with white, later reddish to brownish, straight, dangling tips, up to 1.5cm thick.
Leaves: tough, deep-green, small, up to 6cm long and 0.8cm wide, with bluish undersides.
Location: sunny to half-shade, tolerates warmth.
Winter hardiness: -18°C to -26°C.
Use: as a solitary plant, decorative next to a pond or stream, opaque screen, hedge, takes well to cutting, low-maintenance container plant.

Bamboos

Bamboos figure among the evergreen grasses and provide the garden with some exotic Far Eastern flair.

PHYLLOSTACHYS BISSETI

Bisset's bamboo

Height: 3-7m

Growth: slightly overhanging, dangling tips, dense foliage, bushy, sends out runners.

Stems: young stems dusted grey, fresh green, later shiny olive-green, with age and in the sun yellowish, densely packed at the beginning, up to 2.5mm thick.

Leaves: shiny dark-green, thick; balanced leaf mass.

Location: sunny to half-shade, wind-resistant. Suitable for a harsh climate.

Winter hardiness: -20°C to -80°C.

Use: as a solitary plant, as a windbreak or screen, a cut hedge, takes well to cutting. The winter-hardiest and toughest *Phyllostachys* bamboo. Always use a rhizome block when planting.

PHYLLOSTACHYS NIGRA

Black bamboo

Height: 3-6m

Growth: upright, overhanging tips, produces many runners.

Stems: green, then dark specks, later turning black; there are different clones on the market, not all of which turn completely black.

Leaves: small, shiny, dark green.

Location: sunny, sheltered.

Winter hardiness: -16°C to -22°C.

Use: as a solitary plant, in a grove, as a screen or hedge, takes well to cutting, good container plant. Use a rhizome block when planting.

PHYLLOSTACHYS VIVAX 'AUREOCAULIS'

Golden Chinese timber bamboo

Height: 5-10m

Growth: inclined to begin with, but nearly perpendicular when mature, overhanging, forms strong runners.

Stems: sprout light yellow, later glowing yellow to ochre, irregular green stripes, fluted, often brittle, up to 6cm thick.

Leaves: medium-sized, oblong; decorative lush foliage.

Winter hardiness: -18°C to -22°C.

Location: sunny, sheltered.

Use: as a solitary plant, tall screen, in a grove, good container plant. Use a rhizome block when planting.

Fargesia 'Jiuzhaigou' (opposite)
This new form of umbrella bamboo works extremely well as dense screen hedging.

Phyllostachys aurea (below, left)
Fishpole bamboo is used in the same way as the Golden Chinese timber bamboo, but at 3 metres is markedly smaller.

Phyllostachys bissetii (below, centre)
Bisset's bamboo is a robust species that spreads profusely.

Phyllostachys vivax 'Aureocaulis' (below, right)
Golden Chinese timber bamboo has brightly coloured stems that are unsurpassed when viewed from a distance.

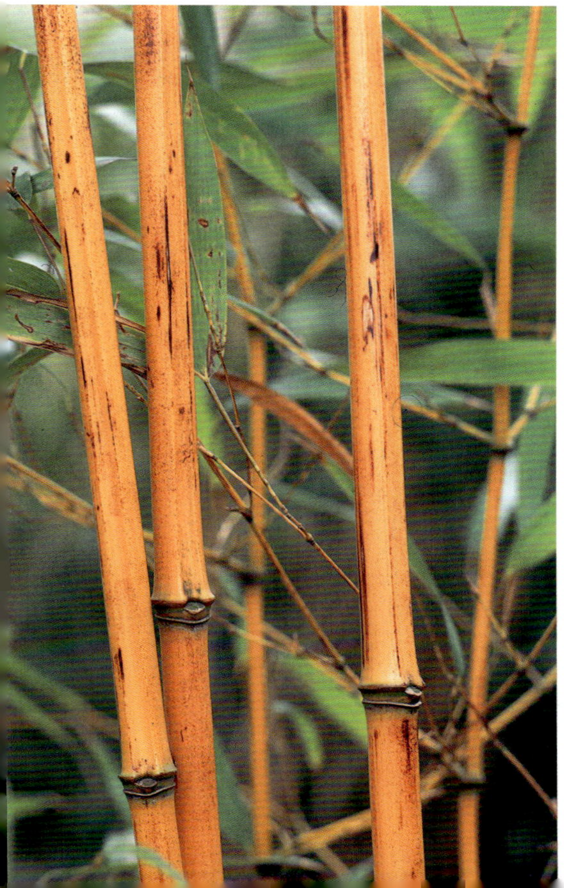

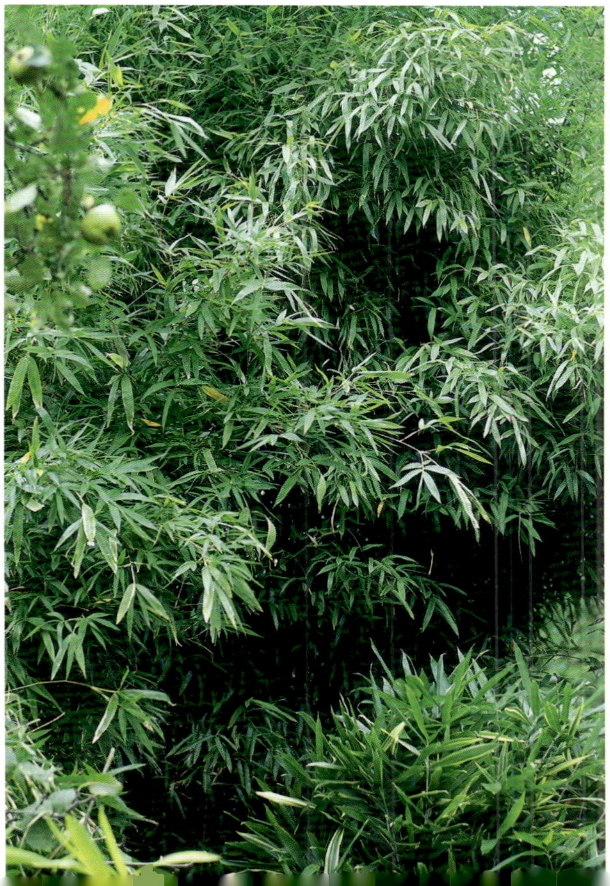

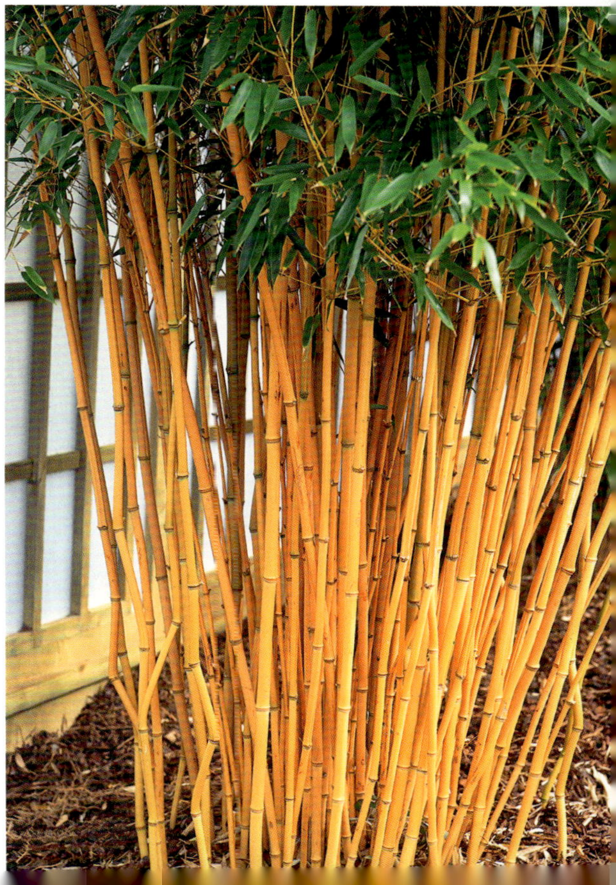

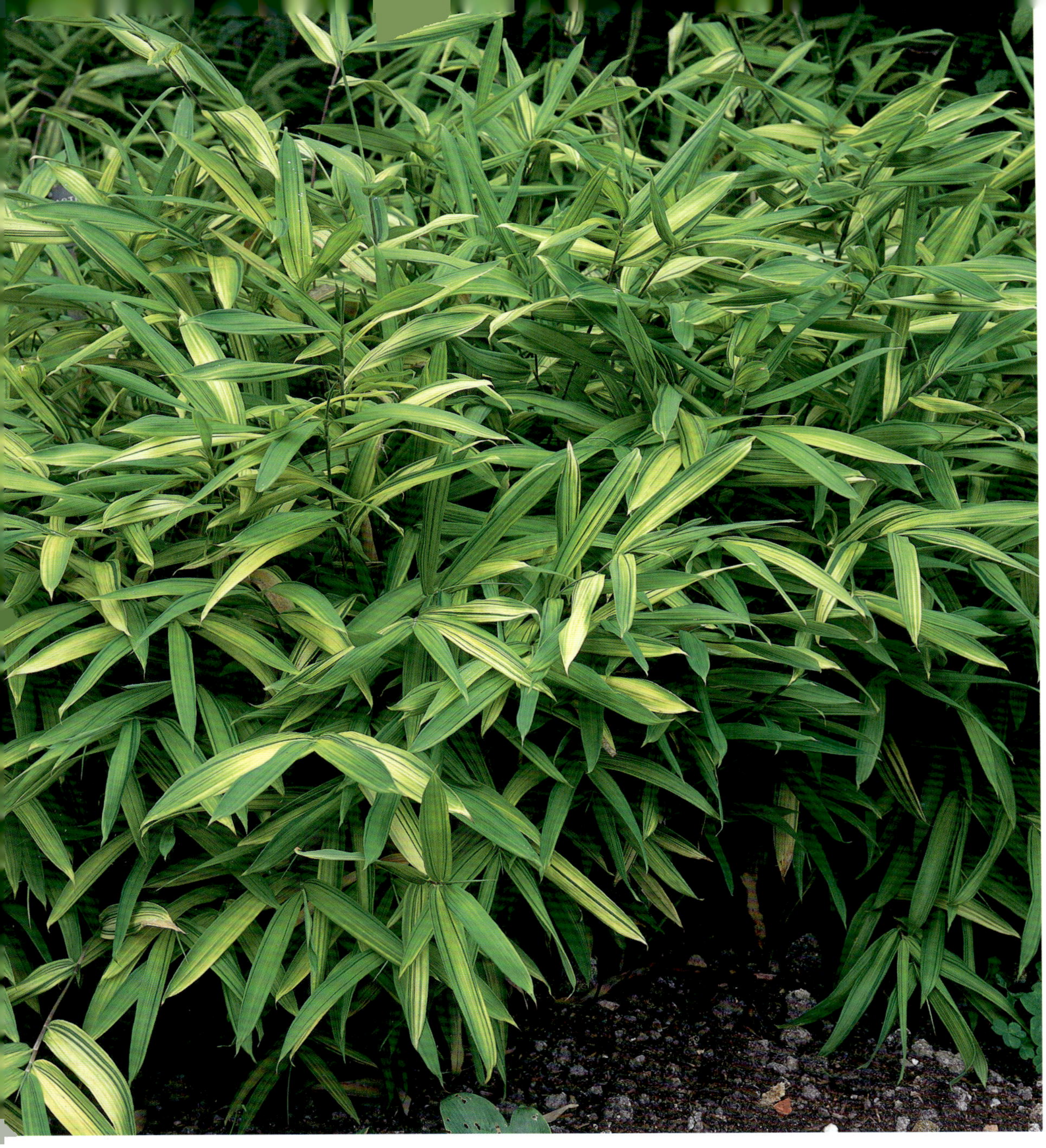

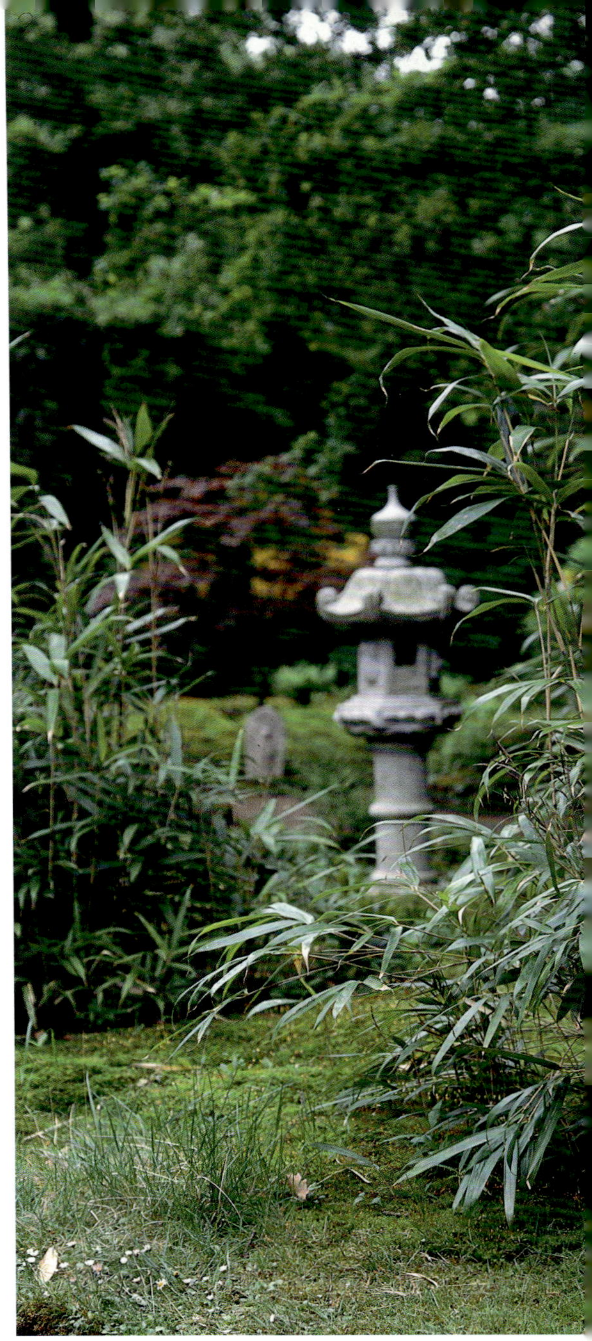

PLEIOBLASTUS VIRIDISTRIATUS
syn. ***Pleioblastus auricomus***
Dwarf greenstripe
Height: 50-100cm
Growth: loose, flat, produces many runners.
Stems: green to reddish, fine, sparse.
Leaves: soft, golden yellow with numerous stripes in different shades of green, bright when sprouting.
Location: half-shade, in warmer regions, also in shaded, protected spots, decorative play of colour from May to September.
Winter hardiness: -16°C to -25°C.
Use: companion to shrubs and trees, decorative container plant. Use a rhizome block when planting.

PSEUDOSASA JAPONICA
Arrow bamboo
Height: 3-5m
Growth: upright, tops overhanging, produces many runners.
Stems: green, turning reddish in summer and yellow with age, strong, up to 1.5cm thick, pale decorative stem sheaths fall off the second year.
Leaves: fresh green, shiny, large, up to 35cm.
Location: half-shade to sunny, sheltered, protect from cold winds and winter sun.
Winter hardiness: -18°C to -27°C, puts on new growth quickly after damage.
Use: as a solitary plant, over wider areas, as a screen or hedge, good container plant. Use a rhizome block when planting.

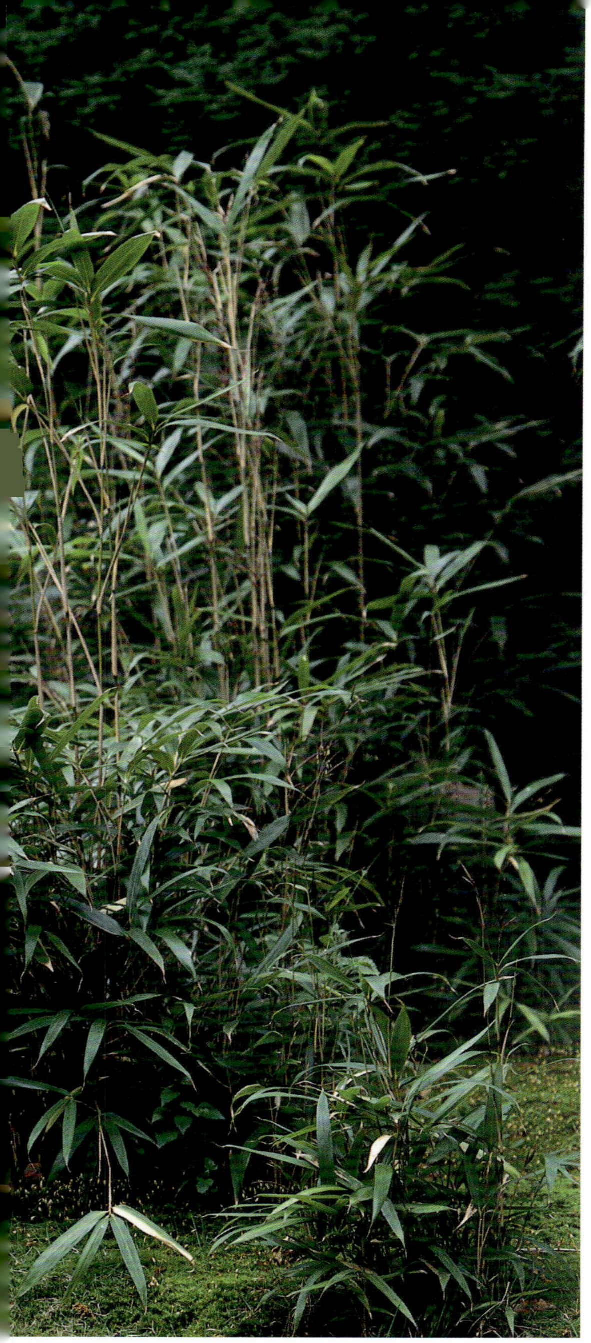

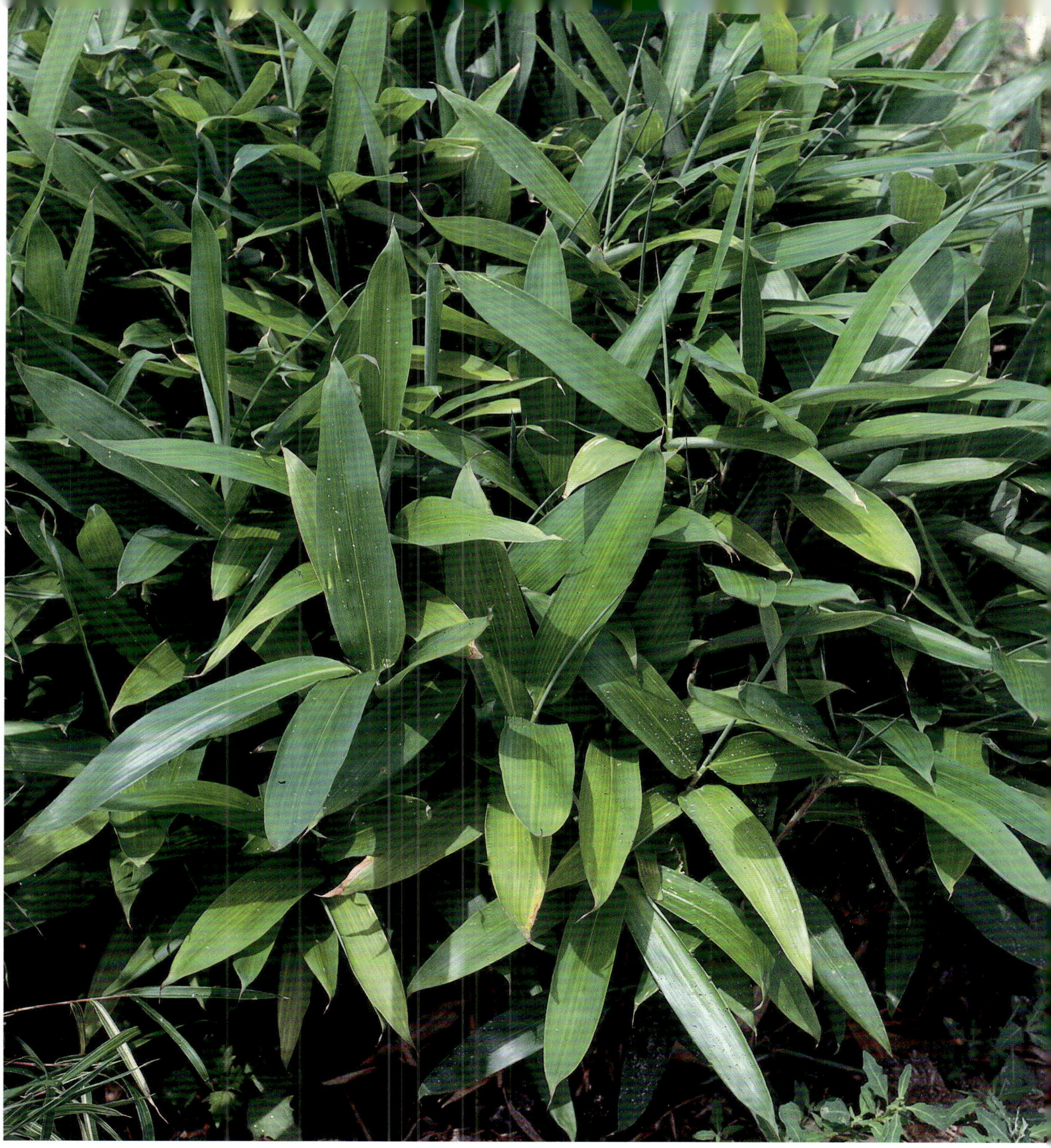

SASA PALMATA

Broad-leaved bamboo

Height: 100–150cm
Growth: extensive, strong, produces many runners.
Stems: green, yellow with age.
Leaves: deep-green, shiny, large, up to 30cm long, finger-like end leaves.
Location: half-shade to sunny.
Winter hardiness: -18°C to -25°C.
Use: underplanting, over wider areas, hedges, robust companion plants for trees and large shrubs. Use a rhizome block when planting in smaller gardens.
Similar variety: *Sasa tsuboiana* grows more extensively and has somewhat darker foliage and darker stems.

SASA VEITCHII

Veitch's bamboo

Height: 40–80cm
Growth: dense, compact, produces many runners.
Stems: dark-green, sparse, solid, very straight.
Leaves: dark-green, shiny; in spring the edges of the leaves dry out and create a variegated effect that remains into the start of the following year.
Location: half-shade to shade, sheltered.
Winter hardiness: -18°C to -24°C.
Use: underplanting, over wider areas, as a companion plant for shrubs, good container plant. Should be pruned before new growth appears to stop the plant acquiring a ragged appearance. Use a rhizome block when planting.

Pleioblastus viridistriatus (left)
Because of its low growth, dwarf greenstripe is also suitable as ground cover.

Pseudosasa japonica (centre)
The large, exotic-looking leaves of the arrow bamboo are a striking feature of this species.

Sasa tsuboiana (right)
The Japanese bamboo needs a lot of space and, like all bamboos that produce runners, should only be planted with a rhizome block.

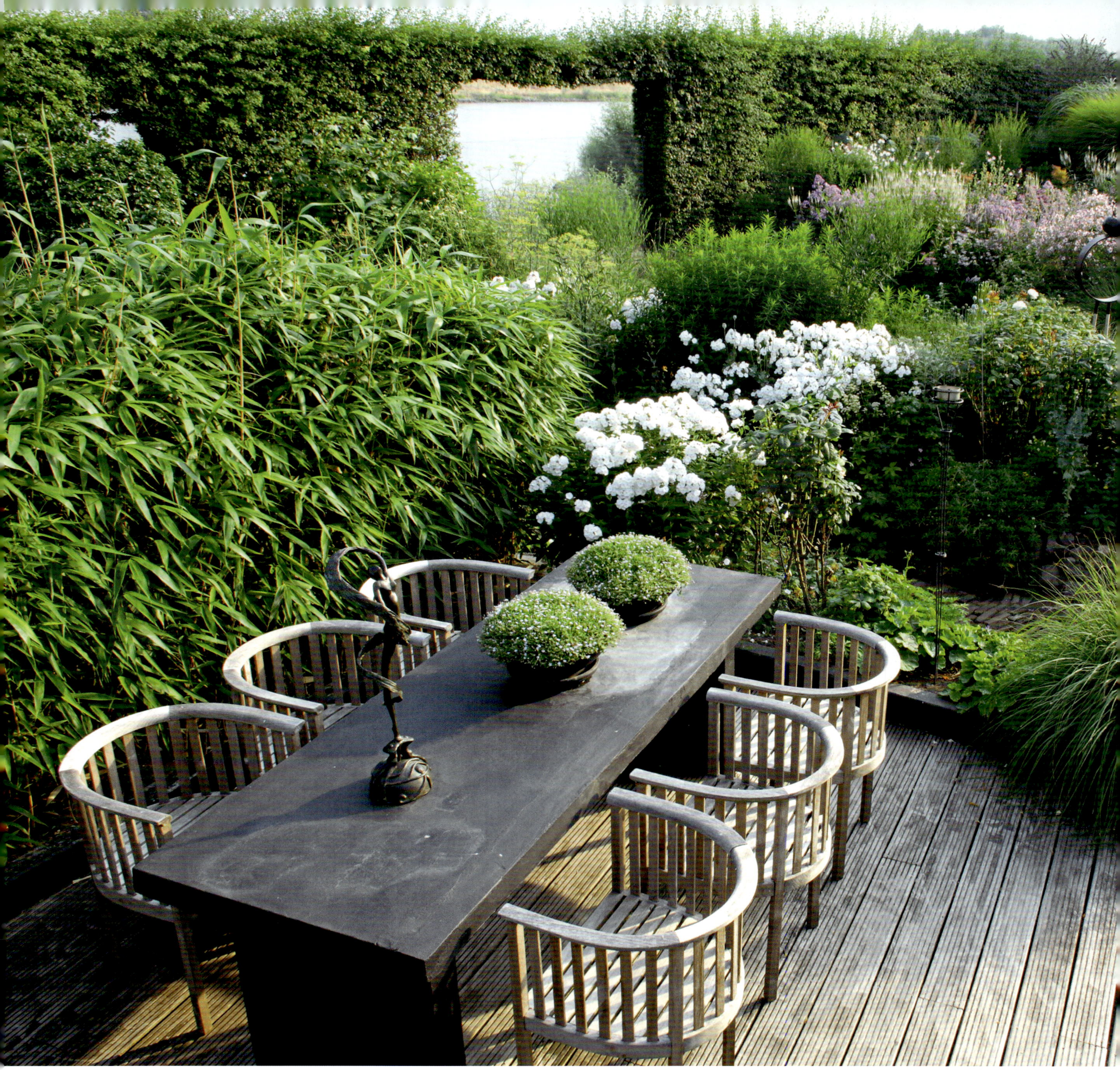

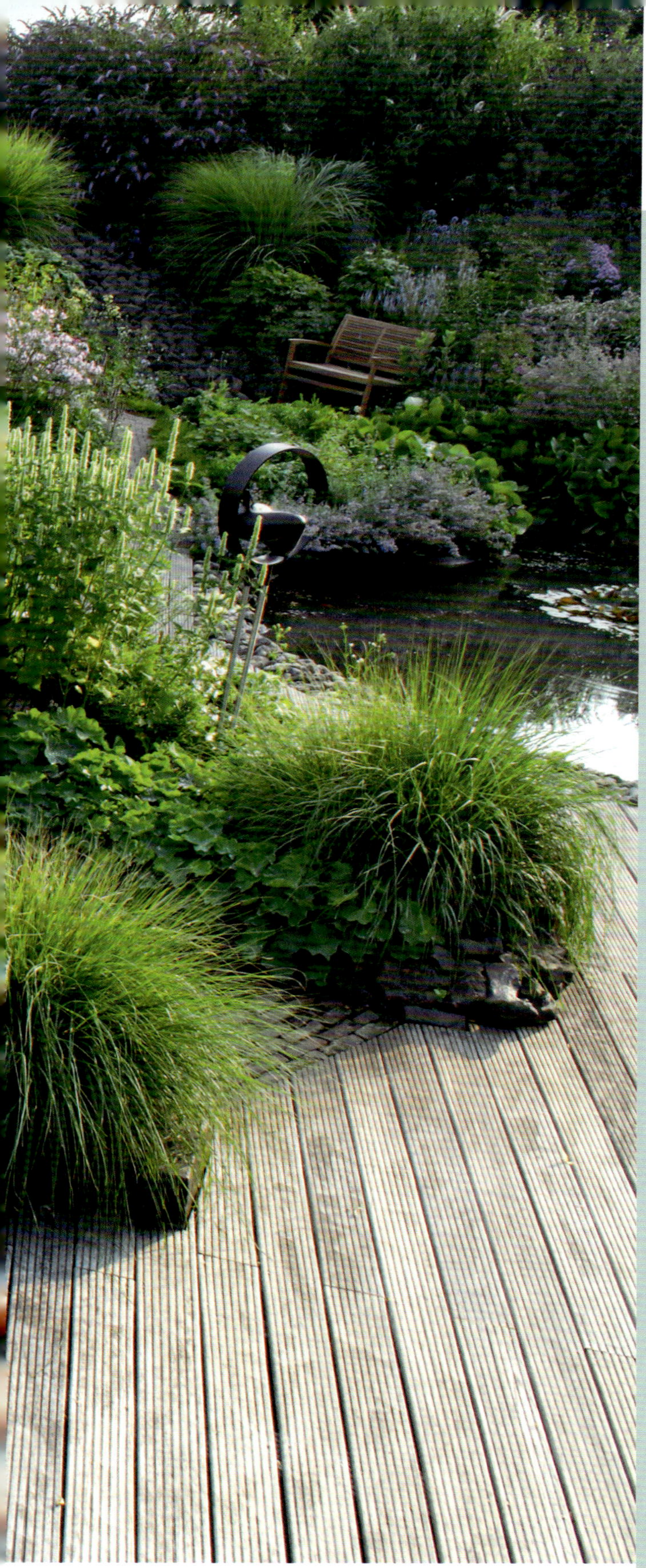

In order to enjoy your grasses for a long time you should check for good quality at the point of purchase. Strong plants with strong, healthy rootballs guarantee luxurious growth and lots of flowers, so long as you provide regular care and sufficient fertiliser.

PLANTING AND AFTERCARE

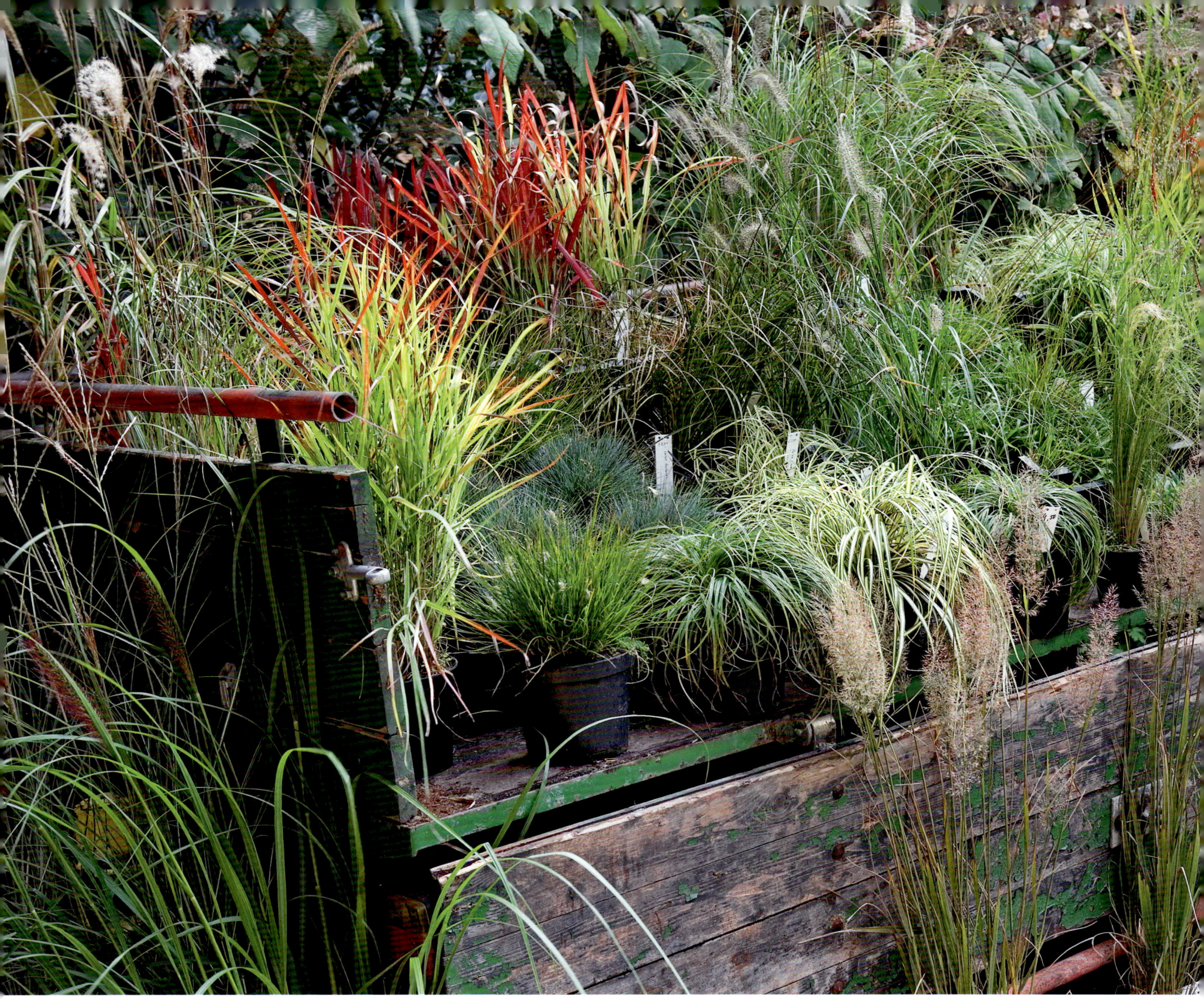

Plant markets and plant fairs
One of the best sources for particular plants are the specialist plant fairs.

Good-quality plants are bushy and have regular-sized shoots. (Long, light shoots that don't have many leaves indicate a plant that has been kept in too dark a location.) They have healthy foliage of the colour that is typical for that species that show no marks, signs of fungal growth or yellowing. Wilted leaves are an indication that the plants have suffered in transit to the point of sale or that they have not been sufficiently watered. Broken stems are a sign of damage done in transit or in storage. Healthy grasses have a well-developed rootball, which should be neither too damp nor too dry. When you pull the plant out of the pot you should be able to see a lot of healthy, light-coloured roots, and the rootball itself should remain intact.

SOURCES

Local nurseries normally have a good standard selection. They usually have good contacts with their customers and are thus well informed about their specific requirements. These nurseries

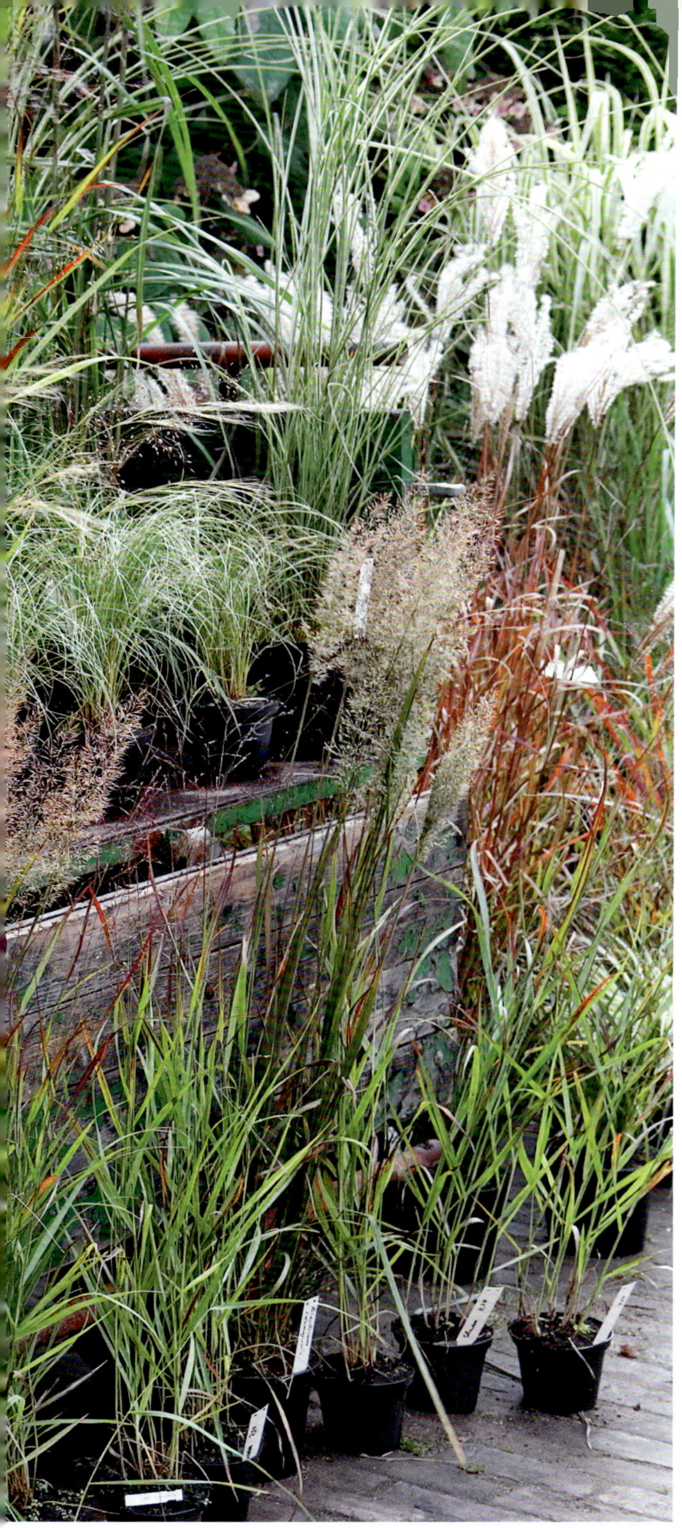

Acquiring Grasses

Garden grasses can be acquired in shrub nurseries, plant markets or garden centres. Even plant fairs and the Internet are possible sources.

usually maintain a very high quality, because they are very focused customer satisfaction as a means of building long-term loyalty. Nurseries usually buy their products directly from the breeders, for example through specialist companies. They acquire young plants and grow them on in order to bring sales-ready plants to market at the start of the season. Nurseries also often cultivate plants that can be propogated from seed.

Garden centres usually hold only a limited selection. Unlike nurseries, garden centres acquire sales-ready plants from large nurseries that can supply these in the required high volume. The quality is normally quite high. What matters is that the plants receive expert personal attention for the time that they are kept at the point of sale. So you should make sure that the plants on offer look fresh and well cared-for.

Ordering plants from a mail-order company involves a certain degree of trust, as you are not able to see the plants before buying them and have to rely on the fact that the quality of the plants matches the description or the illustration. Many companies offer their customers extensive 'guarantees of satisfaction' as well as the option to return goods if they do not correspond to how they have been represented.

Good sources for rarer plants are plant fairs and plant markets. These are mostly organised by gardening clubs or horticultural associations, whose members often collect individual genera, propagate them and sell surplus plants or exchange them for other plants. The dates of these are usually advertised in the daily press, on the Internet or in gardening magazines.

Planting

Once you have acquired your new plants you should plant them in the garden as quickly as possible, in order to ensure rapid growth.

Once you have acquired your plants and prepared the planting area, you can start with the planting itself. Place the grasses and shrubs, which mostly come in pots, next to the bed. If you have already created a planting plan, mark out the sections of the plan on the bed using sand. You can also arrange the pots according to the planting plan, of course not at the prescribed distances apart but bunched closer together. In this way you have the plants handily lined up in the right order. Once you have established the exact order of the plants, place them in their proper locations. After you have done this, remove the plants carefully from their pots. Moist rootballs slide out of the pot more easily. With a small shovel, dig out suitably sized holes and carefully place the rootballs or rhizomes in them so that the plant sits as deep in the hole as it did in its pot. Press down plants with great care, using your hands only. Then pull very gently on the plants to test whether they are sitting firmly in the ground. After planting, water generously – even if it is raining – so that the cavities in the planting hole are flooded and the roots and the soil particles are fused together. In the period following planting you should water regularly and generously in order to ensure good growth.

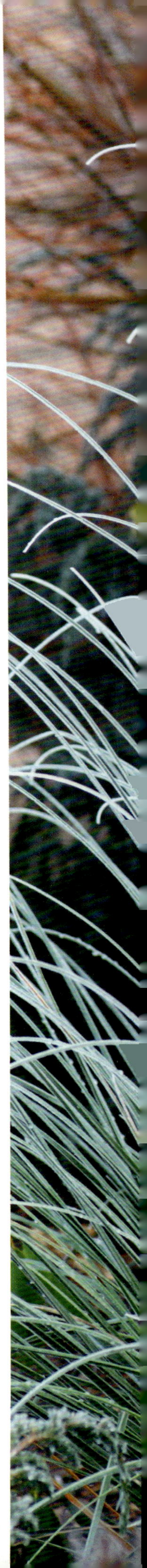

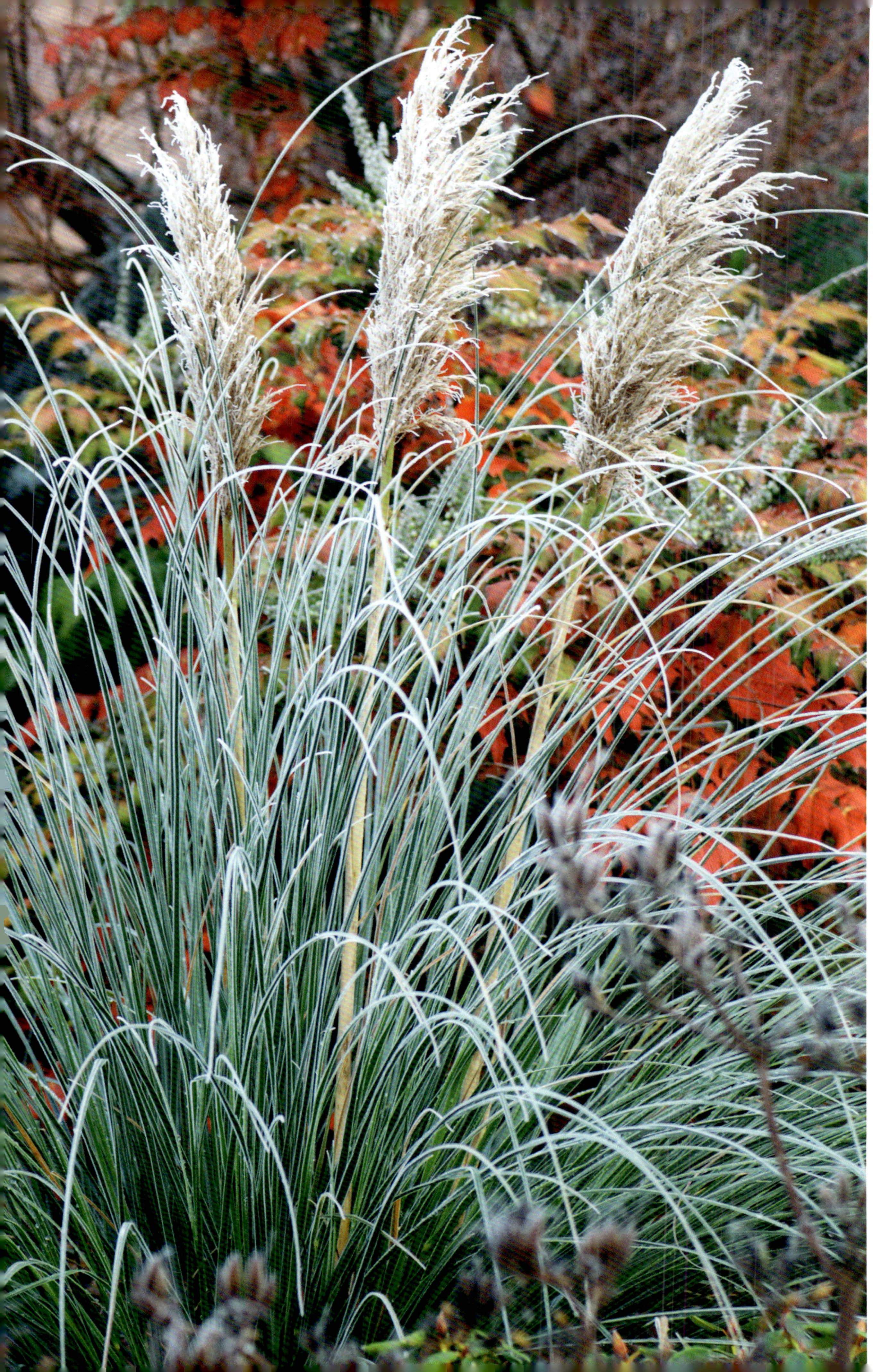

Pampas grass

Only grasses correctly planted in locations suited to them develop into such spectacular plants.

Aftercare

Grasses are among the most straightforward of garden plants. But they repay regular care with luxuriant growth and beautiful flowers.

Pruning at the start of the year
The blooming forsythia marks an important point in the gardening calendar. The dead grass foliage is cut back now, just before the new growth appears.

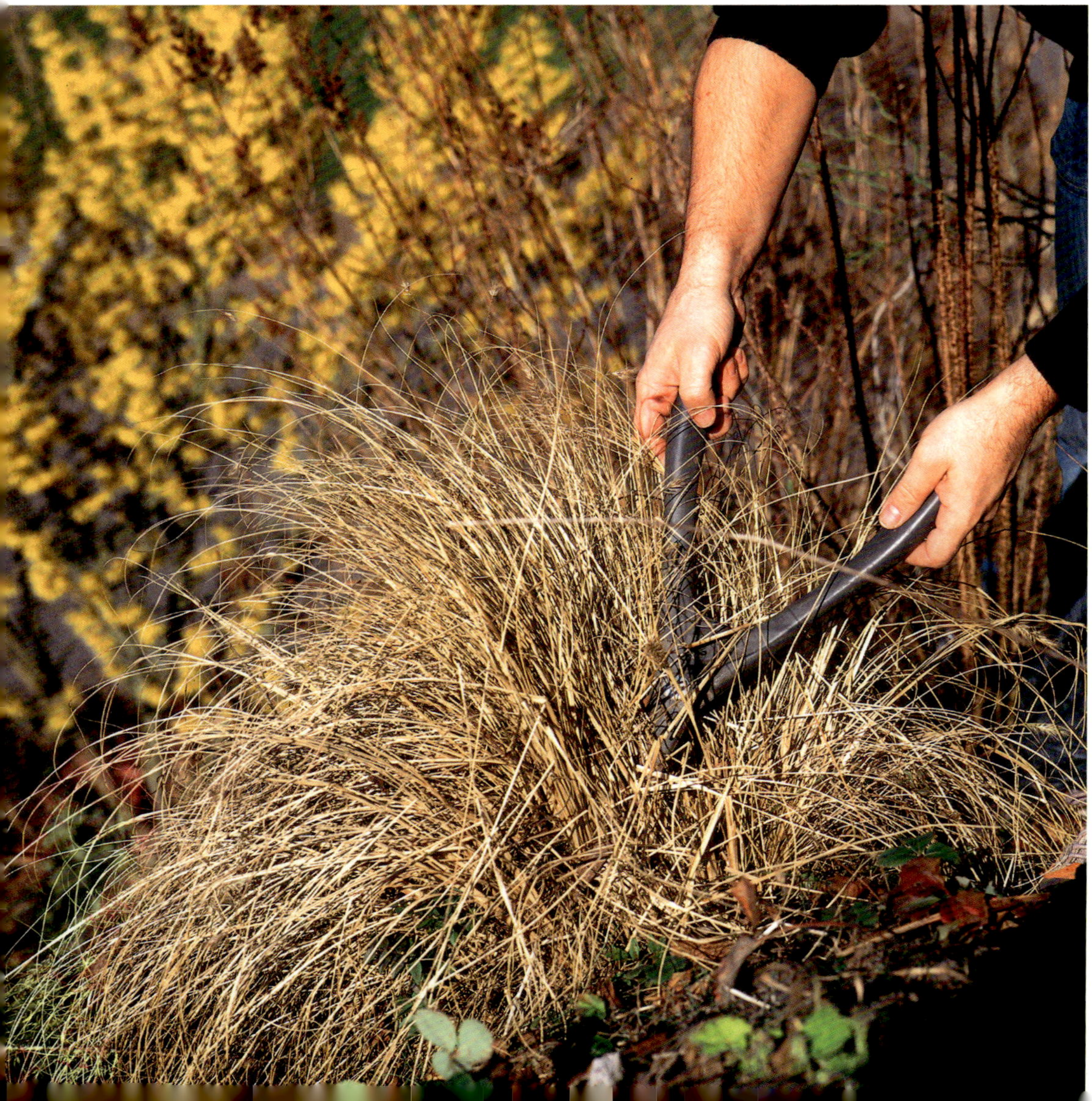

Particularly in the period after planting, when the plants are still small and there are still large gaps in the border, it is advisable to cover the bed in a layer of mulch. This helps both to seal in moisture in the soil and to suppress the growth of weeds. The layer of mulch should be at least 5-7cm deep. Good forms of mulch are well-rotted bark chippings, leaf mould or finely chopped straw, which is best mixed in with some leaves.

It is important to note that as the organic mulch gradually decomposes, the soil organisms will draw the nutrients down, so a supplementary feed of horn chippings is advisable – use about 80g per square metre. After two or three years the mulch layer will have fully decomposed and will need to be replaced.

If you don't mulch, you will need to hoe regularly and remove any sprouting weeds.

During growth plants are constantly drawing nutrients from the soil, so these must be regularly replenished. It is advisable to feed new beds in advance; this should ideally be done with organic material. If you are using compost, ensure that this is not applied too generously. A 1-2cm thick layer dug into the top layer of the soil is quite sufficient.

As a general rule, the soil should only be fed with the same amount of nutrients as the plants take out of it. Too heavy an application of fertiliser can make the soil too salty, and leached nutrients can pollute groundwater. To get specific recommendations on the quantity and composition of your fertiliser you can send soil samples to testing laboratories.

As a rule, pruning of grasses is limited to the beginning of the growing season, i.e. early in the year. Only then should the previous year's flower and seed heads be cut off. Many grasses can be radically cut back to the ground in summer, especially spring-flowering, shade-loving grasses, which can look unsightly after blooming. It can makes sense to cut back flower heads before the seeds ripen, if there is a risk that the plant might produce new and unwelcome seedlings that in the long run will threaten valuable plants nearby.

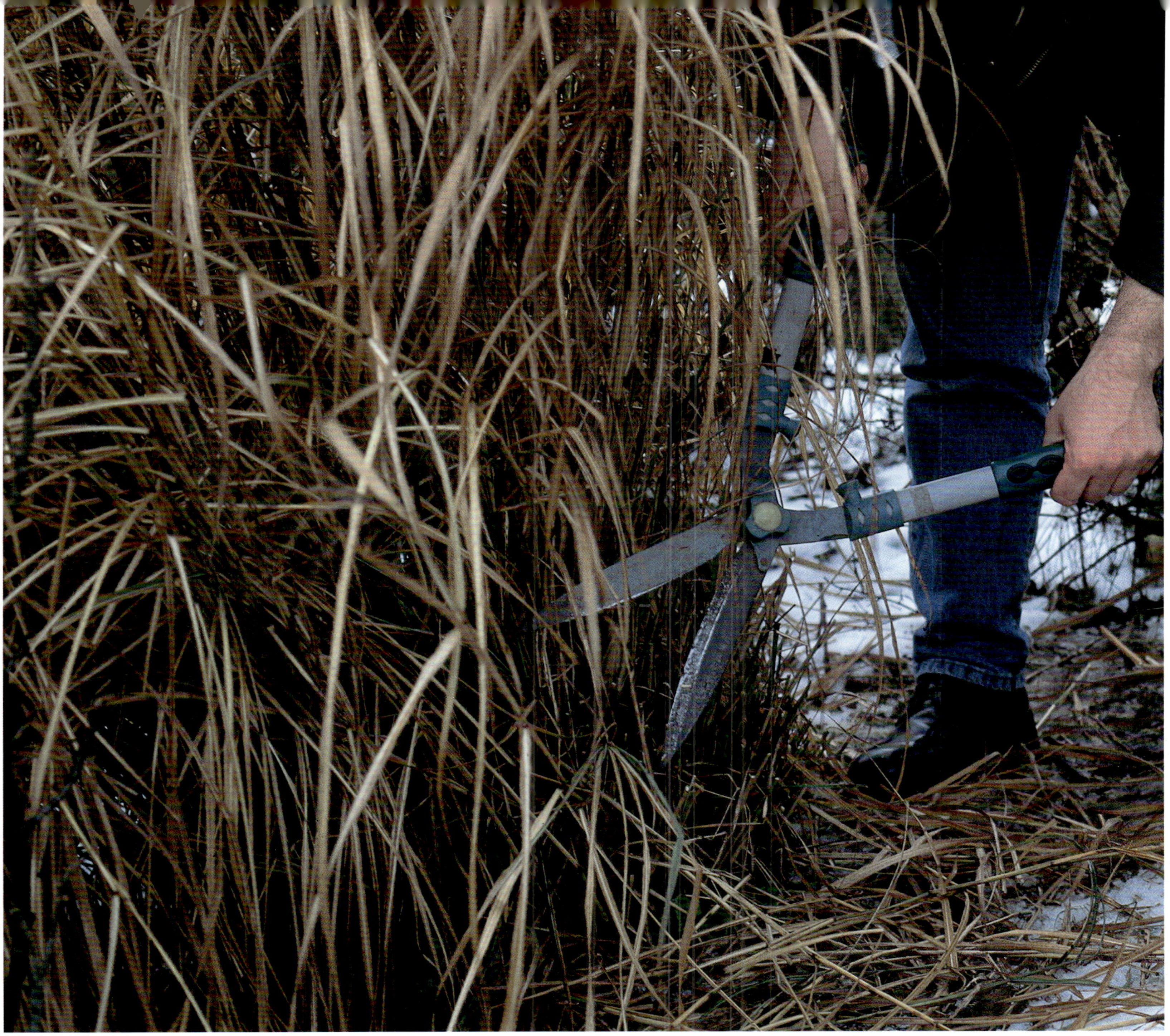

Pruning with shears

The pruning of old stems must be completed before the new growth appears – either in late winter or in early spring.

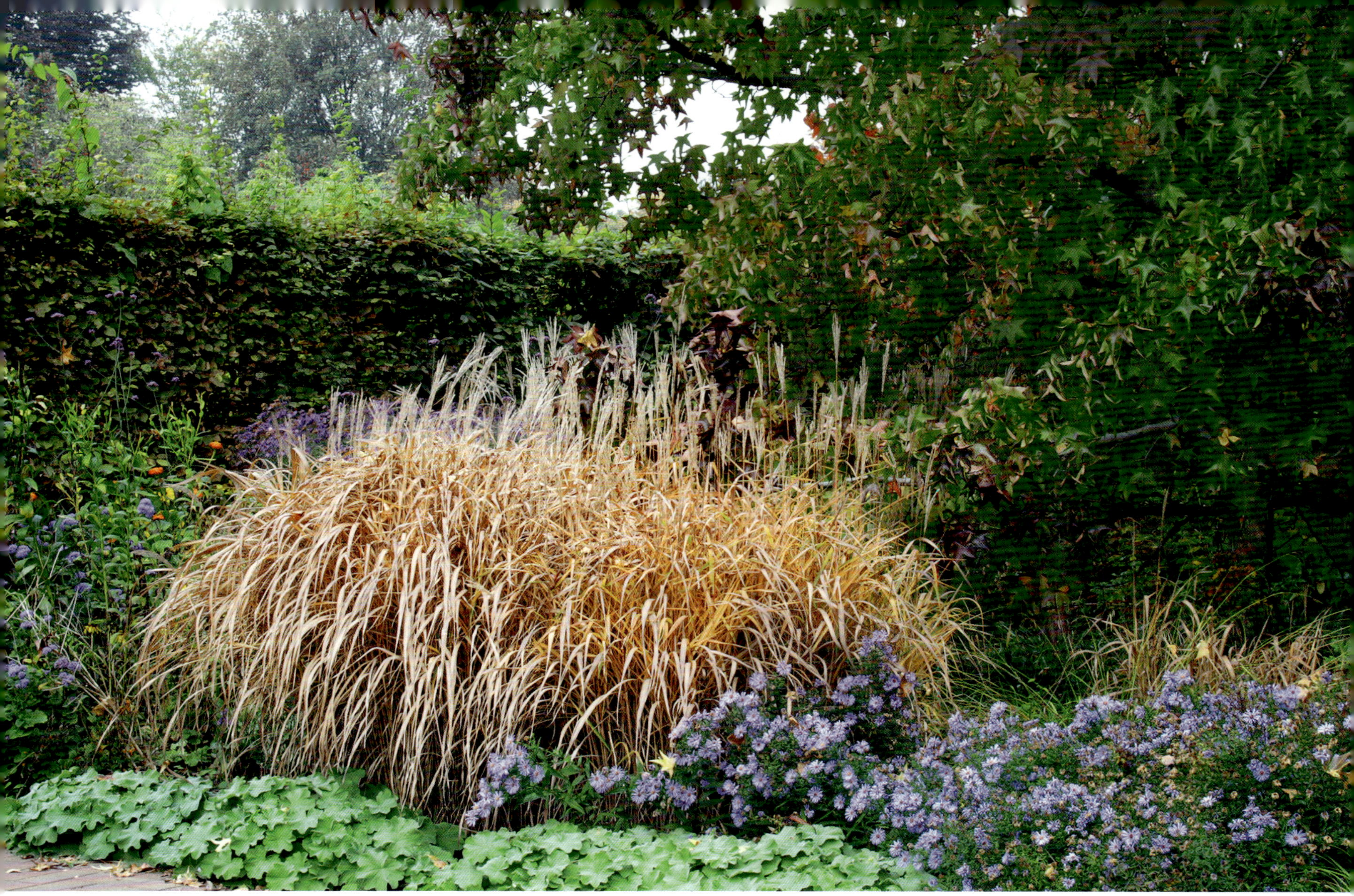

Propagation

Grasses can be propagated by division or by seed.

Most grasses are propagated by division. The felt-like rhizomes can easily be separated into two or more pieces using a spade or a fork. The best time to do this is either early in the year or in autumn. Make sure that the pieces have enough of a root system to grow. Also, the rootballs of the pieces should not be left to lie unprotected for too long, otherwise they might dry out and get damaged.

When dividing grasses you should proceed as follows: push the spade in deep all round the plant and loosen the earth under and next to the rootball. Pull the plant out or try to work the spade underneath and lift it up. Then use the fork to separate the rootstock into different parts, as required. It is best to plant the pieces straight into prepared holes in their new location.

Annual grasses can be propagated by seed.

Cultivars are best divided, but pure species can be propagated equally well by seed as by division.

SOWING ON THE WINDOW SILL

There are a number of receptacles that can be used for sowing on the window sill. If you are only trying to grow a small number of plants, you can use everyday household containers such as yogurt pots or plastic mushroom trays. You should ideally make sure that the seeds are spread out in the seed tray. You can buy special polystyrene trays from gardening outlets, which can be used again and again. These trays usually measure 20 x 30cm or 15 x 20cm.

SOWING IN A COLD FRAME

If you would like to raise a large number of plants, you should consider making a cold frame. It can be easily constructed in a sheltered corner of the border and can be dismantled in early summer, when it is no longer needed. A cold frame consists of a 30–40cm high frame, which is covered with panes of glass. A number of manufacturers offer ready-made cold frames, but anyone with a modicum of DIY skills can make one themselves. You simply need some boards of the requisite size, connecting corners and glass or plastic panes. Old, discarded window panes are suitable for this. When the seedlings have reached an appropriate size and need to be ventilated regularly, you can simply insert spacers between the frame and the glass.

HARDENING OFF AND PLANTING OUT

After the young plants have been acclimatised to the weather conditions in the garden through regular ventilation or occasionally being placed in the open air, you can plant them directly into the border. They will need careful attention until they have become fully established, so that they aren't overrun by weeds or neighbouring plants.

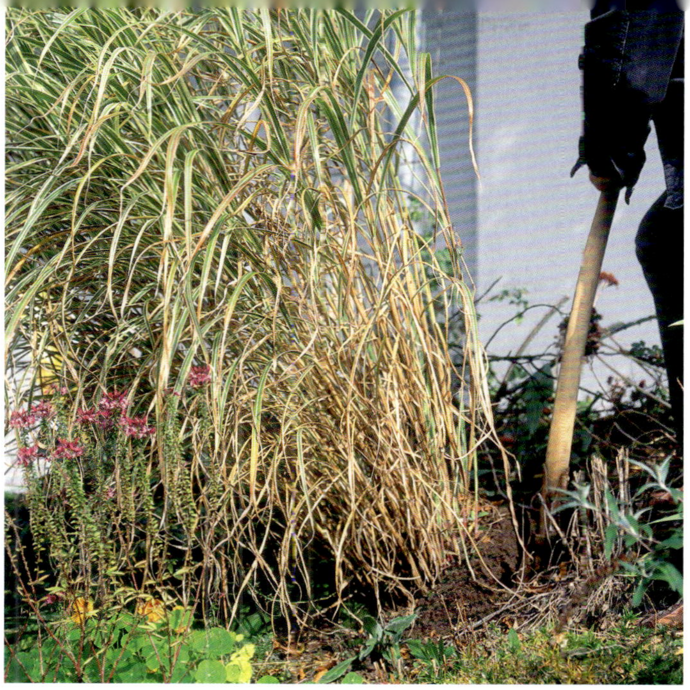

Dividing grasses (1)
The clump is carefully loosened with a spade.

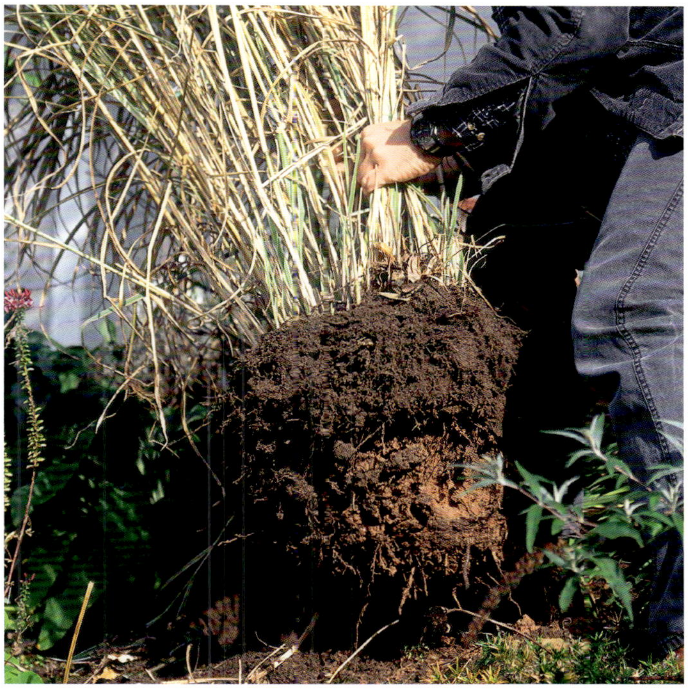

Dividing grasses (2)
When the rootball is separated from the soil, the plant can be lifted from the hole.

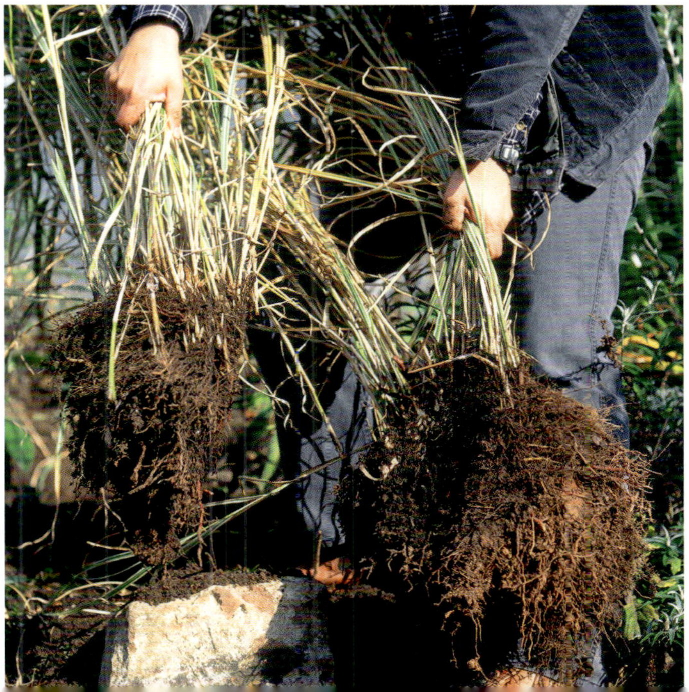

Dividing grasses (3)
Depending on the size of the clump, the plant can be divided into two or more enough large parts, which in turn should be planted in their new locations as quickly as possible.

Grasses for Every Location

Species	Common Name	Location	Height x width (cm)	Recommended variety	Characteristics	Page
Anemanthele lessoniana	pheasant's tail grass	sunny, half-shade, shade	100 x 70	'Golden Hue'	golden-yellow autumn colouring	108
				'Autumn Tints'	Red autumn colouring	108
Arundo donax	giant reed	sunny	400 x 150	'Versicolor'	Expecially winter hardy	108
Bouteloua gracilis	blue grama grass	sunny	40 x 30		well-drained soil	109
Calamagrostis × acutiflora	feather reed grass	sunny	180 x 50	'Karl Foerster'	erect growth	109
				'Waldenbuch'	low, compact growth	109
Calamagrostis brachytricha	diamond grass	sunny, half-shade	120 x 80		early sprouting	110
Carex buchananii	leatherleaf sedge	sunny		f. *viridis* 'Green Twist'	wintergreen	110
Carex caryophyllea	spring sedge	half-shade	25 x 30	'The Beatles'	wintergreen	126
Carex comans	New Zealand sedge	sunny	40 x 60	'Bronze Form'	for more moist locations	111
Carex elata	tufted sedge	half-shade	60 x 60	'Aurea', 'Knightseye'	also for more moist locations	126
Carex grayi	Gray's sedge	half-shade	60 x 50		decorative seed heads	126
Carex morrowii	Japanese Segge	half-shade, shade	50 x 30	'Ice Dance'	ground cover	127
Carex muskingumensis	palm sedge	half-shade, sunny	70 x 50	'Silberstreif', 'Wachtposten'	pondside plant	127
Carex oshimensis	striped weeping sedge	shade	25 x 40	'Evergold'	sensitive to winter sun	132
Carex pendula	weeping sedge	half-shade, shade	120 x 80		very robust, pretty flowers	127
Carex plantaginea	seersucker sedge	shade	30 x 30		wintergreen	133
Carex siderosticha	creeping broad-leaved sedge	shade	30 x 30	'Variegata'	ground cover	133
Chasmanthium latifolium	spangle grass	half-shade	100 x 50		fine autumn appearance	128
Chrysopogon gryllus	French whisk	sunny	180 x 80		likes warmth	112
Cortaderia selloana	pampas grass	sunny	250 x 200	'Pumila'	needs winter protection	113
Cyperus glaber	flat sedge	sunny	50 x 30		annual	134
Deschampsia caespitosa	tufted hair grass	half-shade	100 x 80	'Goldgehänge', 'Tauträger'	compact leaf tufts	129
Fargesia murielae	umbrella bamboo	half-shade, sunny	400 x 300	'Jumbo'	bamboo, evergreen	136
Fargesia nitida	Chinese fountain bamboo	sunny, half-shade	400 x 300		bamboo, evergreen	136
Festuca amethystina	tufted fescue	sunny	50 x 30		wintergreen	113
Festuca cinerea	blue fescue	sunny	30 x 20	'Blauglut', 'Azurit', 'Golden Toupet'	green-leaved varieties can tolerate more damp	113
Festuca gautieri	spiky fescue	sunny, half-shade	30 x 40	'Pit Carlit'	protect from winter sun	114
Festuca mairei	atlas fescue	sunny	100 x 80		companion to roses	114
Hakonechloa macra	Japanese forest grass	half-shade, shade	30 x 50	'Aureola', 'Albostriata'	likes cool locations	129
Helicotrichon sempervirens	oat grass	sunny	120 x 60	'Saphirsprudel'	for poor soils	115
Hordeum jubatum	foxtail barley	sunny	80 x 30		annual	134
Imperata cylindrica	Japanese blood grass	sunny	40 x 30	'Red Baron'	Doesn't flower in Europe	115
Juncus effesus	soft rush	sunny	80 x 50	'Spiralis'	pondside plant	117
Lagurus ovatus	hare's tail grass	sunny	50 x 30		annual	134

Species	Common Name	Location	Height x width (cm)	Recommended variety	Characteristics	Page
Leymus arenarius	European dune grass	sunny	100 x 30		for sandy soils	117
Luzula nivea	snow rush	shade, half-shade	40 x 20		tolerant of dry conditions	133
Luzula sylvatica	great wood-rush	shade	80 x 40	'Aurea', 'Tauernpass'	tolerates root pressure	133
Melica altissima	Siberian melic	sunny, half-shade	100 x 50	'Atropurpurea'	black seeds	117
Melica ciliata	silky spike melic	sunny	60 x 40		likes chalky soils	117
Milium effesum	wood millet	half-shade	40 x 40	'Aureum'	accent plant	130
Miscanthus sinensis	Chinese silver grass	sunny	200–300 x 150	'China', 'Graziella', 'Gnom', 'Flamingo' etc.	important structural plant	118
Molinia caerulea	purple moor grass	half-shade	200 x 70	'Heidebraut', 'Strahlen-quelle', 'Edith Dudzus'	attractive winter aspect	130
Nassella tenuissima	Mexican feather grass	sunny	60 x 60		for free-draining soil; protect in winter	120
Panicum miliaceum	common millet	sunny	100 x 60		annual, good for feeding birds	135
Panicum virgatum	switch grass	sunny	100 x 50	'Heavy Metal', 'Shenandoah', 'Strictum'	attractive autumn colouring	120
Pennisetum alopecuroides	Chinese fountain grass	sunny	80 x 70	'Hameln', f. *viridescens*	long flowers	121
Pennisetum setaceum	African fountain grass	sunny	75 x 50	'Violaceum'	annual	135
Pennistum villosum	feathertop	sunny	60 x 50		annual	135
Phalaris arundinacea	reed canary grass	sunny	120 x 80	'Freesy's Form'	pondside plant, prolific!	121
Phyllostachys bissetii	green bamboo	sunny, half-shade	700 x 300		bamboo, evergreen	137
Phyllostachys nigra	black bamboo	sunny	600 x 300		bamboo, evergreen	137
Phyllostachys vivax	Chinese timber bamboo	sunny	1000 x 300	'Aureocaulis'	bamboo, evergreen	137
Pleioblastus viridistratus	Kamuro-zasa	half-shade, shade	100 x 50		bamboo, evergreen	138
Pseudosasa japonica	arrow bamboo	half-shade, sunny	500 x 300		bamboo, evergreen	138
Sasa palmata	broad-leaved bamboo	half-shade, sunny	150 x 200		bamboo, evergreen	139
Sasa veitchii	Veitch's bamboo	half-shade, shade	80 x 200		bamboo, evergreen	139
Schizachyrium scoparium	blue stem	sunny	120 x 50		attractive autumn colouring	122
Schoenoplectus lacustris	club-rush	sunny	100 x 70	'Albescens'	pondside plant, prolific!	122
Sesleria heufferiana	Balkan blue grass	half-shade	50 x 60		also for rock gardens	131
Sesleria nitida	nest moor grass	sunny	40–80 x 50		for moorland borders	122
Sorghastrum nutans	Indian grass	sunny	150 x 50		late sprouting, for prairie planting schemes	122
Spartina pectinata	gold-edged prairie cord grass	sunny, half-shade	150 x 100	'Aureomarginata'	pondside plant	124
Spodiopogon sibiricus	frost grass	half-shade, sunny	150 x 40	'West Lake'	erect growth	131
Stipa calamagrostis	rough feather grass	sunny	90 x 80	'Algäu', 'Lemperg'	chalk-loving	124
Stipa capillata	bridal veil	sunny	80 x 50		chalk-loving	124
Stipa gigentea	giant feather grass	sunny	200 x 50		wintergreen, likes warmth	125
Stipa pulcherrima ssp. nudicosta	golden feather grass	sunny	100 x 50		for free-draining soils	125

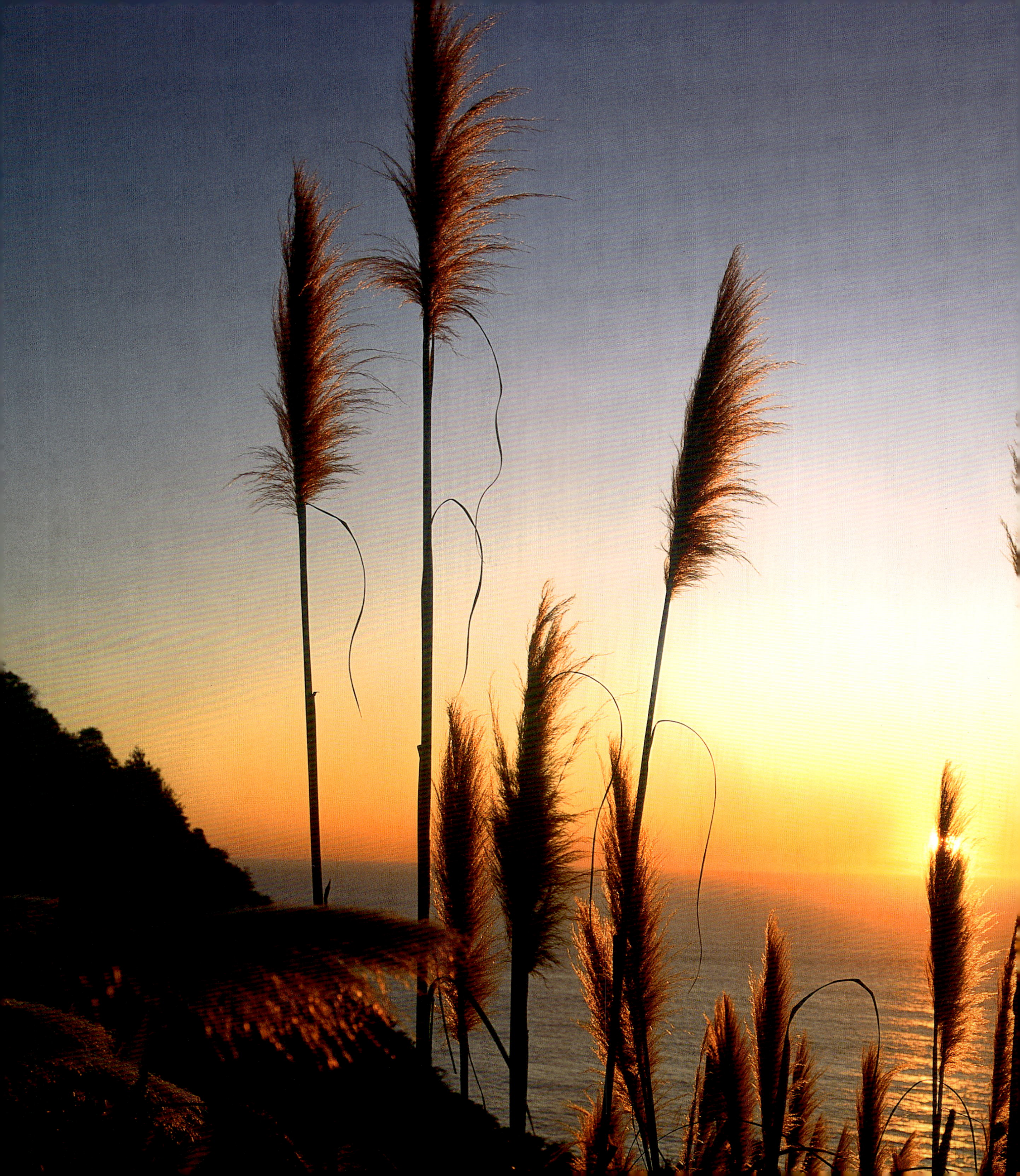

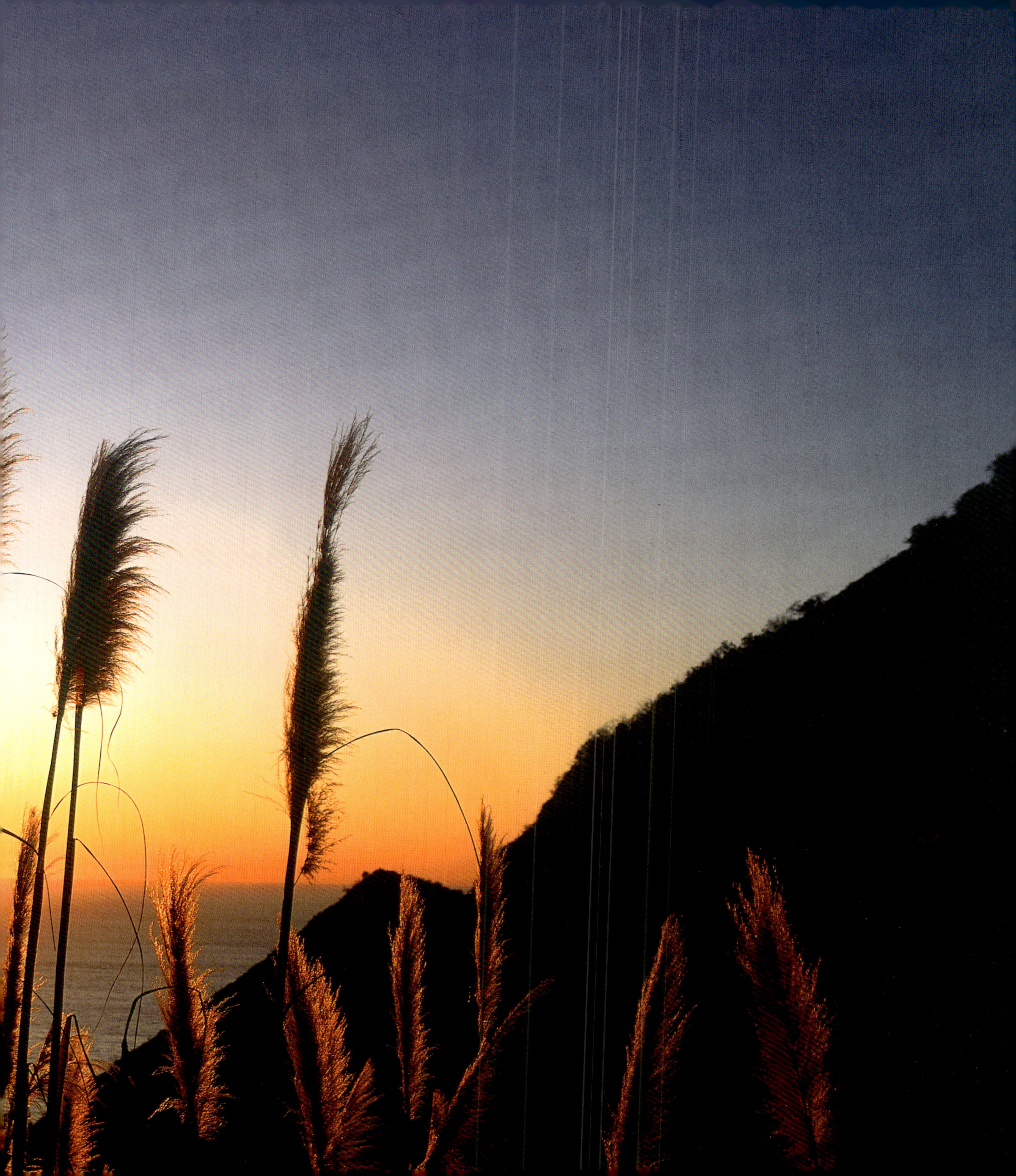

GRASS SUPPLIERS

The plant search facility on the Royal Horticultural Society website – www.rhs.org.uk – features a helpful list of nurseries and suppliers.

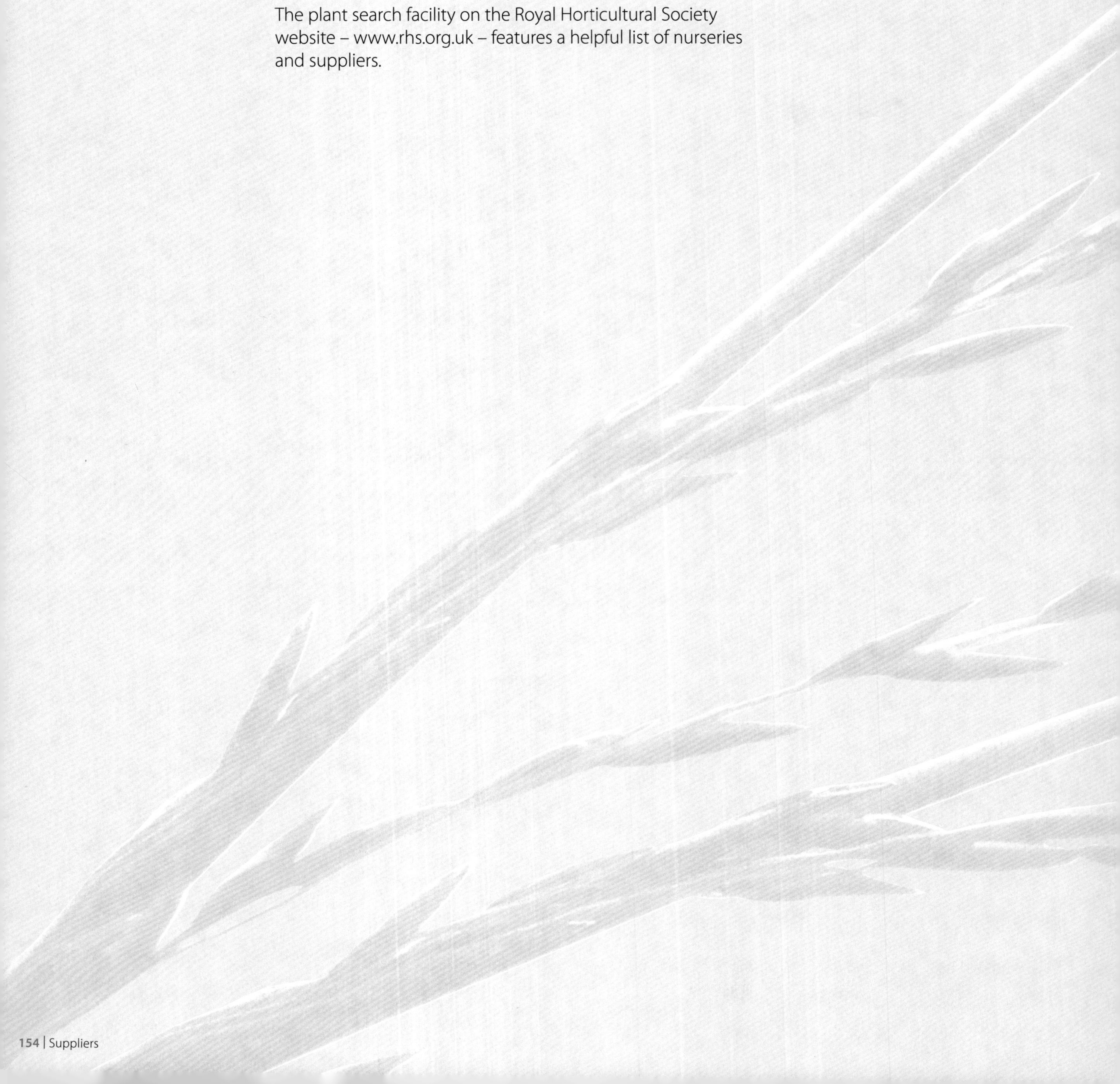

INDEX

Page numbers in **bold type** indicate an illustration

COPYRIGHT

ISBN 978-1-87067-385-3

German edition first published in 2009 under the title Gräser im Garten (ISBN: 978-3-7667-1795-5)
© 2009 Verlag Georg D.W. Callwey
GmbH & Co. KG
Streitfeldstraße 35
81673 München, Germany
www.callwey.de

English edition:
Translation: David Watson
Editor: Susannah Hecht
Designer: Craig Holden

British Library Cataloguing-in-Publication Data
A catalogue record for this book is available from the British Library

Printed in Germany for Garden Art Press, an imprint of the Antique Collectors' Club Ltd., Woodbridge, Suffolk

PICTURE CREDITS

180 photos.

Katharina Adams, Linnich (7): 16, 67 below, 89 right, 55, 56, 135 middle, 148

Jürgen Becker, Hilden (12): 4/5 (Garten Janke, Garden Concepts, Germany), 9 (Design: Oudolf, Netherlands), 28 below (Garten Janke, Garden Concepts, Germany), 48 (Garten Van Steeg, Design: Oudolf, Netherlands), 54 (Gruga Park Essen, Germany), 80 (Garten de Sy/ de Smet, B), 87 both (Garten Oudolf, Netherlands), 95 above (Grugapark, Essen, Germany), 95 below (Garten t Hof, Overwellingen, Netherlands), 104/105 (Grugapark, Essen, Germany), 142/143 (Garten Dahlhuisen, Netherlands)

Daniel Böswirth and Alice Thinschmidt, Vienna (7): 8, 15 above, 23, 32 below, 91, 92, 96/97

Christa Brand, Ismaning (15): 14, 32, 34, 42/43, 46/47, 47, 59 above, 64/65, 67 above, 69, 73 above, 78/79, 88, 98, 100 below

Julia Fink/fotolia.com (1): background grasses on pages 4/5, 40/41, 56/57, 62/63, 76/77, 86/87, 145–159

Modeste Herwig, NL-Soest (56): 93, 106, 107 both, 108, 109 both, 110, 111, 112 both, 113 both, 114 both, 115 both, 116, 117, 118 both, 119 all 3, 120 all 3, 121 all 3, 122 both, 123, 124, 125 both, 126, 127 both, 128, 129 both, 130, 131, 132, 133, 134, 135 left, 135 right, 136, 137 all 3, 138, 139 both

Anne Humburg (3): 10 all 3

Norbert Kühn (1): 76 left

Stefan Leppert, Münster (4): 62 both, 63 both

Marianne Majerus, London (4): 35 below, 44/45, 58, 89 left

Volker Michael, Baesweiler (14): 15 below, 30, 38 above, 44, 49 below, 53, 59 above, 82, 83, 84/85, 86, 90, 100 above, 144

Marion Nickig, Essen (13): 17, 26, 37 both, 38 below, 40, 41 both, 51, 52, 72, 81, 76/77

Reinhard-Tierfoto/Hans Reinhard, Heiligkreuzsteinach-Eiterbach (22): 1, 2/3, 11, 12, 12/13, 18, 19, 20 both, 21, 22, 31, 36, 66, 75, 77, 146, 147, 149 all 3, 152/153

Reinhard-Tierfoto/Nils Reinhard, Heiligkreuzsteinach-Eiterbach (1): 27

Karl-Heinz Rücker, Stuttgart (2): 56 left, 86 left

Annette Timmermann, Kalübbe (18): 6/7, 24/25, 28 above, 29, 32 above, 35 above, 48, 49 above, 49 above, 60/61, 68, 70/71, 73 below, 94, 99, 101, 102/103, 145

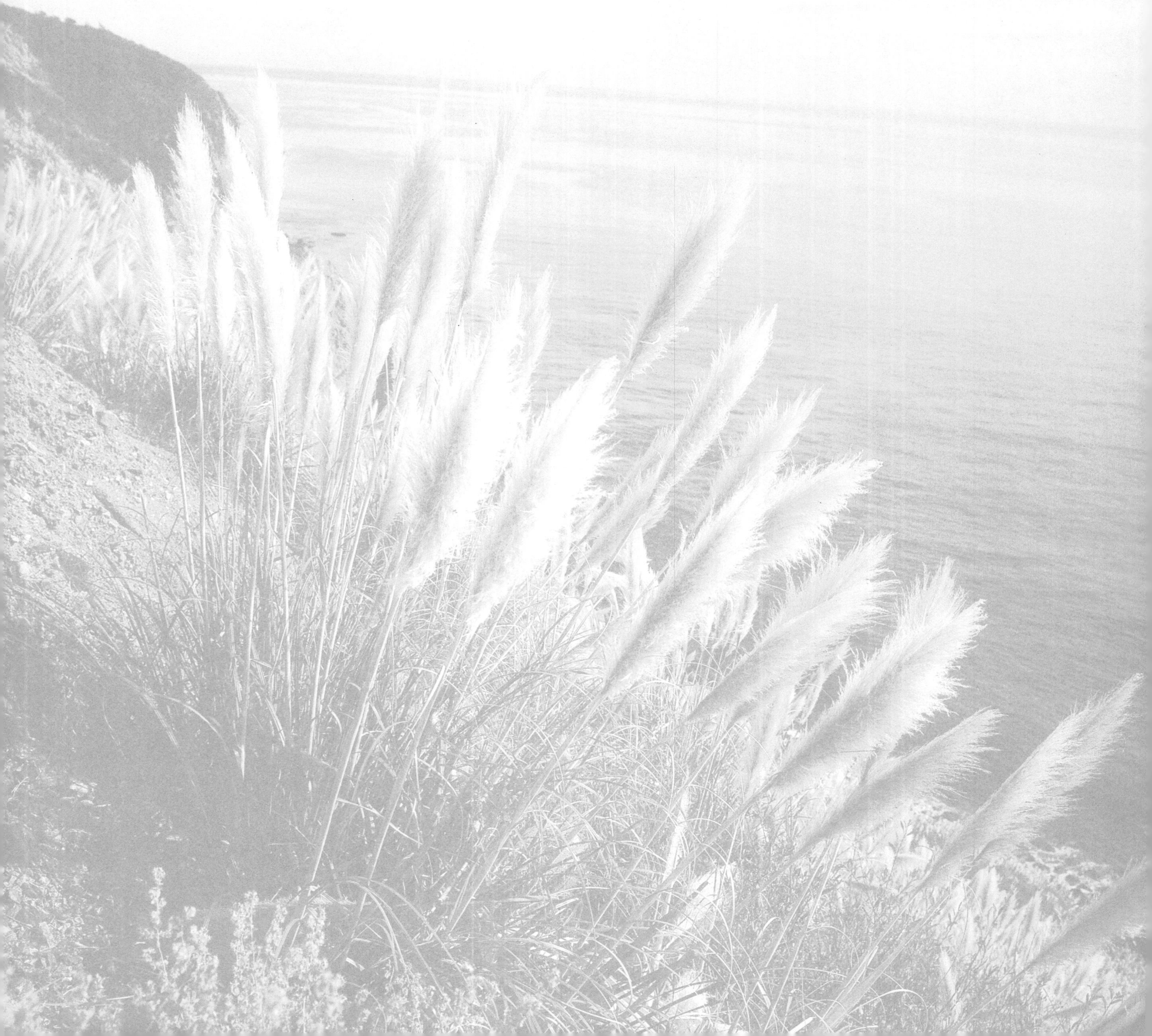